Education in Sub-Saharan Africa

A World Bank Policy Study

*Education in
Sub-Saharan Africa*

**Policies for Adjustment,
Revitalization, and Expansion**

The World Bank
Washington, D.C.

Copyright © 1988 by The International Bank
for Reconstruction and Development / The World Bank
1818 H Street, N.W., Washington, D.C. 20433, U.S.A.

All rights reserved
Manufactured in the United States of America
First printing January 1988

The judgments expressed in this study do not necessarily reflect the views of the World Bank's Board of Executive Directors or of the governments that they represent. The maps used in this document are solely for the convenience of the reader and do not imply the expression of any opinion whatsoever on the part of the World Bank or its affiliates concerning the legal status of any country, territory, city, area, or of its authorities, or concerning the delimitation of its boundaries or national affiliation.

Library of Congress Cataloging-in-Publication Data

Education in Sub-Saharan Africa.

(World Bank policy study)

  Bibliography: p.
  1. Education and state—Africa, Sub-Saharan.
2. Education—Economic aspects—Africa, Sub-Saharan.
I. World Bank. II. Series.
LC95.A357E38 1988   379.67   87-34650
ISBN 0-8213-0996-X

Foreword

Without education, development will not occur. Only an educated people can command the skills necessary for sustainable economic growth and for a better quality of life. Recognizing this, African governments have placed heavy emphasis on expanding educational opportunities from primary school through university in the two or three decades since their independence. The number of students enrolled in African institutions at all levels has more than quintupled since 1960. Indeed, the spread of educational access may be the single most significant development achievement of Africa.

The key role of education in the development process is the reason, too, why the World Bank has put so much emphasis on supporting educational expansion and improvement in Sub-Saharan Africa.

Even so, education in Sub-Saharan Africa is in crisis today. Rapid population growth has resulted in more children than ever seeking places in schools already pressed for resources because of the financial crises of the 1980s. A lower proportion of children and young people are able to obtain places in educational institutions as a result, and the quality of education has dropped as classrooms have become overcrowded and teaching materials increasingly scarce.

Governments cannot be expected to increase substantially the resources they devote to education. Already, many Sub-Saharan African countries allocate over 20 percent of the government budget to education. Further increases would cut too deeply into other pressing demands for public funds. Measures for improving quality and further expanding the education systems, however, will certainly require an incremental flow of resources. Thus African countries will need to strike a balance between demands for education and the scarcity of resources, and they will need to develop country-specific, comprehensive, and internally consistent sets of policies along three dimensions: adjustment to current demographic and fiscal realities, revitalization of the existing educational infrastructure to restore quality, and selective expansion to meet further demands.

The analysis and recommendations contained in this study should contribute to this educational planning process. To this end, the study attempts to diagnose the problems of erosion of quality and recent stagnation of enrollment and to offer a set of policy responses commensurate with the severity of these problems. In doing so, it does not prescribe one set of educational policies for all of Sub-Saharan Africa, as the nature and scope of both the issues and the responses to them differ markedly among African countries. Nor does it propose specific educational investments. Instead, the study presents a framework within which countries may formulate strategies tailored to their own needs and circumstances.

The study has been prepared after very broad consultation both in Africa and in the industrialized countries. In particular, its preparation has benefited enormously from discussions at two conferences of African ministers and permanent secretaries of education planning and finance, convened for this purpose in Côte d'Ivoire and Ethiopia. The comments of many experienced and knowledgeable people helped immeasurably to shape and refine both the tone and the substance of this study on a number of complex issues.

This study will guide the World Bank's lending and technical assistance to Sub-Saharan African education over the next several years. It should serve to provide a common ground for other donors as well, to expand their assistance to education in Africa, and to increase the effectiveness of international assistance for this purpose. But most important, we hope this study will provide insights for our member governments in Africa as they develop their own country-specific plans for educational reform, revitalization, and expansion.

Barber B. Conable
President

The World Bank
December 11, 1987

Contents

Glossary and Acronyms *ix*

Preface *xi*

Summary 1
   Educational Development in Africa *1*
   A Policy Framework *2*
   Formulation and Implementation of National Programs *3*
   Policy Options by Level of Education *4*
   The Role of the International Donor Community *6*
   Why Meet the Challenge? The Expected Benefits of Education *6*

Part I. The Policy Context

1. **The Remarkable Progress of African Education** 11
   Before Independence *11*
   Advances after 1960 *12*
   Expenditure on Education *14*

2. **Education and the External Environment** 18
   The Demographic Challenge *18*
   Macroeconomic Adjustment and Fiscal Austerity *20*
   Investment in Education *21*

3. **The Stagnation of Enrollment and Decline in Quality** 28
   Enrollment Stagnation *28*
   Declining Quality of Education *31*

Part II. Policy Options for African Governments

4. **The Foundation: Primary Education** 39

    Measures for Improving Quality *40*
    The Containment of Unit Costs *46*
    Mobilizing Resources for Primary Education *51*

5. **The Consolidation of Competence: Secondary Education and Training** *54*
    Meeting the Demand for Expansion by Reducing Unit Costs *56*
    Equity Issues: Increased Participation by Females *61*
    Training for Vocational Competence *62*
    Financing Secondary Education and Training *65*

6. **Preparation for Responsibility: Higher Education** *68*
    The Challenge and the Promise *69*
    Issues in Higher Education *70*
    A Program for Structural Adjustment of African Higher Education *77*

7. **Using Resources Well: The Mandate for Education Managers** *81*
    Improving Organizational Structure *82*
    Improving Information: Testing, Statistical, and Accounting Systems *85*
    Strengthening Analytical Capacity *86*
    Development of Managerial Staff *87*
    Priorities and Resource Requirements *89*

Part III. An Agenda for Action

8. **Policy Packages for Educational Development** *93*
    Adjustment *94*
    Revitalization: Restoring Quality *97*
    Selective Expansion *98*
    Policy Design and Implementation *100*

9. **International Assistance for African Educational Development** *101*
    Sources of Aid and Its Recent Use *101*
    The Comparative Advantage of Aid: Past and Present *105*
    New Structures to Support Policy Design and Implementation *107*
    Future Amounts and Targeted Areas of Aid to African Education *109*
    A Call to Action *112*

Bibliography 113

Appendix 119

Maps *following page 185*

Notes on the Data

Most of the discussion and all of the statistics about Africa in this study refer to just thirty-nine countries south of the Sahara, for which the terms Africa and Sub-Saharan Africa are used interchangeably. The appendix lists and provides comparative information on these countries.

    "Dollars" means U.S. dollars.
    "Billion" means one thousand million.

Glossary and Acronyms

Correspondence education. A type of distance education through which students receive textbooks for individual study in their homes and supplementary mass media broadcasts on the subject matter. Each textbook includes exercises to be completed and mailed to a postal tutor, who grades each exercise and provides an individual evaluation to the student.

Curriculum. A set of courses in a field of study, often constituting an area of specialization at the higher levels of education.

Distance education, or distance teaching. An education delivery system that uses a variety of media and a system of feedback to teach people who are unable to attend traditional schools. Distance education usually combines the use of media broadcasts, printed materials, and some kind of face-to-face study. Distance teaching programs can range from in-school programs, in which broadcasts supplement learning activities in the classroom, to out-of-school programs, such as correspondence lessons in which students may never meet their tutors and may have little or no contact with the regular education system.

Diversified secondary education. Education at the secondary level that introduces practical or occupational subjects into an otherwise completely academic program and is thus intended to meet the expected needs of school leavers. Two models are prevalent. The first introduces practical subjects (industrial arts, home economics, agriculture) at the lower secondary level to provide a prevocational orientation and to develop a positive attitude toward work. The second includes a general academic stream plus one or more specialized occupational streams, usually at the upper secondary level, that are suited to economic conditions in the surrounding area.

Enrollment ratio. School enrollment, both public and private, as a percentage of a given age group in the population. The gross enrollment ratio is the total number of students enrolled at a given education level divided by the population of the age group for that level. This ratio may include students who are younger or older than the age expected at that level. The net enrollment ratio is calculated by using only that part of the total number of students enrolled that corresponds to the specific age groups defined for that level.

Equivalency program. A teaching program that provides opportunities for education to students who would otherwise be unable to attend formal schools and that emphasizes the acquisition of knowledge rather than the place where the knowledge is acquired. Equivalency programs exist for all levels of schooling.

External examination. An examination set by an independent organization and administered to a large number of students from different schools to allow comparison of results across schools.

Extramural or external degree or certificate. A degree or certificate awarded by a university to students in equivalency programs who have studied the curriculum on their own and have not attended formal classes.

Incomplete school. A school that does not have the full number of grades for the level of education provided.

Nonformal education. Education and training for out-of-school youths and adults in classes, courses, or activities intended to promote learning but not constituting part of the formal school system and not leading to formal qualifications, such as diplomas or specific trade standards. Nonformal education typically concentrates on short programs of a few months in duration.

Nongovernmental or private voluntary organization. A nonprofit organization with private membership that provides development assistance. Such organizations include foundations, lay and religious aid associations, and nongovernmental cooperatives.

Postsecondary, tertiary, or higher-level education. Education that requires, as a minimum condition of entry, the successful completion of education at the secondary level or proof of equivalent knowledge or experience. Instruction is given in various types of institutions, including universities, vocational and technical training institutes, and teacher training institutes.

Primary or basic education. The first level of education, in which students follow a common curriculum. Primary education offers students instruction in primary or elementary schools that are part of the formal education system. These schools span grades 1–4, 1–5, 1–7, or 1–8 and teach communication, mathematics, and science. Basic education generally refers to instruction in literacy and numeracy skills for out-of-school youths and adults.

Secondary education. Secondary education requires at least four years of primary preparation for entry. Students may follow a general academic program that typically leads to admission to a postsecondary institution, or they may study technical and vocational or agricultural curriculums to prepare for direct entry into a trade or occupation. This level may span any subset of grades 5–12.

Technical education. Training in specialist skills for the higher-level skilled worker. Instruction is typically in preemployment training institutions such as polytechnics; administration is commonly the responsibility of ministries of education, labor, or employment, or comes under the authority of specific industries. Courses of study in technical education usually include a component of general education.

Training. Instruction in job-related skills to prepare students for direct entry into a trade or occupation. Such instruction can take place in training centers, through apprenticeships, or at the place of employment (on-the-job training).

Vocational education. Training in craft or trade skills for the semiskilled worker. Instruction typically occurs in schools and comes under the direction of ministries of education.

World Bank. An international lending institution comprising the International Bank for Reconstruction and Development, which lends to governments of member developing countries on nonconcessional terms for projects and other purposes intended to stimulate economic growth, and the International Development Association, which lends for the same purposes but on concessional terms and only to the poorest member countries.

Acronyms

ADB	African Development Bank Group
ECA	United Nations Economic Commission for Africa
GNP	Gross national product
IBRD	International Bank for Reconstruction and Development
IDA	International Development Association
IEA	International Association for the Evaluation of Educational Achievement
ILO	International Labour Organisation
NGO	Nongovernmental organization
ODA	Overseas Development Administration
OECD	Organisation for Economic Co-operation and Development
OPEC	Organization of Petroleum Exporting Countries
SIDA	Swedish International Development Authority
UNDP	United Nations Development Programme
Unesco	United Nations Educational, Scientific, and Cultural Organization
UNICEF	United Nations Childrens Fund
USAID	U.S. Agency for International Development

Preface

Since their independence, the nations of Sub-Saharan Africa have invested heavily in education. The achievements in the sector have been impressive both absolutely and in relation to other sectors and other countries at other times. In many African countries, however, enrollments have stagnated recently, and the quality of education has apparently declined.

These reversals have occurred in an environment of unprecedented population growth, mounting fiscal austerity, and often tenuous political and administrative institutions. Each of these factors has hurt education in the region, and the ensuing deterioration in educational services has made it more difficult to solve the region's economic and social problems. To break this cycle of eroding prospects for the people of the region, policies need to be identified that will renew progress in Africa's education. The role of human skills in development is critical.

The return to investment in human skills depends, nevertheless, on the macroeconomic policy environment. The United Nations and the World Bank have spelled out the essential ingredients of this environment. And most African governments have initiated the necessary economic reforms—with some good results. In 1986 real incomes per capita rose in low-income Africa for the first time in the 1980s. To sustain this growth in personal income, however, there must be a moderation of the region's unprecedented population growth. The World Bank, in *Population Growth and Policies in Sub-Saharan Africa* (1986), summarized the widely accepted elements of population policy for Africa and noted the very hopeful recent trends in government policy. Clearly, the 1980s mark an important transition as Africa's economic and demographic policies set the context for productive investment.

Any discussion of policies and priorities for a region as vast and diverse as Sub-Saharan Africa naturally runs the risks of overstating commonalities and understating differences. Readers will fully appreciate the enormous diversity that exists among African countries along several dimensions—economic, political, institutional, cultural, linguistic, and educational. And the extent of a country's own internal diversity should not be underestimated.

Most of the discussion and all of the Africa-wide statistics in this study refer to just thirty-nine countries south of the Sahara. (They are listed in the statistical appendix, which provides full comparative information on them.) Whenever the term "Africa" or "African" is used, it refers only to these countries and their residents. The many averages cited throughout the paper, although they reflect the thirty-nine most populous African countries, apply specifically to none. Individual countries, country blocs, and language groups will thus provide exceptions to all conclusions. In the end, national authorities must decide the policies and priorities for educational investments and tailor those investments to specific conditions, needs, and aspirations. For these reasons, there is no attempt here to prescribe an education policy for the continent—that would be inappropriate and futile. Instead, the focus is on generalizations—on addressing trends and issues that, because of their importance in many African countries, assume importance for the whole continent.

This study—on investment in education and training—is the first in a series that the World Bank is preparing to stimulate discussion of sectoral policies for Africa in the 1990s and beyond. It has three main objectives. The first is to identify and describe common problems and issues of educational development in Africa. The second is to provide leaders in each country with comparative data and analytical tools for developing their own policies and priorities. The third is to suggest specific policy directions for consideration by national education authorities and by donors. The key word here is "consideration." This study is about diverse and variably applicable policies for African educational development, not about a monolithic and universally applicable policy. It will meet its objectives if it helps initiate serious reflection and debate in Africa on future directions for the sector.

For broader analysis than could be included here, several important documents are available. The Lagos Plan of Action, adopted by African Heads of State under the auspices of the Organization of African Unity (OAU) in April 1980, analyzes Africa's problems and puts forward a comprehensive plan for addressing them (OAU, *Lagos Plan of Action for the Economic Development of Africa, 1980–2000*, 1981). In accordance with the policies set forth in this plan, the OAU met again and agreed to a set of activities and priorities; these were spelled out in a second document (OAU, *Africa's Priority Programme for Economic Recovery, 1986–1990*, 1985). Subsequently, the U.N. General Assembly adopted a set of resolutions pertaining to African development (United Nations, *Programme of Action for African Economic Recovery and Development, 1986–1990*, 1986). Concurrently with these efforts, the World Bank has published its own series of special reports on macroeconomic issues and development requirements for Africa. The first in this series, *Accelerated Development in Sub-Saharan Africa: An Agenda for Action*, was released in 1981; the fourth and most recent, *Financing Adjustment with Growth in Sub-Saharan Africa, 1986–90*, appeared in 1986.

Education in Sub-Saharan Africa was prepared by Peter R. Moock, task leader, and Ralph W. Harbison under the general direction of Aklilu Habte and the immediate supervision of Dean T. Jamison. Janet Leno drafted many of the boxes and provided writing and editorial assistance throughout. Rosemary Bellew had principal responsibility for preparing the appendix. Birger Fredriksen and John Middleton wrote the initial drafts of chapters 4 and 7, respectively. Others who made important contributions to this effort include Wadi Haddad, Price Gittinger, Kenneth King (University of Edinburgh), and Adriaan Verspoor.

Moreover, a series of background papers was commissioned in preparing the study; authors and titles are noted in the bibliography. Comments on various drafts of the study, by World Bank staff and numerous reviewers in Africa, Europe, and North America, helped to shape and refine the analyses and recommendations. Finally, thanks to financial assistance from the Norwegian Ministry of Development Cooperation, the study benefited greatly from discussion of an early draft by African policymakers at two international meetings held in Ethiopia and Côte d'Ivoire in early 1987, and it was the topic of a conference of international donors to education held in France in early 1988.

The study was discussed by the World Bank's Board of Executive Directors on October 15, 1987.

Summary

African societies have a long and rich history of education and training. Indigenous education among all groups remains an important transmitter of cultural identity from one generation to the next. In addition, Christianity and Islam have for centuries had a pervasive influence on education, community life, and perceptions in many parts of the region.

In the colonial era, missionaries and metropolitan governments opened up a network of Western-type schools in Africa. The administration of education systems was dominated, however, by expatriates, as was teaching beyond the primary level. Moreover, access to education was quite limited, especially in the thinly populated areas of French West Africa. By 1960, the gross primary enrollment ratio in all of Sub-Saharan Africa was still only 36 percent, about half the levels then found in Asia and Latin America. Many countries—including The Gambia, Côte d'Ivoire, and Senegal in West Africa and Tanzania and Somalia in East Africa—had literacy rates below 10 percent at the time of independence.

Educational Development in Africa

The education systems inherited by the African nations at the time of independence were thus quite inadequate to meet the needs of the new countries for self-governance and rapid economic growth. From this low starting point, the progress achieved in African education has been spectacular. Quantitative expansion has been particularly impressive.

Progress since Independence

Between 1960 and 1983 the number of students enrolled in African institutions at all levels quintupled to about 63 million. Enrollments increased about 9 percent annually during the 1970s, double the rate in Asia and triple that in Latin America. At the primary level, the gross enrollment ratio rose from 36 percent in 1960 to 75 percent in 1983. At the tertiary level, the number of students enrolled in African institutions had reached 437,000 by 1983, growing from just 21,000 in 1960. The substantial expansion of education since independence has increased the participation of some groups who had previously had little or no access to formal education.

This massive educational expansion has substantially improved the human capital stock. The estimated average educational attainment of working-age men and women in the median African country increased from less than half a year in 1960 to more than three years in the early 1980s. The adult literacy rate in the median country rose from about 9 percent to 42 percent.

The Current Challenge

The advances since the early 1960s are now seriously threatened—in part by circumstances outside education. Africa's explosive population growth greatly increases the number of children seeking access to schools and increases the number of potential illiterates. Between 1970 and 1980 Africa's population grew at 2.9 percent a year, a full percentage point higher than the worldwide rate. Between 1980 and the end of the century, Africa's population is projected to grow at 3.2 percent a year, its primary- and secondary-school-age population at 3.3 percent. If the growth of educational places is to keep pace with the growth of the school-age population, more schools, teachers, books, and other inputs are required each year. This requirement comes at a time when economic decline has necessitated significant cutbacks in public spending. Public spending on education in Africa has dropped from $10 billion in 1980 to $8.9 billion in 1983. These fundamental facts sharply constrain the options open to policymakers and have serious implications for African education policy.

The main educational issues in Africa today are the stagnation of enrollments and the erosion of quality. Although total enrollments in Sub-Saharan Africa grew at an average annual rate of 6.5 percent during 1960–70 and 8.9 percent during 1970–80, the rate of increase plummeted to 4.2 percent in the first three years of the 1980s. The slowing of enrollment growth affected all levels of education but was most evident at the primary level, where the rate of growth fell from 8.4 percent a year during 1970–80 to 2.9 percent in 1980–83. If the population of primary-school-age children increases at the projected average annual rate of 3.3 percent, a 2.9 percent increase in enrollments will not even keep pace. And as long as enrollments stagnate, current inequalities in access to education are not likely to be eliminated. Male-female differentials remain a particularly serious problem in most African countries, especially past the primary level.

Complicating the problems of stagnating enrollments are the low levels and recent erosions of educational quality. Cognitive achievement among African students is low by world standards, and there is some suggestion of further decline recently. Much of the evidence is indirect: supplies of key inputs (especially books and other learning materials) are critically low, and the use of these inputs has declined in relation to the use of teachers' time and of physical facilities. Less is known about the output—the performance of students. But in the few cross-national studies that have been conducted, academic achievement in Africa has been sufficiently poor to be a cause for serious concern.

Addressing these issues of stagnation and low quality will require additional resources. Equally important, it will require profound changes in educational policy for many countries. Indeed, for most African countries, the first will not be obtainable without the second.

A Policy Framework

Hard decisions on education policy should not be postponed. In most African countries the cost would be continued stagnation of enrollment and decline in quality through the 1990s. This study urgently recommends that each African nation now embrace the task of formulating and implementing an internally coherent set of policies that reflects the nation's unique history and aspirations and that effectively addresses its own recently exacerbated problems in the education and training sector. Although the particulars of the policy packages can be expected to vary from one country to the next, every country-specific package needs to contain, in varying proportions, three distinct dimensions: adjustment, revitalization, and selective expansion.

Although undoubtedly painful and politically difficult, adjustment policies will alleviate the burden of education and training on public budgets. Measures for revitalization and expansion, however, will certainly require additional resources. Thus, in the context of ongoing austerity in Africa, resolute movement toward adjustment is a necessary condition for implementing forward-looking policies on the other two dimensions. Moreover, if new policies are in fact to be implemented, management practices will need to be improved.

Adjustment

Adjustment to current demographic and fiscal realities, though it will be difficult, is essential if the disruptive effects of these external factors are to be minimized in the years ahead. Adjustment will take two main forms:

- *Diversifying sources of finance.* A necessary part of country-specific policy packages, diversification can be achieved through increased cost sharing in public education and through increased official tolerance and encouragement of nongovernmental suppliers of educational services. For many African countries, increased user charges in public education will be inevitable, but this policy should be directed especially at the tertiary level, where more than a third of public expenditure in the typical country now covers student welfare costs, as distinct from pedagogical costs; for most African countries, the scope for further cost sharing in primary education is negligible or nonexistent.
- *Unit cost containment.* In the adjustment process,

the containment of unit costs will be just as important as, and in many countries probably more important than, policies to diversify sources of finance. The most promising areas for containing costs are utilization of teachers, construction standards, and the tendency of students to repeat grades or drop out of school.

Revitalization

Revitalization of the existing educational infrastructure is the second dimension of a properly conceived educational strategy. Renewed emphasis on fundamentals is needed to take maximum advantage of the current capacity of education and training systems. Three kinds of measures are necessary for the restoration of quality:
- A renewed commitment to academic standards, principally by strengthening examination systems.
- Restoration of an efficient mix of inputs in education. A minimum package of textbooks and other learning materials is usually the most pressing need.
- Greater investment in the operation and maintenance of physical plant and equipment, and greater expenditure on other inputs that would increase the utilization of these capital assets.

Selective Expansion

The selective expansion of educational services is the third dimension of any complete strategy for educational development. Measures in this area, viable only after measures of adjustment and revitalization have begun to take hold, will concentrate in four areas; success in all will depend upon a general effort to safeguard the quality of instructional staff at all levels:
- *Renewed progress toward the long-term goal of universal primary education.* Expanding access to primary education should remain a high priority in most African countries. To maintain the high economic and social returns that have accrued to this investment in the past, however, parallel efforts are required to combat the incidence of disease and malnutrition among young children.
- *Distance education programs.* At the secondary level, and later on at the tertiary, expansion of enrollments in selected subjects and streams will be necessary in most countries as soon as appropriate measures of adjustment and revitalization have been put in place. To accommodate these increases in postprimary education, most countries will need to consider alternative ways of delivering educational services that shift more of the burden for learning onto the students themselves. Now is the time to begin planning such programs and developing the correspondence materials, radio programs, examinations systems, and other support that will be needed.
- *Training.* Training for those who have entered the labor force must be increased. This training should serve both school leavers and those who have had no exposure to formal schooling, and it should be designed to ensure that individuals can acquire the necessary job-related skills and renew these skills during their working lifetime in response to changing market conditions.
- *Research and postgraduate education.* Expansion of Africa's capacity to produce its own intellectual talent to fill the highest scientific and technical jobs—in educational establishments, in government, and in the private sector—is a critical matter to be addressed in building for Africa's future. Here, as with programs for distance education, economies of scale are likely to be important, and these will be difficult to achieve fully within a national context except, perhaps, in a few of Africa's largest and wealthiest countries. The pressing need is for Africa to develop, probably with the support of the international donor community, regional and subregional approaches to these particular goals.

Formulation and Implementation of National Programs

For most African countries, the formulation of a comprehensive and coherent educational development program, derived from a balanced package of policies for adjustment, revitalization, and selective expansion, will be a new experience. Each country will organize for the task in its own way. In many countries, however, a fruitful approach to policy design might be expected to include the following: establishing a national commission to oversee the work; constituting a technical staff to support the commission; for both, drawing upon the nation's best political judgment and analytical talent, from the ministries of finance and planning as well as education, and from institutions of tertiary education and research; building a national consensus through public debate of the emerging findings and recommendations; and taking advantage of the experience of other African countries in developing the nation's own educational development program. Budgetary flows would have to be sufficient to cover not only the personnel costs of the national commission but also its operating expenses for travel, communications, publications, and specialized contractual services (such as data collection and processing, expert technical consultants, targeted research, and analysis).

Although the careful elaboration of educational development programs is essential, African capacity for implementation will ultimately determine the effectiveness of the programs. Improvement in education management is a necessary concomitant to policy reform and must be given immediate and continuing attention.

Management at the national level may be significantly improved by delegating various administrative functions. Some functions, however, must appropriately remain with the central ministry, and the performance of these functions will need to be improved. But the toughest challenge to improving management lies closer to the classroom, at the level of individual schools and districts. African policymakers should consider how, with adequate safeguards against abuses, schools and the local communities they serve can be given more authority in the acquisition and utilization of the resources essential to effective classroom teaching and learning.

In addition, central ministries must tend more seriously to the development of their own managerial capacity, especially in monitoring performance and policy planning and analysis. Improvements are needed in examination systems (which was mentioned above with reference both to academic standards and to distance education), in the nature and timely availability of statistical and financial accounting information, and in the number and qualifications of staff engaged in full-time analytical work. Incentives in many ministries of education are insufficient to attract, motivate, and retain able staff. Governments committed not only to the formulation of an educational development program but also to its expeditious implementation will need to be imaginative in addressing the issue of incentives at all levels of the education system.

Policy Options by Level of Education

The mix of adjustment, revitalization, and expansion components that is appropriate in light of country-specific conditions and goals can be expected to differ. Within a country, the mix will differ also among levels of education.

At the primary level in most African countries, there is only limited scope for adjustment in the form of either lowered unit costs or increased cost sharing. There is, however, good potential for improving the quality of output—that is, for revitalizing primary education by changing the input mix to include more textbooks and learning materials. At the secondary level there is far more scope for containing unit costs—partly through making fuller use of available resources and partly through switching to cheaper ways of providing services. Higher education poses a set of problems uniquely its own. Rapid expansion has left in its wake an abundance of institutions, programs, and graduates that are often of low quality and dubious relevance. Modest consolidation, an adjustment measure that would lower unit costs, and increased cost sharing are the first steps on the road to higher education's revitalization, which must be regarded as a prerequisite for any further expansion of the subsector.

Primary Education

During the 1960s and 1970s some analysts warned that Sub-Saharan Africa's preoccupation with the quantity of education would lead to a serious deterioration in its quality. In the countries where educational standards have deteriorated the most, the choice between expansion and quality is no longer an either-or choice. Without some basic revitalizing inputs, particularly textbooks and instructional materials, almost no learning can be expected to occur. Ensuring the availability of essential inputs is a prerequisite both for quality and for expansion. Beyond this minimal level, however, are the questions of finding for each country an appropriate balance of quality and quantity—and of identifying efficient approaches to enhance quality and expand enrollments, and of financing both improvements.

A review of possible measures for improving the quality of primary education yields two broad conclusions:

- First, the safest investment in educational quality in most countries is to make sure that there are enough books and supplies. These materials are effective in raising test scores and, almost invariably, are underfunded currently relative to teachers' salaries. External aid might be used to address this problem in the short run, especially where foreign exchange is a governing constraint. Other possibilities for improving quality are found in school feeding and health programs, intensive use of radio, in-service education of teachers in subject matter, and stronger systems of inspection and supervision.
- Second, some investments are *not* likely to have a noticeable effect on primary school quality despite their potentially high costs. These investments include reducing class size (within the

range of 25 to 50), providing primary teachers with more than a general secondary education, providing teachers with more than minimal exposure to pedagogical theory, constructing high-quality buildings, and introducing televisions or computers into classrooms.

Even with no quality improvements (and assuming no improvements in efficiency), the resources devoted to the primary level would need to increase more than 3 percent a year just to keep pace with population growth. There is, however, little likelihood of significantly reducing unit recurrent costs at this level, especially if countries hope also to improve the quality of education. There is greater scope for reducing unit capital costs, but even so it is unlikely that overall per pupil costs can be reduced very much at the primary level. Thus the further growth of primary education will require additional resources.

Secondary Education and Training

Can adjustment measures at the secondary level generate sufficient savings to provide the necessary books and supplies and, at the same time, significantly expand capacity? Substantial economies are possible in the operation of regular schools. Boarding costs can also be reduced. And, most significant, there can be economies from the creation of distance education systems that combine radio and correspondence techniques and reduce (but do not eliminate) the amount of face-to-face interaction with qualified teachers. Such systems would extend secondary education of reasonable quality to many more communities than could be reached in any other way for the same price.

Beyond this general support for expanding access to secondary education, African governments should give serious consideration to policies designed to remedy existing inequalities in school participation. Females are the largest group underrepresented in postprimary education in Africa. Small, community-based schools (whether or not they rely on distance education) will tend to attract girls more readily than larger schools located in urban centers and at greater average distances from homes. Although smaller conventional schools may imply higher unit costs, this is not necessarily true if larger schools tend to include boarding facilities while smaller schools do not. Increasing the number of female teachers may also attract more girls, especially in Islamic areas.

Another set of issues to be addressed mainly at the secondary level concerns the relevance of the curriculum to the needs of individuals and societies. The main questions that many countries face are when and how to make the transition from programs and subjects that have broad vocational relevance (language, mathematics, and science) to programs and subjects that will prepare individuals for specific jobs or clusters of jobs. International experience shows that a strong general education, which schools can provide efficiently, greatly enhances an individual's future trainability. It also shows that job-specific training is very important. Such training usually is most efficiently provided after initial job decisions have been made and in institutions under, or strongly influenced by, the ultimate employer. Occupation-specific and job-specific training need not provide individuals with degrees or credentials.

Because of the high costs and tenuous vocational relevance of much school-based training for specific jobs and occupations, there is an urgent need to establish industrial training centers and to encourage (through incentives and technical assistance) local enterprises to offer skill development programs and other types of on-the-job training. Governments interested in laying the groundwork for a more technically oriented economy should place heavier emphasis on general mathematics and scientific skills in the secondary and postsecondary curriculum. These programs are relatively inexpensive and are generally more conducive to economic growth than is in-school vocational education.

Higher Education

Preparing and supporting people in positions of responsibility—in government, business, and the professions—is the central and essential role of the continent's universities. In numbers at least, the universities have risen impressively to this challenge. Enrollments grew from 21,000 in 1960 to more than 430,000 in 1983.

Higher education's contribution to development in Africa is being threatened, however, by four interrelated weaknesses. First, higher education is now producing relatively too many graduates of programs of dubious quality and relevance and generating too little new knowledge and direct development support. Second, the quality of these outputs shows unmistakable signs in many countries of having deteriorated so much that the fundamental effectiveness of the institutions is also in doubt. Third, the costs of higher education are needlessly high. Fourth, the pattern of financing higher education is socially inequitable and economically inefficient.

Wherever the foregoing diagnosis of weaknesses in higher education can be confirmed, policy reform should seek four objectives: (a) to improve quality;

(b) to increase efficiency; (c) to change the output mix, which may imply smaller enrollments in certain fields of study; and (d) to relieve the burden on public sources of financing by increasing the participation of beneficiaries and their families. But quality improvements, the first objective, will cost money. Thus, implementing adjustment policies to achieve the other three objectives will, almost everywhere in Africa, be a prerequisite for freeing the resources needed to achieve the first.

The Role of the International Donor Community

This study argues that adjustment measures are needed to alleviate the burden of education and training on public budgets in Africa. The "savings" generated by lower unit costs, increased cost sharing, and greater tolerance of the private provision of educational services can be used to help fund the necessary revitalization and ultimate expansion of the sector.

Regrettably, all such savings from adjustment measures will not be sufficient, in most countries, to cover the substantial resources needed to revitalize and build African education to the extent essential for future development. International aid will remain a critical determinant of the pace of progress of education in the region. However, the rapid evolution of African needs, as summarized in the three dimensional framework for policy reform, demands corresponding changes in the organization and nature (and not just an increase in the level) of international aid for African educational development.

The pressing requirement is for aid in support of policy reform. The international donor community should quickly offer three related kinds of support for the design of national policy.

- The first form of planning support is simple: seed money to cover both the local and foreign costs of developing policies and improving management. The willingness of the international donors to bear a part of these extraordinary expenses, perhaps on a matching basis, would provide an important incentive for African governments to review their policies for the sector.
- The second kind of support that the international community should provide is ready access to the ongoing experience of other countries in formulating and implementing policy reform. Intensive collaboration among countries, so that they share their accumulated experience widely, should pay high dividends as countries grapple with common issues.
- Third, the international donor community should establish and finance a source of high-quality specialized technical expertise without direct financial or political ties to any government or international donor. African governments could call on this expertise for help in formulating policies at the outset, and in monitoring, evaluating, and correcting them during implementation.

Appropriate mechanisms do not now exist for meeting these three interrelated needs for the improvement of policy development. The requirement is for expeditious action to develop them. Any donor initiative in this area that would take more than a year to get started would be an inadequate response to the needs of African governments.

Beyond its assistance in policy design, the international community should help finance the implementation of sound programs. These programs will typically require more resources, for a longer period, than can be mobilized internally. Countries that have demonstrated their willingness to address policy issues should have access to increased, longer-term, and more flexible international aid. To the extent that a country's policy package involves thoroughgoing reform, there are likely to be substantial one-time transition costs to a new and more sustainable policy regime.

The international commitment to the reform program must be seen from the beginning as continuing, a characteristic that has been missing in the past. In addition, the sum total of aid to different levels of education and different expenditure categories should reflect, at least in very rough terms, the priorities given to these levels and categories in the national program. In recent years, only 7 percent of international aid to African education has been used for primary education, compared with 16 percent for general secondary education, 33 percent for vocational and technical education (including teacher training), and 34 percent for higher education. In terms of expenditure categories, only 11 percent of aid has been used to support operational costs (local salaries, consumable supplies, and instructional materials). The donor organizations, both individually and as a group, need to review these allocations to make sure that they are consistent with the programs being formulated by African governments for the development of education and training.

Why Meet the Challenge? The Expected Benefits of Education

Greater investment in education can, at this time in Africa's history, be expected to yield broad economic benefits. These benefits include higher incomes and lower fertility. The research evidence to this effect is compelling. A caveat, however, is in order. The studies examining the welfare benefits of education are based necessarily on education as provided at some historical point in the past. To the extent that the quality of education has declined recently and is allowed to deteriorate further, new investments in the quantity of education may not yield returns commensurate with those in the past. Hence the strong emphasis in this study that quality be enhanced through revitalization as a prerequisite and complement to further expansion.

Assessments of the labor market returns to past investments in education have consistently found rates of return above 10 percent and sometimes above 20 percent—rates that compare favorably with those in most sectors in Africa today. A recent study on the long-term impact of educational investments on development in thirty-one African countries corroborates the microeconomic findings of education's high returns.

Increased investment in the quality and quantity of education can also be expected to reduce fertility. In general, there is a strong negative relationship between how much education a woman receives and the number of children she bears during her lifetime. Men and women with more education, in addition to having fewer children, tend to live healthier and longer lives. And numerous studies have shown that parents' education affects children's survival and enhances their physical and cognitive development.

The benefits of education go far beyond those for income and fertility, however. The rapid transition in Africa from colonial status to self-government to participation in the international arena was possible only because African educational systems produced people to replace expatriates at all levels. The nurturing of leaders who can address the increasingly complex tasks of nation-building is a continuing responsibility of African education. In addition, the stock of human capital in Africa will determine whether Africans can harness the universal explosion of scientific and technical knowledge for the region's benefit—or whether Africa will fall farther and farther behind the world's industrial nations. Above all, education is a basic right, an end in itself, an intrinsic part of life and development. When all the benefits of education are considered, the case for revitalization and expansion of schooling and training in Africa is compelling, even in this period of unusal scarcity.

Part 1

The Policy Context

1

The Remarkable Progress of African Education

Around the time that most countries of Sub-Saharan Africa gained independence from colonial rule, the region lagged far behind the rest of the world on nearly every indicator of Western-style educational development. Efforts since then have been truly dramatic, especially during the 1960s and 1970s, even though they did not close the education gap. The record of this period is a tribute to the determination of African leaders and the sacrifices of African parents in their quest to provide a better standard of living for their children's generation.

Before Independence

African societies have a long and rich history of educational traditions. Indigenous education was offered by all ethnic and linguistic groups and remains an important transmitter of cultural identity from one generation to the next. It aims to instill in children the attitudes and skills appropriate for male and female social roles, emphasizing the duties and privileges derived from cultural values. Imparted through language and example at home as well as in formal lessons and rituals outside the home, indigenous education responds to the concrete problems of local communities. It prepares political leaders and ordinary farmers, and it engenders a sense of citizenship in the people of the community.

Africa's early Christian heritage represents a second important element of education in the region, with roots extending back long before the colonial period. Especially in northeastern Africa and the Nile Basin, Christianity has thrived for more than 1,500 years. In about the year 450, the Ethiopian Christian Church, a prime example, established a comprehensive system of education that provided an underpinning for Ethiopian cultural, spiritual, literary, scientific, and artistic life.

A third major antecedent to the colonial period is the influence of Islam on African education. Arab culture and language were adopted in much of North Africa, and the Islamic faith also won converts in the Sahelian zone, along the coast of East Africa, and in much of the Horn of Africa. Both formal and nonformal school systems were established to teach the ethics and theology of Islam; they included a small number of elite centers of excellence such as the ones at Tombouctou in Mali and at Lamu on the east coast. Designed to impart skills and knowledge within the religious realm, the Islamic education system emphasizes reading and recitation in Arabic.

The Western colonial period in Sub-Saharan Africa began with the arrival of the Portuguese in the fifteenth century and ended only recently. Of the African countries covered in this study, Ethiopia and Liberia alone have been sovereign states for longer than thirty years. All of the other countries achieved sovereign status in the relatively short period between 1957 (Ghana) and 1980 (Zimbabwe). Colonial precedents are still much in evidence in most of Africa, and they sometimes constrain the degree to which governments are free to initiate new policies.

The principal suppliers of Western-style education before independence were the colonial governments themselves and the African missions of the Roman Catholic and various Protestant churches. The division of administrative and financial responsibilities between government and church differed from one colonial regime to the next. The British, for example, were generally more tolerant of religious and local community autonomy than were the French.

In their quest for converts and literate African subjects, the missionaries and colonial governments opened up a network of schools in the region. Many were of a high standard. Yet the curricula were based for the most part on overseas models and reflected little in the way of African content. The administration of "modern" education systems in Africa was dominated by expatriates, as was teaching beyond the primary level.

Nevertheless, the economic changes that the colonial powers set in motion in Africa helped create a demand for Western-style education that, in many areas, seemed nearly insatiable. Education became the vehicle for moving, within one generation, from peasantry and poverty to the topmost ranks of society. This fact of modern-day life escaped few African parents looking for ways to promote a better future for their children.

Access to education was quite limited, however, especially in the thinly populated areas of French West Africa. In 1960, the gross primary enrollment ratio in all of Sub-Saharan Africa was still only 36 percent. This was about half the levels then found in Asia (67 percent) and Latin America (73 percent). The enrollment ratio was 38 percent in the Francophone territories (50 percent in the Belgian colonies and just 31 percent in the French) and 40 percent in the Anglophone. Many countries, including The Gambia, Côte d'Ivoire, and Senegal in West Africa and Tanzania and Somalia in East Africa, had over 90 percent illiteracy at the time of independence.

There were also significant differences in educational access and participation within colonial territories—between urban and rural populations, males and females, and members of different ethnic or religious groups. Such patterns stemmed from a variety of causes. Different African peoples were regarded and treated differently by colonial administrators; the costs of providing education differed, certainly between urban and rural areas; some population groups were more responsive than others to educational opportunities; and most Africans, responding to the incentives imposed by patrilineal customs, preferred education for their sons to education for their daughters. As a result, problems of unequal educational participation frequently transcended colonial boundaries. Participation patterns in northern Nigeria, for example, had less in common with those in the south of the same British territory than with those in the north of neighboring French Cameroon. Such within-country differences and between-country similarities remain evident today.

Transition rates from one educational level to the next were low in 1960, and dropout rates were high. As a result, enrollment pyramids were typically very narrow at the top. Only 6 percent of all Sub-Saharan enrollments in 1960 were at the secondary level, and tertiary education was virtually nonexistent until the very end of the colonial period. The gross enrollment ratio at the secondary level in Africa was 3 percent in 1960, compared with 14 percent in Latin America and 21 percent in Asia. The ratio at the tertiary level was 1 to 500, about one-sixtieth those then found in Asia and Latin America. According to Unesco figures, at the time of independence there were only 90 African university graduates in all of Ghana, 72 in Sierra Leone, and 29 in Malawi. When Botswana became independent in 1966, 96 percent of higher-level posts in the country were filled by expatriates.

Advances after 1960

The systems of education inherited by the African nations at the time of independence were altogether inadequate to meet the needs of the countries for self-governance and rapid economic growth. From this low starting point, the progress achieved in African education has been remarkable.

Quantitative expansion has been particularly impressive. Between 1960 and 1983 the number of students enrolled in African institutions at all levels quintupled to about 63 million students (appendix table C-2). Enrollments increased about 9 percent annually between 1970 and 1980, double the rate in Asia and triple that in Latin America. The substantial expansion of education after independence has increased the participation of some groups who had had little or no access to formal education.

Primary school enrollments increased the most in absolute terms, growing from approximately 11.9 million pupils in 1960 to 51.3 million pupils in 1983 (see table 1-1). The gross primary enrollment ratio rose from 36 percent to 75 percent over this period. In only three of the region's thirty-nine countries (Congo, Lesotho, and Mauritius) was the enrollment ratio higher than 80 percent in 1960; by 1983, sixteen countries had achieved this milestone (see maps 5 and 6 in the appendix).

Table 1-1. School Enrollments and Enrollment Ratios in Sub-Saharan Africa, 1960 and 1983

Level	1960	1983
Primary education		
Enrollment (thousands)	11,900	51,300
Gross enrollment ratio (percent)	36	75
Secondary education		
Enrollment (thousands)	800	11,100
Gross enrollment ratio (percent)	3	20
Higher education		
Enrollment (thousands)	21	437
Gross enrollment ratio (percent)	0.2	1.4
Total enrollments (thousands)	12,700	62,900

Source: Appendix table C-2.

In fact, twelve of the thirty-nine countries now have gross primary enrollment ratios equal to or greater than 100 percent (appendix table A-7). Enrollment ratios in excess of 100 percent arise from the definition of the gross enrollment ratio, which divides the enrollment by the total (male and female) population of school age. The official age range differs from country to country depending on the structure of the education system. The gross enrollment ratio is an accurate measure of the school system's capacity relative to the school-age population. By including students who are outside the official age range, however, it overstates the percentage of this population that is actually enrolled. The net ratio, which excludes overage and underage children, is conceptually superior, but generally this information is not available. (Problems with gross enrollment statistics are further discussed in the technical notes for appendix tables A-7 to A-9.)

Enrollments at the tertiary level increased the most in relative terms, especially between 1960 and 1970. This happened because most African nations were emphasizing higher education in an effort to alleviate manpower shortages and also because enrollments had started from a low base. In 1960 there were only about 21,000 university students in Africa (approximately one in 500 of the age group) and a few thousand studying in foreign universities; by 1983, 437,000 (seven per 500) were enrolled in African institutions, and a further 100,000 Africans were studying abroad. The relative increase in tertiary enrollments was particularly dramatic in French-speaking Africa. In the group of eighteen Francophone countries, there were forty times more students enrolled in higher-level institutions in 1983 than in 1960. By way of contrast, in the sixteen Anglophone countries, where enrollments were much higher initially, enrollments had increased by only a factor of fifteen. For every student enrolled in higher education in the Francophone countries in 1960, there were four enrolled in the Anglophone countries; by 1983, the ratio was only about 1 to 1.5.

The building of schools and training of teachers to accommodate the additional students throughout the region were mammoth achievements. Between 1960 and 1983 the number of primary schools in Sub-Saharan Africa increased from about 73,000 to roughly 162,000, and the number of primary school teachers, from 310,000 to more than 1.3 million. Although the average pupil-teacher ratio remained roughly the same during this period (approximately 39 to 1), the average primary school size increased from 162 pupils in 1960 to 317 in 1983, almost doubling.

The number of teachers employed at the secondary level increased eightfold, going from about 46,000 in 1960 to about 373,000 in 1983. This understates the increase in African teachers, since many expatriate teachers were replaced during this period. At the tertiary level, the number of institutions in Sub-Saharan Africa has more than tripled since 1960 and today exceeds 80. (See appendix table A-10; the numbers of schools and teachers in the preceding two paragraphs reflect reasonable assumptions about missing data in the table.)

This massive educational expansion, which began in some countries in the 1950s and intensified everywhere after independence, has built up the stock of human capital considerably. Using data from countries that conducted censuses about 1980, it is possible to examine the changing educational attainment of successive cohorts of individuals who were of school age at different times during the thirty years beginning in 1950. For the few countries that have collected data, the proportion of males who reached adulthood without having attended school declined from 31 percent in the early 1950s to 22 percent in the late 1970s in six Anglophone countries, and from 59 percent to 42 percent in four Francophone countries. For the same countries and the same period, the proportion of males who *completed* primary school rose from 47 percent to 58 percent in the Anglophone countries, and from 16 percent to 30 percent in the Francophone. Estimated mean years of schooling for the male population (over age 15) increased from 4.6 to 5.4 years in the Anglophone countries and from 2.0 to 3.4 years in the Francophone.

An alternative to using census data for estimating stocks of education is to add up past enrollments. In conjunction with demographic assumptions, this allows estimates to be made, country by country, of the educational attainment of the working-age population. Table 1-2 reports estimates of educational stocks produced in this fashion. The estimated average educational attainment of working-age men and women in the median African country increased from 1.0 years in 1970 to 3.3 years in 1983. The figures in the table underline the wide disparities that remain in this variable, especially between the Sahelian (low-income semiarid) countries and the rest of Africa.

Table 1-2 also shows how literacy rates have risen since 1960. In the median African country, the percentage of adults reportedly able to read and write has increased by a factor of nearly five. This progress reflects both the growth of formal education and, in many countries, the success of programs to promote literacy among adults and young people not attending school. Approximately a quarter of all African countries have launched programs to eradicate adult illiteracy.

Other forms of adult and nonformal education have also been strengthened in the first two decades of independence. Many universities now have departments and institutes dedicated to the production and study of adult education, and nongovernmental bodies concerned with functional literacy and income generation in urban and rural areas have proliferated.

In addition to the remarkable quantitative achievements, many other significant changes have occurred in African education over the past quarter century. Especially at the primary level, Africanization of the curriculum has been widespread. In nearly every part of Sub-Saharan Africa, texts have been adapted and new texts written so that basic skills are now taught with reference to African customs, the local environment, and the area's own history. Twenty-one of the thirty-nine countries in the region now officially begin instruction in one or more African languages, rather than asking children to use a European language as the medium of instruction from their first day in primary school. These transformations have made the African classroom far more conducive to learning and have enabled children to acquire cognitive skills more quickly.

Expenditure on Education

The amount of resources allocated to education reveals the high degree of commitment of African

Table 1-2. Indicators of Educational Progress

Country group	Median estimated number of years of schooling of working-age population 1965	1983	Median literacy rate (percent) 1960	Latest available year
Economic status				
Low-income semiarid	0.1	0.9	2	15
Low-income other	0.5	2.9	10	41
Middle-income oil importers	1.3	4.2	19	72
Middle-income oil exporters	0.7	3.6	16	56
Linguistic				
Francophone	0.5	2.4	7	40
Anglophone	1.2	3.4	18	58
Sub-Saharan Africa	0.5	3.3	9	42

Source: Appendix tables C-3 and C-4.

nations to educational development and explains the significant advances that have occurred in the sector since 1960.

Public Domestic Expenditure on Education

In 1970 the thirty-nine countries of Sub-Saharan Africa allocated approximately $3.8 billion of public domestic expenditure to the education sector. This is a World Bank estimate of total (capital plus recurrent) expenditure (see box 1-1), expressed in constant 1983 U.S. dollars. By 1975 this figure had reached $6.3 billion, up 66 percent over 1970. By 1980 it was nearly $10.0 billion, up another 58 percent. Between 1980 and 1983 public expenditure fell somewhat, down approximately $1.1 billion, to $8.9 billion in constant 1983 dollars. This probably overstates somewhat the decline in real education expenditure since, in most African countries in recent years, teachers' salaries (which constitute approximately 90 percent, 70 percent, and 50 percent of recurrent expenditure in primary, secondary, and tertiary education, respectively) have not gone up as rapidly as prices in general as reflected in the GDP deflator.

Box 1-1. Aggregate Public Domestic Expenditure on Education in Sub-Saharan Africa

The discussion of public education expenditure in the text is based on information provided by Unesco and presented in appendix tables A-14 to A-23. Unesco local-currency expenditure figures were inflated to reflect 1983 prices using country-specific GDP deflators and then converted to U.S. dollars using official 1983 exchange rates. Because, for any given year, expenditure data have been reported for only a subset of countries, the total of public domestic education expenditure for all thirty-nine African countries is not known. For example, 1980 expenditures are known for only twenty-nine of the thirty-nine countries (see appendix table A-14).

In an attempt to bypass this data limitation, the table in this box reports estimated totals of public education expenditure in 1970, 1975, 1980, and 1983 for the thirty-nine countries as a group. These aggregates were arrived at by taking all countries for which actual data were available for the particular year and estimating, for this subset, the average relationship between expenditure and certain other measures including per capita income and enrollment at each of the three education levels. The estimated relationship was then used to impute expenditure figures for the remaining countries for which actual values were not reported. These estimated values were then added to the sum of reported values to arrive at the aggregate values given in the table.

Indexes of Total Enrollment and Expenditure on Education, 1970–83

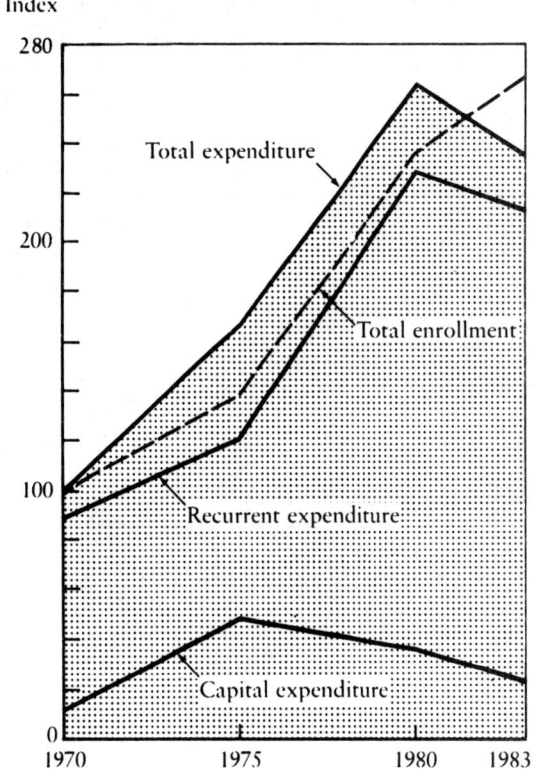

Public Domestic Expenditure on Education, 1970–83

Item	1970	1975	1980	1983
Actual data available (see appendix table A-14)				
Number of countries	27	26	29	28
Percentage of Sub-Saharan African population	60	77	89	75
Estimated expenditure for all 39 Sub-Saharan African countries (millions of 1983 dollars)				
Capital	459	1,767	1,316	865
Recurrent	3,329	4,516	8,636	8,032
Total	3,788	6,283	9,952	8,897

Although data are not available for 1984 and 1985, expenditures may have resumed growth after 1983, when the economic crisis was at its peak.

Since the use of official exchange rates may give a false picture of expenditure over time and may also distort comparisons between regions or countries, an alternative measure of public expenditure on education is useful. Expenditure as a percentage of national income is an especially meaningful indicator of a government's effort in the area of education. Figure 1-1 shows public domestic expenditure on education as a percentage of national income in Africa and elsewhere in four years between 1970 and 1983. The figure shows that Sub-Saharan Africa has been allocating a larger share of total income to education than have the developing countries in general, but still a smaller share than developed countries have managed to do. The figure also corroborates the decline in government expenditure on education after 1980.

Figure 1-1. Percentage of National Income Spent on Public Education in Sub-Saharan, Developing, and Industrial Countries, 1970–83

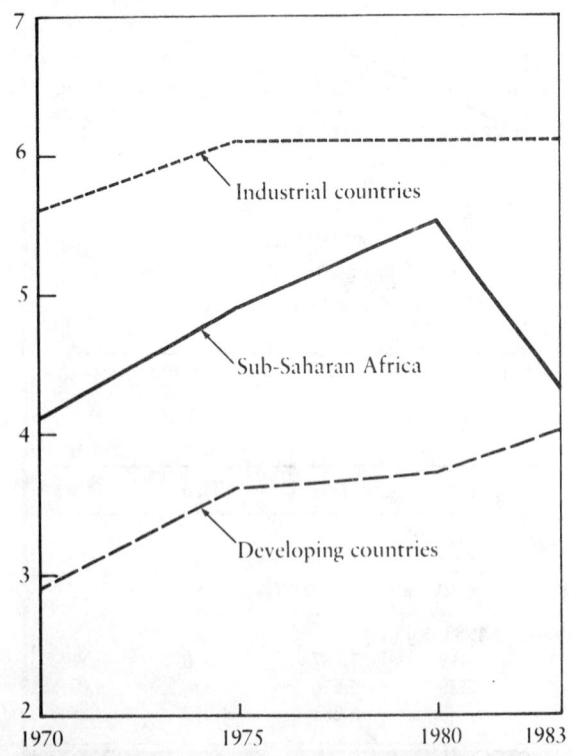

Another way to look at public expenditure on education is as a percentage of total public expenditure. On this indicator, the African countries have clearly treated education generously in the past. The median African country allocated 17.6 percent of the budget to education in 1970, 17.4 percent in 1975, 18.5 percent in 1980, and 15.3 percent in 1983. In terms of weighted means, as distinct from medians, education's share went from above 16 percent throughout the 1970s to below 12 percent in 1983. This more precipitous drop in education's share of expenditure after 1980 reflects, to a very large extent, what was happening in a single large country—Nigeria (see appendix table A-14). At the lower end of the spectrum, Malawi, Nigeria, and Somalia all spent below 10 percent of the central government budget on education in 1983. At the upper end, education's share was above 20 percent in Burkina Faso, Côte d'Ivoire, Mali, Niger, Rwanda, and Togo.

With regard to the distribution of expenditure across levels of education, the recurrent expenditure on primary education was between 43 percent and 49 percent of total recurrent expenditure in the median African country from 1970 to 1983. The share going to secondary education was between 25 percent and 31 percent, and the share going to tertiary, between 13 percent and 18 percent. The "unspecified" category remained nearly constant at about 10 percent (see appendix table A-16); as a residual, it cannot be taken very seriously but would presumably include most allocations for central administrative services and for adult education in ministries of education.

Private Spending on Education

The focus in the appendix tables on government expenditures reflects the relatively better data available on public, as distinct from private, sources of educational finance. Although information on the total of private spending is not available in most countries, it is clear that families and nongovernmental organizations bear a significant and growing portion of the financial burden of education in much of Africa. It has been estimated, for example, that private expenditure accounted for 14 percent of total national spending on education between 1975 and 1980 in the Sudan, 23 percent in Tanzania, 31 percent in Zimbabwe, 48 percent in Sierra Leone, and 53 percent in Ghana.

These figures tend to be larger today than they were in the early years after independence. Government-collected fees (which in official statistics are often counted as part of "public" expenditure on education) have been imposed or increased recently in many African countries. In addition to these fees, there are significant private outlays that are not channeled through government and are difficult to quantify. They include most fees paid to private education institutions; the privately borne costs of such items as transportation, school uniforms, textbooks, and supplies; and, especially important at the primary level, family and community outlays, either in cash or in kind, for the construction or repair of school buildings in public education. Commitment of student time is, of course, another valuable input to the education system, but this study does not attempt to account for it.

During the colonial period, much of Western-style education in Africa was organized and, to a significant extent, financed by missionary groups that often relied heavily on community self-help. After independence, governments assumed responsibility for most such education in nearly every African country, Lesotho being a major exception to this rule. During this period, wherever school fees had been charged, they were often reduced or eliminated. More recently, however, in response to growing fiscal and demographic pressures, African leaders have condoned a reversal of this postindependence trend. In the late 1970s and 1980s students, their families, and communities have been asked to contribute ever larger amounts toward the costs of education. Often, to avoid having to collect school fees, governments have referred to these subscriptions by another name, such as development fund contributions or activity payments.

Foreign Aid Flows to African Education

Foreign aid also accounts for a significant part of total spending on African education (appendix tables A-24 to A-27). In 1981–83, the total of bilateral, multilateral, and private voluntary organization aid to African education granted through central government ministries of education (and not through other departments of government, nor directly to individuals) was estimated to be about $915 million a year. This figure includes about 3 percent from the IBRD of the World Bank Group and from the African Development Bank that was in the form of market-rate loans. The remaining 97 percent can be counted as concessional aid to African education. Nearly a quarter of the total was in the form of scholarships for African students to study abroad; a significant portion of aid to education (about 44 percent) was in the form of technical assistance.

African governments received an estimated additional $394 million of external aid each year to finance project-related training in sectors other than education. In addition, when African students study abroad, the host countries incur indirect costs— nonexplicit subsidies that students, including foreign students, receive at most universities. A very rough estimate of the total of such subsidies to African students who were studying abroad between 1980 and 1982 is $245 million annually.

The total of all categories of external aid to African education and training in the early 1980s was about $1.6 billion annually. This is a significant amount, nearly $4 per capita, but there is no evidence to suggest that external aid has increased in recent years to compensate for the decline in African government expenditures. To the contrary, the total of all aid to Africa for all purposes was smaller in 1983 than the 1980–82 average, and smaller in 1984 than in 1983. Further discussion of external aid to education in Africa appears in chapter 9.

Education and the External Environment

The impressive gains recently won in African education are now seriously threatened by circumstances outside the sector, including Africa's explosive population growth, which swells the number of potential illiterates on the continent, and Africa's recent economic decline, which has necessitated significant cutbacks in public spending. Although economic prospects may have brightened somewhat since 1983 and population growth has begun to slow in a handful of countries, for most of Sub-Saharan Africa current economic and demographic realities undermine both the quantitative and qualitative educational advances achieved since independence. Retrogression in education will, in turn, make the solution of these problems more difficult. And so the pattern is repeated, and it is destined to continue until extraordinary efforts are made to interrupt this cycle of deteriorating prospects.

The Demographic Challenge

Between 1970 and 1980, while the world's population was growing at an average annual rate of 1.9 percent, Africa's population grew at 2.9 percent, one and a half times the world's rate. Between 1980 and the end of the century, Africa's population is projected to grow even faster, at about 3.2 percent a year, while growth rates are projected to decline for the other principal regions of the world.

Africa's high population growth rate reflects the rapid decline in mortality rates in recent years while fertility rates have remained, for the most part, at the same high levels that prevailed historically. In 1960 the crude death rate in Sub-Saharan Africa was twenty-five per thousand and the crude birth rate forty-nine per thousand. By 1983, owing to significant improvements in health care, the death rate had fallen to seventeen per thousand, but the birth rate remained practically unchanged. Birth rates actually increased over this period in a handful of countries.

Africa's rapid population growth creates serious problems for education. For the growth of educational places to keep pace with the growth of school-age children, more schools, teachers, books, and other inputs are required each year. Moreover, because as populations grow the number of school-age children increases more rapidly than the number of working adults, the burden of supporting an expanded education system falls on an adult population that is shrinking as a proportion of the overall population. Sub-Saharan Africa today has the youngest population of any region in the world. One in three persons is of primary or secondary school age in Africa (see figure 2-1), as compared with just one in five persons in Latin America and in Asia, and one in six persons in the industrial countries.

By the year 2000 Africa's primary and secondary school-age population is likely to reach 220 million, which is 90 million, or 70 percent, more than the number in 1984 (see figure 2-2). This massive explosion in the potential demand for educational services is virtually inevitable, given the number of people

Figure 2-1. Population by Age, 1984

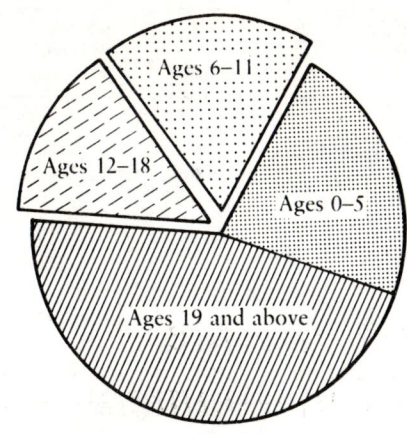

already born who will be of child-bearing age during the period. This inevitability of growth is of fundamental importance. It sharply constrains African planners' options, and its implications color all of the analysis presented here.

For example, there were 51.3 million primary and 11.1 million secondary school places in Africa in 1983. These figures would have to reach 90.7 million and 19.7 million, respectively, by the year 2000 just to maintain participation rates at their 1983 levels (see table 2-1). The goal of universal primary education, which African education planners at one time hoped could be achieved even by 1980, unfortunately from the perspective of the mid-1980s still seems very far away. For the region to have all primary-school-age children enrolled by the year 2000 would require that 131.8 million primary school places be made available, a 157 percent increase in just seventeen years. The 80.5 million additional places required are more than all of the places that exist now after many decades of educational development.

The investment in the construction of new classrooms and the recurrent costs necessary to support such massive expansion in education, while not altogether unreasonable if the achievements of the 1960s and 1970s are simply extrapolated forward, unfortunately do not seem very likely in the context of long-run austerity beginning in the 1970s. Table 2-1 shows that to maintain gross enrollment ratios at their 1983 levels would require the addition of 39.4 million primary and 8.6 million secondary school places by the turn of the century. Assuming that per pupil expenditures will remain at their 1983 levels in constant dollar terms (roughly $50 per primary and $250 per secondary school pupil), the recurrent costs of just the first two levels of education would go up by approximately $4.0 billion, becoming $9.4 billion by the year 2000 (see table 2-2). This amount is already more than the total allocated by African governments to all three levels of education and their central administration in 1983.

In addition to meeting the swollen recurrent costs, government budgets would have to finance school buildings and equipment—both to meet the needs of new students and to replace (at an estimated 2 percent a year) outmoded facilities. Assuming very modest capital costs of $150 per primary place and $1,250 per secondary place (this best-practice scenario involves capital costs well below actual average capital costs in Africa today), the required investment in facilities would be another $1.4 billion annually. The total of recurrent and capital expenditures for primary and secondary education alone would come to nearly $11 billion annually. This is about $2 billion more than the total spent on all aspects of education

Figure 2-2. Growth of School-Age Populations, 1965–80 and Projected to 2000

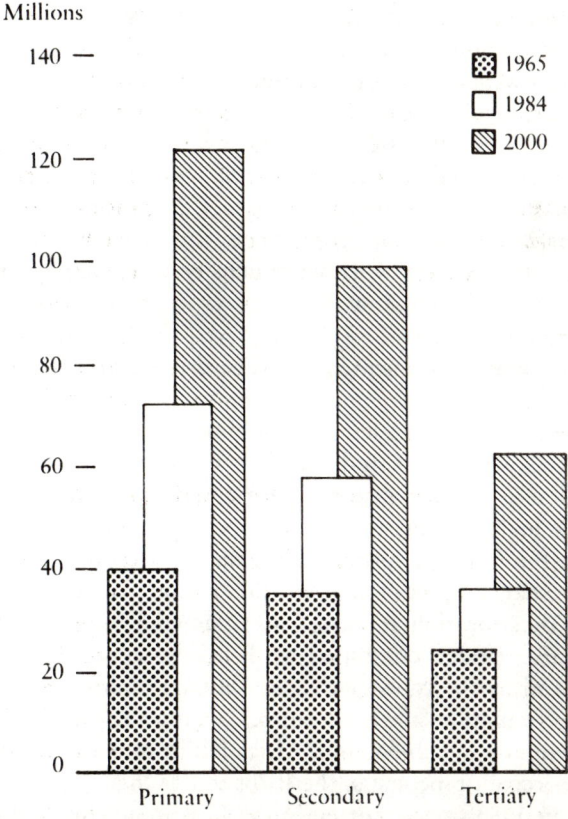

19

Table 2-1. School-Age Population and School Enrollment, 1983 and Projected to 2000

Indicator and date	Primary Millions	Primary Change, 1983–2000 (percent)	Secondary Millions	Secondary Change, 1983–2000 (percent)
School-age population				
1983	68.5	n.a.	55.6	n.a.
2000	120.9	76	98.6	77
School enrollment				
1983	51.3	n.a.	11.1	n.a.
2000				
Assuming enrollment ratios as in 1983	90.7	77	19.7	77
Assuming full enrollment and no repetition or dropout	120.9	136	98.6	788
Assuming full enrollment and repetition and dropout as in 1983	131.8	157	105.5	850

n.a. Not applicable.
Source: Appendix tables A-1, A-2, A-7, A-8, A-12, and B-4.

in 1983. In sum, the demographic tide requires massive efforts just to stay even in terms of enrollment ratios.

Ironically, in addition to explosive population growth, much of Africa suffers from another demographic condition—low population density. The combination of rapid growth and low density may seem strange since, given enough time, the first will eventually eliminate the second. In the meantime, however, low population density often implies high unit costs in education, especially in rural areas, where economies of scale in the provision of education are precluded given present methods for delivering education. At the present, Africa's population density is about nineteen people per square kilometer, compared with a worldwide density of about thirty-six per square kilometer.

Macroeconomic Adjustment and Fiscal Austerity

The late 1970s ushered in an economic crisis that accelerated after 1980 and has left most African economies in serious disarray. Agriculture, which accounts for the largest share of goods produced (about a third of total production), was hurt by the drought that affected much of the region, by a marked deterioration in terms of trade (declining agricultural prices combined with rising energy prices), and by the continuation of national policies that discriminate against the sector. Moreover, the investment rate in Sub-Saharan Africa fell from more that 18 percent of income in the 1970s to less than 15 percent in 1983 and is currently the lowest of any developing region, thus threatening to undermine Africa's long-term productive capacity.

Economic stagnation, combined with rapid population growth, has meant a decline in living standards, a fatal decline for many individuals in those countries worst hit. Overall, income per capita fell nearly 4 percent annually between 1980 and 1984; it is lower in the region today than it was twenty years ago. The external public and publicly guaranteed debt increased elevenfold between 1970 and 1984, and debt service payments more than tripled as a percentage of GNP, from 1.2 percent to 4.4 percent. Central government expenditures increased while revenues remained about the same, and fiscal deficits on the continent rose to about 10 percent of GNP.

Because continuation of these trends spelled economic disaster, African governments recognized that macroeconomic policy reforms were an absolute necessity. In this regard, they have made substantial progress since 1980, along the general lines prescribed at the United Nations Special Session on Africa in May 1986. Thus many governments have reconsidered their exchange rate policies, instituted wage and salary reforms, and begun to eliminate price distortions that penalized farmers. They have also reduced public spending, including spending on education (chapter 3).

It is expected that these structural reforms will gradually encourage higher investment and lead to increased consumption levels. Moreover, in 1986 the drought in Africa abated, and there was an improvement in the region's terms of trade. In that year low-income Africa registered a growth in per capita income for the first time in the 1980s; figures for 1987 are expected to show some further improvement. In sum, there may be room again for cautious optimism with regard to the economic environment and long-

Table 2-2. Enrollment and Recurrent Expenditure, 1983 and Projected to 2000 Assuming Enrollment Ratios as in 1983

Indictor and date	Primary	Secondary	Total
Enrollment (millions)			
1983	51.3	11.1	62.4
2000	90.7	19.7	110.4
Recurrent expenditure (billions of 1983 dollars)			
1983	2.6	2.8	5.4
2000	4.5	4.9	9.4
Required average annual capital investment, 1983–2000 (billions of 1983 dollars)	0.5	0.9	1.4

term growth prospects of the region, but this relative optimism should by no means give rise to complacency.

Investment in Education

Extensive experience from Africa and elsewhere provides strong evidence that increased investment in education and training at this stage in Africa's history can yield broad economic benefits—including higher incomes and lower fertility, both of critical importance in the African context. Although direct evidence for developing areas and especially for Sub-Saharan Africa is less extensive and rich than for the industrial countries, enough information exists to conclude that the direction of the relationship between education and various indicators of economic well-being is the same everywhere and that the positive relationship holds true for both formal general education and for training. The evidence suggests, however, that the impact of education is somewhat larger in developing countries, because of its relative scarcity there.

Education cannot, in itself, bring about economic growth, but the evidence indicates it to be a vital factor. It provides the fertile ground without which other development initiatives will not take root. Education accelerates the growth process; it is an essential complement to other factors. Thus, for example, although education is associated with increases in agricultural productivity, the impact of education is found to be much greater in environments that are already modernizing. Likewise, investments in the provision of family planning services have been shown to have greater effect if the women using the service (or potentially using it) are better educated.

The economic rationale for enhanced activity in African education, elaborated below, may be supported by several broad and politically compelling explanations of why African countries have invested so heavily in education since independence and why they should endeavor to protect and expand their commitment to the sector in the future. First, the essence of sovereignty is the control of nationals over the destiny of their country. The transition from colonial dependence to self-government and to active independent participation in the international arena was possible only because African educational systems were able to produce indigenous personnel at all levels to replace expatriate rule. The qualitative nurturing and quantitative regeneration of that leadership elite, so that it can address the increasingly complex challenges of nation-building in the future, is a continuing requirement for the effective maintenance of sovereignty and, as such, a fundamental responsibility of African systems of education.

Second, the rate and extent of the growth of human capital in African countries, attained through the improvement and expansion of education at all levels, will ultimately determine whether the universal explosion of scientific and technical knowledge can be harnessed for the benefit of the region, or whether Africa will be left behind and denied the enormous benefits accruing to technological change. Finally, education is everywhere a "merit good," a basic human right, an end in itself; indeed, education is an intrinsic element of the development process. It is unthinkable that African governments, and their international partners, would permit a decline in the fraction of the population having access to education's many benefits. And yet that is the specter that now menaces many African countries.

The economic evidence indicating large payoffs to education is of three principal sorts, each providing corroboration for the others. The first two rely on individual-level data; the last consists of macroeconomic evidence. The first one examines the relation between an individual's education level and his or her productivity in the labor market as a wage employee or self-employed worker. The second links the education of individuals to important outcomes of household behavior such as fertility rates or child survival. Finally, macroeconomic evidence relates the growth rates of national economies to prior investments in education and can control for other factors presumed to influence growth. The macroeconomic evidence is an important complement to the individual-level data, particularly the data on education and earnings, in that it provides evidence to assess the view, occasionally advanced, that education improves the lot of individuals by reallocating societal resources but does not increase the overall flow of resources. The remaining pages of this chapter summarize evidence of all three types.

Labor Productivity

Economists have assessed the economic value of education by observing differences in the earnings of workers with different levels of education, having controlled for other differences that exist between the groups, and then comparing the adjusted earnings differences with the costs of the education. The indicator that summarizes the information on costs and benefits is the social rate of return. In technical terms, the rate of return is the discount rate that equates the present value of the economic costs and benefits of an investment. Private rates of return to education are calculated using after-tax earnings differentials and only those educational costs that are actually borne by students and their families. Social rates of return, which are more useful for public policy, are based on before-tax earnings differentials and on education's full resource costs. The full costs of education equal the sum of all private costs plus any subsidies given.

A recent survey of cost-benefit studies conducted in sixteen African countries suggests average social rates of return to investment in African education of the following magnitudes: primary, 26 percent; secondary, 17 percent; and tertiary, 13 percent. Although these rates of return certainly seem attractive in relation to many other forms of investment, they may overstate the actual current returns, because the data on which many of the estimates are based are out of date. The cross-sectional earnings data used in these studies are, on average, ten years old, and there has been considerable educational expansion over the decade since then.

A more recent study from Kenya indicates that rates of return have fallen off somewhat and that the substantial difference (nine percentage points) observed in the past between primary and secondary education may have completely disappeared, which would reflect the declining relative scarcity value of primary education (see box 2-1). Even so, the Kenya study confirms that rates of return to both levels of education, after adjusting for other factors, remain substantial (around 12 percent).

The relatively lower rate of return to education at the tertiary level should not be interpreted to mean that high-level skills are not important in Africa. What the findings reflect most of all are the extremely high unit costs of tertiary education. In addition, most studies ascribe all costs at this level to teaching and none to other outputs of the tertiary system, such as research. If the costs of tertiary education were to be prorated and the value of the research and other outputs of the education were to be assessed broadly to include some that may accrue to society in general, rather than only to the individuals who receive the education, then the rate of return to tertiary education would certainly appear higher.

Many of the early rate of return studies relied on earnings data for workers employed in the formal wage sector. To the extent that the number of primary school leavers able to find employment in the formal sector has declined recently in relation to the number of uneducated people so employed, and to the extent that earnings in the formal sector are "protected" and thus remain higher than elsewhere in the economy, the estimated rates of return might have been inflated. The perceived validity of such benefit-cost studies has been considerably enhanced, therefore, by a number of recent studies of education's impact, including some done in Africa, that are based on information about self-employed workers. Since the self-employed do not receive wages as such, many of these studies have sought to estimate the value of education by looking at the value of what more-educated individuals produce. Most of the research has focused on agriculture, especially on crop production.

A recent review of eighteen studies of farmer education and farm productivity in thirteen countries concluded that farmers who have completed four years of education produce, on average, about 8 percent more farm output than farmers who have not gone to school, controlling for differences in the use of physical inputs. Moreover, the percentage increase in output associated with four years of education is found to be about 10 percent in "modernizing" environments (indicated by such factors as the availability of new crop varieties and reasonable incentives); in more traditional environments, where tech-

Box 2-1. Rates of Return to Primary and Secondary Education in Kenya

Perhaps the most influential fact to emerge from twenty-five years of studying rates of return in developing countries concerns the relative returns to primary and secondary schooling. Most studies, including most of those conducted in Africa, have reported substantially higher rates of return at the primary level. The implication generally drawn is that top priority should be given to primary education as a form of investment in human resources. Recent studies from Kenya throw some new light on this issue.

Returns to education are measured by the gaps in wages, and presumably productivity, between workers with different levels of education. It is often assumed that the average wage of labor with a given level of education measures the wage received by the marginal (most recently recruited) worker with that level of schooling. However, the average may not always indicate the marginal wage.

Because of rapid expansion in the education system, the labor market conditions faced by those just leaving school now are very different from the conditions faced by earlier cohorts when primary school leavers were in short supply. For those entering the labor market a generation ago, a primary school certificate was a passport to a white-collar job, and typically those who obtained jobs at that time remain in them today. But, because the education system has expanded, today's primary school completer is fortunate to get even a menial blue-collar job in the wage sector, and his chance of obtaining a white-collar position is virtually nil.

The process by which successive cohorts of workers at a particular education level enter less skilled jobs is called "filtering down." A recent study took this process into account in calculating average and marginal rates of return in Kenya. The study found that the rate of return to primary schooling is highly sensitive to the distinction between average and marginal rates of return, whereas the rate of return to secondary schooling is not. The average return to primary schooling, as conventionally measured, is 17 percent; the marginal return is 12 percent. The marginal return is lower for two reasons. At the primary level there are both substantial filtering down and large differences in wages by occupation, whereas for the uneducated there is less scope for filtering down and wage differences by occupation are small.

For secondary education, by contrast, the average and marginal rates of return are both 13 percent. Because the degree of filtering down of primary and secondary school completers is similar, the differential in earnings between the two groups is little affected. In Kenya moving from the average to the marginal concept erases the usually reported difference in rates of return: at the margin, the rate of return to secondary education (13 percent) about equals the rate of return to primary education (12 percent).

---

nology and opportunity are changing only slowly, there is little payoff to education. Only one African country, Kenya, was included among the thirteen countries in the review, but the results there were consistent with the general findings. A recent study of this kind based on data from South Asia identifies numeracy and literacy among the critical cognitive skills through which education's effect on farmer productivity is mediated.

One may conclude from all of the available evidence that rates of return to investment at all levels of education in Africa today compare favorably with realized rates in most other sectors, including some sectors for which the World Bank and other development agencies have been providing relatively large amounts of money in recent years. The Bank's experience with project lending reinforces what researchers have concluded regarding the value of education. The probability that a development project in any sector will be successful has been observed to increase as a function of the human capacity available to plan, implement, and benefit from it. The absence of important skills, particularly in project management, is often cited as the primary reason for the failure of particular projects to meet their objectives. More generally, the education level of the entire population involved in a project—farmers who would be using new inputs made available under a project or women who would be visiting a new health or family planning clinic—is often a key element in determining whether the project has a significant impact. Investment in education, in sum, increases the return to investments in other sectors.

There are other ways that education may enhance worker productivity. It has been shown, for example, that education increases the propensity of individuals to migrate. This tendency will increase economic growth to the extent that individuals shift their jobs, as they will naturally seek to do, from less-productive to more-productive sectors. Moreover, employed urban migrants typically remit a part of their earnings to their families back home, and this resource flow has been shown to result in increased investment in Africa's rural areas.

Education may also, under certain conditions, be expected to fulfill equity goals. Since it was first

Box 2-2. Education and the Decline of Mortality: Research from Ghana, Nigeria, and Sudan

A number of survey and census analyses have detected an inverse relationship between a child's chances of survival and the mother's level of education. Data from the 1960 census of Ghana, for example, reveal that the rate of child mortality is almost twice as high for mothers with no education as for mothers with an elementary education, and nearly four times higher for mothers with no education as for those with secondary schooling. The patterns are much the same for children in urban and rural areas.

A more comprehensive study was conducted in Nigeria as part of the 1973 Changing African Family Project Survey. One component of this study was a probability sample of 6,606 Yoruba women between the ages of fifteen and fifty-nine in the city of Ibadan. The second component consisted of a probability sample of 1,499 Yoruba women over age seventeen living in southwestern Nigeria. Analysis of these data allowed for an examination of rural-urban differences, which serve as a reasonable proxy for differences in access to modern health services.

The study considered child survival in relation to a variety of variables, including the quality of medical services at childbirth, the parents' practice of birth control, and the family's income as measured by the father's occupation. The analysis concluded that the single most important influence on child survival is the level of the mother's education. In Ibadan the child mortality index for women with some primary schooling was 68 percent of that recorded for women with no schooling, and the index for women with more than primary schooling was 39 percent of that for women with no schooling. In southwestern Nigeria the figures were almost the same, 68 percent and 41 percent, respectively.

Although the father's education was also found to be significant, it was less important than the mother's in explaining differences in child mortality. Family income, too, was found to be of little importance, after the effects of education were taken into account. Although child mortality was higher in polygamous than in monogamous homes, the effect of a mother's education to the secondary level was at least a 50 percent reduction in mortality in both polygamous and monogamous homes. Once other factors were controlled for, child survival was found to be higher among parents who practiced birth control, which might be explained by the greater care accorded children in smaller families.

Results in the Sudan from the same Changing African Family Project Survey confirmed the findings on the importance of mother's education to child survival.

---

introduced in Africa, Western-style education has been a vehicle by which able children of poor families have managed to move to higher levels in society's occupational and income structure. As access increases, the additional expenditures on education will flow increasingly to the disadvantaged elements of society—the poor, those in rural areas, and girls. The study in box 2-1 compares the experience in Kenya, where secondary education was allowed to expand rapidly during the 1970s as a function of demand, with the experience in Tanzania, where the expansion of secondary education was relatively constrained. Although both Kenya and Tanzania expressed concern over the widely dispersed wage structures that existed, Kenya's policy resulted in substantially greater compression in the distribution of earnings over the period than occurred in Tanzania. In addition, the larger size of the secondary system has meant greater access for the children of the poor and uneducated in Kenya than in Tanzania.

Education yields the recipients other important benefits that are not (immediately) reflected in the form of increased earnings or a more equal distribution of earnings. These benefits have to do with fertility, health, and individual fulfillment.

Lower Fertility and Other Benefits

The more education a woman receives, the fewer children she is likely to bear. Of course, in areas where income is very low fertility may actually increase with the first few years of schooling given to women, because of education's impact on health and fecundity. Nevertheless, research on the determinants of family size in Africa and elsewhere indicates convincingly that raising the educational attainment of women ultimately reduces fertility. This longer-term behavioral change occurs through education's direct effects on individual decisions to have children and through its indirect effects on children's survival and women's employment opportunities.

From the household perspective it is desirable that, through education, women gain the power to control the number and spacing of the children they bring into the world. Moreover, in light of the economic problems associated with Africa's unprecedented population growth rate, the social benefits of education's impact on fertility-related behavior can be expected to be high.

In addition to having fewer children, more-educated men and women are found to live healthier and longer lives. One recent multination study demonstrated that a difference of one percentage point in the national literacy rate is associated with a two-year gain in life expectancy, controlling for per capita income and food energy consumption.

The education of parents, particularly mothers, has been shown to affect the physical and cognitive development of children. This benefit occurs, in part, through education's effect on family income and, in part, through its effects on parents' knowledge and use of good health and nutrition practices. Furthermore, intellectual skills acquired through one's own education tend to "rub off" on one's children. Studies have shown that children of more-educated parents are more likely to be enrolled in school and, once enrolled, are more successful and continue higher up the education ladder.

There is, following from education's effects on nutrition and health, a consistent and strongly positive relationship between parental education and child survival. A review of research in this area concludes that the addition of one year of mothers' schooling reduces child mortality by nine deaths per thousand live births. Box 2-2 summarizes new research from Africa on the impact of maternal education on child survival.

Economic Growth

Microeconomic evidence of the sort just discussed strongly suggests the importance of education in determining economic growth. Yet some concerns may remain. Perhaps education's high rates of return are accounted for, indirectly, by reductions in the earnings of the less well educated. Or, conversely, to the extent that the better educated enhance the productivity of those around them (through their entrepreneurial activities or technical contributions, for example), measurement of income differentials by education level may understate education's impact. To address these concerns, macroeconomic evidence on education and economic growth complements the extensive microeconomic literature.

Macroeconomic analyses attempt to explain differences in growth rates and other development outcomes among countries in terms of differences, among other things, in their patterns of investment in education. The World Bank's *World Development Report 1980* undertook an analysis of this sort and concluded the following: (a) increases in literacy contribute both to increased investment and (given the level of investment) to increases in output per worker; (b) literacy, as well as nutrition and income, affects life expectancy; and (c) variations in life expectancy, literacy, income, and the strength of family planning programs explain most of the variation in fertility rates across countries.

Although the *World Development Report*'s findings on the development impact of investment in education are quite clear, the analysis was undertaken on a sample of all developing countries, and somewhat different results might pertain to Africa. More recent analyses suggest, however, that levels of investment in education are, if anything, more important in explaining differences in growth rates in Africa than elsewhere. Box 2-3 summarizes the results of an analysis, undertaken in conjunction with the preparation of this paper, of the contribution of education to the growth of thirty-one African countries over several decades. The analysis concludes, in short, that investments made in education have contributed significantly to growth in GDP; indeed, perhaps 30 percent of GDP growth has resulted from education investments. The aggregate evidence thus corroborates the microeconomic findings of education's high returns.

Box 2-3. Education and Economic Growth in Sub-Saharan Africa

Between 1965 and the early 1980s Africa invested heavily in education. The growth of primary school enrollments, which rose from 12 million in 1960 to over 50 million in 1983, is one measure of this investment. The average investment in education in Sub-Saharan Africa in recent years has been between 4 and 5 percent of national income, plus direct parental contributions and the potential earnings forgone by students while they attend school.

In order to guide future allocations to the education sector, it is important to evaluate the extent to which African governments' past investments in education have contributed to recent economic growth. Such an analysis was undertaken, using data from the appendix and other World Bank sources. The analysis used a "production function" that relates the GDP of each country in each time period (five intervals between 1965 and 1983 were used) to a number of factors potentially important in determining GDP. These included the size of the working-age population, the area of land under cultivation, the available physical capital stock, and the available human capital stock as measured by the number of years that members of the

(Box continues on the following page.)

Box 2-3 *(continued)*

working-age population attended secondary school. A measure of years of primary school attendance was also available, but since the two education variables are highly colinear, one was dropped from the analysis.

These data permitted use of standard econometric methods to estimate the parameters of the production function that relates GDP to the availability of the determining variables. Specifically, a Cobb-Douglas production function was estimated by examining how changes in input availability resulted in changes in GDP. With an estimated production function and knowledge about growth in the availability of the input factors, it is possible to account for the growth in overall GDP by disaggregating it into components that reflect the rate of growth of each input's availability and the relative importance of that input for determining output, as assessed from the production function.

The table below reports the results of this analysis. The first column of the table lists and defines the variables used in the analysis; the second indicates their growth during 1965–83. For example, for the thirty-one countries included in the analysis GDP grew at an average rate of 4.3 percent a year during the period, and the size of the working-age population grew at a rate of 2.5 percent a year, so that the growth of GDP per member of the working-age population was, on average, about 1.8 percent a year. The third column indicates that the amount of land per worker grew more slowly than GDP per worker, but that physical capital and, particularly, human capital stocks grew much more rapidly.

The final two columns show how these input growth rates accounted for the 1.8 percent growth of GDP per worker. Increases in the stock of human capital accounted for 0.55 of the 1.8 percentage points, or 31 percent of total GDP growth. This is an impressive fraction, indeed, and clearly demonstrates the importance of investment in education in explaining GDP growth in Africa. The most nearly analogous figure from Edward Denison's work on economic growth in the United States between 1929 and 1976 is 26 percent. Growth in the availability of physical capital accounted for 71 percent of the total growth. A "residual" of unaccounted-for growth was actually negative in this analysis, resulting in a decrease of 0.1 percentage points a year in the level of growth that would have been expected on the basis of growth in the measured inputs. This residual (often interpreted as technical and institutional improvement) is positive in studies undertaken with data from the United States and other industrial countries and often accounts for a substantial fraction of total growth. That it has been negative during this period in Africa may be consistent with impressionistic accounts of recent sharp technological and institutional deterioration.

Contributors to GDP Growth in Sample Countries, 1956–83

	Annual growth rate (percent)		Contribution to growth of GDP per member of working-age population	
Variable	Absolute	Per member of working-age population	Percentage points	Percent of total
GDP	4.3	1.8	n.a.	n.a.
Labor (size of working-age population)	2.5	n.a.	n.a.	n.a.
Capital (physical stock)	7.8	5.3	1.25	69
Land (area under cultivation)	3.6	1.1	0.09	5
Human capital (years of secondary education in working-age population)	18.3	15.8	0.55	31
Residual	n.a.	n.a.	−0.09	−5

n.a. Not applicable.

Economic and demographic pressures will, clearly, constrain the capacity of societies—and, even more, of governments—to invest as fully as would be desirable in the education levels of their future populations. Over a period of time, however, governmental policy reform and individual responses to reform, combined with development assistance from abroad, will create an environment in which sustained growth can resume. Indeed, economic statistics emerging since the mid-1980s have reflected a return to growth. To take full advantage of an improving economic policy environment, sustained infrastructural investments must be made, both public and private. The evidence is powerful that education is a key area for such investment. African governments and peoples have successfully implemented massive educational investments, and evaluation of the consequences shows the returns to have been high. We come, then, to the first central recommendation of this report.

Recommendation 1

Because of the unusually favorable rates of return and the feasibility of project implementation, education is prominent among the economic sectors in Africa that call for greater investment. To promote long-term development most African countries should try to increase both public and private expenditures on education. Government expenditure, currently averaging between 4 and 5 percent of national income in the region, should be gradually increased in most countries, particularly those that now dedicate significantly less than this proportion to the sector or that lag far behind on key indicators of educational development. Such increases in public spending are warranted, however, only in conjunction with efforts at all levels to improve education's internal efficiency and financial viability. The broad array of measures appropriate for these objectives will typically include greater nongovernmental provision of education services, thereby raising private resources dedicated to the sector at least in proportion to the increase in public resources.

3

The Stagnation of Enrollment and Decline in Quality

Although African nations have made enormous progress in education as described in chapter 1, much remains to be done. Africa still lags behind other developing regions with regard to most indicators of educational development. Moreover, the external factors described in chapter 2 provide an inhospitable environment for eliminating the education and training gap.

Indeed, because of the invidious combination of rapid population growth and economic stagnation, the gap between Sub-Saharan Africa and the rest of the world appears to be widening; certainly it is no longer closing as in recent decades. Unless steps are taken to address the serious problems in education, this gap will in time become a gulf. Given the vital links between education and a people's prospects for economic growth and development (see chapter 2), this cannot be allowed to happen.

This chapter describes the alarming state of education in Africa along the two principal dimensions of educational output: quantity and quality. On the quantitative side, school enrollments have fallen as a proportion of school-age populations in many African countries; absolute declines have occurred in a few. Although adult education for literacy is an alternative to primary education that can often be justified on grounds of equity (to the extent that it provides a second chance for those who miss the opportunity to enroll in the formal school system), it should be seen primarily as a stopgap solution. For the longer run, the educational goal should remain universal primary enrollment, which ultimately obviates the need for adult education of this kind.

With respect to the qualitative dimension of educational output, although the evidence is limited, it nonetheless points convincingly to the conclusion that the performance in Africa is unsatisfactory and has declined recently.

Enrollment Stagnation

Between 1960 and 1970 total enrollments in Sub-Saharan Africa grew at an average annual rate of 6.5 percent. Between 1970 and 1980 this rate rose to 8.9 percent. During the first three years of the 1980s, however, the rate of increase plummeted to 4.2 percent. (Comparative data more recent than 1983 were not available at the time of this study, but there is evidence of some economic recovery since 1983 that could have led to some recovery in enrollments.)

Although the rate of increase in enrollment declined at all levels of education, the drop was most pronounced at the first level, where it fell from 8.4 percent (approximately 2.9 million additional pupils each year) between 1970 and 1980 to 2.9 percent (approximately 1.4 million additional pupils each year) between 1980 and 1983. Given that the population of primary-school-age children is now increasing at an average annual rate of 3.3 percent, a 2.9 percent increase in enrollments will not even keep pace.

School Enrollments

In nineteen of the thirty-nine countries, the present growth rate of the school-age population exceeds that of primary school enrollments. In these countries, if present conditions continue, gross enrollment ratios must inevitably fall. For the region as a whole, if the growth in primary enrollments continues at a rate below 3 percent, by the year 2000 the gross enrollment ratio will have fallen back below 70 percent, the level of the late 1970s.

Although absolute enrollments continue to rise in most countries, this is no longer the case everywhere. Between 1980 and 1983 first-level enrollments actually fell in four countries—Angola, Mozambique, Somalia, and Togo. Less complete and reliable data for the more recent period suggest that primary enrollments have fallen in Benin, in some states of Nigeria, and in several of the least advantaged parts of the Sahelian countries. Postprimary enrollments also declined between 1980 and 1983 in several countries; in four (Côte d'Ivoire, Ghana, Senegal, and Swaziland) secondary or tertiary enrollments declined even though primary enrollments continued to increase at close to or better than pre-1980 rates.

These declines in enrollment reflect the current economic situation in Africa. Children who might have attended school in better times are kept out or pulled out because they are needed to work at home or, in dire situations such as the recent drought, because their families have been forced to migrate. Family incomes have fallen at the very time that many countries have introduced or raised school-related fees. In addition, the private benefits of education—especially education of inferior quality—may have fallen during the recent economic stagnation, while educational qualifications for many jobs have risen because of the rapid expansion in the number of graduates. Until issues of school quality are addressed and economic recovery is well under way, the demand for schooling in Africa will remain weaker than in the past, when it was extraordinarily strong.

To some extent, the deceleration in the expansion of education in much of Africa is a natural outgrowth of past quantitative achievements in the sector. As described in chapter 1, there was tremendous progress in the first years after independence, and proportionate enrollments in some African countries are already close to world standards, especially at the primary level. The gross primary enrollment ratio for the thirty-nine Sub-Saharan countries as a whole was 75 percent in 1983, and in sixteen of them the enrollment ratio exceeded 85 percent. This level of participation was reached in Latin America and Asia only in the early 1960s.

In general, given a country's present enrollment, the rate of its enrollment growth is closely related to its income per capita. Although this relationship holds in general terms, the country with the fastest growing primary education sector in recent years is Burundi, which is a low-income country according to the World Bank's classification of economies; Burundi's GNP per capita in 1984 was only $220. The country with the most impressive recent gains at all three educational levels is Zimbabwe. Primary enrollments in this country grew at nearly 15 percent annually between 1980 and 1983, secondary enrollments at 54 percent, and tertiary enrollments at 23 percent. Zimbabwe's efforts stand out in marked contrast with the general regional trend toward enrollment stagnation (see box 3-1). It would appear that, over and above the ability to pay, commitment to the sector is an important factor in determining a country's rate of educational expansion.

Adult Literacy and Training

Falling enrollment ratios must result eventually in adult populations less "schooled" and, as a consequence, less productive than those living and working in Africa today. Even before the current fiscal problems, in the early 1970s, widespread concern about education budgets and patterns of inequality in the formal education system led to an appeal for nonformal education for adult literacy and other purposes. Although data are not available on these programs and the extent to which they have grown or contracted, adult programs are important in several countries.

By the late 1970s adult education and training activities included, in most African countries, not only literacy teaching but also some or all of the following: out-of-school training for the informal sector; skill acquisition and income generation for women; the training of trainers for health, nutrition, and agriculture; and a variety of activities designed to provide education equivalent to the several levels of the formal system. Nonformal education in Africa is characterized by the following: It serves mainly young adults, many of whom are the same age as their counterparts in the formal schools; much of the activity is organized locally and takes place with little or no direct subvention and control from the state beyond some minimal registration and supervision; the young recipients (or their families) often pay for courses that are, in some sense, equivalent to those offered in the schools or in formal industrial training; even those who pay for instruction are typically drawn from the poorer elements of rural and urban

> **Box 3-1. The Story of Zimbabwe**
>
> Although primary and secondary enrollment rates have fallen in many Sub-Saharan African countries since 1980, enrollment rates have increased dramatically in Zimbabwe. That year marked the beginning of majority rule in Zimbabwe, fifteen years after a white minority regime had unilaterally declared independence in what was then called Rhodesia.
>
> Rhodesian society—including the education system—had been structured basically along lines of racial inequality. Separate European and African education departments had restricted the provision and lowered the quality of education for blacks relative to whites. Public expenditures per pupil were twelve times greater in the European system than in the African system at the primary level, and nearly three times higher at the secondary school level. In 1979, however, in response to the intensifying war of liberation, the coalition government merged the two education departments and began the racial integration of schools. Although these reforms increased black access to education, enrollments continued to be restricted, especially at the secondary and higher education levels.
>
> After independence in 1980, the new government began to redress the inequality inherited from earlier periods. Reform was based on the premise that education, in addition to contributing to a nation's growth and economic development, was also a basic human right. Education was viewed as an effective vehicle for promoting many of Zimbabwe's goals, including the development of nonracist attitudes, a new national identity, and loyalty to the state. The government gave priority to reopening and reconstructing schools that had been closed during the war (nearly one-third of all primary and secondary schools in rural areas) and to the expansion of education at all levels, with particular emphasis on secondary education.
>
> Parents and local communities supported the expansion by contributing fees and their labor for the construction and rehabilitation of schools. This private support stemmed from the belief that education is the key to obtaining a job in the modern sector of the economy and improving one's standard of living.
>
> Between 1979 and 1985 primary enrollments in Zimbabwe increased about 160 percent and secondary enrollments about 650 percent. The gross primary enrollment ratio now exceeds 100 percent, and given the low reported rate of pupil repetition (1 percent; see appendix table A-12), it seems safe to conclude that Zimbabwe has achieved the elusive goal of universal primary education. The secondary enrollment ratio has shot up also, from below 10 percent before independence to above 40 percent today. Although enrollment has been increased at some cost—larger expenditures and consequently less macroeconomic flexibility—it nonetheless clearly represents a remarkable achievement.

society, and they are often obliged to combine their education or training with work; many of the courses taught, especially those organized through nongovernmental organizations, have been negotiated with the participants or their representatives and, to this extent, reflect the needs of the community.

Many of these characteristics are innovative and likely to induce efficiency. Some are typically absent from—and could, with appropriate modification, be emulated in—the formal education system. The possibilities for change with respect to all elements of the education system will be discussed in part II of this book.

The presence and recent growth of nonformal education programs raise three questions for African governments. First, do the present equivalency programs that offer education and skills outside the formal sector point to ways that would dramatically open up to a wider public many of the currently underutilized institutions of the ministries of education and labor? Second, can the concerns of African governments about the vocational preparation of young people for informal sector employment be met through existing low-cost, out-of-school programs rather than new national schemes for vocational study within schools? And third, to what extent, if any, can the existing nonformal education structures compensate for slowdowns in expansion of school enrollments? These questions are addressed in the chapters that follow. The question of complementarities between the formal and nonformal education systems, however, deserves some brief comment here.

Unlike primary, general secondary, vocational, and university education, adult literacy education is not a regular concern of the ministry of education in most African countries. Usually, it commands attention on an ad hoc basis for a particular campaign or series of campaigns. The tendency has been for the national literacy coordinating committee to use mechanisms that have routinely been associated with other forms of adult and nonformal education—token honoraria for teachers, classes scheduled during students' time off from jobs, school buildings commandeered for evening use. Part and parcel of most successful adult literacy campaigns has been a powerful sense of the commitment of unpaid or modestly paid volunteers. Such relatively low-cost means are much in evidence in the first months or years of the campaign, but in the medium to long term, reliance on volunteers and a campaign spirit probably cannot be sustained. The institutionalization of these efforts continues to be a challenge.

Moreover, the accomplishments of the successful campaigns in, say, Ethiopia and Tanzania, could rapidly become diluted if primary school systems cannot attract and serve the ever larger cohorts of children during the 1980s and 1990s. In countries where the primary system fails to meet this challenge, the call for universal literacy, if issued at all, can never be met in a single campaign. In such an environment the campaign would have to be a perennial event, continued with additional expense and effort until such time as the birth rate stabilizes. Unless the problem of low school enrollment ratios is vigorously attacked, the pool of young adult illiterates will be refilled as rapidly as campaigns to eradicate illiteracy can deplete it.

Adult and child literacy (and illiteracy) are thus intimately connected. Adult literacy campaigns have advanced the cause of universal education in several countries, and more general programs of adult or community education are vital to the maintenance of new schooling traditions in parts of Africa. Campaigns to achieve adult literacy or universal primary enrollment will prove to be poor investments, however, unless they are consolidated by productive opportunities to put new skills to use. Lifelong education opportunities are essential to give individuals the information and skills they need to adapt to changing economic circumstances. The issues relating to vocational education, training, and the learning of occupation-specific skills will be discussed in chapter 5.

Expansion and Equity

The current stagnation of enrollments in Sub-Saharan Africa has critical implications for equity. A great virtue of educational investments that are properly designed is their potential for reducing inequities in enrollments. Conversely, the recent stagnation of enrollments seriously undermines the prospects for eliminating inequities that now exist. In practice it is difficult to separate the fact of unequal participation in education from that of low overall participation. Policies that increase overall participation will necessarily benefit disadvantaged groups, if only in the long run; the status of disadvantaged groups is unlikely to improve if education conditions in general are stagnant or deteriorating.

Ethnic and rural-urban differences in school participation, although considerably attenuated since before independence, remain an issue in most of Africa today. Male-female differences are close to being eliminated at the primary level, at least in the region as a whole (in 1983 girls constituted 44 percent of African primary school enrollments), but the disadvantage of females is still much in evidence at the secondary level (34 percent of enrollments) and especially at the tertiary level (21 percent). Illiteracy is much higher among adult females (73 percent in 1980) than among adult males (48 percent).

Declining Quality of Education

The impact of rapid population growth and economic stagnation on the quantity of educational services in Sub-Saharan Africa is relatively easy to document. Another probable effect of the recent economic and demographic trends in the region is the erosion of quality in education, but this effect is more difficult to measure.

The Nature and Importance of Quality

The quality of a school or education system is properly defined by the performance of its students and graduates—the so-called output. In practice, however, because inputs into the teaching process are generally easier to measure than output, quality is often gauged by the inputs. Although information on the availability of inputs is important, caution is required in drawing conclusions about quality from this information alone. The discussion that follows uses direct measures of both school output and inputs to provide information on quality.

When an attempt is made to measure output as a direct indicator of quality, the most common approach is to concentrate on the scores of cognitive achievement tests. This makes sense to the extent that enhancing cognitive achievement is prominent among education's goals and contributes centrally to a student's ultimate productivity. This study follows the conventional practice because research suggests that cognitive achievement is highly important (see box 3-2) and because most of the same factors that foster quality in learning appear likely to strengthen the school's impact in other domains.

The goals of schooling encompass, however, more than just academic achievement. Quality pertains also to how well the school or school system prepares students to become responsible citizens and instills

Box 3-2. Are Cognitive Outcomes Really Important? The Interplay of Ability, Skills, and Schooling

Earnings go up with education, it is generally believed, because education imparts cognitive skills to workers, and employers pay more for these skills. Critics believe other factors are at work.

If the critics are right, the value of education may well have been exaggerated. Researchers tested the arguments of the critics in a study conducted in Kenya and Tanzania; they assessed the impact on earnings of innate ability, years of schooling, and acquired cognitive skills (such as numeracy and literacy). Their work provides answers to the following questions.

Do acquired cognitive skills and innate ability matter? Workers with high cognitive skills do earn much more than others. But the direct effect of innate ability improves earnings only slightly (although innate ability does have a large indirect effect on earnings by enhancing the acquisition of cognitive skills).

Do cognitive skills affect earnings in each educational category? There are great variations in levels of skill among graduates of both secondary and primary schools. In skill tests, the top third of workers scored 50 percent to 100 percent higher marks than the bottom third in each category. This top third can expect to earn 50 percent more than those in the bottom third in Kenya and 35 percent more than those at the bottom in Tanzania. Moreover, the top third of primary school leavers will earn almost as much as the bottom third of secondary graduates.

How large are the indirect effects of schooling and innate ability? In Kenya, secondary schooling raises earnings directly by 21 percent, but raises them indirectly by 25 percent by improving cognitive skills. The pattern is similar in Tanzania.

The study strongly supports the view that education endows workers with cognitive skills that draw a premium in the labor market. It shows that innate talent is not sufficient—it must be converted to cognitive skills through education; and long years spent at school are not sufficient—they must be used productively to acquire skills.

---

attitudes and values relevant to modern society. Schools do achieve these goals, and they are important ones.

When African children enter school, they frequently face a situation quite foreign to their life at home in a rural village or urban slum. The language used in the school is often different, the method of communication is written rather than verbal, and existence is categorized into subjects that are not referred to at home. A child's major challenge at this stage may not be that of learning new skills, but simply one of adjusting to an altogether different environment. In addition to teaching basic cognitive skills such as literacy and numeracy, therefore, schools have to help children integrate what they already know when they enter school with what they will need to learn as they proceed through the education system. Quality thus encompasses how well the education system does this job of accommodating modern, market-oriented skills to traditional, home-based values and needs. Policies for the achievement of these qualitative objectives include adjusting the school calendar to take account of the child's economic functions at home; giving first instruction in the child's mother tongue; integrating subjects around the life of the child and his community; and involving students in the application of theory so that learning has utility beyond that of qualifying individuals for the next level of education. These changes encourage children to look at and react to their environment in new and more productive ways.

When either academic or postschool performance is used to measure school quality, it is necessary to control for the effect of nonschool factors, such as innate ability, family background, and early childhood education. The impact of school inputs on performance is the gain attributable to these inputs, after controlling for the effects of nonschool factors. Although this study focuses on school factors, the importance of some nonschool factors affecting student performance are considered also, especially the child's health and nutritional status.

What constitutes an acceptable standard of school quality is always a relative matter. As with other services such as housing, nutrition, and health, the appropriate level of quality differs among countries at different levels of development and for any one country over time. For example, when African countries more than doubled their enrollment ratios in a comparatively brief period, it was to be expected that the performance of students would decline on average, simply as a function of the region's having moved from a small system serving the elite to one serving many, including children disadvantaged with respect to the out-of-school factors that affect learning.

It is sometimes argued that this decline in average quality is acceptable as long as the performance at the top of the achievement distribution does not suffer. But in view of the serious deterioration in learning conditions in much of the region (see next section), there is reason to believe that the performance of the highest achieving students has also declined. Certainly, to maintain a constant average quality of education in a rapidly expanding system, the overall effectiveness of the system needs to improve. This need remains to be satisfied in most of Sub-Saharan Africa.

Evidence of Declining Quality

The cognitive achievement of African students is low by world standards, and the evidence points to a decline in recent years. Much of this evidence is indirect, however, and focuses on quantities of particular inputs (especially books and other learning materials, management, and maintenance of capital assets) and their recent decline relative to other inputs (especially teachers).

Information on outputs is limited, but the information that is available is both compelling and disturbing. The International Association for the Evaluation of Educational Achievement (IEA) based in Stockholm, Sweden, has served as the coordinating agency for a number of large cross-national studies of student achievement since the mid-1960s. Although few developing countries participated in the earlier studies, the latest rounds of IEA surveys do include more of them, including some African countries. The second IEA study of achievement in mathematics, for example, which was conducted in 1981–82, includes (in addition to fourteen industrial market economies) information on three upper-middle-income countries and three lower-middle-income countries. In the last group were two African countries, Nigeria and Swaziland, and Thailand.

For the mathematics study, tests in five subfields of mathematics were administered at the end of the 1981 school year to national samples, ranging in size from 800 to 8,000 students, all of whom had reached the age of 13 years by the middle of the school year. Although there were differences among countries, the upper-middle-income countries as a group performed on a par with the industrialized ones (for details see appendix table C-5). The lower-middle-income countries, however, and particularly the two African countries, performed much worse. Students in Nigeria and Swaziland answered just over half as many items correctly as students in Japan, the highest scoring country, and about 65 percent as many items correctly as students in the seventeen better-off countries. These differences are highly significant.

Earlier IEA studies of achievement in reading comprehension and general science included no African countries, but the same tests used in these studies were subsequently administered to a small sample of students in Malawi (appendix table C-5). Although the Malawian students were, on average, six years older than the IEA-surveyed students, their performance was less satisfactory than that of any of the other sixteen groups in reading and lower than all but three in science. On the reading test the Malawian students had just over half as many correct answers as the average number in the IEA- surveyed countries and about 84 percent of the average on the science test.

Examples of specific test items illustrate more concretely the magnitude of the problem. In November 1986, an educational research institute in a Francophone African country administered, to fifth grade students, the same mathematics test that had been administered to all incoming fifth grade students in France a few months before. Three of the questions on the test are translated and substantially reproduced below:

(1) 1322 × 0 = ?
   (a) 0   (b) 1322   (c) 13220

(2) A roast weighs 2kg, 50g or:
   (a) 2050g   (b) 2500g   (c) 250g

(3) A purchase of 4 cartons costs 3.80 francs. A purchase of 8 cartons would cost:
   (a) 30.40 francs (b) 7.60 francs (c) 6.60 francs

Since, for each question, students were given a choice of only three responses, guessing would give a 33 percent chance of choosing the correct response. In fact, only 33 percent of the students were correct on the first item; 30 percent were correct on the second; and 26 percent were correct on the third. Each of the items tested content that the students' teachers believed was covered in the curriculum. On the test as a whole (forty items), the students performed no better than chance would predict, even though the tests had been administered in reasonably good schools in the capital city. The conclusion is inescapable: students in primary education in this country are learning virtually no mathematics.

The general conclusion to be drawn from these studies is that the quality of education in Sub-Saharan Africa is well below world standards. One explanation for this low quality is that expenditure per student, a highly aggregated proxy for educational inputs, is very low by world standards. This is especially true at the primary level. (It becomes less true as one moves up the educational ladder. At the tertiary level, in fact, per student expenditure is on a par with that in the industrialized countries; see chapter 6.) Another explanation for the low quality may be that what little is spent on each student is poorly allocated—that there is internal inefficiency in the education system.

Public recurrent expenditure per student at the primary level in the industrial market economies exceeded expenditure in the countries of Africa by a ratio of 30 to 1 in 1980. The industrial market economies were spending more than $2,200 per pupil in current 1980 dollars (median expenditure in sixteen countries with 1980 data available), and Africa (twenty-three countries with data available) only about $65. East Asia (five countries) was spending about $190 per pupil on the average in the same year, and Latin America (twenty countries) about $155. Only in five countries of South Asia was spending per primary school pupil lower than the African average.

Per student expenditure in African education is not just low, it is declining (see table 3-1). The combination of essentially constant budgets (since 1980) and rapidly expanding enrollments has made the financing of education's recurrent costs ever more difficult. Between 1970 and 1983 recurrent expenditure per student at the primary level expressed in constant 1983 dollars fell from $67 to $48, and at the secondary level from $362 to $223 in the median African country (appendix table C-5). Only in higher education, where there are relatively few students and traditionally high unit costs in comparison with lower levels of education in Africa, was there no obvious downward trend in expenditure per student: for the median country it was $2,462 in 1970, $3,090 in 1975, $2,798 in 1980, and $2,710 in 1983. The weighted mean of expenditure per student did fall sharply, from $6,461 in 1975 (for twenty-three countries where information was available) to $2,365 in 1983 (for twenty-eight countries), but most of this decline was accounted for by Nigeria, a large country where central government expenditure fell from $14,621 to $2,181.

Low expenditure per student has certainly constrained educational achievement in Sub-Saharan Africa. But low quality results also from a misallocation of expenditure. At least until recently, there was a tendency, often encouraged by donor agencies, to emphasize expenditure for development, especially for the construction of new facilities, and to ignore the recurrent costs of new projects as well as the recurrent inputs that would ensure the productivity of existing establishments. For example, the ratio of expenditure on books and supplies to expenditure on teachers' salaries is far lower than most knowledgeable educators would consider optimal. Moreover, because teachers' unions are politically potent and most salaries are protected by contractual obligations, the salary-nonsalary ratio in African public education has tended to increase in recent years as budgets have been cut.

Data for the most recent year available show that teachers' salaries and benefits in Sub-Saharan Africa account for about 90 percent of recurrent education expenditure at the primary level, 70 percent at the secondary, and 50 percent at the tertiary (weighted means; see appendix tables A-20 to A-22). Even if all of the rest were available for the all-important teaching materials, not much would be left for them or for the maintenance of school buildings and equipment. At the secondary and higher levels, where transfers to students for welfare costs (food and lodging) claim significant sums, the crunch on nonsalary inputs is even tighter than the figures suggest.

Table 3-1. Public Recurrent Expenditure per Student in Sub-Saharan Africa, 1970–83
(median values; expenditure in constant 1983 dollars)

Expenditure	1970	1975	1980	1983
Per primary student	67	61	51	48
As percentage of GNP per capita	16	19	16	15
Per secondary student	362	308	195	223
As percentage of GNP per capita	111	93	62	62
Per tertiary student	2,462	3,090	2,798	2,710
As multiple of GNP per capita	11	12	7	8

Source: Appendix tables A-17 to A-19.

Educational materials account for just 1.1 percent of the recurrent primary education budget in the median African country (appendix table A-20). This allocation amounts to less than $0.60 per pupil a year, which buys very little in the way of books, slates, wall charts, and writing implements. Even if some educational materials are purchased out of development budgets (because of the unwillingness of many donor agencies to finance recurrent costs), and notwithstanding the fact that some materials (perhaps significant amounts in some places) are purchased privately by students for their own use, the picture remains stark in comparison with other places. The developed countries spend a larger percentage of a much larger budget on instructional materials, close to 4 percent at the primary level, which amounts to about $100 per pupil a year. With only $0.60 spent per pupil a year on educational materials in Africa, even the most ingenious teacher would find it hard to teach children very much. Only when a substantial multiple of this amount is made available for teaching materials—either by shifting funds from other expenditure categories or by mobilizing additional resources—can teachers in African schools again become pedagogically productive.

Part II

Policy Options for African Governments

The first three chapters in part II deal, successively, with primary, secondary, and higher education. Because the problems encountered at these three levels differ, the substance and structure of the chapters differ accordingly. But common issues do recur in each chapter, and these are discussed in general terms here.

Chapter 3 raised concerns about recent trends in both the quantitative and the qualitative outputs of African education systems. Quantity and quality outputs may be undesirably low for either of two reasons: inefficiency or an inadequate flow of financial or other resources. This book argues that both factors operate, but it places particular emphasis on the importance of strengthening management to reduce inefficiency. Because of the crucial importance of management improvement, chapter 6 is devoted to this subject.

The first set of issues to be considered concerns efficiency in education. Efficiency has to do with how well inputs into the educational process are used in producing desired educational outcomes. It is achieved when the maximum output is obtained from a given budget or when the minimum budget is used to achieve a given output. Educational output can be measured quantitatively or qualitatively. It is usually measured quantitatively by the number of students who pass successfully (however this is defined) through the educational process—and qualitatively by gains in cognitive achievement. In light of these two dimensions of output, any discussion of policies to increase the efficiency of education should distinguish between policies that would involve additional participants in the system, given the average gain in achievement, and policies that would raise achievement, given the number of participants.

Savings realized through more efficient production methods may become available for redeployment. Those realized in a given school or educational subsystem can be put back into the same unit to increase the unit's output, or they can be shifted elsewhere in the economy—to another unit within the same sector or to a different sector. Although in any particular instance there may be good reasons for doing the latter, policymakers should first consider returning the savings to the unit where they were made, to give managers an incentive to reduce costs.

The second cluster of policy issues relates to the other factor that limits the output of the system—adequacy of finance. Especially when economic or political criteria call for an increase in the quantity of education provided (whether an increase is defined as additional students or as higher achievement by students), the financial question looms large on the policymaker's agenda. How can a society mobilize additional resources for education? There are three possible answers: government can allocate additional public resources to education, communities and families can provide additional local or private resources, and the international donor community can make additional resources available.

Given the importance of education to development, African education will need additional resources from all sources—public and private, domestic and international. But in many countries public budgets have already been stretched close to the limit. For most African countries, under the conditions of austerity prevailing on the continent today, the strategy of utilizing resource flows more efficiently offers the greatest potential for ameliorating problems of access and quality. This book accordingly emphasizes management and efficiency. It is also important, however, to diversify sources of finance instead of relying only on the public budget. The forms of cost sharing that might be appropriate to each level of education will be discussed in the chapters that follow.

A third set of issues concerns the relevance of the curriculum to the needs of individuals and societies. The main issues that many countries face in this domain concern when and how to make the transition from subjects that have broad vocational relevance, such as language and science skills, to programs and subjects that will prepare individuals for specific jobs or clusters of jobs. Several lessons can be taken from international experience. A strong general education, which schools can provide efficiently, greatly enhances the future trainability of an individual. Job-specific training is also important, and such training is usually most efficiently provided after initial job decisions have been made and in institutions that are under the strong influence of the ultimate employer. Occupation- and job-specific training need not provide individuals with degrees or credentials.

It is no longer seriously disputed that the main emphasis of the primary and lower secondary curriculum should be on imparting the basic skills of language and mathematics and a basic knowledge of the social and natural environment. At this level these are the skills and information that are most relevant to future productivity, and the chapter on primary education does not discuss this issue further. At the upper secondary level, however, there is a real trade-off between continuing with education that is generally relevant and introducing a more specialized curriculum. And as specialization becomes preferable for an increasing proportion of students, the question arises of whether schools are efficient institutions for providing specialized training or whether such training is better done by institutions at or close to the ultimate work site. The answer may well differ for different occupations and perhaps for different countries at different times. Chapter 5 discusses these difficult issues further, and chapter 6, on higher education, deals with closely related questions—for example, the relative importance of producing lawyers or engineers.

A fourth class of issues involves equity. Since independence, African governments have stressed, almost uniformly, the importance of poverty reduction—of eliminating extremes in the distribution of income and achieving broad participation in the development process. The experience of the World Bank has shown that giving the poor a productive asset such as education is one of the most effective ways to address their needs—more effective than transferring income to them directly. Fortunately, many education policies that serve important equity objectives have other significant benefits. The further extension of primary education—perhaps the most important educational policy for addressing unequal income distribution—also has a high rate of return. Education that empowers women enhances their productivity, both as income producers and in the management of the household. And policies that reduce subsidies to relatively well-to-do students not only further equity goals but also improve efficiency in the provision of learning opportunities. A great virtue of properly designed educational investments is their potential for reducing inequity; this point is illustrated frequently in the pages that follow.

Because this is a policy study, the discussion inevitably focuses on what those responsible for education policy must consider doing. To the extent that they can put their own house in order, the claim that the sector can legitimately place on national resources will be strengthened. In the end, of course, the success of policy reform in education will depend greatly on the adoption of appropriate complementary policies for other sectors and for the macroeconomic framework within which all sectors operate.

4

The Foundation: Primary Education

The growth in primary school enrollments in Sub-Saharan Africa during the 1960s and 1970s may be unparalleled at any time or place in history. Throughout this period, however, some analysts warned that the region's preoccupation with quantitative growth would lead to a serious deterioration in the quality of education. Warnings of falling quality have become even more persistent in recent years as the financial squeeze between ever tighter budgets and ever larger pupil cohorts has starved education systems of essential operating inputs such as textbooks and facility maintenance. Poor quality in primary education is a serious matter because this is the only formal education that most of today's African children can hope ever to receive and because the quality of primary education plays a great role in determining the quality of all higher levels of education.

Even so, the extent to which any particular country can increase the relative emphasis given to the quality of education in the near future depends on the progress already achieved with respect to quantity. In this regard, the diversity within the region is considerable. The gross enrollment ratio for the ten lowest primary enrollment countries ranges from 21 to 49 percent, with a median value of 37 percent. The enrollment ratio for thirteen middle enrollment countries ranges from 53 to 79 percent, with a median of 67 percent. Finally, the enrollment ratio for the sixteen highest enrollment countries ranges from 87 percent to well above 100 percent, the median being 106 percent (see appendix table C-6).

Furthermore, within every country there are large enrollment disparities among different population groups. In thirteen of the thirty-nine African countries, the share of girls in primary enrollments is less than 40 percent. Much larger than the disparities between girls and boys at the primary level are those between rural and urban areas. In most countries there are, in effect, two education systems, one urban and the other rural. The former has close to universal enrollment; in the latter the schools are scattered and may not offer all grade levels, and enrollment ratios are much lower. A recent survey in Côte d'Ivoire, for example, showed enrollment ratios in Abidjan and other urban centers that were 30 percentage points higher on the average than those in the countryside. Thus, regardless of the overall enrollment ratio in a country, increased coverage may well involve the addition of children who are more difficult to attract to school (because of high opportunity costs or negative parental attitudes toward school) and for whom it is more costly to provide coverage because of the scattered population.

At first blush, the tradeoff between improved quality and further expansion of primary education seems stark. The possibility of increasing efficiency in education, however, offers policymakers some hope of achieving gains on both fronts simultaneously, even when budgets are tight. If by increasing the annual flow of certain crucial inputs (such as instructional materials) pupils can be brought up to the same level of competence as before in fewer years than before (or to a much higher level of competence in the same number of years), savings can be made on the use of other, much more costly factors, notably capital costs and teachers' salaries. Seen in this light, there is a cost associated with low-quality instruction, and the tradeoff between quantity and quality becomes less dramatic.

In the countries in which educational standards have deteriorated the most, there is no longer an either-or choice between expansion and quality. Without some minimal package of basic inputs, including, most important, textbooks and other instructional materials, virtually no learning occurs. Under these conditions, ensuring the availability of essential inputs is a prerequisite both of quality improvement and of expansion. For the remaining countries, however, a balance must be found that takes into account current levels of enrollment and quality. The remainder of this chapter discusses efficient approaches to increasing quality, expanding quantity, and financing both kinds of improvement.

Measures for Improving Quality

Six areas that affect educational quality are identified, five of which are discussed in this section: the training and use of teachers (reviewed under the headings of class size, teacher training, and teacher morale); instructional materials; school buildings and facilities; the language of instruction; and the nutrition and health of children. The sixth important ingredient in improving quality is a strong examination system. External examinations contribute importantly to quality improvement through performance measurement and curriculum improvement. Since examinations are essentially a management tool, they are treated in chapter 7.

The potential for adjusting any of these inputs to improve quality efficiently varies, and the purpose of the discussion that follows is to summarize what experience has to say about the effectiveness as well as the financial and administrative feasibility of the alternatives. In the final analysis the effectiveness of any input depends on how it is used in conjunction with all other inputs; an effective school is one that offers a coherent package of inputs.

The Training and Use of Teachers

Two dimensions of the costs associated with teachers may be distinguished: quantity, as reflected in class size, and quality, as reflected by such factors as the length and content of the training received and teacher morale.

CLASS SIZE. Substantial evidence from research supports the proposition that within broad limits (between 25 and 50 pupils) changes in class size influence pupil achievement modestly or not at all. But since most classrooms are not designed for more than 50 pupils, and since discipline can be a problem, classes much larger than 50 pupils should probably be discouraged.

In primary schools that operate under a single-shift system, the pupil-teacher ratio is a good proxy for class size. The median pupil-teacher ratio in Sub-Saharan Africa is 39 to 1. This suggests that class size is, on average, acceptable. For classes that are at or close to this number, it is likely that only a substantial reduction in class size, too costly to be considered by any country at present, would raise achievement.

Even in countries in which the average class size is below 45 pupils, however, many classes, especially in urban areas, are much larger than the average, and in such cases overcrowding may detract from learning. Moreover, nine of the thirty-nine African countries report average pupil-teacher ratios of more than 50 to 1. In such settings, modest reductions in class size (or larger classrooms) could prove to be cost-effective, especially if this strategy were accompanied by other measures to increase the average number of classes per teacher (for example, through double shifts).

TEACHER TRAINING. The increasing body of evidence on the payoff on various amounts and kinds of teacher training indicates that for primary school teachers preservice training that consists of more than general secondary education and a minimum exposure to pedagogical theory is not cost-effective. Long residential courses tend to be expensive to produce, and teachers' salaries are usually closely tied to the amount of such training received. In recognition of these two cost factors and the difficulty of changing them, policymakers in some countries (for example, Burkina Faso) have chosen to shorten the duration of preservice training for primary school teachers. In other countries the cost of preservice training has been substantially lowered in recent years through the use of distance teaching (that is, correspondence education supplemented by radio and tutorial sessions). Nigeria, Tanzania, and Zimbabwe have all successfully applied distance teaching methods to preservice teacher training. Box 4-1 summarizes Tanzania's experience.

The optimal mix of training modes (general education, preservice classroom study, supervised teaching practice, learning on the job, and in-service training) depends on the relative costs of the various

> **Box 4-1. Distance Learning for Teachers in Tanzania**
>
> In 1974 Tanzania mounted an effort to achieve universal primary school enrollment by 1977, despite serious resource constraints. It was estimated that 40,000 teachers would be required to reach this goal and that it could not be accomplished through conventional teacher training methods. Furthermore, the pool of secondary school leavers who might be pressed into service as primary school teachers was small because the government had focused on developing primary and adult education. Thus Tanzania needed a new strategy to fill its ranks of primary school teachers. It chose to use primary school graduates with some experience in adult education and to train them on the job.
>
> Trainees had to be between 17 and 28 years old, live in an area where teachers were in short supply, and have taught adult literacy for at least two years. The strategy consisted of providing an initial six-week residential training course followed by supervised primary school teaching. While working in the schools and teaching twenty-two periods a week, trainees followed correspondence courses and listened to related radio programs. In addition, opportunities were provided for them to meet with fellow trainees and supervising head teachers to discuss their work. Trainees were examined each term, and a final national examination was administered at the end of the three-year course. Of the 45,534 students who began the course between 1976 and 1978, 37,325 (82 percent) completed it, and 35,028 (77 percent) passed their final examinations, thus becoming qualified teachers.
>
> A comparison of these trainees with a control group who attended a regular teacher training program found that the first group performed slightly worse on academic knowledge but better on measures of classroom behavior. Because they were recruited locally, their level of motivation may have been higher. The combination of the practical classroom apprenticeship with study at a distance appeared to be an effective way to respond to the critical shortage of primary teachers. Furthermore, the strategy realized important savings, since teachers were employed during their training period and the costs of residence at training college were minimized. The cost of the distance teaching strategy in Tanzania was calculated to be approximately one-quarter the cost of conventional teacher training.

modes and on the salary structure for teachers. In many countries an emphasis on in-service training over preservice training has been found to be cost-effective provided that there is constructive supervision of the training. Some countries (for example, Botswana, Ghana, Kenya, Lesotho, and Malawi) are now successfully using distance teaching methods to upgrade the pertinent knowledge and skills of incumbent teachers.

Perhaps more cost-effective than training in itself as a way of raising the professional quality of the teaching force may be the introduction, where labor market conditions permit, of more selective criteria for admission to the profession. The recent increase in unemployment among secondary school leavers and university graduates in the liberal arts should help to attract more able individuals to the sector. Many potentially able teachers may lack formal credentials. It might be desirable to admit individuals to the profession on the basis of performance on subject-matter tests and then to provide them with brief initial and in-service training.

In summary, in many African countries ineffective teachers are a constraint on learning, and this problem deserves attention from policymakers. In most of these countries in-service training is likely to prove more cost-effective than alternative programs of preservice training in ameliorating this problem.

TEACHER MORALE. The teacher's use of time and other classroom resources is known to be a principal determinant of pupil achievement. To the primary school teacher falls the important task of turning into reality government-imposed strategies for improving quality. But for this to happen, the teacher must be motivated and dedicated. In the past the title "teacher" was a term of considerable respect. The profession commanded high status in the community, and positions were eagerly sought. Today, in contrast, primary school teachers are often a beleaguered and dispirited force, their status much eroded and their working conditions poor.

The lifting of teachers' morale is a great challenge, since most countries cannot afford additional monetary incentives. But not all measures to regenerate teachers' professional pride and enthusiasm need be costly. Increased provision of instructional materials and better support and supervisory services from inspectorates and ministries will help improve working conditions, particularly for the many teachers who must work in the relative isolation of rural areas.

Instructional Materials

There is strong evidence that increasing the provision of instructional materials, especially textbooks, is the most cost-effective way of raising the quality of primary education. The scarcity of learning materials in the classroom is the most serious impediment to educational effectiveness in Africa. It is certainly here that the gap in educational provision between this region and the rest of the world has grown widest.

Given that many primary school teachers in Africa have less formal education and teacher training than is usually the case in more developed regions of the world, the use of teachers' guides and other materials designed to assist teachers in the organization of classroom activities could prove especially cost-effective. The advantage of such materials is that they supplement the teacher's own knowledge and promote the proper sequencing of learning activities in the classroom.

The availability of all such instructional materials has declined in recent years as increased fiscal stringency has led to severe cuts in nonsalary expenditures. The problem of the scarcity of appropriate teaching materials, however, goes well beyond the availability of funds. Most African countries have yet to develop a national capacity for the development of low-cost teaching materials that are pedagogically sound and relevant to the national curriculum.

An objective common to all African countries should be to develop national skills for adapting and editing written materials. For most countries, in addition, an increased capacity to write and publish classroom materials is a feasible short-term objective. Printing, however, need not necessarily be done locally, since small countries with limited educational markets are particularly costly to serve with local presses. The economies of scale that can be achieved through a combination of sophisticated (and very expensive) high-speed multicolor presses and relatively inexpensive but highly skilled labor make it more economical for most African countries—and for many American and European publishing houses as well—to print textbooks for mass circulation abroad. In those African countries in which the local printing industry is reasonably developed and efficient, the awarding of contracts for paper procurement and textbook printing through international competitive bidding will ensure that the prices paid do not exceed the lowest prices obtainable elsewhere by more than the normal margin of domestic preference accorded to goods and services of national origin. Cooperation among groups of small African countries affords the possibility of economies of scale in printing, as well as the possibility of producing materials in local languages that cut across national borders.

Once on hand, instructional materials need to be stored adequately and distributed to schools in a timely manner, and teachers need to be trained in their use. All this requires organization and planning and, above all, funds for transport, an item in short supply.

Exercise books and pencils are basic to the learning of literacy and numeracy skills. To recover costs, some countries have transferred to parents the costs of these basic supplies. An advantage of this approach is that it safeguards the provision of these relatively inexpensive but pedagogically crucial inputs during periods of financial stringency.

Apart from tangible instructional materials, radio broadcasts to the classroom have proved to be effective in some countries (for example, Ethiopia, Kenya, and Tanzania). In primary education the use of radio is usually an added cost. (In secondary and higher education radio can be used as a partial substitute for teachers; see chapter 5.) In return for a modest increase in unit costs, the use of radio in primary schools can yield significant gains in learning, especially where highly skilled teachers are in short supply. In Kenya, for example, an experiment to use radio to help teach English to primary school students in regions where English was not widely spoken showed substantial learning gains, according to a careful evaluation (box 4-2). Elsewhere in the world experience with the use of radio for teaching mathematics in primary schools has been very favorable; the radio package (including workbooks) substituted for textbooks for little more than textbooks alone would have cost.

Radio, when thoughtfully used, has an important potential for improving school quality, but there is no evidence that more costly technologies (such as television) have any advantage over radio. Indeed, the cost and the complexity of implementing the once massive television system for primary education in Côte d'Ivoire eventually led to its abandonment.

Physical Facilities

Dilapidated buildings, missing or broken desks and chairs, and a lack of good ventilation and sanitation facilities are commonplace in African schools, especially in rural areas. Not much is known about how construction standards, school upkeep, and the presence and condition of other school facilities affect the quality of education as indicated by pupil achievement. One effect of low-standard, poorly maintained

> **Box 4-2. Interactive Educational Radio in Kenya**
>
> Interactive radio differs dramatically from traditional educational broadcasting in its reliance on student participation in, or interaction with, the program. Unlike the instructional design of traditional educational radio, which encourages passivity as students listen to lecture-style instruction, the design of interactive programs makes creative use of radio. The Kenya Radio Language Arts Project (RLAP), a good example of interactive radio, involved primary school children as active participants in a pedagogically sound dialogue for teaching the language curriculum.
>
> What might have looked like pandemonium in an RLAP classroom was actually a well-designed, tightly controlled lesson called "English in Action" that involved students actively in the learning process. The thirty-minute daily broadcasts, which were punctuated by music and little dramas, incorporated regular pauses for the children to respond and receive immediate reinforcement for answers. Responses could be sung, spoken, written, or acted out. Typically children were given the chance to respond over one hundred times during each thirty-minute period. Careful evaluation of students' learning gains after the introduction of radio found highly significant increases. The cost of extending RLAP to additional students is estimated to be considerably less than $1 per student per year.
>
> The effort to involve children in a conversation with the radio demands precise timing and careful observation of how children respond to radio prompts. RLAP designers achieved this precision through trials, observations, repeated pretesting, and classroom monitoring. Teachers tended to be supportive of the interactive radio experiment; they saw the program as a way to supplement their work, not as a way to replace them in the classroom. With assistance from teachers' guides, they worked along with the radio programs, calling on individual children as cued by the radio, overseeing written responses, and providing closer overall supervision than would be possible without interactive radio.
>
> Kenya's RLAP drew on the successful experience with Radio Math in Nicaragua. That program's use of interactive learning produced consistently superior results among children in radio mathematics classes compared with children in conventional classes.
>
> Experience has shown that interactive radio can be used effectively by untrained classroom monitors as well as trained teachers, with little training or special support. Furthermore, once radio lessons are developed, the annual per pupil cost is modest, since few supplementary learning materials are required.

facilities may be to discourage pupil attendance. For those who attend, little can be learned, surely, on a rainy day under a leaky roof or with no roof at all.

The current budgetary crisis has aggravated the problems of inadequate plant maintenance and missing or broken furniture because in most African countries the responsibility for maintenance rests with the central government. The general trend toward greater local financing of the capital costs of education, if extended to include capital maintenance, might alleviate these problems somewhat, and the use of more local materials for school buildings and classroom furniture may make it possible to reduce their costs. Whether the central government or a local authority is responsible, the failure to maintain physical facilities not only curtails learning but can also increase overall costs because it can lead to premature replacement of the facilities.

The Language of Instruction

The diversity of linguistic backgrounds in Sub-Saharan Africa greatly complicates teaching. Linguists identify over 1,250 languages in use today in the region, and only nine of these are spoken as a first or second language by as many as 10 million people. The African educator's response to this challenge has reflected in part colonial precedents and in part a healthy pragmatism. Although literacy in one or more African languages is an explicit goal of the education system in some countries and not in others, the combination of the colonial heritage and the relative absence of published materials in these vernaculars has led most African countries to adopt the language of the former colonial government (the metropolitan language) as the national language and to introduce it as the medium of instruction at some level in the formal education system.

Differences in school language policy have to do with when and how fast the transition to the national language takes place. The colonial powers in Africa pursued different policies with respect to media of instruction in schools, and African nations have often kept these traditions after independence. As shown in table 4-1, eleven of fifteen former French colonies and all three former Portuguese colonies officially begin instruction in the national language from the first day of primary school. In contrast, thirteen of

Table 4-1. Language of Instruction in the First Year of Primary School, by Former Colonial Status
(number of countries)

Former colonial status	Metropolitan language only	One or more African languages
Belgian	1	2
British	2	13
French	11	4
Portugese	3	0

Source: Appendix table B-2.

fifteen former British colonies begin instruction in one or more African languages and teach English at first as a subject; only later is English introduced as the medium of instruction.

Although the decision to use or not to use an African language for instructional purposes often echoes the colonial past, the feasible choices also depend on the number of speakers of the language in the nation. An examination of current school language policies among African countries suggests convincingly that the size factor has influenced policymakers. In twenty-one countries that utilize one or more African languages for instructing beginning primary pupils, the most widely spoken African language is the first or second language of more than 5 million people in the median case. In sixteen countries in which a European language is used as the medium of instruction, the number of speakers of the most widely spoken language is only about 2.5 million. (These figures are derived from appendix table B-2.)

The policy regarding the language of instruction—whether and when to use the national language or an African language—must be devised by African governments themselves on the basis of political as well as economic imperatives. For most African countries a central objective of primary education is that pupils emerge orally fluent and literate in the national language. Fluency in the national language may help to promote political stability and build national unity as well as serve economic purposes.

On purely pedagogical grounds, however, the benefits of using the mother language for instruction in the initial years of primary school now seem to be established even when literacy in the national language is the ultimate objective. Current research suggests that (a) the acquisition both of oral fluency and of literacy in a second language is most successful when there is a strong foundation in the first language; (b) conversational skills in a second language are learned earlier than is the ability to use the language for academic learning; and (c) academic skills learned in school transfer readily from one language to the other, so that skills taught in the first language in transitional programs do not have to be relearned in the second language.

In light of the above, most linguists agree that even where instruction is ultimately to be given in a language other than the child's mother tongue, the most effective policy educationally is one of initial instruction using the mother language, followed by a gradual transition to the national language as medium. Ideally, study of the first language, as a subject at least, will continue after the transition is complete. The pedagogical advantage of this approach is more pronounced during a transition period in which the teachers themselves are not particularly fluent in the national language—a situation that is fairly typical in many African primary schools today.

The effectiveness of this kind of bilingual education policy in relation to the costs involved depends both on the size of the population group being educated and on the degree of linguistic heterogeneity within individual classrooms. In Uganda, for example, perhaps an unusual case, 47 percent of primary school classrooms contain students who speak four or more different mother tongues; in this type of environment instruction in English from the outset may be the only feasible approach. Experience from the Rivers State of Nigeria demonstrates, however, that it is possible to prepare textbooks in the mother tongue of many small language groups, if that policy is chosen. Country-specific circumstances will be decisive.

In many countries the principal problem will not be providing initial literacy in the African language but, rather, effectively introducing a national language that many of today's primary teachers speak and read only poorly, if at all. Good materials are important for rectifying this, as are teacher training and selection. The use of radio also has a particular comparative advantage in language teaching; the success of the Radio Language Arts Program in introducing English into rural Kenyan primary schools (box 4-2, above) shows the potential of radio.

Nutrition and Health: Ensuring Teachable Pupils

The recent drought in much of Africa and its immediate impact on nutritional status and human survival rates received widespread, if belated, international attention. But the drought was a more or less temporary problem. Unfortunately, serious nutritional deprivation predates the recent crisis and is prevalent in many parts of Africa even when harvests are normal. Childhood malnutrition and the concomitant debilitating diseases are certain to continue well into the foreseeable future as perennial problems.

The incidence of malnutrition and disease is especially high among preschool children. By the time such deprived children reach school age, a large proportion are physically stunted (below normal in height), a condition frequently accompanied by impaired mental ability. Many of those who are malnourished and sick will never attend school. Those who do enroll tend to be listless from hunger and weakened from their frequent bouts with diarrhea and fever; their attendance and academic achievement obviously suffer. The high benefits predicted to accrue from investment in education are never realized in the case of these sick and malnourished children.

To the extent that health problems continue and imbalances between food supply and population persist (or worsen), it will be essential to ascertain what remedies there are for children and what the consequences of failing to adopt those remedies will be, for the education system and for society in general. There is potential for high returns in programs for family planning and primary health care (including prenatal care), nutrition education for mothers, preschool education for children, and in-school feeding of children. Because they do not fall neatly within any one ministry's responsibility but overlap ministerial responsibilities, programs that address the complex of problems linking health, nutrition, and intellectual development, especially as they affect those not in school, tend to fall between the bureaucratic cracks. Governments may wish to consider giving more attention to preschool child development, especially to nutrition and primary health care, so as to identify approaches that are effective and feasible within particular national contexts.

School feeding programs that target those at greatest nutritional risk could, under some circumstances, provide the most effective means for improving a child's ability to learn. The food required for such programs is often available in kind from external sources such as the World Food Programme.

Summary

This review of measures for improving the quality of primary schools has yielded only a limited number of attractive options. There are two principal conclusions.

- The safest investment in educational quality in most countries is to secure adequate books and supplies. These are effective in raising test scores and, almost invariably, have suffered from underinvestment in relation to investments in teachers. This is also an area in which external aid has a comparative advantage. Other areas that appear to have potential include school feeding and health programs, the intensive use of radio ("interactive radio"), in-service education of teachers in subject matter skills, and strengthened inspection and supervision systems.
- The following kinds of investment are *not* likely to have any noticeable effect on primary school quality despite their potentially high cost: reducing class size, providing primary teachers with more than a general secondary education, providing teachers with more than minimal exposure to pedagogical theory, procuring high-quality buildings and furniture, and introducing classroom television or computers.

Although these conclusions may pertain to developing countries in general, they are particularly valid today for the countries of Sub-Saharan Africa. Indeed, the current severe shortage of teaching materials in African primary schools—in African schools at all levels, for that matter—gives particular force to the conclusion dealing with textbooks and materials. In terms of rectifiable inefficiency, the relative imbalance of inputs to the detriment of critical learning materials stands out as a pervasive problem. This leads to recommendation 2.

Recommendation 2

A prerequisite for both quality improvement and system expansion in African education is the assured availability of nonsalary recurrent inputs. In countries in which recent fiscal constraints and persistent pressures to expand enrollments have combined to distort the balance between salary and nonsalary expenditures, governments should take steps to re-

store an efficient mix of inputs into the educational production process. The provision of a minimum package of textbooks and instructional materials is usually the most pressing need in this respect, and this is critically important if productive use is to be made of the other (much more costly) recurrent inputs into education, namely, teachers' and students' time. The problem of inadequate supplies of books and materials exists at all levels of education, but it is particularly acute (and relatively inexpensive to rectify) at the primary level, where an annual expenditure of about $5 per pupil should meet minimum requirements. Similarly, with regard to physical plant and equipment in African educational institutions, the balance between development outlays and maintenance expenditure should, in most countries, be adjusted to give relatively more weight to the latter to ensure that full benefit is derived from existing facilities.

The Containment of Unit Costs

The preceding section reviewed options for improvements in quality and argued that a minimum package of textbooks and teaching materials is a prerequisite both for improvement of quality and for further expansion of enrollment. To help finance this minimum package, it is essential to identify all possible ways of containing unit costs.

To demonstrate the importance of containing unit costs, it is worth recalling the enrollment disparities noted at the beginning of this chapter and the fact, noted in chapter 2, that in nineteen of the thirty-nine countries dealt with in this book primary enrollment ratios have actually declined since 1980. In at least four of these countries not only enrollment ratios but also the absolute numbers of enrollees have declined.

To address these problems, this section reviews the possibilities for reducing unit costs, stressing those measures that preserve quality. The concluding section turns to a discussion of the scope for mobilizing additional resources for primary education.

Teachers' Salaries

The salary bill for teachers typically accounts for between 85 and 95 percent of the recurrent budget for primary education in an African country. Any discussion of strategies for cost savings must include an examination of the scope for reducing what the average teacher gets paid.

The severe scarcity of teachers over much of the past three decades, the hitherto attractive alternative employment opportunities for persons with the educational qualifications of teachers, and the heavy political and economic power of the teachers' labor organizations all tend to contribute to high salaries for teachers in relation to average earnings in Africa. It is not surprising, therefore, that international comparisons of primary teachers' salaries in relation to per capita incomes reveal that primary school teachers in Africa, especially in the Francophone countries, earn relatively more than their counterparts in other regions.

In the late 1970s the average primary teacher's salary as a multiple of per capita income was 2.5 in the OECD countries, 2.4 in Latin America, and 2.6 in Asia. About 1983, for twenty-two African countries for which information was available, the average primary teacher's salary was 5.6 times GNP per capita in the median case (appendix table A-23). For the ten Francophone countries the figure was 8.8 times GNP per capita, and in one, Mauritania, it was a remarkable 15 times. For the twelve Anglophone countries, by contrast, the average teacher's salary was only 3.6 times GNP per capita; in Uganda the two were practically on a par. Couching the comparisons in terms of a technically more appropriate (although not readily available) indicator, such as the average teacher's salary as a multiple of nonagricultural GDP per capita or the average wage in the modern sector, might attenuate the overall differences and reorder the ranking of individual countries, but it would not alter the general conclusion that teachers are expensive in the skill-short African context.

This is not to say that teachers are necessarily "overpaid"—that is, compensated more than is necessary to keep them in teaching, given the employment opportunities open to them elsewhere in the economy. There are reports of serious teacher shortages and absenteeism, especially in remote rural primary schools, and of teachers leaving the profession, particularly from secondary schools and universities, to take up more remunerative opportunities in other sectors of the economy. At the same time, in most African countries many adequately educated young people are actively seeking employment, and they provide a pool of talent that (with appropriate hiring and in-service training policies) might welcome reasonable downward adjustments in teachers' salaries if this policy opened up employment possibilities. Despite the problem of low teacher morale and the political difficulties involved in cutting nominal salaries, there may be some scope for lowering the overall structure of hourly earnings for primary teachers.

Even in labor markets in which the salary of a teacher trained to a given level cannot be reduced, it is possible and perhaps desirable to recruit teachers who are less well trained and hence less costly, as has been done in Burkina Faso (see box 4-3). Data for six Francophone countries show that the difference in the starting salaries of teachers with two and with four years of preservice training (following completion of junior secondary education) is 40 percent at the median. In view of the modest effects on educational quality (as measured by pupil achievement) of the duration of professional pedagogical training for teachers, recruitment of the more trained group of teachers is not likely to be cost-effective in these countries. Indeed, the average cost per teacher could be reduced by using as primary teachers essentially untrained but educated young people. These might be A-level or baccalaureate graduates who teach before (or instead of) entering the university, or university graduates who are fulfilling a national service obligation. This option, particularly if it were combined with intensive short-course pedagogical training, would probably not involve any sacrifice of quality.

Finally, a country could reduce the average rate at which teachers move from step to step on the salary scale. At present in most countries salary increments are more or less automatically given every two years or so. As an alternative, a new norm of four or five years between promotions might be established. This time could be reduced by two or even three years for primary teachers willing to teach in rural areas, for postprimary teachers in subjects that are difficult to cover (such as the sciences), or for teachers with outstanding attendance records. In general, a strong case can be made in theory for the rationalization of salary structures—for rewarding with higher pay those characteristics of teachers that are in short supply instead of rigidly linking salary progression to age, seniority, and entry qualifications. Certainly a start in the right direction could be made simply by associating a below-norm time-in-step with rural

---

Box 4-3. Reducing Teacher Costs in Burkina Faso

Efforts to expand the provision of primary education in Burkina Faso through the reduction of unit costs have been hampered by the relatively high cost of teachers. Although primary teachers' salaries are modest by international standards, they are high in comparison with the country's income level—more than 10 times GNP per capita, as against 2.4 times in Latin America and 2.6 in Asia. In light of the fact that 98 percent of the primary education budget goes for teachers' salaries, any attempt to reduce the costs to the subsector had to address this central issue.

The primary teacher work force consists mainly of two categories: *instituteurs-adjoints* (level B2 in the civil service salary scale), recruited from graduates of the lower secondary schools and trained for two years, and *instituteurs* (level B1), recruited from graduates of the upper secondary schools or through promotion by examination from the *instituteur-adjoint* level. Liberal standards for promotion from the B2 to the B1 level added to the budgetary pressure by driving up teachers' salaries at a fast pace.

Efforts to reduce teacher costs by increasing the pupil-teacher ratio were not attempted, since at 65 to 1 the national average was already quite high. Instead, Burkina Faso is lowering unit costs by restructuring the primary teacher corps and improving internal efficiency through better-focused teacher training. It has been demonstrated that by reclassifying newly recruited *instituteurs-adjoints* from level B2 to C1 and reducing training for this group from two years to one, unit costs can be brought down significantly. Implementation of these policy changes, combined with a revision of current fellowship and subsidy policies, would produce resource shifts in favor of expansion of primary education. The country could thereby attain its unofficial enrollment target of 60 percent by 2000 while simultaneously realizing improvements in quality through an increase in teaching materials. If no policy changes were implemented, the gross enrollment rate would rise only in proportion to overall budgetary growth, falling far short of the 60 percent target.

The new *instituteurs-adjoints*, who will make up the standard teacher category in primary education, will receive training at the National Primary Teachers College in Loumbila. The course consists of pedagogical training (40 percent), general subjects (40 percent), and complementary courses such as agriculture and physical education (20 percent). These teachers are to receive field assistance through the provision of textbooks and teaching materials, regular pedagogical support, and a gradual decrease in class size.

In addition, the examination for promotion of primary teachers is being upgraded through the inclusion of general subjects to introduce a measure of selectivity into the process. This is expected to raise promotion requirements, thus slowing the overall rate of promotion and leading to a gradual reduction in the average teacher's salary.

service or with the successful completion of in-service training programs.

More Intensive Use of Teachers

The salary bill required to sustain a given enrollment is defined by the average salary per teacher and by the average ratio of pupils to teachers. Given the difficulties involved in reducing teachers' salaries, the more intensive use of teachers appears to offer greater scope for reducing salary costs per pupil. As shown in appendix table C-5, the pupil-teacher ratio differs considerably among African nations. Of the thirty-eight countries for which 1983 data are available, eighteen had ratios of 37 or below, and seven of these had ratios below 32. In these eighteen cases at least, it should be possible to increase the number of pupils without increasing commensurately the number of teachers. The extent to which this can be done will, of course, be greater, the greater is the population density in a particular country.

Even a modest increase in the pupil-teacher ratio can lead to dramatic savings. For example, in a system in which the ratio is currently 35 to 1, a 20 percent increase would make the ratio 42 to 1. If there are 1.4 million primary-level students in the system (an average size system for the region), the same number of teachers (40,000) could accommodate an additional 280,000 students under the new ratio. Where teachers' salaries now account for 90 percent of the recurrent primary education budget, if the pupil-teacher ratio were not increased but were kept at 35 to 1, adding the same 280,000 students to enrollments would add a full 18 percent to the budget. This difference is not trivial when one is talking about an annual primary education budget in the tens or hundreds of millions of dollars.

There are three ways to increase the pupil-teacher ratio: (a) increase the average teaching load of teachers—that is, the number of classes taught per school year; (b) reduce the average attendance load of pupils—the number of classes attended per school year; and (c) increase the average class size—the number of pupils in a class. (Theoretically, a fourth way to reduce the pupil-teacher ratio is to reduce the number of teachers in each class. It is assumed, however, that each primary school class already has only one teacher.)

Teaching loads can be increased by increasing the number of classes taught per week or by increasing the number of weeks in the school year. The latter measure offers particular promise in a number of African countries in which the school year is now quite short. Of course, for these measures to increase the pupil-teacher ratio, the number of classroom hours must be extended only for teachers and not for pupils. This implies some system of double shifts (that is, splitting the school day, week, or year), with each of the two sessions catering to half of the total number of pupils enrolled. Such measures may be impossible to implement without compensating teachers financially, which tends to defeat the original purpose, but they can still reduce average per pupil cost if the increase in the pupil-teacher ratio is greater than the increase in teachers' salaries and if the heavier teaching load does not seriously undermine the average teacher's effectiveness in the classroom. The assumption used here is that in many instances teachers will be willing to accept a reduction in hourly earnings if they have an opportunity to increase their annual earnings by teaching more hours per year. In the interest of reducing unit costs and extending enrollments, Senegal recently decided to implement double shifts (see box 4-4).

In addition to raising teaching loads, countries should make every effort to enforce whatever teaching loads are officially on the books. Absenteeism is widespread in many countries. Enforcement of discipline with respect to duties is essential for efficiency; it may entail replacing slack teachers with currently unemployed graduates. In addition, countries should minimize the extent to which those trained and paid as teachers are assigned to other, extraneous duties. Many teachers perform office and supervisory tasks that could probably be performed less expensively and at least as satisfactorily by somebody trained for such work.

Reducing the average attendance load of pupils, either by decreasing the number of classes attended per week or by reducing (for pupils) the number of weeks in the school year, is the second principal strategy for increasing the pupil-teacher ratio and thereby reducing salary costs per pupil. The savings generated by such measures must be weighed against any loss in the average achievement of pupils. For some countries, present financial constraints may necessitate that the tradeoffs be at least considered. In particular, countries in which all primary grades now have instruction for the same number of hours per week might consider reducing the length of the school day for, say, the first three grades to permit a second shift. The most vocal opposition to a shorter school day is likely to come from parents employed in the urban wage sector, who may have to make alternative after-school or before-school child-care arrangements. Parents in rural areas may welcome a shorter school day, which would reduce the opportunity cost of children's school attendance.

The third way of increasing the pupil-teacher ratio is to increase the average class size. Even in countries

> **Box 4-4. Reducing per Pupil Costs through Double Shifts in Senegal**
>
> The gross primary enrollment ratio in Senegal was expected to fall from around 50 percent in 1986 to below 40 percent in 2000 owing to increases in the primary school population and growing pressures to contain public expenditure on education. In an effort to prevent this decline, the government of Senegal is planning to introduce measures that would lower the unit costs of primary education and increase the share of primary education in the education budget.
>
> Senegal ranks first among low-income African economies in the average cost of primary education, which was $101 per student in 1983 (appendix table A-17). Teachers' salaries, which are between seven and nine times GDP per capita, account for much of the problem. Another factor is that student-teacher ratios are significantly lower in rural areas than in urban areas. Unit costs vary by as much as 110 percent in some cases. The use of teachers in administrative positions also contributes to the high unit costs.
>
> One way to lower unit costs, increase enrollments, and reduce the amount of overcrowding in urban schools (which, it is believed, has contributed to declining pass rates in the primary completion examination since the late 1960s) would be to introduce a system of double shifts. Under this scheme a teacher who taught two shifts would receive 25 percent of his or her base salary as extra pay. In the double shift schools, classroom hours for students would be reduced from 28 hours a week to about 20; as partial compensation, the school year would be extended by 30 days and teachers would be given special training on how to utilize classroom hours more efficiently. If the double shift system were implemented in about 20 percent of the overcrowded classrooms and if it were initiated at grade 1 in the first year and extended to grades 2, 3, and 4 over a four-year period, the number of student places would increase by approximately 33,000 (6 percent of current enrollment) by 2000.
>
> To have an even more pronounced impact on enrollments, double shifts could be implemented as part of a broader policy package for reducing unit costs. Other cost-saving elements that Senegal plans to introduce include increasing the proportion of *instituteurs-adjoints* (who have less training and are therefore paid less than *instituteurs*), redeploying 400 teachers from administrative positions to classroom teaching, and mixing two or more grades in underutilized rural classrooms (multigrade teaching).
>
> In addition, Senegal plans to reduce the growth of expenditures for secondary education, higher education, and administration, reduce public funding for education fellowships, and limit the budget for campus services at the University of Dakar. These policies would yield substantial annual budgetary savings that could be reallocated to primary education.
>
> If all of these policy measures, including double shifts, were implemented as a package, and if recent rates of real growth in the education and government budgets continue, an estimated 877,000 children could be enrolled in primary education in 2000, compared with 667,000 children if no new policies were introduced. This would mean a slight increase in the enrollment ratio between 1986 and 2000 rather than the precipitous decline that was projected.

in which the average class size appears "about right" (in the 35–45 pupil range), the average usually masks large differences between urban and rural areas. In urban areas classes of 50, 60, and even 75 pupils are not uncommon. In such settings smaller classes should probably be the objective. This can be achieved by double shifts, with pupils attending school only half of each day or every other day.

In rural areas the problem is usually not overcrowding but the reverse—classes that are uneconomically small. In these areas special efforts should be made to increase class size. Several approaches should be considered. The first is careful planning of the location of any new schools. A second approach, which to be successful would probably require special materials and training for teachers, is multigrade teaching. A third approach, which is more controversial but easier to implement, is to admit pupils only in alternate years, as is done now in rural areas of Mali. That is, the birth dates of children entering the first grade in a particular community in a particular year would span two years instead of one, and in any given year only three years of a six-year primary cycle would be taught (that is, in year 1 new students would be admitted and grades 1, 3, and 5 would be taught; in year 2 no students would be admitted to first grade and grades 2, 4, and 6 would be taught).

Reductions in Repetition and Dropout

Even where the cost per pupil-year is reasonable owing to the cost-efficient utilization of teachers, the cost per completer of the primary cycle is everywhere higher than need be because many pupils repeat grades and others drop out before they complete the cycle. For Sub-Saharan Africa as a whole, repeaters account for 16 percent of primary enrollments (23 percent in Francophone and 8 percent in Anglophone countries), and because of dropout only 61 percent of those who enter the first grade reach the final grade of primary education (these are median values; see appendix table A-12). As a result, it is estimated that the cost of each completer in the median country of Africa is 50 percent higher than if there were no repetition and dropout. In general, the lower the income of the country, the worse is the situation. In ten out of twenty-four low-income economies (countries in which GNP per capita was below $400 in 1984), the cost per completer is more than double what it would be without repetition and dropout. Although it is useful to note these high costs per completer, it is essential to bear in mind that even quantitative measures of educational output have a qualitative dimension: the number of repeaters (and, to some extent, the number of dropouts) can change with promotion standards. Ultimately, the efficiency of these and other policies can be assessed only in terms of their impact on learning gains.

Dropout occurs for a variety of reasons, the relative importance of which varies among countries and individuals. Students may drop out because they fail a grade or have for other reasons become discouraged about their chances for success, because the opportunity costs of continuation have become too high, or simply because of lack of opportunity to continue in systems in which many schools offer only some primary grades. Although some benefits undoubtedly accrue to pupils who drop out before completion, it can be assumed that these benefits are small if dropout occurs before the attainment of basic literacy and numeracy at about the fourth grade. Beyond that, there is little evidence of any inefficiency associated with dropping out before the completion of a cycle.

The extent to which repetition should be regarded as waste is a controversial point. The proponents of repetition claim that it is useful in that it remedies inadequate achievement and helps pupils who are emotionally and intellectually immature when they enter school. Critics of repetition claim that achievement depends principally on nonschool factors, that valid tests cannot be developed to separate failures from those who are promoted, that repetition does not improve the achievement of slow learners, and that repetition, by calling attention to the repeaters' poor performance, hurts their self-image and their prospects for future success. Most important in the developing-country context, repetition extends the duration of study and hence raises the cost per year of school finally completed. Critics of repetition propose that pupils be promoted automatically from one grade to the next. The proponents of repetition oppose this policy on the grounds that it lowers academic standards, destroys pupils' incentive to learn and teachers' incentive to teach, and creates pedagogical problems by increasing the ability range within the classroom.

One reason that pupils repeat grades, especially toward the end of a cycle, is that they believe this will improve their chances of passing the examinations for entry into the next level of education. Accordingly, a useful strategy for reducing dropouts is to separate the primary school leaving examination from the secondary school entrance examination. Under this arrangement pupils take the school leaving examination at the conclusion of the cycle and, if they are successful, receive a diploma certifying that they have completed primary school. The secondary school entrance examination is taken independently. Individual students can try to improve their chances of success on the entrance examination through independent study or private tuition, but not by prolonging their time in a government primary school.

Significant reductions in dropout and repetition rates could be achieved, but that would require sizable and costly improvements in the school and classroom factors that cause pupils to repeat or drop out. Thus, at least in the short term, the areas of repetition and dropout probably offer little opportunity for cost savings.

Appropriate Construction Standards

There is potential in many African countries for the development and use of new school designs that meet minimum standards but are much cheaper than those typically used at present. The cost of facilities is now often a substantial fraction of the economic cost of providing primary education. Annualized capital costs are in some cases the equivalent of 80 percent of annual recurrent costs. Strategies to increase teacher utilization would be facilitated in the future through the choice of appropriate construction designs. In addition, appropriate standards would emphasize the use of local materials, and this, in addition to reducing building costs, would facilitate the ongoing transfer of responsibility for primary school construction and maintenance from the central government to local communities.

In many cases greater reliance on local materials is also a way of improving the quality of construction. For example, in Niger the cost of a classroom made of concrete is five times that of one made of *banco*, the most commonly used construction material in rural areas. Yet the latter is cooler in summer and warmer in winter than the former.

Box 4-5 describes a project recently implemented in Senegal that demonstrates the feasibility of using low-cost school construction techniques on a large scale.

Mobilizing Resources for Primary Education

Although there are some policies by which countries can improve the efficiency of resource use in primary education, when all is said and done there is little likelihood of significantly reducing unit recurrent costs at this level, especially if countries also hope to improve the quality of education. There is more scope for reducing unit capital costs, but even so, it is unlikely that overall per capita costs can be reduced much at the primary level. The principal reason for the low quality of primary education in Africa is the comparatively low use of resources per pupil. In 1983 the median per pupil public expenditure was under $50. By comparison, public spending per pupil was approximately 2.5 times this amount in East Asia and Latin America and over 30 times in the industrialized countries. Moreover, real per pupil expenditure declined nearly 30 percent in Africa between 1970 and 1983 (appendix table A-17).

Thus further growth of primary education will inevitably require that additional resources be mobilized. Even with no quality improvements (and assuming also no improvements in efficiency), the amount of resources devoted to the primary level would need to increase by more than 3 percent annually just to keep pace with population growth. In principle, these additional resources can be made available either by reallocating resources within the education sector in favor of the primary level or by increasing the total allocation to the education sector. The latter could be achieved through an increase in public or private spending or through an increase in foreign aid for education. In the recent past only about 8 percent of foreign aid to the education sector in Africa went to the primary level. Although this is partially understandable in an aid environment that emphasizes discrete project investments, a more program-oriented pattern of aid flows would provide

---

Box 4-5. Low-Cost School Construction in Francophone Africa

The high cost of classroom construction in Senegal in past years has stemmed from reliance on expensive imported materials, designs, and techniques that are inappropriate to the local setting, from inefficient procurement methods, and from the rapid deterioration of facilities because of insufficient maintenance. Despite efforts over the past fifteen years to bring construction costs down, in 1985 the government was still facing initial investment costs of around $300 per student place. A recent pilot project undertaken by the government has brought the cost per student place down to $155.

Eighty-six primary school classrooms in the Kolda and Tambacounda areas were constructed under this project. A number of strategies were used to hold costs down. The tendering procedure made use of a bidding process organized as a competition among partnerships of architects and contractors. The outcome was a replicable, low-cost, low-maintenance construction technology that is labor-intensive and maximizes the use of local materials. Fully 80 percent of total construction materials are locally available. The foreign exchange component of this technology represents approximately 28 percent, compared with about 52 percent for classical construction methods.

The project relies on a general contractor to provide transport, technical know-how, and skilled labor and to train local unskilled labor as masons and bricklayers.

The additional income generated for the community from wage receipts, at the prevailing wage of $4 per day, is $1,800 per classroom constructed. Through the training of unskilled labor on the job, local artisans and craftsmen will emerge and a new regional employment market will be developed. Furthermore, the design's high thermal mass will counteract the uncomfortable daytime temperatures common in Senegal and thus provide a better environment for learning.

Similar projects are currently under way in Burkina Faso, Central African Republic, Mali, and Niger. The implementation of such pilot projects has given governments experience in managing programs for the construction of small buildings on large numbers of widely scattered sites with the use of a new technology. At the same time, education financing studies have pointed out the difficulties that central governments are likely to face when they assume full responsiblity for financing capital investment in the sector, particularly with respect to the construction of primary schools. Funds generated through local taxes are likely to be increasingly important in this regard. Thus the task for central governments and their ministries of education will be to manage and monitor existing education facilities, provide incentives to regional authorities, and ensure that minimum standards are met.

a more generous share to the primary level. Chapter 9 deals with foreign aid for primary education; the remainder of this chapter discusses the mobilization of domestic resources.

In many African countries a good case can be made for gradually increasing the proportion of public education budgets allocated to primary education. (An increase in the proportion of the public education budget allocated to the primary subsector does not mean that public expenditures on secondary and higher education must necessarily decline in absolute terms; they can remain the same or even go up while the share of primary education is going up, as long as the total public budget for education is growing. As is argued in chapter 6, however, most of the increase in total resources for higher education, which is urgently required in most countries, will have to come not from growth of the public budget but rather from increased private financial contributions to the subsector.) An increase in the share of primary education in the budget is particularly defensible in countries with low primary enrollments, where the median share of education spending going to the primary subsector is only 34 percent (appendix table C-6). Here an adjustment in favor of primary education would be both profitable to the national economy and equitable, since the expansion of primary education benefits less advantaged population groups disproportionately. As the data in table 4-2 clearly suggest, inadequate relative allocations within the education sector may be an important reason for low enrollment levels.

Although adjustment of shares may be desirable on grounds of efficiency and equity, politics could stand in the way. Obviously, if the share of primary education is to be increased, the share going to something else must be diminished. An economically attractive source of public funds would be the budget for living-expense subsidies to students at the tertiary level. The effect here could be significant. A study based on twelve African countries indicated that, on average, primary enrollments could increase by a remarkable 18 percent with the public funds saved if university students paid their own living expenses.

Increased total public spending on education would have to be financed either through increased economic growth (maintaining constant the share of resources devoted to education) or by an increase in the share of education in the total budget. As regards the former, the growth prospects for Sub-Saharan Africa for the foreseeable future are modest at best. In *World Development Report 1986* the World Bank examined scenarios of average annual rates of GDP growth ranging from 3.2 percent ("low case") to 4.0 percent ("high case") for the low-income African countries over the next ten years. If the low case is the more accurate projection, these countries may suffer another decade of falling real incomes per capita. Even in the high case, GDP growth will barely keep pace with the projected population increase. Thus over the next decade the additional resources required for doing more than simply maintaining present educational coverage and quality will not be derived from economic growth.

In 1983 education received 15.3 percent of total public expenditure in the median African country (appendix table A-14). Whether this figure is high, low, or about right depends on one's assessment of the relative profitability of public spending in different areas. There are in any case marked differences between African countries in the priority given to education. Whereas one out of five countries allocated more than 20 percent of public expenditure to education in 1983, one out of three countries allocated less than 13 percent. Countries in the lower half of the distribution might wish to review whether

Table 4-2. Primary Enrollment Ratios and the Share of Primary Education in the Education Budget
(percent)

Country group[a]	Median gross primary enrollment ratio	Median share of primary education in recurrent education budget
Low primary enrollment	37	34
Medium primary enrollment	67	45
High primary enrollment	106	46
Thirty-nine Sub-Saharan African countries	77	43

a. Low primary enrollment: gross primary enrollment ratio of less than 50 percent (ten countries); medium primary enrollment: 50–80 percent (thirteen countries); high: more than 80 percent (sixteen countries).
Source: Appendix table C-6.

education is really getting its appropriate share of total expenditure or whether a higher budgetary priority for the sector might be warranted, as was recommended in chapter 2.

Various strategies can be used to mobilize additional resources for primary education by recovering the costs of education from the recipients of the service. Educational costs may be recovered through school fees or other monetary levies, or they may be repaid in kind—for example, in the form of free labor for school construction and maintenance. It is estimated that private expenditures now cover about 6 percent of costs in East Africa and 11 percent in West Africa. (These percentages are only about one-third as high at the university level.)

A distinct trend in recent years, particularly in the Anglophone countries but elsewhere in the region as well, has been the shift of the main responsibility for the construction and maintenance of primary school classrooms from the central government to parents and local communities. Driven by the inadequacy of government funds to support the sizable capital budget for primary education, many African governments have been willing to accept greater involvement by the recipients of educational services. This policy has enabled primary school development programs to proceed at a more rapid pace than would have been possible otherwise, and it has tended to ensure that new schools are opened where the demand for primary education is the strongest.

For items other than classroom construction and maintenance, private financing is less significant in African primary education. This is as it should be, since if fees are charged it is likely that the very poorest African children will be deprived of any education at all. Recent African experience suggests that parents are much less willing to pay for basic tuition than for institutional materials; where tuition fees have been imposed in public primary schools, some enrollment declines have been experienced. Very few countries anywhere else in the world charge for public primary education.

As further justification for subsidization of primary education costs, there is increasing evidence of large externalities that accrue to investment at this level. A recent study of education and production in Nepal showed that farm yields depend not only on the farmer's own educational attainment but also on the average educational attainment of the community in which the farmer lives. A recent evaluation of Bank-financed project-related training suggests that the effectiveness of such training is high in countries in which the adult literacy rate is greater than 50 percent and much smaller in countries in which the rate is less than 50 percent.

Although charging primary pupils for instruction should generally be discouraged, there may be situations in which the judicious use of modest fees might be used for the explicit purpose of increasing accountability in education. For example, a purchase fee or rental charge for textbooks and other materials that are crucial to high levels of pupil achievement would help to ensure that these inputs are not eliminated from the budget during times of fiscal austerity. Another efficiency-increasing mechanism would be for parental groups to "top up" primary teachers' salaries in proportion to the time that teachers actually spend in the classroom; this would be an incentive to reduce absenteeism.

Private school enrollments account for about 6 percent of total primary enrollments in the median African country. Private education plays a somewhat larger role in Anglophone Africa (22 percent of enrollments) than in Francophone Africa (3 percent). A "private school," however, is a school that is managed by nongovernment authorities; the financing of private education can come from public as well as from private sources. Indeed, much private education in Africa is at least partially subsidized by the government. Hence data on enrollments give an exaggerated idea of the extent of private financing of primary education. Nonetheless, a greater degree of tolerance than many African governments have shown in the past for private alternatives to public education at the primary level would almost certainly facilitate expansion.

5

The Consolidation of Competence: Secondary Education and Training

Secondary education, building on the foundation laid at the primary level, seeks to strengthen the general intellectual skills that are relevant to many occupations and to subsequent education. Its goal is to prepare individuals for adult responsibility and for the world of work, where most job-specific skills will be learned. Quality improvement was identified in chapter 4 as the immediate objective for most African countries with respect to primary education. The quality of secondary education is also a great concern since, as in the case of primary education, the amounts of essential nonsalary recurrent inputs being provided are not adequate. For nearly all African countries in the years to come, however, the biggest challenge with respect to secondary education will be expansion—how to satisfy the burgeoning demand for a limited number of secondary school places.

As recently as 1960 only two of the thirty-nine countries of Sub-Saharan Africa enrolled more than 6 percent of the relevant age group in secondary education. These two were Mauritius and Ghana, where the gross enrollment ratios were 22 percent and 19 percent, respectively. For the rest of the region, secondary education remained highly selective.

Today participation in secondary education varies greatly from country to country (see appendix table C-7). Of thirty-nine Sub-Saharan African countries, ten had gross secondary enrollment ratios that were considered low (less than 10 percent in 1983), sixteen had medium enrollment ratios (between 10 and 20 percent), and thirteen had high enrollment ratios that surpassed the 20 percent mark, an impressive accomplishment in the light of historical precedent. (Virtually none of the now developed nations of Europe and North America had secondary enrollment ratios of more than 10 percent at the beginning of this century, and for the most part ratios of more than 20 percent were achieved only after World War II.) Three of the high secondary enrollment countries—Congo, Mauritius, and Zaire—already have secondary enrollment ratios of more than 50 percent.

As would be expected, gross secondary enrollment ratios are related to per capita income. Nine of the thirteen high enrollment countries are classified by the World Bank as middle-income economies (economies with a 1984 GNP per capita of $400 or more). Conversely, all ten low enrollment countries are low income (GNP per capita of less than $400). The eighteen Francophone countries are equally distributed among the three secondary enrollment groups. The sixteen Anglophone countries are skewed toward the high end of the enrollment spectrum; seven of them are in the high enrollment group, six are in the medium category, and only three are low secondary enrollment countries.

Table 5-1 shows how the three country enrollment groups differ with respect to other important indicators. Those with higher enrollment ratios not only are richer, they also spend a larger proportion of national income on education. The greater emphasis on secondary education has come at the expense of

Table 5-1. Median Enrollment Characteristics and Education Expenditure by Secondary Enrollment Group
(percent)

Country group	Gross secondary enrollment ratio	Public expenditure on education as percentage of GNP	Expenditure on secondary education as percentage of public recurrent expenditure on education	Ratio of secondary to primary enrollments	Progression rate from primary to secondary	Females as percentage of secondary enrollments
Low secondary enrollment	5	3.3	30	10	16	32
Medium secondary enrollment	15	4.0	30	21	45	33
High secondary enrollment	24	5.3	35	23	54	39
Thirty-nine Sub-Saharan African countries	16	3.9	31	20	40	33

Note: Low secondary enrollment: gross primary enrollment ratio of less than 10 percent (ten countries). Medium secondary enrollment, 10–20 percent (sixteen countries). High secondary enrollment, more than 20 percent (thirteen countries).
Source: Appendix table C-7.

primary education. Among the thirteen high secondary enrollment countries the proportion of public expenditure on education that is allocated to secondary education ranges from 16 percent to 56 percent, with a median of 35 percent, whereas among the ten low enrollment countries this figure ranges from 14 to 40 percent, with a median of 30 percent. In the high enrollment group the ratio of secondary enrollments to primary enrollments ranges from 0.13 to 0.57 (median 0.24), whereas at the low end the ratio ranges from 0.02 to 0.26 (median 0.10). The rate of progression from the last grade of primary school to the first grade of general secondary education was 54 percent for the median high secondary enrollment country, compared with only 16 percent for the median low secondary enrollment country.

Even in countries in which secondary participation rates are below the Africa-wide average, the growth of the secondary education subsector in recent years has often been robust. Of the three main education levels, the secondary level appears to have been the least affected by the recent economic depression. The rate of growth of secondary places, which had been 12.4 percent between 1960 and 1980, fell to only 10.9 percent after 1980, about a 12 percent decline in the growth rate. The growth rates of postsecondary and primary enrollments fell much more precipitously—by 39 percent and 59 percent, respectively (appendix tables A-1 to A-4). Reflecting this shift in favor of enrollments at the secondary level, public expenditures on secondary education increased in relation to expenditures on primary and tertiary education in a majority of African countries between 1980 and 1983 (appendix table A-16).

Political pressures have contributed to this reallocation. The earlier rapid expansion of primary education in African countries resulted in an ever larger pool of primary school leavers, many of whom could no longer find the jobs in the modern wage sector that they had come to expect. The heightened scramble to fill the limited number of secondary school places generated political pressures for expansion. Generous public subsidies further fueled the demand for secondary school places.

The case for the expansion of secondary education, however, is more than just political. There is a strong economic rationale for expanding secondary education in most African countries as long as hard measures are taken to increase the efficiency and equity of the systems. Chapter 2 reviewed evidence that the social rates of return to investment at the secondary level are high in comparison with most alternatives in the region, including many educational alternatives. Although much of the research to date has shown even higher rates of return for primary education (owing, at least in part, to the much lower per student costs at the primary level), recent evidence, reviewed in box 2-1, suggests that the differential between rates of return to primary and to secondary education in Africa has narrowed considerably over time, increasing the relative economic attractiveness of the secondary level.

In assessing the economic consequences of a substantial expansion of secondary education, it is interesting to compare the recent experiences of Kenya and Tanzania. Kenya has pursued a relatively expansionary policy with respect to secondary education, whereas Tanzania's approach has been much more restrictive. Box 5-1 suggests that an important part of Kenya's more rapid growth in average wage levels can be attributed to its investments in the quantity and quality of secondary education.

Secondary education will and should continue to expand in Sub-Saharan Africa for sound economic and political reasons. A prerequisite to the further expansion of secondary education in today's economic climate will be the rigorous containment of unit costs, the subject of the next section.

Meeting the Demand for Expansion by Reducing Unit Costs

Secondary education is often expensive in Africa, in both absolute and relative terms (appendix tables A-17 and A-18). Public recurrent expenditure per secondary student ranged from less than $50 in Ghana and Guinea-Bissau to more than $700 in Côte d'Ivoire and Tanzania and was $223 in the median African country in 1983. This per student cost equaled 62 percent of per capita GNP in the median African country, and here too the range was substantial, from about 20 percent in the Central African Republic, Ghana, Kenya, and Mauritius to well above 300 percent in Tanzania. What is spent on each secondary student in the median country could be used to educate four additional primary pupils at current spending levels.

Public spending per student tends to be highest in those countries in which enrollment ratios are the lowest. Appendix table C-8 compares unit costs and some key determinants of this variable for low, medium, and high enrollment countries. (Caution must be exercised in interpreting the comparative cost data. In addition to the usual problems associated with the use of exchange rates to convert local currency figures into U.S. dollars, there are many gaps in the data on costs. This is because the collection of statistics on education has evolved largely as

---

Box 5-1. Policies toward Secondary Education

Significant differences between education policies in Kenya and Tanzania, particularly with respect to secondary education, emerged in the late 1960s. In Tanzania the government reduced the share of public spending allocated to secondary schooling and, until recently, also restricted the establishment of private and community secondary schools. In contrast, the Kenyan government encouraged the growth of both public and private secondary education. By 1980 these divergent policies had led to secondary school enrollment ratios that were six times greater in Kenya than in Tanzania.

Important qualitative differences in secondary education also emerged during this period. Tanzania placed greater stress on the teaching of agriculture and other vocational skills, thus diverting time from general academic skills. The Tanzanian system also greatly emphasized the use of Swahili at the primary level, which may have made it more difficult for students to learn in English in secondary school. Research indicates that for any given combination of inputs of individual ability and years of secondary schooling in the two countries, cognitive outputs (as measured by scores on academic achievement tests) are substantially higher in Kenya than in Tanzania.

Given the differences in the quantity and quality of secondary education, it was to be expected that over time the cognitive skill level of the average employee in Kenya would rise in relation to that of the average employee in Tanzania. Indeed, results of cognitive tests reveal that Kenyan employees score higher on tests of literacy and numeracy than their Tanzanian counterparts despite the fact that the average scores of Kenyans and Tanzanians on tests of reasoning ability are essentially the same. Since analysis has shown that workers who are more literate and numerate are more productive, one may conclude that Tanzania has paid a price in output forgone by restraining the growth of secondary education and reducing educational quality.

One way to quantify this price is to estimate how much greater the cognitive skill and productivity of the Tanzanian labor force would be if the quantity and quality of education were increased to the Kenyan level. Such an analysis shows that a simultaneous increase in quantity and quality would increase the cognitive skills of Tanzanians by 31 percent and their earnings by 13 percent. Roughly 40 percent of the current difference in mean wages between Kenyan and Tanzanian workers can be accounted for by the lower cognitive skills of the Tanzanian labor force. Differences in the quality of education account for more than half the difference in the skill level and thus in the mean earnings of the labor force.

This suggests that the opportunity cost to Tanzania of its policy regarding secondary education has been substantial. The divergence between Kenya and Tanzania in educational policy in the late 1960s appears to have been an important factor in their differing economic performances.

a by-product of education administration rather than in response to a policy concern about analyzing and controlling costs.) In both absolute terms and with respect to per student expenditure as a percentage of GNP per capita, the low secondary enrollment countries spend more on secondary education than do countries in the two higher groups. But most striking is the fact that secondary per student costs in relation to primary per student costs are much higher in the low enrollment countries than in the other two groups. In the typical low enrollment country, expenditure per student in secondary education is 9 to 10 times that in primary education, whereas in the rest of the region the ratio is just above 3.

Given the tight limits on public resources in Africa and the competing claims on these resources by other parts of the education system, the key to satisfying the high demand for secondary education in Africa lies in greater cost sharing at this level combined with substantial reductions in unit costs. Cost sharing is the subject of later sections of this chapter. Cost containment is discussed here.

This book's conclusions concerning unit cost containment at the secondary level parallel those for primary education. Chapter 4, on primary education, reviewed a variety of measures that could save on the training, salaries, and utilization of teachers and on capital costs and thereby reduce per pupil costs. Most of these suggestions apply to secondary education, and there is no need to repeat the entire analysis here.

The difference between the two levels is that there is usually much greater scope for unit cost reduction at the secondary than at the primary level. In particular, there is evidence from many parts of Africa today that capital and teachers are relatively underutilized at the secondary level. The median student-teacher ratio in Sub-Saharan Africa is 39 in primary education but only 23 at the secondary level. There is no pedagogical rationale for a difference of this size (although in some cases there may be a logistic one). Policies to increase student-teacher ratios at the secondary level could substantially reduce unit costs. The principal means that policymakers may wish to consider for raising this ratio include larger classes, heavier teaching loads (obtainable through double shifts and extensions of the school calendar), and specialization of teachers in several subjects rather than in only one.

In brief, there is substantial potential in most countries for reducing unit costs at the secondary level by improving efficiency within the existing system. African leaders will need to implement firm policies in this regard. A substantial part of the savings will have to be redirected to increasing recurrent inputs (the inadequacy of instructional materials and consumable supplies is a problem at the secondary level, although less so than at the primary level), but some resources may be left for expansion. In addition, and in contrast to the situation in primary education, there is a potential for achieving expansion at the secondary level through a substantial modification of the existing system. This could result in a dramatic reduction in unit costs, to perhaps half their current levels. This possibility is the subject of the following discussions on the introduction of distance education programs and on the transition from boarding schools to day schools.

Distance Education: Self-Study Schools and Extramural Programs

Given the unsatisfied demand for secondary education and the fact that the pool of eligible primary school leavers grows inexorably larger every year, policies that incrementally increase student-teacher ratios and the utilization rates of facilities and incrementally reduce unit capital costs will never completely remedy the shortage of second-level places and eliminate the political pressure on African governments to expand the capacity of the system. To achieve a quantum increase in secondary enrollments without a commensurate increase in total costs or a serious decline in educational quality will require radical changes in educational practices in Sub-Saharan Africa. New means of education are required to reduce substantially the dependence of students on face-to-face contact with teachers. These methods, which typically involve some combination of radio and correspondence techniques, reduce the amount of contact with qualified teachers, but they should never, or only in extraordinary circumstances, be allowed to eliminate such contact.

Distance education has been defined as "an educational process in which a significant proportion of the teaching is conducted by someone removed in space and/or time from the learner" (Perraton 1982, p. 4). The use of textbooks in conventional classrooms is one of the simplest and most proven examples of distance education. Properly designed distance education projects combine the strengths of different media—"print for permanence, broadcasting for immediacy, face-to-face learning for individuality and feedback" (Perraton and others 1986, p. 6). The essence of distance education is that a small number of teachers produce course materials that are made available in quantity as printed matter, through broadcasts, or through some other medium that does not involve direct contact with the original producers. Economies of scale, which are not very practical in face-to-face teaching, become possible under such a system.

At the primary level printed materials and broadcasting are used, for the most part, to enrich the instruction provided by teachers in classrooms, and distance methods nearly always represent an added cost. But at the secondary level and above (including preservice training and, especially, the in-service upgrading of primary school teachers), students have already acquired the basic study skills and maturity to make use of a variety of educational media on their own, with a minimum of individual supervision. Beginning at this level, the potential of distance education to reduce costs by substituting for the time of highly skilled teachers makes it an attractive alternative to conventional instruction for low-income countries, especially in Sub-Saharan Africa. Table 5-2 describes two kinds of distance education that can be used to save on teacher costs—self-study schools and extramural programs—and contrasts them to the enrichment and quality enhancement modes, which typically do not reduce costs.

Distance education is already helping to widen the opportunities for secondary schooling in a number of African countries. Some Anglophone countries— Zambia is a good example—have established extramural programs that are run by the government or by universities. Several Francophone countries have set up teaching programs modeled on the French Centre National de Télé-Enseignement. One reason for establishing such colleges has been to reduce the amount of foreign exchange spent on correspondence courses from Europe.

Initially the intended target group for the distance education programs often consisted of people with primary education and perhaps incomplete secondary education who were employed in the formal

Table 5-2. Main Modes of Distance Education

Mode	Description	Costs and effects
Enrichment and quality enhancement	Radio or television broadcasts are provided in one or two subjects for between 15 minutes and 2½ hours a week. Many countries, including Ethiopia and Kenya, use limited amounts of time for enrichment. More substantial use sometimes carries the main burden of instruction in a subject (see box 4-2 on interactive radio).	The use of radio for enrichment is inexpensive but has relatively little impact on learning. More substantial use, as in interactive radio, increases costs but produces strong positive effects on learning in mathematics and the national language. Enrichment and quality enhancement are particularly suitable at the primary level.
Self-study schools	Students attend "school" but classes are led by an older student or community member. Radio or television carries the main burden of classroom instruction in all subjects, and students are expected to rely heavily on their textbooks. The world's largest educational institution, the Chinese Television University, uses this model, which emphasizes postsecondary instruction, as does the Malawi Correspondence College at the secondary level (see box 5-2.).	Self-study schools reduce costs by 20 to 30 percent—more if they use regular classroom space after hours. They can extend access by providing very small schools in individual communities, which is particularly important for increasing female access and reducing reliance on boarding schools. Costs are higher for television than for radio, and the gains in learning outcomes are minimal with television.
Extramural programs	Extramural programs rely principally on print to convey instruction, but, to the extent feasible, they frequently supplement print with radio or television broadcasts and tutorial meetings. (The latter are particularly important where change of assignments through the mails is slow or unreliable.) The British Open University is perhaps the best-known extramural program today. The University of Zambia operates a small-scale (but long-established) extramural program, and Tanzania had marked success with correspondence education for in-service teacher training (see box 4-1.)	The potential for cost savings with extramural programs is even greater than with self-study schools. The cost per student per course may be expected to be 10 to 25 percent of conventional instruction. Extramural programs have the added advantage of allowing students to pursue their studies while employed. Their disadvantage is the demand they make on student motivation (although this is arguably a good criterion for student selection). Extramural programs have their main roles in higher and in-service education, but they are also an option at the secondary level.

wage sector and needed educational qualifications for promotion. Very soon, however, the programs also began to attract recent primary school leavers who had not succeeded in being admitted to secondary school and were not yet gainfully employed. Because of the selection process, the students enrolled in the distance education programs were on average less academically able than those enrolled in the regular schools. Accordingly, to provide increased support for such students and raise their chances of passing national examinations, some countries supplemented the correspondence methods with study centers in which students could receive instruction by radio and work on their correspondence materials during scheduled times under the guidance of supervisors. In this fashion a number of extramural programs that relied exclusively on correspondence and broadcasting methods have evolved into self-study schools.

The classroom supervisors in self-study secondary schools are not usually secondary school teachers, although some may have qualified as primary school teachers. Typically they lack the background to teach the students, but they are able to help them with the organization of their studies and advise them on how and where to seek further assistance. The Malawi Correspondence College is an example of a distance teaching program that has been adapted to resemble more nearly a regular school program. Students in this program may choose to study part-time or full-time, relying heavily on radio broadcasts and self-study printed materials but enjoying the benefits of a classroom in which to study and a supervisor to oversee their work (see box 5-2).

Extramural programs such as the one in Zambia and self-study schools such as the Malawi Correspondence College can be seen as ways of promoting equity in education, in that they provide a second

---

Box 5-2. An Alternative Route to Secondary Schooling in Malawi

In 1965 the government of Malawi created the Malawi Correspondence College (MCC) as an alternative to the formal system, which could enroll only 9 percent of primary school graduates. The MCC evolved gradually over twenty years as the government recognized that it offered a relatively inexpensive way to respond to the growing demand for secondary education. The recurrent cost per student in an MCC study center is less than one-fifth of the recurrent cost of a student in a government secondary school, and the cost per graduate is slightly less than the cost per secondary school graduate.

The system is based on radio, correspondence, and the use of not fully qualified teachers who work with students in special study centers and in regular secondary schools at night. The only entrance requirements are a primary school leaving certificate and payment of a fee for correspondence materials. More than 80 percent of MCC students enroll at the junior secondary level and the rest at the senior secondary level. Although the MCC centers were originally designed to serve working youths on a part-time basis, over 70 percent of all students are now studying in classrooms for over five hours a day. By 1985 the MCC was enrolling more than 10,000 new students a year and providing to its approximately 19,000 active students fifteen hours of radio programs a week, correspondence materials, and a service that reviews and marks students' correspondence lessons.

MCC centers are generally located in simple buildings, often constructed by the community next to a primary school, and are frequently accompanied by simple housing facilities for students and teachers. In some cases centers make use of primary school buildings in the late afternoons and evenings. The teachers, who may have only a primary teaching certificate, are selected by local supervisors on the basis of their skills and interests. They are paid by local education authorities and are responsible for the general supervision of the classes. The MCC also provides classes in regular secondary schools after hours. These classes are often taught by regular secondary school teachers, who receive supplementary payments through the MCC.

Overall pass rates for MCC candidates on the National Junior Certificate Examination have been between 10 and 22 percent over the past few years. These pass rates are low compared with those of regular secondary schools, but they are satisfactory in the light of the MCC's much lower admissions standards.

The program became more attractive to students when the government made places at regular senior secondary schools available to all MCC students who passed the examination for the full junior certificate in one sitting and at the university to all who earned a full Malawi certificate of education in one sitting. This policy has been changed somewhat, and MCC graduates now have to compete on an equal footing with graduates of the regular secondary schools.

chance for those who would not otherwise have access to secondary education. But the evidence suggests, not surprisingly, that this is a more difficult route to secondary qualifications than the conventional one. Those who do well in their primary school leaving examination now go to regular schools; those who do less well must settle for a method of study that is intrinsically more difficult. If a country wishes to promote full equity and at the same time expand secondary education by taking advantage of the low costs of distance education, the most desirable system may be one in which all second-level students do some of their study through distance education (preferably in self-study schools, using textbooks and submitting homework to be checked by a marking service) and some of their work in regular schools face-to-face with qualified teachers. Alternatively, students in regular schools might be charged some fraction—say, 50 percent—of the additional cost of regular schools as compared with the cost of self-study schools or extramural programs. The most likely pattern, however, is for self-study schools to serve smaller communities during school hours and, in urban areas, to offer evening or weekend study in existing school facilities for individuals who are already employed.

Day Schools

The transition from a system of boarding schools to one of secondary day schools is another approach to reducing both the capital and the recurrent costs of secondary education. Although the savings would be less dramatic than those achieved by moving to a full-fledged distance education system, they can nevertheless be substantial in countries in which boarding schools are now prevalent. The advantages of small day schools that cater to individual communities over large boarding schools that draw students from greater distances are stronger at the junior secondary than at the senior secondary level. Especially when implemented in conjunction with distance education, which reduces the need for large boarding complexes at any level, a system of small day schools can significantly reduce the unit costs of secondary education. (In addition to the higher monetary costs of boarding schools, there can be serious social costs when young students, especially girls, live away from home.)

Boarding schools are sometimes justified on nation-building grounds because they bring together students from different regional and ethnic backgrounds. In addition, they may offer economies of scale with regard to teacher utilization, and they avoid the daily commuting costs associated with day schools. But in some African countries the housing and feeding expenses in boarding schools are as high as all of the instructional costs, and since in many countries these extra costs are fully subsidized, boarding schools in fact shift the basic welfare costs of children from families to the public education budget. Government expenditures per student tend to be much higher in boarding schools than in day schools—by as much as three and a half times in Somalia, for example. The result is that for a given amount of money the government can offer many fewer places. Table 5-3 illustrates this by comparing the costs of boarding schools in Malawi with the costs of regular day schools and of the Malawi Correspondence College.

From the standpoint of equity, there is some concern that exclusive reliance on day schools reduces the access of rural families (and, conversely, increases the access of urban families) to secondary schooling. As the secondary school network in a country grows and coverage in rural areas improves, the transition from a system of boarding schools to one of day schools becomes increasingly feasible. The widespread introduction of small radio correspondence schools would facilitate the transition. Where board-

Table 5-3. Per Student Costs of Day Schools, Boarding Schools, and Self-Study Schools for Secondary Education in Malawi
(1984 kwacha)

School	Capital cost	Annual capital cost	Annual recurrent cost	Total annual cost Amount	Total annual cost Index
Boarding	5,800	530	750	1,280	7.5
Day	3,880	360	204	564	3.3
Self-study (Malawi Correspondence College)	1,180	114	56	170	1.0

Note: Calculations do not include the opportunity cost of student time, but the boarding school costs do include food. Capital costs include construction (depreciated over thirty years) and furniture and equipment (seven years) and are annualized with the use of a 7 percent discount rate.

ing facilities are still regarded as necessary for reasons of equity, the most equitable policy of all is to charge parents the full costs of boarding and feeding (with reduced charges for academically able students from poor homes), since this measure generates revenue and allows for a larger total number of students in the system.

To sum up, substantial savings can be realized through economies in the operation of regular schools, through reduced reliance on boarding, and most significantly, through the creation of distance education systems that take advantage of radio and correspondence techniques. Distance education would permit the expansion of secondary education of a reasonable quality to many more communities than can be reached in any other way for the same price. This leads to recommendation 3.

Recommendation 3

In most African countries it will not be possible to expand secondary and tertiary education significantly—in particular, enough to reach far more females and more people from remote rural areas and disadvantaged social classes—unless policies are adopted to substantially reduce unit costs. Fortunately there is considerable scope for such reductions. The key is to identify and implement new instructional methods that rely much more heavily than in the past on the input of students' time and motivation and that economize on expensive capital inputs and teachers' time. The increased availability and use of self-study schools and extramural programs that employ varying combinations of radio broadcasts and correspondence materials can dramatically lower costs by reducing the need for skilled teachers and by allowing the extension of educational services even to very small communities; this in turn reduces the need for expensive boarding facilities. An increased use of fees for services in both public and private schools would also lower unit costs and enhance efficiency in education to the extent that individuals are more cost-conscious when spending their own funds than when making use of a "free" public service.

Equity Issues: Increased Participation by Females

Beyond general support for expanding access to secondary education, African nations should give serious consideration to policies designed to remedy existing inequalities in school participation. Females are the largest underrepresented group; others include the children of families in remote rural areas, especially nomads, and the children of political and economic refugees. The last group is, unfortunately, a rapidly growing and often neglected element of African society. Unequal access to educational services is not only inequitable; it is also inefficient if those less able to benefit from education gain access ahead of those who are more able.

The differential between male and female school enrollments is no longer particularly pronounced at the primary level—girls account for 44 percent of primary enrollments in Africa today, compared with 43 percent in Asia and 48 percent in Latin America. The difference between male and female enrollments remains high, however, in postprimary education. At the secondary level female enrollment is 34 percent of enrollments, compared with 39 percent in Asia and 50 percent in Latin America, and at the tertiary level it is only 21 percent, compared with 33 percent and 45 percent. Moreover, in many African countries repetition and dropout rates are somewhat higher for females than for males, contrary to the situation in most other parts of the world.

Although female enrollments have grown steadily as a proportion of total enrollments in most African countries since independence, the proportion has actually fallen at the secondary level in the three former Portuguese colonies, and it has been almost stagnant in Benin, Burundi, Rwanda, and Togo. Even where substantial progress has been made, female enrollments continue to lag behind male enrollments. (The only real exceptions are Botswana, Lesotho, Madagascar, Mauritius, and Swaziland, where female enrollments now make up more than 45 percent of secondary enrollments; in Botswana, Lesotho, and Swaziland virtual parity had been attained by 1960.)

Women in Africa spend, on the average, less of their lives in wage employment than do men, and some observers have therefore concluded that the return on investment is smaller for girls' education than for boys'. But this reasoning ignores the significant self-employment of African women, the now proven links between mothers' education and the health and educability of their children, and the connection between education and reduced fertility (see chapter 2). Many studies have shown that female secondary education and the final years of primary education have the greatest impact on these variables that are indicators of household productivity. Moreover, a recent study in Botswana reports higher monetary rates of return for the education of females than for that of males except in the most traditional parts of the country, where women seldom enter the paid labor force.

Given these findings on the returns to girls' education, special efforts should be made, particularly at the secondary level but extending to the tertiary, to raise female enrollments. It may not be obvious, however, how policymakers can influence the participation of females relative to that of males. Rarely in Africa would it be correct to attribute the lag in female enrollments explicitly to government policy. Rather, to identify the principal causes of differences between male and female enrollments, one needs to look primarily at the demand side. Where, for example, the school is far from home, as in many rural areas, parents are afraid for their daughters to walk alone, and a girl may be kept out of school unless there is someone, preferably an older brother, to accompany her. (Distance education, by promoting the geographic dispersion of secondary education, can help to expand educational opportunities for girls.)

When a choice must be made between sending a son or a daughter to school, African parents, like parents in many other parts of the world, usually send the son. The important social benefits derived from female education are not likely to have much impact on a family's private investment decisions. In patrilineal societies the opportunity costs of a daughter's time when she is attending school and such other costs as school fees are borne by her parents, whereas the benefits of her education are thought to accrue principally to her future husband's family. Recently, however, in some areas where a bride-price has traditionally been paid to the bride's family by her husband's family, studies have shown that a woman with more education may command a higher bride-price. This is an example of how families try to capture for themselves the returns to their educational investments.

A key issue from the policy perspective is how to bring private decisions regarding the education of girls in line with what is best for society as a whole. Nothing is likely to change unless explicit attention is given to this goal, and there are indeed policy measures that will increase the willingness of families to allow daughters to attend school.

Small community-based schools, whether or not they rely on distance education, tend to attract girls more readily than do large schools located in urban centers and at greater average distances from home. Although one might expect smaller conventional schools to have higher unit costs, this is not necessarily the case, at least from a fiscal perspective, especially if large schools tend to include boarding facilities and smaller schools do not. Increasing the number of female teachers may also attract more girls, especially in Islamic areas. Governments can reduce the private costs of girls' education in relation to boys' by, for example, providing girls with free books and other instructional materials, charging them lower tuition fees, recovering from families less of the cost of boarding and welfare services for girls than for boys, and offering a school meal program for girls. (Incentive programs targeted to girls may be less feasible where coeducation is the rule than where single-sex schools prevail.)

Training for Vocational Competence

Of central importance to a country's total factor productivity and economic growth is the stock of human capital embodied in the country's working population. Investment in human capital includes—in addition to learning general cognitive skills and maintaining good health—acquiring specific job-related skills and developing reliable work habits and positive attitudes toward work of all kinds. All of these attributes are important to an individual's successful integration into the labor market and lifetime performance at work.

There is little if any disagreement with the proposition that general cognitive skills such as reading, writing, mathematics, and scientific understanding are taught most efficiently in a formal school setting. Virtually every society has developed a school system to transfer these general skills, which are important both for individual self-fulfillment and as the foundation for all subsequent learning, including that pertinent to specific occupations. Although there is no disagreement, either, about the importance of occupation-specific skills, positive attitudes to work, and good work habits, the most efficient timing, methods, and venue for imparting these more narrowly vocational attributes are subjects for debate. Is it most cost-effective for the individual to acquire job-related skills in school, after completion of school but before taking a job, or after securing a job? For those already employed, should training be provided in regional centers that serve large numbers of workers in a particular industry, or should it be given by the individual firm? What is the optimal mix of theoretical instruction and practical work experience?

Different countries have had success with different strategies for transferring occupation-specific skills to the work force. The cost-effectiveness of different methods of acquiring skills depends on many complementary factors; what works well in one country may be poorly suited to another. Moreover, specific programs may require time in which to evolve and mature before they are effective in serving the goals for which they were intended, and in some instances it may be more cost-effective to modify existing institutions than to invent new ones.

Finally, and an important consideration, although it may be cost-effective to have the schools provide instruction in certain widely applicable skills (for example, bookkeeping, typing, and accounting) that are comparatively inexpensive to teach, more specialized and technical skills might be taught more cheaply and effectively within firms, where the equipment and expertise are already on hand and where the identification of needed skills is driven by production requirements. Between these two extremes, in many African countries industries consist of many small firms, none of which is large or developed enough to provide effective skills training. Here the answer is likely to be industrial training centers, typically operating under government control but ideally financed by taxing the beneficiaries in proportion to the benefits received. As a rule of thumb, schools should provide general skills that are applicable in a wide range of jobs and household situations; training centers should concentrate on more specific skills that are applicable within particular occupations; and firms can best provide job-specific skills.

From early colonial days in Africa there has been pressure to increase the vocational content of the school curriculum. Since most secondary school students will not continue their formal education, it is argued that secondary schools should provide specific vocational training that will give them immediate prospects for good jobs on their completion of school. This rationale is put forward most strongly in countries in which the industrial base is still very small and employers have abandoned traditional apprenticeship practices—that is, where there seem to be few ways to acquire technical skills outside school. In such circumstances, it is reasoned, the formal education system has an obligation to impart the attitudes and specific job skills that prepare students for work. In the postcolonial era, many African governments have accepted this reasoning.

One way of incorporating more vocational training into secondary education has been to set up specialized vocational schools—an independent system of technical, agricultural, and commercial schools that parallels the general system. A second method, the diversified secondary school approach, involves inserting into the core curriculum a number of vocational (or, as they are sometimes called, prevocational) courses. Both approaches have been tried extensively in Africa and have received substantial support from international funding agencies, including the World Bank.

Rigorous evaluation of both kinds of vocational education has not been common in Africa. There is a clear need to assess how different types of general and vocational education have performed in relation to their costs and to examine how they have been sustained under the increasingly austere financial conditions of recent years. Such studies need to be conducted several years after the institutions have been established and after they are no longer dependent (if they ever were) on external sources of finance. Also, because it takes time for graduates to find regular work, tracer studies of graduates' experience in the labor market should ideally not be conducted until some years after completion of the course.

Studies along these lines are now being undertaken, some under the auspices of the World Bank; indeed, the Bank is planning to issue a policy study on vocational education and training before the end of the 1980s. In the meantime a few existing findings are reported here, not with any intent to show that in-school programs for teaching vocational skills should be avoided by all countries and under all circumstances but simply to raise warnings that policymakers may prudently bear in mind when the introduction or expansion of such programs is being considered.

First, there is an apparent tendency, particularly in developing countries, to overstate the need to acquire specific skills before employment. Most entry-level jobs require relatively little in the way of specific skills, and even where the reverse is true, adequate on-the-job training can usually be provided by employers, by itself or in some combination with classroom instruction. There is, of course, the problem of how very poor economies can provide skills for an industry that is only emergent or as yet nonexistent. This is a classic "chicken and egg" problem. Teaching high-technology skills cannot bring into being a modern high-technology industry if the other preconditions for the development of the industry are lacking.

Second, there is a tendency to overstate the power of the schools to shape attitudes and behavior in ways that will facilitate the transition from school to work. It is true that certain behavioral characteristics that are emphasized in schools, such as punctuality, persistence, and willingness to accept instruction, are also rewarded in the workplace. If schools do not actually impart these desired behaviors, at least they select for them. But there is scant evidence to suggest that training for a particular occupation will in and of itself predispose an individual to seek employment in that occupation. Indeed, the history of African education is replete with examples of vocational school programs whose principal attraction has been that they offered students a second chance to reenter the academic stream and qualify for high-paying jobs, not necessarily in the occupations for which the vocational schools were designed to provide training. Moreover, the attitudes that are learned in school vocational programs are not always appropriate ones. For example, the credentialed graduates of such programs may have unrealistic expectations concerning pay and status for entry-level personnel.

Third, there is mounting evidence that, for many occupation-specific skill categories, the training provided in schools is generally less useful (that is, the market demand for it is less strong) than training provided on the job or in specialized training centers. The reasons are easy to comprehend. Schools have trouble recruiting and retaining competent instructors, especially in those fields in which market demand is strongest, and school administrators are generally not able to offer different compensation to instructors in different fields. In addition, since vocational schools are separate from the industries for which they train, they generally find it difficult to provide realistic work experience. For the same reason, instructors find that their own skills quickly fall out of date. Equipment, too, tends to become technically obsolete, especially in times of fiscal austerity, when schools experience budgetary pressures that might not be felt in industry. Unlike much industry, schools are slow to adjust to changing market conditions and to change the mix of skills provided. Even when good labor market information is transmitted to those who run training establishments, curriculum changes are inherently difficult to effect within the formal education system.

There are exceptions to the general rule that the formal school system is an inhospitable venue for occupation-specific training. The Federal Republic of Germany offers one such counterexample. There preemployment training within the formal school system is emphasized much more than in—to take a comparable example—Japan, which has a system of broad general education followed by heavy investment by enterprises in on-the-job training. Both countries are extraordinarily successful industrial economies, and both approaches produce trained people who bring a high level of technical competence to the job. Both systems are also capable of adapting swiftly to change, and herein probably lies the secret of their success.

Finally, policymakers should remember that most attempts to increase the amount of vocational training in the curriculum, in Africa at least, have proved expensive in relation to the cost of providing general education. Some of the difference in unit costs occurs because many vocational education institutions and programs in Africa are not large enough to benefit from economies of scale. Also, in most industrial fields and (to a much lesser extent) in commercial fields as well, vocational education is inherently more expensive than general education because of its greater reliance on specialized equipment, parts, and consumable supplies and its need for smaller classes.

At the secondary level the cost per student of specialized vocational schools has been at least twice as much in many African countries as the cost per student in general education, and in some countries it has been more than fifteen times as much. A recent evaluation of the World Bank's experience with the alternative approach of diversified secondary schools, which combine vocational and academic subjects, found that unit costs, although not as high as in specialized vocational schools, are still higher than under a general curriculum. In spite of the higher costs, the employment and earnings experience of diversified secondary school graduates seems much the same as for those who graduate from the general curriculum stream. (The study, however, followed students for only a few years after graduation.) If further research corroborates these findings, it would seem, on the face of it, that diversified secondary schools are not worth their higher costs. This is a sad lesson for the many African countries that invested in such programs and a sobering experience for the technical experts (often from international funding agencies) who advised them, but it is a lesson nonetheless and one to be heeded as policymakers consider directions for the future.

Because of the high costs and apparent lack of vocational relevance of both of the school-based approaches to the acquisition of skills, there is an urgent need to develop, through incentive schemes and technical assistance, the capacity of industry to provide on-the-job training and other enterprise-based programs for skills development. Experience with these should be evaluated with reference to all of the alternatives, including postprimary and postsecondary industrial training centers.

While additional information is being gathered on the relative outcomes in the labor market of different types of education and training, policymakers should at least be aware of past differences in per student costs between general and vocational secondary education and should recognize that a policy of increasing vocational content in the curriculum inevitably implies that fewer students can be given access to education. Governments that are interested in laying the groundwork for a more technically oriented economy in the future should place heavy emphasis on general mathematics and science in the secondary and postsecondary curriculum. These subjects are relatively inexpensive to teach and are likely to promote economic growth more efficiently than can in-school vocational education.

At the same time, policymakers should be exploring all of the macroeconomic policy instruments that may help to raise the volume of training provided throughout the economy. Out-of-school training for those already in the labor force has two important advantages over in-school vocational education. First, it has the potential of reaching all workers—those who have never attended secondary schools as well as the minority (in most African countries) who have. Second, it has the potential of continuing throughout an individual's entire working life, thereby allowing the worker to renew skills that become rusty and to replace skills that become obsolete. Among the macroeconomic policy instruments for encouraging in-service training for workers are investment codes, wage structure regulations, tax writeoffs, and apprenticeship guidelines.

Financing Secondary Education and Training

Given the large unmet demand for secondary school places, a natural starting point for promoting the further growth of the subsector is to raise student fees. Another, indirect, way for governments to expand secondary enrollments without increasing the burden on the public budget is to encourage private schools—that is, schools that are managed by nongovernment authorities.

Cost Sharing in Public Secondary Schools

Current levels of subsidization in secondary education are high in Sub-Saharan Africa. This is especially true in the Francophone countries, where in most cases fees were never charged, but it also holds in Anglophone Africa, where fees have typically declined as a percentage of full educational costs in the years since independence.

Obviously, the introduction or raising of fees can relieve the public financial burden of providing secondary education. As a by-product, this policy reduces the difficult administrative chore that educational authorities now face of having to ration a limited number of school places among a much larger number of academically qualified applicants. Evidence from countries that have recently raised student fees indicates that the dropout rate of those already enrolled is smaller than might be anticipated and that the impact on overall enrollment tends to be nil, as those who drop out are replaced by others who wish to enroll.

A recent study in Malawi showed that the 1982 fee of 101 kwacha (30 kwacha for tuition and 71 kwacha for boarding), which represented a cost recovery of about 40 percent at the time, could be increased substantially before all excess demand for places would disappear. Between 5,000 and 11,000 additional places could be financed by this change alone. (The number, which depends on the exact price elasticity of demand assumed, represents 20 to 50 percent of secondary enrollment in 1982.)

To the extent that higher fees would discourage students with less academic ability and hence a lower probability of success from enrolling in secondary education, they would increase efficiency within the subsector. There may be concern, however, about the impact of the policy on equity, since for any given ability level the higher fees would tend to increase the ratio of high-income to low-income applicants. This would exacerbate the existing situation whereby the substantial subsidies to secondary education benefit high-and middle-income groups disproportionately, since enrollments are already skewed toward these groups.

The adverse equity effects of existing fees and of any future increase in fees can be offset by providing scholarships for talented low-income students. It is not inconsistent to endorse a general policy that devolves a higher proportion of secondary education costs onto users while advocating that the fees charged low-income students remain the same or be reduced.

Even in countries in which politicians have taken a stand against user fees in public education as a matter of principle, it is still possible for the government to pass on more of the costs currently shouldered by the ministry of education. First, if care is taken to distinguish between educational services and the welfare, boarding, recreational, and other services that secondary schools provide, it may be possible to charge for the latter without violating the principle of free public education. Moreover, education authorities can rely, more than in the past, on community participation in the construction and maintenance of school buildings. That communities should assume considerable responsibility for the capital costs of primary education is now widely accepted in Africa, and the process of transferring this burden from the central government to local authorities is already far along in many countries, as was discussed in chapter 4. Box 5-3 gives an example, from Zambia, of a parallel process at the secondary level.

Box 5-3. Community Financing of Secondary Schools in Zambia

Since independence in 1964, the government of Zambia has worked to provide basic education to all children. In support of this policy, the government in the 1960s phased out all school fees and provided free board and lodging to all secondary boarding school students. Revenues from mineral export sales met these costs. By the mid-1970s, however, Zambia faced a dramatic economic downturn, which led to severe reductions in public expenditures for education.

As public allocations for education have declined over the past ten years or so, a number of actions have been taken to pick up the slack. To increase the number of secondary school places, the government in 1975 began to encourage individuals and organizations to operate private schools that charged fees. By the mid-1980s the government was also requiring all non-Zambians whose children were being educated in the country to pay tuition and boarding fees and was allowing Parent-Teacher Associations (PTAs) to levy a boarding supplement to improve pupils' diets.

An important element in the mobilization of non-public resources to support education was official encouragement for the establishment of self-help schools in the late 1970s. Community reaction has been positive: between 1981 and 1984 sixty-two self-help secondary schools were created. Contributions of cash, materials, and labor by local communities have greatly expanded access to secondary education. Communities may also offer accommodations for weekly boarders in residents' houses while school dormitories are being built by the community, construct living quarters for teachers, and make private contributions in other ways; one PTA decided to pay teachers' rent. In addition, levies are made on pupils in the community schools to help finance projects and programs.

In government schools and in schools aided by grants, some recurrent educational expenditures have unofficially been transferred from the public budget to parents or other recipients of educational services. Textbooks, exercise books, rulers, erasers and other supplies, and school uniforms are now being paid for by the recipients. Parents of boarding school pupils pay for bedding and for soap and other toiletries. Parents also contribute to cover the costs of such items as entertainment, sports, and school development and maintenance.

Although private contributions have been essential to the education system, the government's response has been ambivalent. No guidelines have been issued regarding the items for which schools may charge parents, and for the most part school authorities and their PTAs have been left to determine the size of contributions to various funds. Some observers fear that the lack of monitoring by the government might lead to financial mismanagement and argue that a clear-cut official policy is needed. In light of Zambia's continuing economic difficulties and the growth of the school-age population, however, government responsibility for education is likely to decline further and private support is likely to become increasingly important in the financing of education.

Another cost-recovery mechanism that may merit more use than is made of it at present is to open secondary schools in more populated areas to evening students. Although this system would serve fewer additional students than a full second shift in the afternoon, it does provide access to secondary schooling to young people who are already working and whose fees can be used to give regular daytime teachers an incentive to return in the evening.

The Role of Private Schools

"Private" schools include schools that are sponsored by religious or other special-interest groups, schools run by labor organizations or business enterprises, private proprietary schools, and fully autonomous or semiautonomous community schools. African governments took over the running of many private schools soon after independence, but private school students still accounted for more than 25 percent of all secondary-level enrollments in 1970. By 1983 this number had decreased to fewer than 15 percent. The usual practice has been to subject education to strict controls, which has tended to stifle private provision and to prevent individual providers from responding to the changing needs of their constituent populations.

Government control over private education ranges from outright prohibition in a few countries to, in most countries, regulations that cover such things as the level of fees, the qualifications of teachers, and the content of curricula. It is argued, on the one hand, that such regulations are necessary to protect families from unwittingly choosing an inferior private alternative to public schools and, on the other hand, that they are needed to prevent the development of a high-priced educational alternative of superior quality that only the rich can afford.

Whatever the merits of these opposing arguments,

many countries seem willing today, in the light of the current financial situation, to reconsider their policies regarding private education. If the restrictions were eased, new providers would be encouraged to enter the educational marketplace. The harambee (self-help) secondary school movement in Kenya contributed importantly to the rapid growth (over 15 percent a year) of secondary enrollments during the latter half of the 1960s and the early 1970s. In contrast, in neighboring Tanzania the expansion of secondary education was deliberately curtailed, and a recent study attributes at least some of the differences in present economic vitality between these two countries to the earlier differences in their policies with regard to secondary education (see box 5-1 above).

It is often assumed that in the African context a greater reliance on private schools should involve some type of accreditation system imposed by the government. These systems, however, are difficult to implement and indeed are unreliable because they depend on such external surrogates for educational quality as teachers' qualifications, student-teacher ratios, and school building standards. A better means of evaluating schools is through national or regional examinations, which can be used as powerful vehicles for shaping curricula and for promoting (not simply monitoring) quality in education. Results on examinations can be used by consumers as a basis for choosing among educational alternatives. When alternatives are available, schools cannot take students for granted. Competition for students will tend to encourage experimentation in public and private schools alike, and the result should be increased efficiency in the education system.

To minimize differences in the private educational costs encountered by households that send children to different kinds of schools, governments may choose to give partial subsidies to private education to the same (presumably reduced) extent that it does to public education. In many African countries today there is a wide range of financial arrangements, from the public schools (where subsidies are usually the highest), to partially aided private schools, to completely unaided private schools.

Financing for Training

In general, the governance (ownership) of vocational training should parallel the pattern of its financing. If training is supported through taxes and other levies on employing enterprises, these enterprises should have a large role in the management of expenditures. Frequently this will mean that training institutions are owned and managed by individual large enterprises or by associations of employers with common needs for skills. A similar model can be applied to public sector institutions that are large enough to own and manage specialized training centers and schools.

Relaxed regulation of proprietary schools and vocational training centers is another option. Again, although proprietary schools have worked well in other contexts, it is not clear how well they might function in many situations in Africa. Such institutions may be more productive in the services sector than in training for industry because capitalization costs are less for training in services. Subsidized training managed by public agencies may continue to be required in agriculture, where the incomes of potential clients are relatively low.

Where proprietary schools generate revenues by charging fees, their management is heavily influenced by consumer preferences as informed by government accreditation. Schools that fail to meet quality standards or that cannot provide training at acceptable prices will not long survive. Under such conditions, schools are encouraged to adjust their curricula in response to demand in the labor market and to seek the lowest-cost methods of training.

Public financing and management of vocational training institutions may, however, continue to be the most feasible option in economies or skill areas where private enterprises are relatively small and lack management and training capacity. In such cases economies of scale may be realized through training institutions that serve a number of firms, particularly if schools and training centers are located close to employers. Institutional arrangements that give small employers a voice in the curricula and management of these training institutions in return for even modest financial contributions should be considered, both to increase the immediate responsiveness of training to demand and to provide a starting point for stronger roles for enterprises in the future.

Policies that alter the way in which training is coordinated entail some implementation costs. The transfer of the ownership of specialized secondary vocational schools from the ministry of education to another organization, for example, involves transition costs for the establishment of new coordinating procedures and units and for the training needed to implement the required changes both in the schools and in the new organizational home. Some of these costs merely represent a shift of costs from one organization to another; others are start-up costs that will disappear after the initial period. Cost savings may eventually develop as the new system becomes increasingly efficient.

6

Preparation for Responsibility: Higher Education

Higher education is of paramount importance for Africa's future. Africa requires both highly trained people and top-quality research in order to be able to formulate the policies, plan the programs, and implement the projects that are essential to economic growth and development. Preparing individuals for positions of responsibility—in government, in business, and in the professions—is a central role of the continent's universities; supporting these individuals in their work—with research, advice, and consultancy—is another equally important role.

The leadership of the region's institutions of higher learning has spoken forcefully and eloquently at meetings in Mbabane in 1985 and Harare in 1987 about the urgent need for these institutions to produce graduates who can tackle the complex problems that confront the continent. Pronouncements at these meetings were consistent with the aspirations and African-articulated policy framework enunciated by the Organization of African Unity in its *Lagos Plan of Action for the Economic Development of Africa 1980–2000* (1981) and in its *Africa's Priority Programme for Economic Recovery 1986–1990* (1985) and endorsed by the United Nations General Assembly in its *Programme of Action for African Economic Recovery and Development 1986–1990* (1986).

University programs of research and teaching that support the rehabilitation and further development of the agricultural sector are particularly important within the framework of the *Lagos Plan of Action*. These programs include many applied areas, such as soil and water conservation and drought and desertification control, and the natural science and engineering disciplines upon which progress in all such applied areas depends. Of equal importance to Africa's future is its capacity to plan and direct the process of development. To achieve this capacity, Africa's institutions of higher learning must produce manpower trained in the disciplines of the social sciences and management, conduct timely research, and provide advisory services in such fields as economic planning, finance (including debt management), and public administration.

Although these tasks are essential to growth and development, they cannot be accomplished unless fundamental changes are made in higher education—changes that will dramatically improve its quality. If African universities are to provide graduates, research, and services that can respond adequately to the demands of Africa's modernizing societies—if they are to produce the research scientists and university teachers who can interpret the latest technology and harness it for the African continent—then resources for higher education must be increased, and they must be used more productively.

This study contends that resources can be increased and used more efficiently to improve the quality of higher education, despite limited economic prospects and the unremitting need for public austerity. It also suggests that the successful implementation of policies to improve higher education may eventually help to ease the constraints on educational development at the lower levels. Higher education in Africa can be adjusted to serve changing imperatives for development, and that adjustment need not be at the expense of priority objectives in other subsectors.

The Challenge and the Promise

The development challenge posed for tertiary education is in one important respect more daunting than that posed for lower levels. The real growth of public resources for the education sector as a whole in most countries is unlikely to keep pace with the growth of school-age populations, which is likely to mean a decrease in real expenditures per capita on public education. Even with the vigorous application of recommended reforms, the primary and secondary levels of the education system will require additional resources just to keep enrollment rates and quality standards from deteriorating from their current modest levels. But if public resources for education are at best constant in real terms, where will the additional resources for primary and secondary schooling be found?

A portion of those resources can appropriately be supplied by the private beneficiaries of primary and secondary education and their families. It is probably inevitable that parents' contributions to the costs of their children's education, particularly secondary education, will increase, despite concerns about how this increase will affect overall equity and efficiency. But, even with greater private contributions, education systems will not be able to ensure the increased stocks of human capital required for continued development, especially in those African countries where enrollment rates are lowest and where the expansion of access to primary and secondary education remains an urgent priority.

The conclusion is harsh and inescapable: to meet minimally acceptable targets for coverage and quality of lower levels of education in most countries, the share of stagnant real public education expenditures devoted to tertiary education cannot expand further and in some cases may have to contract. Savings must be sought at this level from improvements in efficiency, increases in private contributions, and constraints on the growth of output. Total savings from such measures, plus resources mobilized from the international community, must generally be sufficient to finance the indispensable improvements in quality in the tertiary subsector in the short run, as well as its expansion in the long run. In some cases, such as the Sahelian countries where the crisis in primary and secondary coverage is most acute, these savings may need to be substantial enough to free up funds for the lower levels as well.

It will take years of dogged determination and profound changes in the way higher education is organized, managed, and financed to achieve the needed savings. In particular, unless managers of higher education are presented with compelling incentives to improve efficiency, impose quantitative limits on enrollments, and mobilize resources from the private sector, the required savings will not materialize. The most powerful incentive is to ensure that savings realized through wise and courageous leadership in any specific institution are in significant measure available for redeployment in the same institution. Conversely, policies that expropriate savings obtained by sacrifice in individual institutions and transfer them to a central authority for redistribution will be self-defeating because they destroy the incentive to look for savings. Until those savings are obtained, the limits on quality at the tertiary level and on coverage and quality at both the primary and secondary levels will be tighter, and the long-term prospects for development in Sub-Saharan Africa more constrained, than need be.

The challenge, then, is to design and implement with persistence, over many years and in circumstances of severe austerity, policies that generate the resources needed to revitalize the subsector. If the challenge can be met, these policies can increase the contributions of higher education to national development in three critical ways.

First, tertiary institutions prepare the people needed to fill high-level scientific, technical, professional, and managerial jobs—that is, they educate the elite leadership of a nation's development effort. Of special importance is the preparation of teachers, scholars, and managers for the education sector itself, especially for its most advanced teaching and research functions. These people are the core of national capacity for producing trained manpower, setting standards, maintaining quality, and adjusting the education system to changing circumstances. Second, African countries look to higher education institutions to generate the knowledge and innovation needed for development, through indigenous scientific research and as agents for the acquisition, adaptation, and dissemination of scientific and technical knowledge developed elsewhere. Third, African universities as institutions and their faculties as individuals can provide necessary services needed for development in both the public and private sectors.

In addition, tertiary education in Africa as elsewhere is a source of analytical perspective on social problems and their possible solutions that is independent of and, often, a usefully pluralistic counterpoint to political and religious authorities. Higher education institutions also encourage indigenous self-expression, conserve and adapt local traditions and values, and constitute important symbols of national prestige and attainment.

Issues in Higher Education

At least with respect to the preparation of high-level personnel, tertiary education's contribution to Sub-Saharan African development since independence has been remarkable. The rapid growth of universities and enrollments was sketched earlier (chapter 1). In 1960 tertiary institutions in Africa graduated about 1,200 degree and nondegree holders, equivalent to one person trained at that level for each 168,000 inhabitants; the 70,600 graduates in 1983 represented a ratio of one per 5,800 inhabitants.

With this notable easing of the high-level manpower constraint, however, the relative importance of tertiary education's other functions has increased. Today, higher education's continuing contribution to development is threatened by four interrelated weaknesses. First, the mix of outputs of the higher education system is no longer well suited to the requirements for development. Second, the quality of those outputs shows signs of having deteriorated; in many instances the fundamental effectiveness of the outputs may be in doubt. Third, their costs of production are needlessly high (where cost is measured as the other output forgone because resources currently going to higher education were not applied elsewhere in the educational or economic system). Finally, the financing of the outputs is socially inequitable and economically inefficient.

The comments in this chapter on the costs and financing of higher education are based on robust empirical evidence. Findings on the outputs of higher education, however, must be offered more as hypotheses worthy of further study in individual countries than as incontrovertibly demonstrated facts. Except for simple head counts of graduates, there is presently a dearth of reliable data on the levels of outputs from the higher education system and especially on changes in those levels over time. African governments and their international partners in development should launch the necessary activities to generate and analyze data and should be prepared to act promptly on their results.

Inappropriate Mix of Outputs

HIGH-LEVEL MANPOWER. Of the three principal outputs of tertiary education—high-level manpower (including scholars and teachers for the education sector itself), knowledge and innovation (research), and development advisory services—Sub-Saharan Africa today generally produces relatively too much of the first and not enough of the second and third.

The proportion of tertiary graduates in African populations of age twenty-four and older (now about 0.4 percent) is still small compared with other developing regions (on average perhaps 6 percent). The proportion of scientific, technical, and professional positions filled by expatriates remains substantial in many countries, especially in the education sector. Over the long run, Africa can survive and prosper only by fully developing its major resource, people, especially those with skills acquired in tertiary education.

Nevertheless, short- to medium-term overproduction of high-level manpower—at least of the requisite quality—is suggested by the growing problems of unemployment and underemployment among graduates. Although reliable figures are not generally available, recent conversations with officials of African ministries and universities points overwhelmingly to surpluses of manpower trained at the tertiary level. Other considerations (such as physical capital stock) aside, the incidence and size of the surpluses are likely to be greater in countries such as the Congo, Gabon, Guinea, Lesotho, and Swaziland, where about one of every 2,000 inhabitants was awarded a degree from tertiary institutions in 1983, than in Burundi, Mozambique, or Tanzania, where the rate of production of tertiary graduates in recent years was only about one for every 17,000 inhabitants.

Data problems notwithstanding, long and lengthening periods of job search have been reported among graduates in Nigeria and Zaire. In Kenya a 1985 longitudinal study of University of Nairobi graduates between 1970 and 1983 documented job searches lasting from one to three years and in addition found that over the course of the study graduates became more likely to accept temporary employment and less likely to use their formal training on the job. Manpower forecasts for Lesotho show an excess of graduates, particularly outside the teaching profession. In Somalia demand for tertiary graduates around 1990 is estimated at 150 annually, although the anticipated output of Somalian institutions, net of students returning from abroad, is more than five times that amount. Fewer than 15 percent of the approximately 1,100 graduates of tertiary institutions in Mali in 1986 can expect to find employment in the public sector, and private sector opportunities are certainly no greater; the conclusion is that at most 30 percent of the graduates will find work appropriate to their level of training. If the base for these figures were to include Malians returning from training abroad, the picture would be even gloomier. In Guinea a 40 percent reduction in enrollment in higher education was deemed necessary to bring the annual production of graduates in line with the absorptive capacity of the public service, essentially the only employer of high-level manpower.

What accounts for this situation, now an essentially universal phenomenon on the continent? Several hypotheses are worthy of testing in the light of country-specific circumstances.

To some extent, the apparent surpluses represent not so much overproduction as a general failure by African countries to nurture conditions in which individuals with tertiary education can be productive. Political philosophies and development models that place primary reliance on the reasonably unfettered interplay of market forces, internally and internationally, generate by their very nature incentives that reward skills acquired in tertiary education. As African economies succeed in their efforts at liberalization through structural adjustment, their ability to get the most out of high-level manpower will be enhanced. However inevitable it may turn out to be, this increase in the capacity of African economies to use high-level manpower productively is unlikely to become noticeable before the end of the century. If recent experience is any guide (see box 6-1 for a case in point), structural adjustment in the short run exacerbates rather than ameliorates the problem of unemployment among graduates, especially since the graduates' aspirations about occupational status and wages are much slower to respond to new economic parameters than the demand for their high-level skills.

The more immediate explanation for the surplus is that, on the one hand, the demand for graduates contracted suddenly in both the public and private sectors. The economic downturn of the 1980s and the pressure to contain public employment arrived just as African civil services, almost everywhere the largest employer of high-level manpower, had largely completed the process of replacing expatriates with newly qualified nationals and were consequently reducing their hiring rates. Other aspects of adjustment to the downturn—including the retreat from import substitution as a strategy for industrialization, the shift away from nontradables (construction, bank-

---

Box 6-1. Employment and Earnings of University and Technical Graduates in Côte d'Ivoire

Between 1982 and 1984 Côte d'Ivoire experienced a severe recession that reduced GNP per capita by almost 50 percent. Many jobs were lost, especially in the modern private sector, but the system of higher education was not able to adjust sufficiently to accommodate the changing demand for its graduates. A 1985 survey in Côte d'Ivoire revealed that 37.5 percent of people with university diplomas in Abidjan and more than half of such people in other cities were economically inactive or unemployed. More than half of them had been in that situation continuously for the full year before the survey. Among people with vocational and technical diplomas, the situation was only marginally better: 33 percent of them were without jobs in Abidjan, and 26 percent in other cities. The reduced ability of the formal sector—the traditional outlet for university and technical graduates—to absorb such graduates, especially in Abidjan, has induced about 10 percent of them to take up work in the informal sector, mainly as self-employed entrepreneurs.

For those graduates who do find jobs in the formal sector, the private returns to their education are still quite high. Each year of postsecondary schooling adds an average of 17 percent to an employee's earnings. This figure is higher in Abidjan (19 percent) than in other cities (15 percent). For technical and vocational education, the increase in earnings is about 9 percent for each year of schooling, with no difference between Abidjan and other cities. Such elevated returns to education in combination with high unemployment among university and technical graduates are signs of an imperfectly functioning labor market. In particular, it appears that, as a result of the recession, the number of jobs has been reduced while the salary levels of those workers still employed have been maintained.

Graduates who become self-employed in the informal sector sometimes earn even more than their wage-employed peers. For example, in Abidjan, the average self-employed person with a vocational or technical diploma earns an income almost one and a half times that of a government worker with the same diploma and more than three times that of a self-employed person with only a primary school diploma.

These findings suggest the importance in the short run of adjusting university output to levels that the labor market can absorb. At the same time, they point to the need for adjustment mechanisms that will eventually allow full (or fuller) utilization of university graduates as the economy recovers and as labor market performance improves. The high productivity of graduates working in the informal sector, in particular, indicates that (even though new graduates may have to adjust occupational expectations downward) college education is of broad vocational value.

ing, insurance), and the scrutiny of staffing levels following privatization of parastatals—may also have slowed private sector demand for high-level manpower, which in any event was often much less significant than demand from the public sector.

On the other hand, the economic downturn coincided with the coming into production of the remarkable program that was undertaken in the 1970s to expand the capacity of tertiary education. Between 1980 and 1983 enrollments in African institutions of higher education increased 30 percent (from 337,000 to 437,000, not including the additional 100,000 African students enrolled in foreign universities) and graduates increased 70 percent (from 41,500 to 70,600). In short, the supply of graduate manpower mushroomed.

In addition, the emerging imbalance between supply and demand was exacerbated by structural rigidities in the education system. A good example is the remarkable stability in the relative number of graduates in the arts, humanities, and soft social sciences. In 1960, reflecting the need for indigenous administrative personnel and the less onerous requirements for costly facilities in liberal arts programs than in the sciences and engineering, African institutions of higher education enrolled 60 percent of their students in the arts and humanities and 40 percent in the sciences and engineering. Today, the Africanization of public service positions and (at least in some places) of management positions in the private sector is quite advanced, and as a consequence the demand for arts and humanities graduates is less robust. By contrast, the demand for high-level manpower in scientific and engineering professions is, in most places, much more substantial. Yet the 60 to 40 ratio is the same as it was in 1960. Enrollment patterns have not responded to shifting labor market demands. The rigidity of enrollment patterns is further accentuated by the lower proportions of students actually graduating in the sciences and engineering than in the arts and humanities.

In a few countries unemployment and underemployment among graduates of programs in the agricultural sciences, the physical and life sciences, and engineering suggest that, in addition to structural rigidities in enrollment patterns, the overall size of the system may have exceeded the current requirements of economic growth. The continuing reliance on expatriates to staff scientific and technical positions, especially in the education sector itself, suggests that inadequate quality may also impede the absorption of graduates of African universities into the labor force.

Finally, public subsidization has so far kept the direct costs of higher education close to zero for the individual student. Yet, as tables 6-1 and 6-2 make clear, wage differentials remain substantial for labor trained at tertiary institutions. As a consequence, the private rate of return to tertiary education is on the order of 30 percent, higher than for any other region of the world, and it shows no sign yet of decline. In response, the number of secondary school leavers with hopes of acquiring higher education grows larger each year. The result is a paradox of more graduates in many fields than the economy can usefully absorb, combined with undiminished pressure to expand opportunities for higher education.

LEADERSHIP IN EDUCATION. Although an overproduction of graduates may now have become the rule in many African countries, an excess demand for

Table 6-1. Graduate Starting Salaries as a Multiple of Per Capita Income in Selected Countries, circa 1979

Country	Salary as multiple of per capita income
Gambia	11.1
Ghana	3.6
Kenya	14.6
Liberia	11.1
Sierra Leone	5.1
Somalia	8.3
Tanzania	14.2
Zambia	12.0
Mean	10.0
Median	11.1

Source: International Labour Office (1982).

Table 6-2. Index of Starting Salaries in Public Service by Education Level in Selected Countries, circa 1979 (O level = 100)

Country	A level	Degree level
Ghana	120	169
Kenya	127	269
Liberia	.	339
Sierra Leone	229	342
Somalia	128	171
Tanzania	148	323
Zambia	116	169
Mean	145	254
Median	128	269

. Not available.
Source: Derived from International Labour Office (1982).

graduates still exists in some fields of study. These include specific scientific and engineering fields, in which focused expansion of capacity in tertiary education will often be required. But usually the greatest exception to the general rule of overproduction of graduates is to be found in the education sector itself. In eighteen countries for which data are available, expatriates constituted on average 35 percent of secondary school teachers at the end of the 1970s (see appendix table C-9); the proportion is much higher in some fields (for example, science, mathematics, and technical education). Despite sizable staff development efforts, including programs for training in foreign countries, many tertiary institutions are still critically short of African staff, especially in the senior academic positions of teaching and research leadership. In Nigeria, which is ahead of most countries in the Africanization of staff, about 20 percent of the teaching positions in tertiary institutions were still filled with expatriates in the early 1980s. Data for ten other countries at the end of the 1970s suggest that expatriates on average filled 50 percent of tertiary teaching posts (see appendix table C-9).[1] And postgraduate programs, especially those involving rigorous research training, remain in their infancy, in part because requisite staff with doctoral qualifications and adequate experience are not available.

Indeed, the least recognized but perhaps, over the long run, the most devastating damage to African higher education since 1980 was to the promising efforts begun in the 1970s to build an indigenous African capacity to produce tertiary teachers, research scholars, and top-flight analytic personnel for the public services. In Nigeria, for example, the erosion of progress will mean that only one-third of the new academic staff required by universities over the next few years is expected to be forthcoming from existing postgraduate and staff development programs. The shortfall is greater, of course, when doctoral-level staff requirements in research and professional occupations outside of universities are also considered.

RESEARCH. Although substantiation depends more on anecdotal than empirical evidence, African university staff uniformly report that research in their institutions withered in the 1980s. As the financial crisis of tertiary education deepened, research budgets were typically subject to early and severe cuts. The feasibility of offering good postgraduate education also declined, since a significant part of postgraduate (especially doctoral) training involves student participation as apprentices in faculty research and ultimately the solo undertaking of a dissertation project.

Stagnation or outright decline in research output and in the capacity to produce future researchers jeopardizes Africa's long-run ability to take advantage of the worldwide advance in science and technology. Africa need not be consistently in the forefront of all scientific and technological advance, and well into the next century a sizable fraction of Africa's Ph.D.s will still undoubtedly be trained in foreign institutions. But the continent nevertheless already needs to increase its capacity to absorb and use new knowledge, and that capacity is in large measure developed through indigenous postgraduate teaching and research programs. For example, advances in genetic engineering and other areas of biotechnology are potentially applicable to problems of plant and animal health in Africa; the impact on production of food crops and on export agriculture could be sizable. The argument can be extended to human health and even industrial processes—and to such areas as microelectronics and materials science (ceramics and metallurgy).

The central point is that without African mastery of the underlying science of such developments and the techniques to adapt them to local problems and conditions, the potential benefits to Africa of these advances will likely be lost in large measure and certainly will be late in arriving. World-class university-based programs of both basic and applied research and of postgraduate education are the breeding grounds for the mastery of science and technology. They are the key to sophisticated consumption of mankind's exploding stock of knowledge. They are a necessary condition for African escape from intellectual dependency. Ironically, no African nation can afford to have such programs in the short run, yet none can afford not to have them in the long run.

CONSULTANCY AND ADVICE. Even in their current depressed and fragile state, universities in Africa represent a nation's largest reservoir of expert knowledge and cosmopolitan experience. And here is another paradox. The continuing demand for expatriate technical assistance from both public and private sector organizations suggests that there is no lack of tasks requiring the highest levels of academic training and professional experience. Yet, with few exceptions, African universities as institutions and their faculties as individuals do not allocate much time and effort to direct service activities, except for special training programs. Much applied work currently undertaken by foreigners could as well be done by African university staff, who in the process would enrich their own research and teaching by gaining more thorough grounding in present-day African realities.

Low Quality

Direct and hard evidence is not available on the quality of the outputs of African higher education. That African graduates may not be as knowledgeable as their peers elsewhere in the developing world may be suggested by results of the Graduate Record Examination: the scores of African students on the verbal, quantitative, and analytic sections are uniformly lower than those of Latin American, Asian, or Middle Eastern students. Although the significance of this finding is subject to varying interpretations, there is no reason to believe that the cultural disadvantage of African students on such foreign examinations is any greater than that of students from other developing regions. The low (and possibly declining) standard in African higher education is now pervasively bemoaned by teacher, student, employer, and government official alike.

Nor could the situation be otherwise, since indirect evidence of a crisis of quality in African education is overwhelming. A tragic consequence of the economic downturn—and of the concomitant constriction in public budgets and reduced access to foreign exchange—has been the virtual disappearance from higher education institutions in many African countries of exactly those inputs that make physical plant and highly trained academic staff educationally productive (see box 6-2).

These inputs include spare parts for equipment maintenance and repair; routine replacement and upgrading of equipment; reagents and other consumable supplies; acquisitions of monographs and multiple copies of textbooks for libraries; subscriptions to scientific journals; functioning computation facilities; maintenance, gas, and oil for vehicles used in faculty research and student field trips; other research support to faculty, including travel; even routine upkeep of physical plant (for example, sanitary facilities and telephone exchanges) and public utilities (for example, sewerage, water, and electricity).

The level of deprivation of these nonsalary operating expenses varies from place to place on the continent, but appendix table A-22 suggests that, on average, less than 2 percent of total recurrent public expenditures on tertiary education is available for these crucial purposes. Campus visits make clear that the situation prevalent into the 1970s has now reversed: the scarcity of nonsalary recurrent inputs, not the number or level of training of academic staff, is today the governing constraint on quality in African higher education in nearly every country.

Box 6-2. The Crisis of Quality in Higher Education

The scarcity of funding for capital investment and nonsalary operating expenses has seriously undermined the quality of education in African universities. The situation at Nigeria's University of Ibadan illustrates the problem.

> For several months now we have been expected to run a physics laboratory without electricity, perform biology and zoology experiments without water and get accurate readings from microscopes blinded by use and age. Chemicals are unimaginably short. The result of all this is a chemistry laboratory that cannot produce distilled water and hundreds of "science graduates" lacking the benefits of practical demonstrations (Osundare 1983, p. 2122).

Ghana provides other examples. At the University of Science and Technology, no equipment for the electrical engineering department has been purchased since 1962, and most equipment in the civil engineering department dates from the 1950s. Such old equipment, including the university's computer, is rarely in working order; it requires regular routine maintenance, including replacement parts, for which funds are not available. The same university has been characterized as "grossly short of... books, paper and food" (Tipple and Tipple 1983, p. 1654). Similarly, reports from the University of Ghana's faculty of science tell of shortages of chemicals and other consumables necessary for laboratory classes and note that the scarcity of foreign exchange precludes the supply of essential materials from abroad. Lack of funds also means that some universities are operating without the vehicles necessary for field trips and data collection and that others do not have the resources to repair broken telephone systems.

In many countries throughout the Sub-Saharan region, the lack of capital funds has left construction work unfinished on classrooms, laboratories, workshops, libraries, and residence halls. A 1981 report from the Nigerian Commission on Salary and Conditions of Service of University Staff states: "The Commission was horrified to witness the disgraceful spectacle of students in the corridors and outside lecture theatres struggling to comprehend the proceedings inside." Reports from the University of Ibadan are also discouraging: "Everything in the University today points to an agonizing decline. Students swarm from their hostels where there are six in a room designed for two, into a dingy lecture room where a teacher shouts his notes across a hall of five hundred listeners" (Osundare 1983, p. 2122).

The most immediate consequences of the drying up of nonsalary inputs to higher education are that research ceases and instruction is reduced to little more than rote learning of theory from professorial lectures and chalked notes on blackboards. Chemists who have not done a titration; biologists who have not done a dissection; physicists who have never measured an electrical current; secondary science teachers who have never witnessed, let alone themselves actually conducted, the demonstrations central to the curriculum they teach; agronomists who have never conducted a field trial of any sort; engineers who have never disassembled the machinery they are called upon to operate; social scientists of all types who have never collected, or conducted an analysis of, their own empirical data; specialists for whom the programming and use of computers is essential who have never sat before or tested a program on a functioning machine; lawyers who do not have access to recent judicial opinions; medical doctors whose only knowledge of laboratory test procedures is from hearing them described in a lecture hall—qualitatively deprived graduates such as these are now appearing in countries that have been hardest hit by the scarcity of nonsalary inputs. Complicating the situation further in many institutions are student numbers in excess of the carrying capacity of crucial components of the physical plant, particularly living accommodations and library study space.

As a consequence, the skills most relevant to development, those acquired when theory is confronted with the exigencies of the real world, are exactly the ones that do not get learned. The result is that, in its stock of high-level skills and in its ability to generate knowledge and innovation, Sub-Saharan Africa is falling further behind despite the increasing numbers of higher education graduates. Tertiary education discharges ever less effectively its principal responsibilities.

High Costs

Not only does higher education now produce too many graduates in many fields, too few high-level personnel for postgraduate education and research, and not enough research and development advisory and consultancy services. Not only are all those outputs of lower quality than in the past. But the costs per graduate—some of whom are not needed and many of whom are inadequately trained—are exorbitantly high. As a percentage of GDP per capita, which is a reasonable proxy for affordability, unit costs (costs per student-year) of public higher education are between six and seven times more in Sub-Saharan Africa than they are in Asia and nine times more than in Latin America (see table 6-3). As a multiple of the cost of a student in primary school, a plausible measure of opportunity cost, the unit cost of publicly supported students in higher education is about sixty times that of primary students (see table 6-4). In Asia and Latin America, however, unit costs for students in higher education are between ten and fifteen times those for primary students.

There are two parts to this problem of internal efficiency, both reflecting fundamental shortfalls in African higher education. First, wastage—and thus cost per graduate—is high. Data for seven countries suggest that between one-third and two-thirds of the initial entrants to tertiary education fail to complete their studies or complete them behind schedule. Thus, a sizable portion of student places are occupied by repeaters or future dropouts, with the result that

Table 6-3. Unit Costs of Public Education at the Various Levels as a Percentage of Per Capita GNP in Selected Country Groups

Country group	Primary	Secondary	Higher
Sub-Saharan Africa	15	62	800
Francophone	23	86	1,000
Anglophone	12	51	600
Asia			
Southeast Asia and Pacific	11	20	118
South Asia	8	18	119
Latin America	9	26	88
All developing countries	14	41	370
Industrial countries	22	24	49

Source: Appendix tables A-17 to A-19 and Mingat and Psacharopoulos (1985).

Table 6-4. Public Expenditure per Student in Tertiary Education as a Multiple of That at Lower Levels in Selected Country Groups
(medians)

Country group	Tertiary as multiple of primary				Tertiary as multiple of secondary			
	1970	1975	1980	1983	1970	1975	1980	1983
Low-income	68	57	61	60	12	12	18	14
Middle-income	55	50	43	50	7	10	10	7
Francophone	40	55	44	61	9	12	18	13
Anglophone	79	68	50	52	11	11	11	12
Sub-Saharan Africa	55	55	50	59	11	12	14	13

Source: Appendix tables A-17 to A-19.

many more years of student services are required to produce each graduate than the length of the cycle would optimally require. Among the factors contributing to repetition and dropout are: insufficiently developed selection mechanisms for students aspiring to enter higher education (in some countries it remains the case that all who graduate from secondary education are assured a place in higher education); the dearth of nonsalary quality-enhancing inputs (noted earlier), which makes learning difficult, unstimulating, and unrewarding; and the absence of sanctions for poor performance of students and teachers, so there is no incentive to strive hard for results.

Second, resource costs per student-year of higher education services provided are needlessly inflated. Although not uniformly present in every country, several factors typically contribute to the unnecessarily high costs of tertiary institutions borne by the education budget of African nations.

SMALL INSTITUTIONS. Within a sample of fifty African universities at the end of the 1970s, twelve had enrollments under 1,000 students, while only thirteen had enrollments over 5,000 (and several of these had students dispersed over more than one campus). This proliferation of small institutions precludes exploitation of the well-documented economies of scale in higher education (and, in addition, means forgoing the academic advantages of critical mass concentrations of highly specialized staff). Explicit understandings on appropriate divisions of labor—in large countries internally among the tertiary institutions and in small countries across international boundaries—could greatly reduce this cause of high costs.

SUBSIDIES FOR STAFF. In many countries, universities were established initially as self-contained communities on vast tracts of land outside large urban areas. This approach involved heavily subsidized provision to all staff members of housing, standard municipal services, and even welfare and social services (clinics, schools, clubs). The huge sunk costs of this infrastructure prohibit starting afresh, and the ongoing costs of this legacy must somehow be met. With few exceptions, the public budget picks up the tab.

LARGE STAFF. On the basis of personnel listings of approved positions, the ratio of students to academic staff is 13 to 1 in a sample of Francophone African universities and about 7 to 1 in Anglophone Africa, where it ranges from 3 to 1 on the low side to 12 to 1. By way of comparison, the ratio of students to academic staff in British and French universities, in some sense the models for their counterparts in former colonial possessions, is 13 to 1 and 25 to 1, respectively. In some countries, where erosion of salaries and deterioration of working conditions have resulted in an exodus of the most highly qualified academics from the universities, the actual ratio of students to academic staff may be somewhat above the approved ratio. Still, staffing is generous by comparison with industrial countries, where the student-staff ratio is more typically twice that in Africa. One reason is the propensity of African universities to offer a very wide range of programs and courses in each institution, resulting in wasteful duplication. Course enrollment of fifteen students is not unusual.

African universities also usually employ large numbers of nonacademic staff, especially to operate municipal and student welfare services and to care for the campus. An example from Ghana illustrates the general nature if not the exact quantitative dimensions of the problem. In a British university, reasonably analogous to Ghana's three universities together in size, age, and location (on the periphery of a large city), there are over six students for each member of the nonteaching staff and the ratio of nonteaching to teaching staff is 1 to 6. However, nonteaching staff in the three universities of Ghana outnumber students and the ratio of nonteaching to teaching staff is 14 to 1. Most of the difference is in service areas. Guards, ground crew, and maintenance personnel totaled 902 in one of the Ghanaian universities and 166 in the British university. A second example is the University of Nigeria, which employs 52,000 staff for a student population of 77,000.

SUBSIDIES FOR STUDENTS. None of the twenty-four African countries for which recent data are available has a general policy of charging tuition fees that are not covered by a government subsidy in some form. The essentially universal policy of charging no fees for higher education means that the publicly borne unit costs are much higher than they would be if a significant part of the burden were borne by students and their families. But the no-fee policy contributes indirectly to high unit costs as well, since students and their parents have no incentive to contain costs. If instead of fee-free higher education, students and their parents had to shoulder a significant proportion of the total cost, pressure would surely develop to contain unessential expenditure and, in general, to increase efficiency.

In a similar vein, the long-standing practice of providing either free room and board on campus or an allowance to all students, thereby shifting to the public "educational" budget the considerable sums required to cover living expenses of students, greatly inflates publicly borne unit costs of higher education in Africa. Although several countries have begun to phase out support for the living costs of students, fellowships to students still constitute half the public expenditures on higher education in a number of African countries. The scope for reducing such public expenditure is particularly broad in many Francophone countries.

INEFFICIENT USE OF RESOURCES. Finally, unit costs are inflated by the failure to make maximum use of expensive teaching personnel and physical facilities, which is manifest in light teaching loads, in restricting class and laboratory hours to a specified portion of the day, and in letting the entire plant and staff lie idle at least twenty weeks a year. The scope for adding evening and vacation students to increase access to universities has almost nowhere been exploited, the University of Zambia being an important exception. With universities effectively closed to all but the fortunate few full-time students, there is a substantial population of students taking courses at their own expense overseas.

Inequitable and Inefficient Finance

Unlike the situation in some other parts of the world, tertiary education in Sub-Saharan Africa is overwhelmingly public in ownership and operational control. Private institutions of higher education are often explicitly proscribed in fundamental legislation and administrative regulation. Public ownership and control of higher education in Africa has meant for all practical purposes that tertiary education—including the living costs of its students, which are not properly an education expense—is entirely financed by the public budget. With few exceptions, students, their families, and their future employers are spared having to make any contribution to the costs of higher education beyond the general incidence of the tax system and the income forgone while studying. The extent to which the private rate of return to higher education exceeds the social rate of return is a useful index of public subsidization of education, since most of the difference between the two is due to including the state's contribution to costs in the social rate calculation and excluding them in the private rate calculation. The available evidence suggests that in Africa private rates of return to higher education are, conservatively, 150 percent greater than social rates, a multiple more than three times higher than in Latin America or in industrial countries generally and more than fifteen times higher than in Asia.

There are two undesirable consequences of this insulation of the beneficiaries of higher education from its heavy costs. Income inequalities are increased by the sharply regressive effect of higher education expenditures; the system ensures that the rich get richer and the poor get poorer. And perhaps more important, within the education sector as a whole and within higher education as a subsector, resources are allocated inefficiently.

A Program for Structural Adjustment of African Higher Education

If the preceding diagnosis of weaknesses in higher education in Sub-Saharan Africa were to be confirmed through careful analysis of the situation in individual countries, the four objectives to be sought for the short term through reformed policies would be clear enough: (a) improve quality, (b) increase efficiency, (c) constrain output, especially in those fields that do not directly support economic development, and (d) relieve the burden on public sources of financing by increasing the participation of beneficiaries and their families. But quality enhancement as the first objective will cost money. Thus, implementation of policies to achieve the last three objectives will, essentially everywhere in Sub-Saharan Africa, be a prerequisite for freeing the resources needed to achieve the first. The four objectives would, of course, be pursued with differing mixes of policies appropriate to the circumstances of particular countries. The sequence of policy implementation would also depend upon the needs of each country; gradual phasing in of new policies, in stages over some years, would have to be the rule, not the exception.

Improved Quality

A quantum increase in the quality of tertiary teaching and research is the first objective. Long-term development goals cannot be met without it. Improvements in quality, however, are unavoidably expensive. So, given the requirements of other parts of the education system and the environment of constrained public resources, no advance here is possible without significant progress toward the other three objectives of resource conservation.

Better quality could be achieved through a variety of measures. Most immediately necessary are the establishment and gradual implementation of standards of provision for the full range of vital nonsalary inputs to teaching and research. Supplying libraries with multiple copies of basic textbooks, as well as supplementary books and periodicals, is the highest priority, closely followed by supplying laboratories and workshops with consumables and materials needed for equipment maintenance and repair. Resuscitation of long-term efforts to upgrade the academic qualifications of staff is also essential. Formal postgraduate training in masters and doctoral programs, for the time being mostly outside of Africa, is an essential part of this effort. But the need extends much further, to postdoctoral fellowships, faculty exchanges, collaborative research, and other professional links with foreign universities through which African academics are exposed to new developments in research and curriculum in their fields. Twinning arrangements, between a department in an African university and the same department in one or more foreign universities, are an especially attractive device for staff development at these sophisticated levels and can also profitably involve the service of foreign university staff in African institutions. For maximum productivity, such arrangements need to be sustained over many years.

Quality in tertiary education is also improved by rigorous testing programs administered independently of the universities and involving external examiners. Such testing is an essential ingredient in setting standards of performance to which individuals and institutions can respond. Independent performance measurement also creates an ambient in which efficient independent study programs can develop.

Finally, in the longer term, improvements in quality will be realized and sustained through the establishment of programs—and, in some cases, centers—of excellence for postgraduate education and research. These programs or centers could concentrate staff and resources into a critical mass. Participants at the Mbabane and Harare conferences on higher education have voiced their support for an appraisal of the advanced teaching and research capabilities and capacities of African universities, as a first step toward identifying potential sites for research and postgraduate teaching in priority areas. By establishing such specialized, high-quality programs and institutions, African governments would provide able African students with an attractive alternative to (more costly) foreign study, create incentives for university researchers to pursue their work on the continent, and in so doing address two aspects of the serious problem of "brain drain."

Increased Efficiency

Reduction in unit costs (per student-year of educational services provided) is the second challenge. This reduction would be achieved within existing institutions through measures such as the following.
- establishing and gradual phasing in higher numbers of pupils for each member of the academic staff
- setting minimum standards for class or course size
- reducing the ratio of nonacademic support staff to academic staff (perhaps in part by using student labor in some campus jobs)
- increasing the hours per week and weeks per year that academic staff and physical facilities are utilized
- expanding access for part-time, fee-paying students
- introducing self-study methods (for example, use of radio and correspondence) to teach low-enrollment courses
- gradually assigning to nonpublic sources the full cost for housing, food, and other welfare services provided to staff and students
- where feasible within countries—and prospectively even among countries—rationalizing programs and faculties and consolidating institutions, so that diseconomies of small scale are mitigated.

No country is likely to be able to implement all of these measures, but all can potentially reduce unit costs of tertiary education by developing a coherent policy package that selects among them. The potential role of international collaboration should obviously be pursued as well.

Another approach to reducing unit costs that deserves more widespread use is the extramural degree program. Such programs have demonstrated the capacity for reducing costs per student to a fraction of the levels typically found in on-campus programs. Extramural degree programs rely on books, correspondence materials, radio broadcasts (or audio cassettes), occasional on-campus meetings, and most important, student time. Essential to the success of such programs is the existence of an independent examination or accreditation system (further discussed below) to measure and certify quality. Greater reliance on extramural degree programs frees governments from providing boarding facilities and covering the cost of transport, allows fuller use of existing classroom and laboratory facilities, and allows students to work while studying. Avoiding large concentrations of full-time students, typically in capital cities, may in some instances also lower the potential for political turbulence.

Constrained Output

Reduction in the annual number of (publicly supported) tertiary education graduates in some fields, together with deceleration in the growth of graduates in most others, is the third challenge to address. Some selective increases may be needed, of course, in particular countries and fields, the most important of which may be teacher training and graduate education programs in the physical sciences, engineering, and the social sciences.

Output could be reduced through a (more than proportionate) reduction in the intake of students. The intake to tertiary institutions could be limited by a mix of such measures as tightening up selection criteria by instituting stiffer entrance examinations; establishing a system of differential availability of scholarships, or even outright quotas, by region and field; and initiating cost-sharing more aggressively in the disciplines with highest graduate unemployment. Smaller entry cohorts composed of students of higher quality would help to reduce costs per graduate by saving some of the resources now lost when students repeat or drop out of courses. The congestion of physical facilities, now a problem in some countries, would also be relieved.

In addition, the numbers of graduates can be further reduced, their overall quality increased, and important resources freed for investment in quality-enhancing inputs by conditioning the continuation of scholarships on fully satisfactory academic performance. Failure in a course could entail a repetition fee, and failure in too many courses could result in denial of the privilege to return the following year under any circumstances.

In pursuing constraints on output, policymakers should realize that in individual tertiary institutions that have yet to expand to the threshold of diminishing average cost, such constraints imply higher unit costs. In these cases consolidation of small institutions into larger ones should be aggressively explored as a way of constraining output without sacrificing the unit cost advantages of large institutions. The potential payoff to international cooperation in consolidating tertiary education is high.

Of course, in purely economic terms, recourse to such direct measures to control the number of graduates should not be necessary. If markets generally, and the higher education market in particular, functioned properly—that is, if prices (especially wages) were unregulated, if information were comprehensive and readily available, and if the entry and exit of firms (including higher education institutions) to the market were uncomplicated and expeditious—supply and demand for higher education graduates would equate themselves without public intervention. As structural adjustment of African economies is achieved and liberalization is institutionalized, markets will work better and the need to rely on public intervention to control enrollments in higher education will diminish.

For the moment, however, the necessary conditions do not obtain. In their absence, and despite the imperfect wisdom of the authorities in designating the fields for expansion (or contraction) and in implementing appropriate measures (or incentives), public intervention is justifiable. During a potentially lengthy and painful transition to a more market-oriented system of higher education, direct action may offer the only practical short-term possibility for limiting educational outputs.

Expanded Cost-Sharing by Beneficiaries

Recovery of some greater portion of the real costs of providing tertiary education is the fourth imperative. This would be achieved through such measures as:
- allowing the establishment of privately owned and financed institutions of higher education operating under state-set standards of quality
- introducing fees in public establishments, initially for noninstructional services such as food and lodging and then as tuition for instruction

- imposing national service obligations—for example, to teach school, work in distance education centers, or participate in adult literacy campaigns—before, during, and after enrollment in higher education
- promoting an educational credit market
- imposing a special tax on earnings of tertiary-level graduates during a transition to an effective system of graduated income tax.

Expansion of cost-sharing to include the beneficiaries of tertiary education and their families does not mean that governments should lessen their financial support to the subsector. Rather, promotion of broader financial participation should be seen as one way in which governments can help ensure the increase in financial flows necessary for the improvement and ultimate expansion of higher education.

Feasibility

The structural adjustment of higher education involves identifying the educationally and economically correct mix and then determining the optimal sequence and phasing of policy measures in the light of specific country circumstances. This task will not be easy either in its design or in its implementation. First, it will require analytical and planning capabilities that are nowhere plentiful, in some countries exceedingly scarce, and everywhere untested on a task of this complexity.

Second, political considerations will inevitably limit the feasibility of some desirable elements and sequences of measures, many of which will be perceived in the short term as threats to deeply ingrained interests of powerful groups in society (civil servants, professors, and students). Determined and very high-level leadership will be needed to overcome resistance.

Third, actual implementation will demand a level of managerial competence that is uncommon. The program will have to incorporate actions to support management, especially by developing capabilities to monitor and evaluate the impact of new policies and to adjust and fine-tune their implementation.

Fourth, very little can be expected to happen quickly, for institutional change of the magnitude required is always excruciatingly slow. Great persistence will be required.

Finally, and perhaps most important, a fundamental dilemma must be overcome. Rapidly applied, highly visible, and quick-yielding measures to reverse the precipitate decline and ensure the long-term improvement in the quality of African higher education are likely to be a necessary (although not sufficient) condition for acquiring social acceptance of the painful measures that will have to be taken to achieve the three objectives for conserving resources. But it is only after those conservation objectives have been achieved that resources will be available for the sustained maintenance and improvement of quality. Bilateral and multilateral agencies could address ways to resolve this dilemma of transition as a first step in the restructuring of international collaboration on higher education in Africa.

Academics, university administrators, public sector managers, and students share an acute recognition of the intolerable situation of African higher education. In most countries measures to increase efficiency, constrain output, and diversify finance are already under consideration, and in some places they are beginning to be implemented. As such measures take hold, the possibilities for introducing urgently needed improvements in the quality of higher education will grow. Recommendation 4 summarizes the approach.

Recommendation 4

Recent deterioration threatens the ability of most of Africa's institutions of higher education to contribute to the region's development. The quality of these institutions must first be restored and then improved, so that the region can extract maximum advantage, for its own purposes, from the accelerating worldwide advance of science and technology. In most countries, however, a period of adjustment to changed economic circumstances is a short-term prerequisite for improving higher education. Some tertiary institutions, individual campuses, academic departments, and teaching programs need to be amalgamated into larger units of economically viable size. Personnel reductions, especially of nonteaching staff, are indicated in some countries but should be sought in such a way as to increase the average level of relevant training and experience of those who remain, particularly those in academic positions. The number of students at most institutions needs to be stabilized, by tightening admission and performance standards and by eliminating living allowances and free room and board; the inequitable effect of this final measure can be mitigated by the provision of scholarships based on need. Such consolidation in higher education will help to reestablish an economically and pedagogically viable base from which to expand the number of graduates and the scope of research and community service.

7

Using Resources Well: The Mandate for Education Managers

Although enrollment stagnation and low quality can ultimately be traced to demographic and economic adversity, they are exacerbated (and their resolution hampered) by the inefficient use of available resources. Inefficiency is seen in the widespread underutilization of facilities, high levels of absenteeism of teachers and students, and a general lack of order and discipline in the operation of education systems. Administrative and logistical infrastructures originally created for systems of quite limited size cannot cope with the vastly expanded structures of today. This constrains the ability of governments to plan, implement, and monitor policy changes that would address the obstacles to higher quality and wider coverage in the education system. Although appropriate policy changes are necessary to improve education in Sub-Saharan Africa, they alone will not suffice. They must be coupled with measures to strengthen management if the benefits of the policy changes are to be realized. Initially, the managerial capacity to deliver traditional educational services needs to be strengthened, then the capacity to design and implement change and innovation.

Despite more than two decades of investment in education, management capacity remains strained and insufficiently developed for a combination of reasons. There have been relatively low investments in this area; the efforts of governments and funding agencies have been so fragmented that sustained institutional development has been inhibited; multiple and sometimes conflicting policies and procedures have often consumed a disproportionate share of managerial time and attention; and there have been difficulties in adapting modern forms of organization to the values and patterns of allegiance in many African cultures. Central, therefore, to the mandate of educational managers will be the strengthening of their own capacity to use available resources well.

The discussion that follows is concerned with management at three levels: schools, policy implementation, and policy development. In recent years educational policy analysts have developed a strong consensus around the importance of the school-level manager—the principal, headmaster, or headmistress, referred to here as headteacher—and the community environment in which the headteacher operates. Linking the headteacher with the policymaker is a structure for policy implementation, which involves incentives and local politics, budgetary choice and project development, teacher training and teacher supervision. At the top is management of policy development for the national system.

Shaping managerial performance at each level are four factors: (a) the managerial and organizational structure itself; (b) the student testing, general statistical, and accounting systems that provide information to managers; (c) the analytical capacity of those who generate and evaluate options for managers at all levels, but particularly for managers at the policy level; and (d) the quality and training of managerial staff. These four factors are subject to direct improvement:

the policy levers for enhancing managerial capacity thus lie in these domains. The remainder of this chapter discusses these four factors and what is now known about the potential for their improvement.

Improving Organizational Structure

Organizational structures establish predictable relationships between people and tasks and thus channel the processes of getting things done. They are intimately connected with the distribution of power and authority, and they have considerable impact on decisionmaking and resource allocation. The need for structures appropriate to the management of African education is acute. Although the issues and their resolution are complex and interrelated, three areas of policy concern stand out: school management, decentralization, and structural simplification.

School Management

School management is a crucial component of effective teaching and learning. Effective schools have several characteristics in common. First, they display an orderly environment. Teachers and students attend regularly, records are kept, and buildings and grounds are clean and adequately maintained. Second, such schools emphasize academic achievement. Students progress systematically through the curriculum, they use the materials that are available, take tests, and profit from the results. Third, teachers and principals expect high levels of student achievement. Teachers give students regular feedback on their performance and remedial assistance. Students come to believe that work and effort are more important than luck in helping them to get ahead. Fourth, headteachers pursue an activist policy for effectiveness. They have high expectations for the performance of both staff and students. They take an interest in classroom activity and provide professional advice to teachers. They take initiative in acquiring resources for the school. They interact effectively with higher authorities and with the community.

The structure of education organizations can help support effective school management by granting schools the authority to generate and use local resources. Schools that are able to invest locally generated resources in school improvement are able to show parents a return on their financial sacrifice and, thereby, to ensure continued parental support. School supervision provides technical and administrative assistance for these activities. Headteachers can be given responsibility for these tasks, as well as for the quality of classroom instruction. If the school is too small to be assigned an adequately qualified headteacher, a first-line supervisor might be given these managerial responsibilities and become, in effect, the itinerant headteacher for a number of schools. Alternatively, a classroom teacher might be designated to be in charge and either released part-time from classroom responsibilities or provided additional remuneration for school management activities.

The successful implementation of a school improvement policy will demand the establishment of strong and permanent structures for school support and supervision. These structures should allow for regular supervision of schools, permanently available opportunities for in-service teacher training, and frequent upgrading programs for first-line supervisors designed in conjunction with national policy and research institutions.

Decentralization of Policy Implementation

With some notable exceptions, such as Nigeria, education systems in most of Sub-Saharan Africa are highly centralized, and this tendency has become more pronounced, if anything, in the years since independence. The rapid expansion of schools, combined with the increased importance of central control of funding and expenditure, has led to an increasingly centralized system of education management. Resources are controlled at the center, and lower-level managers typically pass along all decisions to higher levels. Centralized control in education is not, in and of itself, necessarily to be avoided, and indeed a convincing case is often made for it, especially in newly independent countries where a strong sense of nationhood has not yet been developed. A centralized system of education may be more efficient for some purposes than a very decentralized one, to the extent that it results in less duplication of effort.

Within the African context, however, there are good reasons for believing that education systems could be made more efficient if certain functions and responsibilities were devolved away from central ministries of education and manpower development. The arguments in favor of greater decentralization have to do with the characteristics of most African countries: long distances between individual schools and the center; great ethnic and linguistic diversity; and relatively poorly developed systems of communications—inferior transport (the absence of all-weather roads, few functioning vehicles, and a central government budget that is inadequate to keep the vehicles on the road), an incomplete and frequently nonworking telephone system, and a slow and unreliable postal service. Under such conditions, the flow of resources and information between the central ministry and individual institutions is frequently interrupted or halted. An increased reliance on local initiative might obviate the need for such flows or alleviate the consequences of their not occurring.

Decentralization can be pursued in two ways. The first and more obvious way is by changing the structure of authority and responsibility in the ministry that deals with public education or with public training so as to increase the autonomy of units at lower levels. As implied above, rigid centralization in Africa has tended to block the flow of information and decisions, to alienate schools from their local environments, and to limit their ability to respond to local needs and resource opportunities. Decentralization can, by supporting school autonomy, contribute significantly to better school management and increase the responsiveness of the school to the local community—and of the community to the school.

Second, governments can decentralize by relaxing restrictions on the activities of private schools and training institutions. These include schools and institutions run by church groups and other voluntary organizations as well as many types of nonformal fee-paying education and training schemes operated by private concerns. Expanding the range of educational services in this way would shift more of the costs of education to the beneficiaries. Government subsidies to privately run institutions, perhaps through scholarships based on students' needs, can help ensure equity and quality at relatively low unit costs. The efficiency of such schools is determined in the marketplace, by the willingness of students or their parents to pay for the services offered. Public investments to support decentralization of this kind include the publication of examination results and pass rates, the importance of which is further discussed later in this chapter. The effectiveness of such schools can be "managed" through examinations, the setting of standards, and inspections. Such mechanisms help to enforce standards and disseminate information to the public on the status of individual institutions.

Decentralization through deregulation of private initiative is likely to be most effective in countries where private institutions exist but do not flourish because of restrictions. Such decentralization will work better in urban areas, where family income is often high enough to permit increased expenditure on education, and at the secondary and postsecondary levels where the private returns to education are greatest.

Planning for decentralization in a given education system is a complex task. The purpose should be clear: decentralization is not an end in itself, but a means to the more effective administration of some specific activity or set of activities. Many things can be decentralized, to different degrees and in different ways. Work, decisions, responsibility, and authority can all be assigned to various levels. In a bureaucracy, what to assign, when, and for what purposes are key issues. The size of the country, the nature of the political system, and the effectiveness of communications are also factors to be considered; the advantages of decentralization loom larger with greater geographic dispersion, more pluralistic institutions, and weaker communication systems.

Effective decentralization requires explicit definition of the roles of units at various levels and the effective flow of information between them. The successful management of educational reform in Ethiopia (box 7-1) illustrates the care with which appropriate tasks were decentralized and others were maintained at the center.

In general, central ministries should retain policy, planning, and monitoring functions. In most countries, curriculum policy and development, together with the production of materials, will continue to be centralized, unless and until the capacity for curriculum development is established at lower levels, and even then if the maintenance of national standards is desirable for nation-building. Administrative support (such as supervision of the payroll, procurement, and school construction), teacher training and certification, and statistical services may or may not be fully centralized, depending on the degree to which public administration is generally (and effectively) decentralized to states or provinces.

The functions of intermediate levels of administration are also crucial to effective decentralization. The supervision of schools should be expanded to include technical advice and training for new functions, such as resource generation, and not be seen narrowly as visits from the center to collect statistics. To the extent that nonformal and private education are encouraged by a government ministry, supervision systems must expand to cover new types of institutions and tasks. Communication links to move information both ways between schools and higher authorities increase in importance. For vocational and technical education, staff should be responsible for establishing and strengthening linkages between schools and employers—a specialized task for which training and resource support may need to be centrally provided.

At the school level, where responsibility for the quality of instruction lies, headteachers should be given the authority necessary to achieve such quality.

> **Box 7-1. Management of Reform in Ethiopia**
>
> Education reform in Ethiopia illustrates an organizational strategy that made use of both the central and local levels of the education system. At the center, the Ministry of Education and the Office of the President took responsibility for establishing the overall framework for change. Subsequently, a number of important tasks were delegated effectively to the local level. This combination of strong central control backed up by local involvement and initiative created an environment for the successful implementation of the reform program.
>
> The goals of the reform were the expansion and improvement of education in rural areas through the construction of schools and the complete revision of the curriculum. A series of education projects begun in 1966 and the 1972 Education Sector Review supported a long-term strategy for meeting the country's socioeconomic needs. The institutional capacity for educational planning, project management, curriculum design, and the development and distribution of educational materials was gradually developed over a ten-year period. These resources in the education system served as the foundation for further reform.
>
> In 1974 the new government strengthened the official commitment to the reform of Ethiopia's education system. In the context of fundamental changes in the social, economic, and political development of the country, the government viewed education as a vehicle for social change and made educational development a high priority. Implementation of the reform relied on three well-established institutions at the center: the Ethiopian Building Construction Authority, which had implemented three earlier projects supported by the World Bank; the National Curriculum Development Center (NCDC), which was well-equipped to write and test curriculum materials; and the Educational Materials Production and Distribution Agency.
>
> Although the reform was very much directed by the central government, implementation was highly decentralized. At the local level the Awraja (district) Pedagogical Centers provided a permanent base for the training, support, and supervision of teachers. The management strategy also provided for the incorporation of local input. Technical feedback from administrators and teachers on the new curriculum and materials proved to be keys to the project's success. Curriculum and textbooks were tested in seventy experimental schools before they were adopted nationwide. Teachers and administrators also provided feedback to NCDC staff, who conducted an evaluation of the project. Moreover, community support and participation played an important part in project implementation. Student commitment was fostered by work in the community that taught additional practical skills and gave students a chance to apply what they had learned in the classroom. This work was supervised by farmer associations, school management committees, and local political units known as *kebeles*.

The headteacher should have a genuine voice, if not the final say, in all of the following: the appointment, discipline, and dismissal of teachers; the adaptation of curriculum and classroom schedules to local circumstances; the establishment of effective relationships with community organizations; the generation of local resources; and, most important, within centrally provided guidelines and a system of accountability, the use of locally generated revenues.

Structural Simplification for Policy Development

Structural simplification can support decentralization and school management as part of a broad strategy for structural reform. As certain administrative duties are delegated to lower levels, central ministries can devote more attention to their principal functions: broad policy planning; designing policy implementation strategies; monitoring the consequences of policy implementation through observation, testing, and evaluation; and adapting policy in the light of its evaluated impact. Delegating to school or intermediate-level officials the power to appoint and dismiss teachers greatly simplifies the responsibilities of the central ministry. The gathering of statistical data is a second case in point: as the capability to gather and aggregate data is decentralized, the tasks of the central unit are simplified and reoriented toward quality control, analysis, and dissemination.

In support of this more focused role of central government, two sorts of structural simplification will often be in order. First, those countries with more than one ministry dealing with education (or ministry-level entity such as Ethiopia's Higher Education Commission), and certainly those few African countries with three or more such ministries, will wish to consider consolidating these entities into a single ministry. This will encourage the more cohesive development of education policy.

The second sort of structural simplification will be the establishment of an entity responsible for overseeing training with a view to the needs of the national economy. It would track how training activities relate to educational activities and how they relate to employers, and it would develop appropriate policies toward training. Such a training policy unit might be housed in a ministry of education, an expanded ministry of education and labor, or a national planning ministry. In any case its work would both facilitate and be facilitated by consolidation and streamlining of the ministry of education.

Improving Information: Testing, Statistical, and Accounting Systems

Each management level—from formulating policy to running an individual school—requires information for its own use and for dissemination to the larger social system. In general, the education sector needs to be concerned with two main types of information. The first is information on the quality of student performance as revealed by achievement tests; the second is descriptive information concerning the numbers and types of institutions, personnel, and students in the system, their geographical distribution, and the financial flows that affect them. These data are used at all levels for planning and resource allocation; they are a necessary input into the analytical function discussed below. Test data also play a key role in the certification of individual students and their selection for the next level of education.

Educational Testing

There is a long history of educational testing in Africa, beginning in the colonial era with extensive use of examinations administered from Europe. After independence, such multinational groupings as the East and West African Examinations Councils helped to develop a cadre of African psychometricians and other professionals experienced in testing. External examinations (that is, those administered outside the individual school) are important today in a significant number of African countries.

The role of external examinations should be fourfold:

- First, if properly designed, examinations measure performance in the system as a whole and in individual districts and schools; this can allow tracking of performance over time, international and interregional comparisons, and school-level accountability. This accountability function is best served by regularly publishing appropriate aggregations of scores. These measures of performance can also be used for analyses of the education system—for example, the careful evaluation of new projects or reform efforts.

- Second, well-designed examinations help to improve the curriculum. They encourage teaching and learning of the designated curricula in the classroom, since teachers teach and students study for the tests, however they are designed; if the tests are well designed, teachers teach and students learn what they are supposed to. Both curriculum improvement and performance measurement—the first two roles of examinations—are central to improving educational quality.

- Third, examinations allow objectivity in the selection of students for the next cycle of education or for appropriate training.

- Fourth, external examinations allow the objective certification of students at the completion of an educational cycle; such certification is essential for the widespread implementation of independent study programs that were identified in chapter 5 as being highly cost-effective.

Performance can be measured by testing only samples of students at selected times. To a lesser extent, the testing of samples may be sufficient for purposes of curriculum enhancement as well. The selection and certification of students, however, will usually require testing all students at appropriate points in their progression through school, although it may be desirable to give different tests for each purpose. Most external examinations in Africa today are mainly for selection. Although this provides a base upon which to build, further development of education testing systems should ensure that examinations serve all their important functions.

To do this, and particularly to improve the curriculum, examinations must cover the full range of cognitive achievement specified in the curriculum—not only the requirements for the minority of students who proceed to the next level, but also those for the majority of students who do not continue. If the examinations fail to test the skills that will be useful for the latter group, there is little or no incentive for schools to teach such skills, nor for students to learn them. As a result, primary education is then treated mainly as a preparation for secondary education (and secondary as a preparation for tertiary), and not as a provider of worthwhile skills for those who do not go on with formal education.

Kenya has shown that it is possible to shift from an examination system that merely screens pupils to one that stresses the full range of skills deemed appropriate for primary school pupils (see box 7-2). Experience there also shows that examinations can be useful in monitoring and ultimately (through constructive feedback mechanisms such as newslet-

> **Box 7-2. Reform of the Examination System in Kenya**
>
> To be admitted into formal, government-funded secondary education, secondary technical schools, and some training schools, Kenyan students are required to pass the Certificate of Primary Education (CPE) examination. The test covers mathematics and English and includes a general section on history, geography, and science (nature study, agriculture, and health). During the 1970s there was concern that the test had limited relevance for those students who would not go on to secondary education, and that it rewarded memorization rather than reasoning ability. Critics charged that the CPE thus discouraged curriculum reform and imaginative teaching methods.
>
> In response to these problems and to the demand for equal access to secondary education, the government introduced a new exam system. It attempted to make examination questions more relevant to the life experiences of Kenyan students and to test for thinking ability. In addition, the new system disseminated data on examination performance to schools to help them prepare pupils to meet the new intellectual demands being made of them. An annual newsletter, distributed to all schools, field officers, professional educators, the teachers' union, and the press, explained the changes being made in the exam, identified key topics and skills that had caused candidates particular difficulty, and suggested ways in which teachers might help students improve their performance. Related changes were gradually incorporated into textbooks and teaching materials as well. Merit lists of schools and districts were publicized, thereby making CPE performance an important public issue.
>
> Thus the new examination gave teachers an incentive to develop in their pupils relevant skills and knowledge and thus to improve the quality of basic education. The new CPE was intended to promote the development of skills that would be useful not only to those entering secondary school but also to those who would not. In particular, the new system attempted to reduce differences in quality among schools by encouraging and assisting the less successful ones. And by basing questions on material relevant to the experience of most students and testing for reasoning ability, the new exam was fairer to underprivileged groups.

ters and regular supervision) attenuating differences in achievement among schools and districts.

Statistical and Accounting Systems

Investments in testing should be accompanied by the creation of strong monitoring and information systems that provide limited but strategically useful information on schools, classrooms, teachers, students, materials, and finances to managers at all levels. These systems should emphasize simplicity and practicality in the gathering and use of data, and they should be based on careful analysis of information needs at different levels. They should be integral parts of the organizational structure, and the necessary tasks should be defined in position descriptions and supported with training. In many countries the management of these functions should be closely tied to the education policy and planning unit.

Information should flow both up and down the administrative hierarchy of the education system. The relevance of statistics for improving the quality of education in the classroom must be made clear to school-level personnel responsible for collecting the raw information and entering it into the statistical pipeline. School personnel should receive analyses of data in time to be useful in their classes, and they also need information about the larger education system.

Testing and monitoring systems may require significant investments in facilities, equipment, and staffing. These investments must address current problems of data reliability and timeliness. With the recent development of microchip technology, the capacity to analyze data should not remain a major constraint, even in very poor societies, and the timely collection of information assumes even greater importance than in the past.

Strengthening Analytical Capacity

Analysis and planning are central to the efficient allocation of resources and, therefore, to the achievement of quality education under conditions of austerity. Educational leaders must be able to assess the performance of their systems and gauge the effects of their policies. This takes expert analytical skills organized in strong, well-staffed central policy and planning offices. In larger countries some of these functions may be decentralized to states or districts.

The work of the policy and planning staff must be well integrated with the policymaking process. In many countries the lack of staff, information, and resources has reduced such units to the status of statistics offices, concerned primarily with meeting the information needs of external funding agencies. Such units are not able to use information to generate a range of policy options for review or to monitor—and thus learn from—the implementation of policy decisions.

Considerable effort, centered mostly around training, has been made to develop planning offices and research capacity. The record, however, is not encouraging. To attract and retain good planners, education organizations need to provide adequate compensation and career opportunities. Planning must be supported by effective information systems, as discussed above, and adequate operational resources. The planning unit should have clear access to the highest levels of policymaking and not be located in a temporary project management unit. In short, an effective analysis and planning unit must be an integral part of the overall organizational design. Ad hoc arrangements that train a few planners under project funding and that fail to provide continuing support within the structure of the education system will not work. Here again improvement requires sustained (although not large) investment accompanied by whatever structural changes are necessary to make the investment productive.

Another element of strengthening analytic capacity, and a crucially important one, is the development of applied research as the basis for policy analysis. African education research institutions should, of course, play a key role in helping to ensure that research is timely, relevant, and of high quality. Since such institutions are only just beginning to appear in much of Africa, investment to strengthen their capacity and willingness to conduct research in these areas should be high on the agenda for action. Three lines of research stand out as particularly important.

First, more descriptive operations-related research is urgently needed on the cost, finance, and running of education and training systems. How much do different types and levels of education and training cost? How are they financed? Who provides and who uses them? What materials are available to students and who provides them? How much time do teachers and students actually spend in school, and how do they spend that time? Are schools orderly and disciplined? Simple though such questions are, answers are frequently unknown; either quantitative or qualitative answers would clearly be relevant to improving operations. A great deal can be learned by making selective improvements in information that is routinely gathered on performance and expenditure and by making more intensive analytical use of these data. When these data are combined with performance data from the examinations systems, vital questions of cost-effectiveness can be addressed.

The second type of research involves surveys to assess the internal efficiency of education. The International Association for the Evaluation of Educational Achievement (IEA) provides important tools for the analysis of internal efficiency; its tests measure the quality of schools in terms of their success in raising achievement in such core areas as mathematics and science. Levels, trends, and determinants of academic performance can now be tracked almost routinely. Such objective feedback on performance is the key to introducing accountability and improving quality in education. The wide and periodic application of IEA-type instruments offers great potential for improving the allocation of resources through better-informed decisionmaking. Research here is dependent on strengthening the testing system, as discussed above.

A third, relatively routine line of research deals with external efficiency—that is, with the assessment of the labor market performance of graduates of different levels and types of education. The Living Standards Survey (LSS) approach—pioneered with World Bank assistance in Côte d'Ivoire and Peru—provides an instrument for assessing performance in several dimensions (see box 7-3). Plans are now being developed for ten other African countries to begin use of LSS techniques. LSS serves a very broad range of purposes, and it will be important to ensure that its potential for illuminating educational policy is in fact realized.

Development of Managerial Staff

Lack of skilled managers and low morale are fundamental constraints on African education at all levels. Past efforts to address these constraints have not been successful. Training has generally not been tied to clear long-term strategies for organizational development. As a result, training has been general in nature and not well linked with the need to develop managerial skills. Training opportunities have been provided principally for higher-level staff (often trained abroad), not for school personnel.

A broader policy approach to the development of management skills is needed in most countries. Fundamentally, this will require the development of strong management institutions—a relatively long-term solution. Meanwhile, governments should consider a number of immediate options. In view of the difficulty of attracting highly qualified individuals to the education sector, priority should be given to developing and advancing talented persons who are already working in the sector. Management development must then be seen as a systemwide activity that promotes good managers from the schools through intermediate levels toward the center. Training should be seen as one of several inputs. The others include the resources necessary to make staff effec-

> **Box 7-3. Living Standards Surveys (LSS)**
>
> Although national data that measure macroeconomic growth are available in most countries, the data for assessing the distribution of the fruits of economic growth and the share accruing to the poor are usually much weaker. To remedy this situation, the World Bank launched the Living Standards Measurement Study (LSMS) in 1980. The goal was to set up a data system for monitoring the well-being of households and individuals in different socioeconomic groups in the course of development. Unlike standard household surveys, which typically make data available only years after collection, the LSMS system was designed to produce information quickly and in a form readily suitable for analysis that could directly inform economic and social policies.
>
> The three key features of a proper Living Standards Survey (LSS) are the comprehensive coverage of the many dimensions of well-being, the emphasis on quality control, and speedy data processing. Living Standards Surveys collect information on the demographic characteristics of household members, their educational achievement, health condition, migration history, use of time in the home and the labor market, and earnings. The household's housing condition is surveyed, as are its ownership of assets and enterprises (and the earnings they generate) and its expenditures, borrowings, and savings.
>
> If survey information is to be useful for policymaking, it must be current and of high quality. To ensure quality the LSS system includes extensive training and refresher courses for enumerators (those who collect the data), a higher than usual supervisor-to-enumerator ratio, use of personal computers in the field for continuous data entry and instantaneous checks on range and validity, and verification of identified errors and inconsistencies by the enumerator in a second round of data collection. Analysis in the LSS system can thus take place while data are being collected. As each new wave of data reaches headquarters, tables can quickly be updated. Experience in the Côte d'Ivoire and Peru, where the LSS system has been tested nationwide, has shown that tables can be produced within three to four months after data collection.
>
> The LSS data base covers many aspects of education. In addition to educational attainment, the education module includes self-reported literacy and numeracy, formal and informal vocational and technical training, and the schooling of children who have left the household. All this is useful for studying the total returns on the household's investment in education. For currently enrolled students, information is gathered on the type of school, distance and travel time to school, out-of-pocket costs, and scholarships. Opportunity costs can be derived from the employment data. This permits a study of private returns to different types of education. The availability of information on other aspects of well-being can throw light on the links between education and policies in other areas such as health, labor markets, and migration. How do graduates of different curricula fare in obtaining jobs? Does better education improve one's use of health facilities? Conversely, does better health improve educational attainment? How do parental characteristics and migration history affect access to education? Should fees be charged for schooling? How much can poor people afford to pay for primary schooling?

tive, incentives to hold them in the system, clearly defined career paths, and systems for assessing performance. A teacher should enter service with a clear idea of the opportunities for advancement and of the kinds of performance and training that will be necessary to move ahead.

Management development in the central ministry should parallel development at lower levels. Training across levels (for example, of headteachers and district officers together) should take place frequently to strengthen relationships and coordination.

Management development is constrained, however, by the quality of those who enter the profession. One policy option would be to enhance the incentives and career opportunities for highly skilled education staff in order to attract talented nationals. Such a policy is difficult to implement for a single sector and is more likely to succeed when applied across sectors with careful controls. Governments and funding agencies alike might well review current practices with regard to technical assistance to see if ways can be found to divert resources from expatriate expertise, with its very high unit costs, toward hiring talented nationals.

Reliance on expatriate assistance, however, is likely to continue in many countries in the short term.

Experience has demonstrated some measures that can be taken to ensure that such assistance is effectively used. First, expatriate assistance should be incorporated within a long-term plan for the development of human resources in the sector (as is current practice in a number of African countries). Such planning can give the government a clear sense of control over the use of high-cost expatriates and the assumption of their roles by national staff.

Second, expatriate staff should be assigned to line operating units— not isolated in project implementation units—working and sharing their expertise with national counterparts. Expatriate assignments should be carefully planned by governments and funding agencies alike so that expatriates' responsibilities include giving both formal and informal training and their performance is evaluated on the basis of how well they have taught their national coworkers. In some cases a training specialist should be included on expatriate advisory teams to ensure that foreign expertise is used effectively in training programs and in the production of training materials.

In the short term, the best combination of policies is one that will (a) promote the recruitment, development, and retention of skilled national staff; (b) base the use of expatriates on broad plans for the development of human resources; and (c) emphasize the training role of advisors. In the longer term, a permanent capacity for management development is needed and, ultimately, African institutions need the ability to provide the full range of management development services, including first-rate research.

Priorities and Resource Requirements

Substantial resources will be required to create a management environment in which African education can be improved. The policies recommended above envisage significant investments in more attractive incentives and career paths for managers, in training and analysis, and in the creation or strengthening of units for testing, accrediting, monitoring, planning, and training. Management development institutions will require substantial financial support. Most measures will also incur significant recurrent costs.

Such investments pose difficult tradeoffs in the current financial and economic climate, in which resources for the management of education systems have stagnated or declined in many countries. However, substantial investment in management capacity is important to the success of other reforms, including financial reforms considered necessary for establishing efficiency and equity within education. Some of these costs may be financed out of savings generated through policy reform. Others may have to come from other important areas, which means that difficult choices will have to made.

A large share of these resources will have to come from external funding agencies. The pattern of this support for education management, however, will have to change significantly if these resources are to be effectively applied. A much higher level of coordination among the external agencies will be required; this in turn will call for longer-term plans for management development in a given country or region. Episodic project-related investments will probably need to be replaced by long-term investments in management capacity per se and in well-designed management development institutions.

The scarcity of resources in the face of large needs argues strongly for a strategic approach to education management that recognizes the validity and urgency of short-term needs but does so in the context of longer-term goals for institutional development. In such circumstances a strategy for management development must be forged from the range of options— for organizational structure, testing and information systems, analytical capacity, and staff development— that were discussed in this chapter. At the outset, however, as a top priority, this strategy should identify the investments, activities, and support systems necessary to achieve acceptable levels of school management. This leads to recommendation 5.

Recommendation 5

A policy framework to make the use of education resources more efficient is generally designed at the national level, but successful implementation of policies will usually depend, in the final analysis, on the strength of managerial capacity throughout the education system, and especially in the individual schools. Among the essential ingredients of this managerial capacity are school leaders who possess analytical skills, the freedom to act on behalf of their school clients, and the relevant information on which to base their decisions. Accordingly, the top priorities for education management should be, in most African countries: (a) the improvement of programs for selecting, training, and supervising school headteachers and principals, combined with greater institutional autonomy; and (b) the development and implementation of achievement testing systems that provide feedback on institutional performance to individual schools, their supervisors, and the communities they serve.

Part III

An Agenda for Action

An extensive menu of policy options for African educational development has been presented in the preceding chapters. The adoption and implementation by any one African country of all of the policies discussed is probably neither desirable nor feasible. The educational achievements and aspirations of individual countries and their socioeconomic and political constraints vary too much for any single comprehensive set of measures to be completely or uniformly applicable. This study is about diverse and variably applicable policies for African educational development, not about a monolithic and universally valid policy.

Nonetheless, the analysis of the predicament of African education and training systems in part I and the discussion of policy options for different levels of education and for sector management in part II do imply a generally applicable three-dimensional framework for the design of educational policies in the region. Although specific details will differ from one African country to the next, elements of all three dimensions are certain to be found in any carefully conceived policy package tailored to the particular circumstances of any country in the region today. The three dimensions, to be elaborated upon in chapter 8, are labeled adjustment, revitalization, and selective expansion.

Although undoubtedly painful and politically difficult, adjustment policies will alleviate the burden that education and training place on public budgets. Measures for revitalization and expansion, in contrast, will certainly require incremental resources. Thus, in the context of ongoing austerity in Africa, resolute movement toward adjustment is a necessary condition for implementing forward-looking policies in the other two dimensions. Savings generated from adjustment will be needed to help fund educational improvement and expansion.

Regrettably, all such savings from adjustment measures will not be sufficient to cover the substantial resources needed to revitalize and build African education to the extent essential for future development. International aid will remain a critical determinant of the pace of progress in education in the region. However, the rapid evolution of African needs, as summarized in the three-dimensional framework for policy reform, demands corresponding changes in the organization, nature, and level of international aid for African educational development. Chapter 9 reviews the pattern of public international development assistance in the early 1980s, and it sketches the modifications necessary to make future assistance fully responsive to and supportive of Africa's determination to make education work better for development.

8

Policy Packages for Educational Development

Hard decisions on education policy can be postponed—but only at the cost in most African countries of continued stagnation in enrollment and decline in quality through the 1990s. Part II of this study has reviewed a series of policy measures—some of them admittedly difficult—that hold the promise of restoring quality and resuming an orderly expansion of enrollments. This chapter suggests that each African country should now embrace the task of formulating and implementing an internally coherent set of policies that will reflect the country's unique history and aspirations and effectively address its own recently exacerbated problems in the education and training sector. Although the particulars of the policy packages that emerge from this exercise would vary from one country to the next, it is nonetheless clear that every country-specific package will need to contain, in varying proportions, elements of policy along three distinct dimensions. These three are adjustment, revitalization, and selective expansion. Moreover, if new policies are in fact to be implemented, management practices need to be improved.

The three dimensions of policy are defined below and further elaborated in the course of the chapter. The closing section of the chapter discusses organizational issues associated with next steps in policy development and implementation.

Adjustment to current demographic and fiscal realities, though it will not be easy, is essential if the disruptive effects of these external factors are to be minimized in the years ahead. Adjustment will take two main forms:
- The diversification of educational finance will be a necessary part of country-specific policy packages. This diversification can be achieved through increased cost-sharing in public education and through increased official tolerance and encouragement of nongovernmental suppliers of educational services.
- The rigorous containment of unit costs will be just as important as the diversification of finance, and in many African countries may be more important, in the adjustment process.

Revitalization of the education infrastructure that now exists in order to restore quality is the second dimension of a properly conceived educational strategy. This dimension gives renewed emphasis to the fundamentals of providing education services, so that maximum advantage is extracted from the current capacity of education and training systems. Three kinds of measures are necessary for the restoration of quality:
- Textbooks and learning materials must once again become generally available in African classrooms.
- There must be a renewed commitment to academic standards, principally through strengthening examination systems.
- Greater investment must be made in maintenance of physical plant and equipment and in operational expenditures.

Selective expansion to address needs for additional education services is the third dimension of any complete strategy for educational development. These measures, viable only after measures of adjustment and revitalization have begun to take hold, will concentrate on four areas; success in all will depend on a general effort to safeguard the quality of instructional staff at all levels.

- Renewal of progress toward universal primary education is the new investment that will bring the highest economic and social returns in many countries.
- At the secondary level, and later at the tertiary, expansion of enrollments in selected subjects and streams will be necessary in most countries in the years ahead. To accommodate these increases in postprimary education, most countries will need to consider alternative delivery modes that shift more of the burden for learning onto the students themselves; now is the time to begin planning for such programs and developing their requisite support infrastructure (correspondence materials, radio programs, and examination systems).
- The amount of training that occurs once individuals have entered the labor force must be increased; this training should serve both school leavers and those who have had no exposure to formal schooling, so that individuals can acquire the necessary job-related skills and renew these skills during their working lifetime in response to changing market conditions.
- Expansion of African capacity to produce postgraduate intellectual talent to fill the highest scientific and technical jobs in education establishments, in government, and in the private sector is an important matter to be addressed in building for Africa's future.

The message here is contained in recommendation 6.

Recommendation 6

To maximize education's contribution to economic growth in the years ahead, African governments should design and begin expeditiously to implement long-term education sector development programs. Each government will need to select, from among the many policy options available (including, but not restricted to, those discussed in this study), a consistent package of policies that effectively addresses country-specific problems and serves country-specific goals. Although the optimal policy package will differ from one country to the next, no country can afford, in light of education's high costs and its crucial role in the development process, to neglect this task. The policy package that emerges will, in every country, contain elements of three strategic dimensions—adjustment, revitalization, and selective expansion. Given the pressure of population growth and fiscal constraints, most countries will need first to implement painful adjustment measures so as to generate the necessary resources for quality-enhancing revitalization, and adjustment and revitalization should be regarded as prerequisites for the longer-term return to selective expansion of the educational system.

Adjustment

The two elements of an adjustment program for education and training are diversifying the sources of finance and containing unit costs.

Diversifying Sources of Finance

The imperative here is to acquire from the beneficiaries of education and training a much larger share of the real costs of providing these services. With regard to training, an increase in cost-sharing is a normal concomitant of moving the locus of training closer to the workplace, a move justified on other grounds elsewhere in this study. With regard to education, the rationale for increasing cost-sharing is strongest at the tertiary level but may, in some countries, be pertinent at lower levels as well.

Increased cost-sharing can be achieved through a variety of measures. First, countries might consider encouraging the establishment of, and relaxing regulations that currently constrain the operation of, privately owned and privately financed institutions of secondary and higher education. Encouraging and facilitating the efforts of local groups or NGOs to construct, finance, and operate schools, especially at the primary and secondary levels, can be expected to result in more resources to and better management of education in response to local needs.

Second, there is a clear rationale in secondary and tertiary education in many African countries for making students or their families more responsible for the costs of food, lodging, and other living expenses unrelated to instruction. These are costs that must be borne whether or not individuals are enrolled in school. There is little if any justification for financing these costs out of the public budget, especially in poor countries where only a minority (and, nearly always, a relatively well-to-do minority) is enrolled at secondary and tertiary levels.

In addition to (or instead of) requiring students and their families to bear these costs, students themselves could be required to perform a variety of instruction-related support tasks now assigned to nonteaching staff (custodial care of teaching facilities, upkeep of the grounds, clerical and secretarial assistance, and other administrative support). Student provision of such services in kind, a widespread practice in many industrial and developing countries, is a potentially important approach to alleviating the public financial burden of secondary and tertiary education.

Finally, some countries will need to introduce or raise tuition fees in public establishments to cover at least part of the costs of instruction. Especially in higher education, however, full cost-sharing could result in many potential students finding themselves excluded from education because of their families' inability to pay. To the extent possible, ability to pay should not be a factor that determines who receives education and who does not.

Therefore, alternative modes of financing the increased private costs of education would need to be introduced. Possibilities include: opening opportunities for students to get tuition waivers by making commitments to national service (for example, to teach school) before, during, or after enrollment; promoting student loans and other education credit markets; and, during a period of transition to an effective system of graduated income taxation, imposing a special tax on the earnings of graduates of tertiary institutions. For most policies intended to decrease the government's share of full educational costs, implementation would need to be phased in gradually over a period of some years. And legitimate concerns on the policies' effects on equity would need to be addressed.

Containing Unit Costs

The containment of unit costs, the most important component of adjustment in much of Africa, should be aggressively pursued at all levels of the education system in both the capital and recurrent accounts. The goal here is to reduce the economic costs per student, or per completed cycle, at each level (and not necessarily to reduce the total aggregate expenditure at any level).

Reducing construction costs and raising utilization rates for physical facilities offer considerable potential for reducing unit capital costs. Since annualized capital costs can account for 40 percent or more of the direct economic costs of education in Africa, careful attention to capital costs is a high priority. Too many existing educational facilities (particularly those financed in part through foreign assistance) cost a sizable multiple of what best practice has shown to be possible. Chapter 2 projected the probable magnitude of capital expenditure in education budgets in the coming years under the assumption that best practice would prevail. In order to contain construction costs to the levels there indicated, it will be necessary to minimize expenditure on pedagogically redundant civil works (such as boarding facilities, auditoriums, cafeterias, and sports complexes) and to use low-cost construction methods and local materials. In addition, particularly at the secondary and tertiary levels, there is scope for more intensive utilization of existing facilities through extension of the teaching calendar. There is little or no justification in most cases for the current practice of closing down facilities in the evenings and during the long vacation periods. In the absence of compelling extenuating circumstances, new construction should be deferred until full utilization of existing capacity, including facilities under construction, is reached.

Because personnel remuneration is the largest single item of education costs at all levels, changes in how teachers and nonteaching staff are paid and employed could be an important element of any strategy to contain recurrent costs. Recent experience has demonstrated that in some countries there is a large payoff to purging from the educational payrolls so-called ghost teachers—those who are not actually assigned to classroom duties or are not fulfilling their assigned duties. There likely remains a significant potential to be exploited in this sensitive area, at least within the primary and junior secondary subsectors.

Everywhere, reductions should be pursued in the typically high numbers of nonteaching staff in African secondary and, especially, tertiary education institutions. Students should be given significant responsibility for performance of essential instruction-related custodial and administrative support services, as has been discussed among the finance diversification measures. In addition, such categories of personnel as messengers, drivers, watchmen, stewards, and sweepers can usually be reduced without sacrifice of educational quality. But because salaries at this level are low, even very sharp reductions will have only a limited, although nonetheless positive, impact on unit costs.

Reduction of teachers' pay is also a policy option that should be considered in countries where it can be demonstrated that a sufficient supply of teachers of comparable quality would still be forthcoming. Inflation has undermined teachers' salaries substantially during the past two decades, as it has all public sector wages in the region. Even if it were politically feasible, further reduction in real rates of pay for teachers alone (in isolation from other civil servants) could lower the quality of education in some African countries. Certainly outright cuts in nominal wages would appear to be undesirable everywhere because of the adverse impact on teachers' professional motivation and commitment. Nonetheless, the growing numbers of unemployed secondary school leavers and of university graduates and dropouts in Africa suggests a potential pool of labor with adequate motivation and intellectual skills for teaching; they ultimately may be prepared to accept wages somewhat lower than those currently prevailing in the teaching profession. This reduction in pay would be facilitated if certification requirements for the teaching profession were relaxed, a point closely related to entry qualifications, to which we now turn.

Although still difficult and controversial, another policy option, especially at the primary and lower secondary levels, is to reduce the minimum entry qualifications for teachers. If less preservice education and training were required of new teachers, they could be paid less than they must be paid under the existing compensation structure. Too many children in the world's least developed countries are denied access to schooling because their governments are trying to match the preservice educational requirements typical of the world's most developed countries. This denial of opportunity is unjustified for two reasons. First, marginally lower entry qualifications—for example, one or two fewer years of schooling and preservice training for those teaching the early primary grades—may not diminish what pupils learn in the classroom, especially in Africa today where the governing constraints on learning are the lack of instructional materials and lack of effective time on task. Second, given the relative costs of providing preservice and in-service teacher training and given the salary structures that prevail in most places, in-service training is usually the more cost-effective means of raising the quality of classroom instruction. For primary school teachers especially, many African countries should consider imposing further limitations on the quantity of preservice education and training, and coupling this with a policy of frequent in-service courses to upgrade and refresh teachers' skills, with particular attention given to subject-matter competency and the proper use of instructional materials.

More intensive use of teaching staff is potentially the most fruitful approach for reducing unit recurrent costs. Savings are possible so long as the increase in teaching time is greater than the increase in salaries needed to motivate and compensate the teachers for their greater effort—that is, so long as teachers can be induced to accept some reduction in hourly wages in the context of an increase in their total earnings. Even in the absence of other measures affecting teachers' compensation, the more intensive use of teachers as teachers (as distinct from implicitly condoning their performance of other activities, such as tending to the family farm or small business) may allow unit costs to be reduced.

As indicated in chapters 4–6, many options can be explored to make greater use of teachers. They include lengthening, through a variety of schemes, the teachers' (but not the students') school day; holding classes six days a week in primary schools that do not already do so; increasing the teaching hours per week in secondary and tertiary institutions to levels more closely approaching norms outside Africa; reducing vacation periods so that teachers (and facilities) are employed much more than the thirty-six weeks a year now common; and increasing the minimum number of students in a class, especially in secondary and tertiary institutions where courses are often thinly subscribed. In addition to all such measures, each of which would result in some modest reduction in unit costs, most developing countries, if they aspire to bring about nonincremental changes in educational access over the next several decades, will need to consider some fundamentally different alternatives for the delivery of educational services (see the discussion below on extramural study programs).

An analysis of tertiary education in Africa leads to a special conclusion about the utilization of teachers at this level. For reasons discussed in chapter 6, it would be desirable in most African countries to stabilize or even reduce the number of university students in the short term (that is, the next five to ten years). This adjustment would be achieved by contracting relatively low-priority faculties (for example, arts and law) and by consolidating the number of institutions and academic programs within a country or across several small countries. This contraction and consolidation would allow for a substantial improvement in the use of facilities and the size of classes in core programs on the consolidated campuses, thereby increasing the productivity of the teaching personnel employed there. A painful—but absolutely necessary—concomitant of this adjustment measure in higher education will be reductions in faculty numbers beyond what would occur through normal attrition. Substitution of African academics for expatriate professors will in many fields make it possible to avoid dismissing currently employed teaching staff. However, in selected disciplines in arts and humanities, where overproduction of personnel trained at the tertiary level is most severe, the redundancy of African teaching staff is inescapable and must be squarely faced.

Revitalization: Restoring Quality

The second dimension of an education strategy for Africa involves revitalizing the infrastructure now available for education and training in order to restore and improve quality. The focus should be on the fundamentals: instructional materials, academic standards, and the maintenance of equipment and physical plant. Students and teachers waste their time (at great cost) for lack of textbooks and other learning materials and for lack of effective examination systems to set and maintain standards. School supervision systems, vital to education performance, come to a halt when there is no money to operate vehicles or pay for telephone and other communication services. In addition, buildings and equipment deteriorate for lack of maintenance, and expensive laboratories are not used for lack of reagents and spare parts. These items of nonsalary recurrent expenditure have been highly vulnerable when budgets had to be cut, even though they amount to only a small fraction of total education expenditures. Appropriate balance in the use of inputs must be restored immediately. If efficiency and quality in education are to be achieved, systematic and sustained measures to revitalize the existing infrastructure are essential supplements to adjustment policies.

Instructional Materials

The top education priority in Africa today is to ensure that every child in every classroom has access to the pedagogically necessary minimum of instructional materials. What that means in pratice will of course be different for the several levels and within levels will vary by grade and subject. Methods of production, distribution, and finance will also vary from country to country. But only those countries that accord central importance to the provision of instructional materials can be judged to have put in place adequate strategies for educational development.

Difficult issues will have to be confronted: what pedagogical material to develop locally and what to purchase from abroad; whether to purchase higher-cost local printing or least-cost printing elsewhere in the region or, more usually, outside Africa; and how to make the best use of nontraditional media such as radio. In a recent policy paper on education, the African Development Bank emphasized the importance of considering instructional materials within the overall context of restoring nonsalary recurrent expenditures to adequate levels:

> The supply of appropriate teaching materials is particularly inadequate in large parts of Africa. While this is to some extent a question of finance, the issue of producing and distributing adequate teaching materials for African schools goes much beyond the question of funds. As there is an urgent need not just for any teaching materials and textbooks, but for materials that are more closely in tune with the realities and needs of African societies, a major field of lending activity opens up here. Bank Group loans will support, not just some of the technical assistance needed in modifying and adapting existing textbooks and materials and preparing new materials, but also the production and distribution of these materials in Africa. Educational Resource Centers in areas where there is a particularly serious shortage of instructional materials could be another example of this general thrust. In this area of quality and internal efficiency, as the majority of the nonsalary inputs have a direct effect on the qualitative aspects of education, the Bank Group will give priority to [helping] regional member countries identify and maintain minimum standards for nonsalary inputs. (African Development Bank 1986, pp. 15–16.)

Academic Standards

The restoration and clarification of standards of academic performance are key to improving the quality of education at all levels. Academic expectations for students and schools should be high, and they should be clear. By providing signals on performance to which teachers, students, and parents can respond, the examination system is both a measurement and incentive device that should be used explicitly to raise academic standards. But to perform this function, most African examination systems need to broaden their tests to sample the full range of cognitive competencies sought by the nation from a given level of the education system. Now the tests often concentrate narrowly on those skills most needed for success at the next level. If examinations were more broadly structured, they would be more pertinent for assessing the skills of the majority of students who will not advance to the next level.

Operation and Maintenance of Physical Plant and Equipment

Preventive maintenance and repair of physical plant and equipment, another item of nonsalary recurrent expenditure, is an essential ingredient for revitalizing

African education systems. Quality education is just not possible in laboratories and workshops that have no electricity or water because wiring, fuses, and plumbing have deteriorated, and where equipment does not operate because spare parts and consumable supplies are lacking. Maintaining door and cabinet locks, replacing broken windows, repairing leaky roofs, changing the oil and filters in heavily used field vehicles—these may be simple things to do, but they are not getting done. Failure to do them means that vital equipment is not available and functioning when needed, and unit costs are inflated when premature replacement is the consequence.

Once plant and equipment are restored to fully functional status and their maintenance attended to on a routine basis, money is also needed to ensure that these resources do not sit idle. Reestablishing adequate budgetary provision for such simple items as gasoline, postage, and telephone service is essential if school supervision systems at the primary and secondary levels and fieldwork at the tertiary level are to make their intended contribution to educational productivity.

Selective Expansion

The third dimension of an overall strategy for education and training in Africa entails the considered and deliberate expansion of selected education services. Public support for the sector has been threatened recently, and will continue to be threatened, by the fiscal austerity that grips the region. Wise leaders, however, will do what they can to protect from debilitating cuts those long-term education investments that promise the most for their nations' future.

Most forward-looking education programs, although they will differ from one African country to the next, will need to put some emphasis on each of the following: renewed progress toward universal primary education; new programs of extramural study at secondary and tertiary levels; development of a broadly based system of training; and improvement of graduate education and research capacity.

Safeguarding the quality of instructional staff will be essential at all levels during any selective expansion and will require special attention. Motivated, knowledgeable, and pedagogically competent teachers are essential components of educational quality. The revitalization efforts described earlier focus on eliminating current constraints on teachers' effectiveness, such as the shortage of instructional materials. But beyond such efforts, as selective expansion again becomes economically feasible to encourage, African education systems will need to provide for constant professional renewal of the teaching force, particularly if the standards for teachers' years of preservice education are relaxed in order to contain costs.

In order to maintain the quality of instructional staff, the design and implementation of cost-effective systems of continuous in-service training for primary and secondary school teachers should be part of every country's education policy package. This training should focus on upgrading and updating teachers' knowledge of subject matter and mastery of improved pedagogical methods embodied in widely available instructional materials. Distance education is likely to be the most attractive delivery mode for much of this activity. Furthermore, teachers' progression through the salary scale should depend on their successful completion of such regular in-service courses, thereby ensuring that pay is more closely related to potential classroom productivity than it is now. For the tertiary level, much on-the-job professional improvement can be achieved in the short run by reestablishing the flow of standard textbooks, new monographs, and journals, but ultimately the upgrading of teacher quality will entail increased investments in formal postgraduate education.

Renewed Progress toward Universal Primary Education

For many countries, the most important long-term investment—in both its economic and social returns—will be to renew, after adjustment and revitalization measures have begun to take hold, national progress toward universal primary education (UPE). Renewing progress toward UPE will inevitably require the mobilization of substantial new resources, including—but not limited to—increased commitments of public resources. Chapters 2 and 3 showed how costly and difficult is the task of merely keeping up with population growth. Yet, two lines of evidence suggest that in many countries very high priority should be accorded to the goal of continued progress toward UPE, while in a few countries universal provision of nine years of education may already be an appropriate goal. First, compared with projects and investments in other sectors, investments in education have an unusually good record of implementation and sustainability; absorptive capacity has been demonstrated. Second, there is strong (and mounting) economic evidence indicating high returns to investment in education, particularly primary education.

Those returns will be greatly attenuated or never materialize at all if the incidence of disease and malnutrition among young children goes unchecked. Policy packages for educational development must consider how to ensure not only that pupils are well taught but that they are teachable, a point of increased importance since serious nutritional deprivation has become a perennial problem in many parts of Africa. However, the links between child health, nutrition, preschool intellectual development, and attendance at and performance in school are particularly complex and only imperfectly understood. Regional and international collaboration in the search for more complete answers offers the best hope of developing practical policies to remedy the situation.

Distance Education Programs

New extramural study programs are perhaps the only viable way to address the massive problems of access to secondary and postsecondary education for students and to continuing education for teachers. Accreditation examinations allow certification of an outside student's "equivalency" to having completed a conventional program. Students can thus acquire diplomas and degrees by independent study, typically guided by correspondence materials supplemented by radio broadcasts. The replicability of high-quality teaching materials allows high performance standards to be set and maintained in the equivalency system. Moreover, by their very nature, equivalency programs tend to favor the most persistent and motivated students. Often extramural programs actually use existing campus facilities during evenings or vacation months for tutorial sessions and laboratory work, although sometimes equivalency education takes place in specially created institutions.

The unit costs of instruction in extramural programs are typically only 20 percent to 40 percent of the unit costs of conventional instruction. In addition, there are often substantial savings in student transportation and (public budget) savings in living costs. During the present period of adjustment and austerity in Africa, a country's rationale for incurring the high construction and incremental costs of the "bricks and mortar" approach to educational expansion deserves to be scrutinized.

Training

Occupation-specific training is essential for African development. The question is not whether to train, but rather when, where, and how to do so in the most cost-effective way. Experience suggests that African policymakers, like their counterparts in other parts of the world, may be tempted to adopt questionable policies by the undeniable urgency of the need for occupation-specific skills. As summarized in chapter 5, there are numerous pitfalls to be avoided, but only a few bedrock principles upon which wise policymakers can rely for guidance.

One such principle is that formal schools are, generally, neither the only nor the best place in which to train students in most specific vocational skills. With the possible exception of some commercial skills (such as typing and accounting) that have wide applicability and low requirements for expensive equipment and facilities, vocational training is best provided after students have secured initial employment. And it is best conducted in venues closer to the workplace and more directly under the control of employers than are formal schools. The emphasis in Africa should be to design for each country a system of vocational training founded on this principle.

This difficult task will be greatly facilitated by ensuring that there is a single place in the government—and not necessarily, or even desirably, in the Ministry of Education—that is charged with formulating, monitoring, and evaluating training policy. In this process, macroeconomic policies that stimulate provision of job-specific training—in such areas as wage regulations, investment codes, tax incentives, and apprenticeship rules—have a crucial part to play and should be prominently included in an overall policy package for improvement of education and training.

Meanwhile, the education systems of most African countries already include schools whose mission is to provide occupation-specific training for agriculture, industry, and the services. These schools must be encouraged to operate as efficiently as possible, even while other, fully coherent training systems are being developed. Typically, a great deal can be accomplished by ensuring that expensive facilities and equipment are fully utilized, curricula are maximally responsive to the (often changing) skill requirements of employers, and teachers are well endowed with real-world experience in the jobs for which they provide training.

Research and Postgraduate Education

The adjustment and revitalization measures for tertiary education proposed in this study will, when implemented, go far toward addressing problems related to the efficiency and quality of undergraduate programs. But better undergraduate programs, in themselves, will not increase Africa's scientific and technological self-reliance in the next century. Ultimately, Africa will continue to develop only to the extent that it can take advantage of the worldwide explosion of knowledge and itself generate knowledge pertinent to African problems. These functions require Africa's top intellectual talent: the people with master's and doctoral degrees whose careers are in university teaching and research and in the most sophisticated knowledge-intensive scientific and technical positions in government and the private sector. In fields central to African development, such as agriculture, health, engineering, and management, and in the basic natural and social sciences that underlie applied work in those areas, the continent must intensify efforts to develop its own capacity not only to produce these people but also to sustain professional environments in which such highly specialized talent can be productive.

Thus the questions arise whether, when, and how Africa can develop, in a few institutions of higher learning, programs of postgraduate education and research training comparable in quality to the best available outside the continent. Can African postgraduate education be expanded and upgraded to produce a substantial fraction of the continent's top professional talent and more research of the highest international standards? This question (like the one mentioned earlier about the importance of childhood nutrition and health for learning) is unfortunately one in which the dimensions of the problem are far more clearly defined than the solution.

Nonetheless, the solution is of critical long-run importance to all countries, although none can reasonably address it alone. Given the continent's limited resources and the unavoidably costly sums required to ensure high-quality efforts, international cooperation—among African countries, and between them and their partners in other regions of the world—to establish a coherent set of programs of excellence in national institutions will have to be central to any solution. Country-specific policy packages for educational development should include practical mechanisms for encouraging and effectively supporting regional and international initiatives to address such transnational issues.

Policy Design and Implementation

For most African countries the formulation of a comprehensive educational development program, derived from a balanced package of policies for adjustment, revitalization, and selective expansion, will be a new experience. Each country will organize for the task in its own way. In many countries, however, a fruitful approach to policy design might include the following: establishing a national commission with political clout to oversee the work; constituting a technical staff to support the commission; drawing for both upon the best political judgment and analytical talent of ministries of finance and planning, as well as education, and of the nation's institutions of tertiary education and research; building a national consensus through provision of ample opportunity for public debate on emerging findings and recommendations and on their rationale; and taking advantage of the experience of other African countries in formulating educational development strategies.

All such activities would, of course, need to be financed. Budgetary resources would have to be sufficient to cover not only the personnel costs of such a national commission and its staff but also their operating expenses for travel, communications, publications, and specialized contractual services (such as data collection and processing, expert technical consultants, and targeted research or analysis).

Although careful elaboration of education development programs is urgent and essential, the impact of such programs will ultimately depend on African capacity for implementation. Thus improvement in education management is a necessary concomitant to policy reform and must be given immediate and continuing attention.

The most important measures to improve management involve the potential returns to downward and outward delegation of various administrative functions. Some functions, of course, must appropriately remain within the central ministry, and the performance of these functions will need to be improved. The toughest challenge to improving management, however, lies closer to the classroom, at the level of individual schools and districts. African policymakers should consider how, with adequate safeguards against abuses, headteachers and the local communities they serve can be given greater authority in the acquisition and use of the resources essential to effective classroom teaching and learning.

In addition, central ministries must tend more seriously to their own management development needs, especially in the areas of performance monitoring and policy planning and analysis. Improvements in examination systems (which were already mentioned with reference both to academic standards and to distance education), in the nature and timely availability of statistical and financial accounting information, and in the numbers and qualifications of staff engaged in fulltime analytical work are among the necessary measures. Incentives in many ministries of education are insufficient to attract, motivate, and retain able staff. Governments committed not only to the formulation of an educational development program but also to its expeditious implementation will have to address imaginatively the issue of incentives at all levels of the education system.

9

International Assistance for African Educational Development

Chapter 8 recapitulated the detailed discussion of policy options for African education and training and recast the various options within a three-part framework that decisionmakers in each African government could use to develop a policy package for their own country. Chapter 9 analyzes the volume and distribution in recent times of public international development assistance for African education and training, and it offers suggestions for making such assistance more effective in the future. It advocates an enlarged and better coordinated international effort, responsive to and supportive of the efforts of African governments as they design and implement new policies for adjustment, revitalization, and selective expansion of their education systems.

Sources of Aid and Its Recent Use

Relative to its population, Sub-Saharan Africa has recently commanded a sizable share of public international development assistance—commonly called "international aid." With only about 11 percent of the population of the world's developing countries, Sub-Saharan Africa in the early 1980s was receiving about 22 percent of international aid. The annual allotment of such aid to Sub-Saharan Africa for all purposes, education included, is equivalent to about $19 per inhabitant, compared with $8 per inhabitant in the other developing regions. Aid for education averages about 11 percent of this total, above 20 percent in Chad, Kenya, and Senegal, and above 30 percent in Nigeria and Swaziland (see appendix table A-25).

As defined here, international aid comprises all flows of resources, financial and in-kind, originating from OECD and OPEC sources, both bilateral and multilateral, and containing a concessional element of at least 25 percent. It includes, therefore, in addition to grants, all loans carrying repayment terms that are so much lower than those attainable commercially that the grant component exceeds 25 percent. Excluded under this definition are nonconcessional loans from bilateral organizations and the multilateral banks (the World Bank and the African Development Bank) and, of course, all loans from private commercial banks. Also excluded from this definition are all flows from Eastern Bloc countries (which do not routinely divulge the pertinent figures) and flows from private, nongovernmental organizations. Nonconcessional and Eastern Bloc aid accounted for only about 7 percent of flows to the education sector in 1981–83, so the definition of aid used here encompasses virtually all flows. Data on aid flows are not notable for their accuracy or consistency, however, and figures given here should be interpreted as rough approximations rather than exact magnitudes.

Analysis of public international development assistance to education in Africa in the early 1980s yields a number of interesting results, the most salient of which will be summarized here (detailed data are in appendix tables A-24 to A-27). Because comparable information on aid flows is extremely difficult to develop, and in any event is not available except with substantial lags, two general caveats are important. First, despite the care taken in preparing appendix tables A-24 to A-27, the reported distribution of aid by use, level, and expenditure category may be distorted because resource flows to education are often integral parts of bilateral arrangements for budgetary support, and it is difficult to obtain an accurate accounting of them. Second, the data say nothing about trends since 1981–83. In response to the deterioration of African education, several important providers of international assistance for the sector have introduced fundamental changes in their aid distribution policies which are not yet reflected in the data. Caution is therefore appropriate when considering the points in the paragraphs that follow.

External resources are critically important to African educational development. In the early 1980s public international development assistance to education and training in Africa from OECD and OPEC sources—"education aid" as defined here—averaged $1.3 billion a year (table 9-1). This was the equivalent of about 15 percent of African domestic public expenditure on education. If one adds to this amount the aid flows from the Eastern Bloc countries, those from private, nongovernmental organizations, and the nonconcessional flows from the multilateral banks ("hard" loans from the World Bank and African Development Bank), the grand total of external flows to African education and training comes to nearly $1.6 billion annually. This is the equivalent of about 17 percent of African domestic public expenditure on education.

Of the $1.3 billion of education aid from OECD and OPEC sources, $367 million (28 percent) was used to finance training sectors other than education. Another $190 million (14 percent) was in the form of hidden subsidies incurred by countries that hosted approximately 100,000 African students in educational institutions abroad. The remaining $757 million (59 percent of the $1.3 billion in total aid to African education and training and the equivalent of about 8 percent of African domestic public expenditure on education) is the subject of the following analysis—the amount actually channeled through education ministries and expended directly by the education sector itself. It will be referred to henceforth as direct education aid (table 9-1).

Direct education aid to Africa has come from

Table 9-1. Estimated Annual Flow of External Resources to African Education and Training by Source and Use, 1981–83 Average
(millions of current U.S. dollars)

Source	Education sector[a]	Project-related training[b]	Cost of hosting African students abroad[c]	Total
OECD and OPEC members	785	394	190	1,370
Concessional flows ("aid")	757[d]	367	190	1,314
Bilateral	507	247	190	944
France	206	.	73	279
Belgium	58	.	7	66
United Kingdom	40	.	24	64
Other and not distributed	203	247	85	535
Multilateral	250	120	0	370
International Development Association	128	54	0	183
African Development Fund	34	15	0	48
Other	88	51	0	139
Nonconcessional flows[e]	28	27	0	56
East European nonmarket economies and Cuba	40	.	55	95
Nongovernmental organizations	90	.	0	90
Total	915	394	245	1,555

. Not available.
Note: Columns and rows may not add because of rounding.
a. Disbursements to central ministries of education.
b. Aid for training in sectors other than education.
c. Host country subsidization of African students studying abroad, over and above any fellowships.
d. "Direct education aid," the term used here to describe concessional flows to the education sector.
e. Loans from the IBRD and the African Development Bank.
Source: Appendix table A-24.

several sources. Three former colonial powers (Belgium, France, and United Kingdom) account for about 40 percent of it; France alone contributes more than a quarter. In the early 1980s, the dollar amounts of direct education aid provided by the United Kingdom and the United States were roughly the same, but each was less than 20 percent of France's aid. All other bilateral sources together supplied 22 percent, and multilateral sources provided 33 percent.

The French Ministry of Cooperation has stated that the correct figure for France's direct aid to African education in 1981–83 is $236 million, which is 15 percent higher than the $206 million reported in table 9-1. The discrepancy, which may well apply in the case of some other donor countries, probably reflects a lag between the disbursements of aid, as reported by the donors to the Development Assistance Committee of the OECD, and their official receipt, as reported by the receiving countries to the UNDP office on external aid.

Direct education aid for the purchase of recurrent items was equivalent to roughly 17 percent of domestic recurrent expenditure on education in the median African country, and aid for the purchase of capital items was about 30 percent of domestic capital expenditure (table 9-2). Both proportions decrease steadily as countries become more developed. For the median low-income semiarid African country, direct aid is 30 percent of recurrent and 55 percent of capital expenditures, whereas for the median middle-income oil-exporting country, the corresponding figures are only 4 percent and 3 percent.

But direct education aid is less rationally distributed on a per capita basis (see figure 9-1). The median low-income African country receives $2.94 per capita while the median middle-income country receives $4.07; the median middle-income oil importer receives $4.16 (see appendix table A-25). Analysis of the country-level data shows that neither level of development (GDP per capita) nor magnitude of educational need (enrollment rates for the three levels) is a significant determinant of education aid per capita. Indeed, among the variables included in the analysis, only the size of the country (population) was a significant predictor of per capita education aid, with smaller countries getting more.

The distribution of direct aid by level of education is heavily skewed toward higher levels (figure 9-2 and table 9-3). Only about 7 percent ($56 million a year in the early 1980s) of all direct aid to African education is used to finance primary education, whereas 34 percent ($259 million) goes to the tertiary subsector. Per student the results are staggering—direct education aid to primary education amounts to $1.10 per student, to secondary education approximately $11, to teacher training $78, and to secondary technical education $182; aid to higher education is $575 per student, which is well over 500 times the amount per primary pupil. In round numbers, direct education aid to primary education covers only 2 percent of the cost of sending an African primary pupil to school; aid to general secondary education and teacher training covers about 4 percent of the cost of each student, and aid to secondary technical and tertiary education about 50 percent. Among bilateral donors, the lack of balance is even more dramatic: less than 4 percent

Table 9-2. Direct Education Aid by Recipient Group and Expenditure Category, 1981–83 Average

Recipient country group	Aid for recurrent expenditures as percentage of domestic recurrent education budget[a]	Aid for capital expenditures as percentage of domestic capital education budget[a]	All direct education aid — Total (millions of dollars per year)	All direct education aid — Percentage of external aid in all sectors[a]
Economic status				
Low-income semiarid	29.5	54.9	99	9.9
Low-income other	17.0	47.7	477	13.1
Middle-income oil importers	11.1	28.0	118	10.7
Middle-income oil exporters	3.9	2.9	64	14.0
Linguistic				
Francophone	18.7	49.9	363	13.0
Anglophone	11.9	24.2	330	11.3
Other	16.4	18.4	65	9.6
Sub-Saharan Africa	16.7	30.5	757	13.1

a. Medians within country groups.
Source: Appendix table A-25.

Figure 9-1. Direct Education Aid Per Capita, by Sub-Saharan Country Group, 1981–83 Average

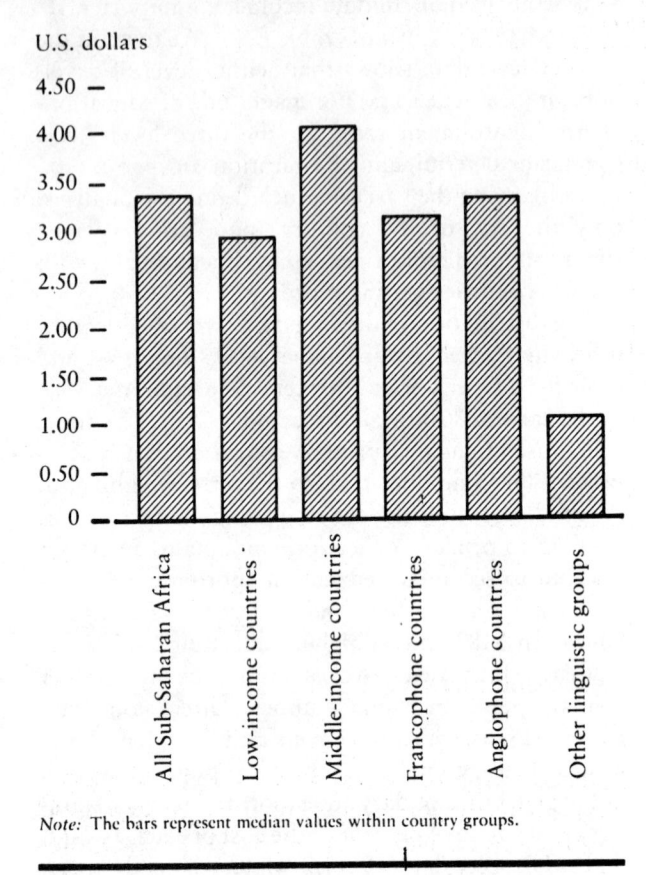

Note: The bars represent median values within country groups.

of their direct aid goes for primary education and 42 percent for tertiary. A notable exception to this general pattern is the program of the Swedish aid agency, SIDA, which devotes 30 percent of its African education assistance to primary education. Among multilateral agencies, UNICEF allocates 39 percent of its assistance to primary education, and the International Development Association of the World Bank, 28 percent (see appendix table A-26).

The distribution of direct education aid by expenditure category is notable for the small proportion dedicated to financing operating costs, which comprise salaries of nationals of the country, consumable supplies including public utilities, and all instructional materials (figure 9-2 and table 9-3). This allocation was especially remarkable in 1981–83 when the absence of nonsalary recurrent inputs to education had become the governing constraint on educational performance at all levels. Only 11 percent of direct education aid is allocated to operating costs. By contrast, 17 percent of aid supports fellowships for African students to study abroad, and no less than 44 percent goes for technical assistance in its narrowest sense of providing foreign experts. (There is an inconsistency between tables 9-2 and 9-3 in the breakdown of direct education aid between capital and recurrent expenditures, and this is due to differences in the sources for the two tables and in the way these sources treat technical assistance; some technical assistance for building capacity is classified by some sources as an investment item rather than as recurrent expenditure.)

Figure 9-2. Direct Education Aid, 1981–83 Average

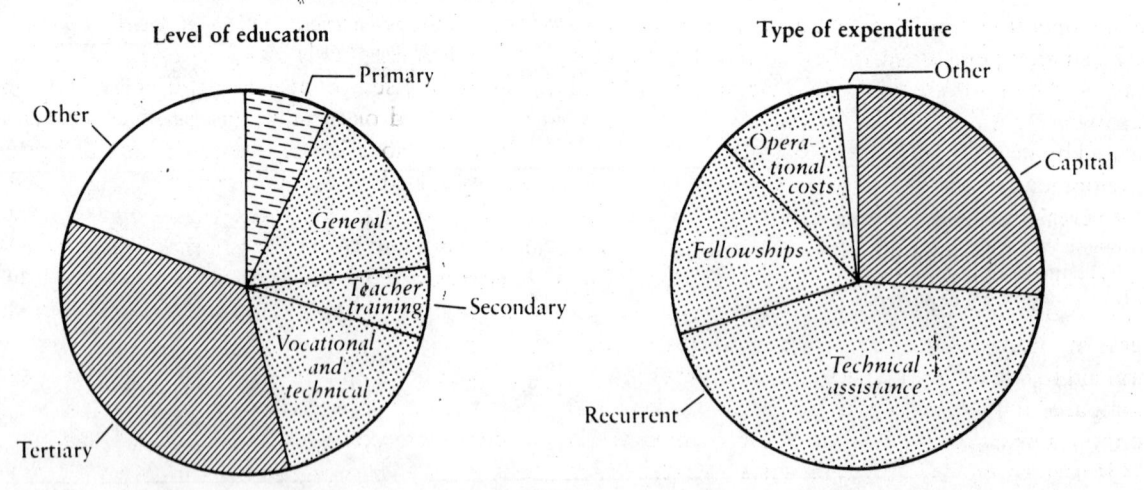

Table 9-3. Direct Education Aid by Level of Education, Expenditure Category, and Source, 1981–83 Average

	Percentage of bilateral aid ($507 million)	Percentage of multilateral aid ($250 million)	Percentage of all direct aid ($757 million)
Level of education			
Primary	3.4	15.7	7.4
Secondary	38.8	39.7	39.1
General	20.9	6.1	16.0
Teacher training	3.0	12.7	6.2
Vocational/technical	14.9	20.9	16.9
Tertiary	42.4	17.5	34.2
Other	15.4	27.1	19.3
Expenditure category			
Capital	7.4	64.9	26.4
Recurrent	90.7	34.2	72.1
Technical assistance[a]	57.5	17.4	44.3
Fellowships	20.5	9.6	16.9
Operational costs[b]	12.7	7.2	10.9
Other	1.9	0.9	1.5

a. Includes provision of teachers as well as other foreign experts.
b. Includes salary support for nationals, utilities and supplies, and instructional materials.
Sources: Appendix tables A-26 and A-27.

The predilection for technical assistance is most marked in the case of the bilateral donors. Each of the four major bilateral donors dedicates at least 55 percent of its direct education aid to technical assistance, which in essence provides employment in Africa for its own professionals; France supplies so many teachers in secondary and tertiary institutions that an astounding four-fifths of its aid goes for this purpose. (As noted above, for various reasons these figures may not give a completely accurate picture of current reality, but the overall conclusion would probably not change even with more complete data.)

Only 13 percent of bilateral aid is used to finance operating costs. Bilateral donors also allocate a smaller percentage of their direct education aid than do the multilaterals to system management and to capacity-building activities. These activities, unallocated by level, are crucial to long-term educational development.

Whereas the bilaterals devote a disproportionately large share of their direct education aid to technical assistance, the multilaterals devote a disproportionately small share of theirs to noncapital expenditure items of all kinds. Only 35 percent of direct multilateral aid to education finances recurrent expenditures (compared with 92 percent in the case of the bilateral donors). Only about 7 percent of direct multilateral aid is used to finance operating costs. UNICEF, which focuses on nonsalary recurrent inputs, is a notable exception to the general rule.

The Comparative Advantage of Aid: Past and Present

Caution is appropriate in drawing negative conclusions about the effectiveness of direct education aid to Africa on the basis of the above facts. The apparent inconsistencies between Africa's current needs and the recent distribution of aid do not, in and of themselves, constitute evidence that aid in the past has been either misdirected or unproductive. The evolution of the context for aid and the comparative advantage of national governments and donors as sources of finance for different purposes must enter into any assessment.

When essentially all direct education aid to Africa was for discrete investment projects, the concentration of aid on small countries, tertiary institutions, and the provision of foreign experts and fellowships for study abroad was understandable and may even have been rational. In general, external sources of finance enjoy a comparative advantage over national governments for investment projects that are capital-intensive; foreign-exchange-intensive; limited in the number, scope, and geographic dispersion of their components so that implementation places a minimal burden on scarce managerial resources; and heavily dependent on the expertise of donor country professionals (including teachers) and on study abroad for recipient country nationals. The distribution of recent direct education aid by expenditure category (table 9-3 and figure 9-2) was broadly consistent with this assessment of donors' comparative advantage.

So too was the distribution of direct education aid by level (table 9-3 and figure 9-2). Intrinsic lack of interest—on the part of the donor and sometimes the recipient—in the primary subsector compared with the more visible interventions in tertiary education and failure on both sides to appreciate the singular importance of primary education in African development affect the way aid is distributed by level of education. But to some extent the relative neglect of primary education can be explained also by differences in the way resources for primary and higher levels of education are generated and utilized and by the implications of these differences for the comparative advantage of national versus external financial support.

School construction and teachers' salaries typically account for more than 95 percent of expenditures in the primary subsector. But primary schools are highly dispersed, the cost of an individual school is minuscule from the perspective of an international donor, and no single school enjoys high visibility or a separately identifiable impact. Moreover, the clear trend is toward using local materials in primary school construction and relying on local communities to finance those materials and to provide the necessary labor. African governments and the external funding agencies that work with them can therefore make only a limited contribution to primary school construction. This is even truer today than it was in previous decades. Although African central governments do contribute relatively more to teachers' salaries than to construction at the primary level, the international community has generally hesitated to finance local salaries as part of conventional investment projects.

For tertiary and secondary technical institutions, the situation is quite the opposite. There are few establishments. Their size and location make them highly visible. Each has a discernible impact on the educational landscape. Typically, these subsectors are directly and wholly dependent on resources from the central government. A significant portion of the capital costs of construction and equipment involve foreign exchange. And many external funding agencies find it easy to support staff development by financing graduate study abroad and either providing expatriate professors outright or supplementing institutional budgets so that African institutions can hire expatriates directly.

In a period characterized entirely by project-focused aid, the distribution of direct education aid by level and expenditure category may have been a rational reflection of comparative advantage. The current challenges facing educational development in Africa, however, suggest that patterns of aid should now change in a number of significant ways. The immediate requirement is policy reform to support (a) adjustment of the education sector to harsh new fiscal and demographic constraints, (b) revitalization of the education system to enhance its quality and efficiency, and (c) carefully targeted and cost-effective expansion of the education system. This leads to recommendation 7.

Recommendation 7

The aggregate amount of external aid to African education has been substantial—the equivalent (depending on what is counted) of between 8 percent and 17 percent of what African governments themselves spend on education. In most countries, however, external sources of finance have tended to focus on discrete investment projects, with little or no effective coordination among donors in support of a coherent national strategy for education. Moreoever, in view of current African needs, a disproportionate fraction of aid has been allocated to higher education rather than primary education; in the case of multilateral donors, a disproportionate share has gone to capital expenditures rather than recurrent expenditures; and in the case of bilateral donors, the imbalance has supported technical assistance and overseas fellowships at the expense of other forms of recurrent expenditures. The organizational forms and the targeted areas of external aid to African education should be adapted to the new imperative for African governments to design and implement country-specific educational development programs that support policy reform. As the policy context develops, the overall volume of aid to education should increase in real terms.

This is not to say that support for discrete investment projects in the education sector has no place in any African country now or in the foreseeable future. It does mean, however, that in most countries for the remainder of the century aid should predominantly support the design and implementation of policies to put the education sector on a viable long-term footing, as well as carefully selected investment projects that will serve as instruments of policy reform. After measures of adjustment, revitalization, and preparation for cost-effective expansion have been implemented over a period of years, the policy environment may again be congenial for a concentration on conventional project assistance for educational expansion. Conversely, and with few exceptions, African countries unwilling to embark upon sectoral development programs are unlikely to be attractive candidates for conventional project assistance.

The design and implementation of such programs along the three dimensions of adjustment, revitalization, and selective expansion represent an unprecedented challenge to African policymakers. How can the international community best assist African countries in meeting the challenge? The answer has two parts. First, new structures are needed to facilitate international cooperation for African educational development. Second, adjustments are needed in the established amounts and targets of aid to African education. A new era in international assistance for African education and training must commence before the end of the decade. The final sections of this chapter suggest how this can be achieved.

New Structures to Support Policy Design and Implementation

When an African government decides to address the issues of adjustment, revitalization, and selective expansion, it will have to confront two immediate tasks: developing the policies and implementation mechanisms for national programs, and mobilizing resources to pay for them. For both these tasks, new forms of international support will be helpful. There are a variety of ways in which this support might be organized. None is perfect in every respect, but change is essential if assistance is to be made more effective. As starting points for more systematic discussion, two sets of ideas on international assistance are outlined below.

The Design of National Programs

A sound country-specific educational development program that will support policy reform is difficult to design. It entails the careful selection of specific policies from the full array of options and then phasing and linking these policies to achieve a variety of goals: contain costs, diversify sources of finance, supply vital nonsalary inputs to learning, ensure adequate standards of performance, operate and maintain physical plant and equipment, expand primary schools, develop distance education systems for secondary and tertiary education, expand training opportunities, strengthen postgraduate education and research capacity, and improve management, giving special attention to the incentive structure for managers at all levels and the knowledge base for decisionmaking. As noted at the end of chapter 8, African governments can address the task of program design in various ways. In many countries, however, this complex task may possibly require a more intensive application of more experience and analytical talent, in more professional disciplines, than local resources alone can supply, at least in the short run.

The international community should offer three related kinds of support for the national process of policy design and implementation sketched in chapter 8. The need is for expeditious action. Any initiatives in these areas that would take more than a year to be adopted and implemented cannot be judged an adequate response to the needs of African governments.

• The first need is simple: seed money, quickly provided, to cover both local and foreign costs of policy development and management improvement activities. Where budgetary resources do not begin to cover the minimal operational needs of the education system, finding funds for a national task force, technical staff, and consultants' services can be a lengthy and ultimately unproductive process, especially if foreign exchange is needed and if budgets other than that of the education ministry are involved. The willingness of international sources of finance to bear part of these extraordinary charges, perhaps on a matching basis, would provide an important incentive to African governments.

Central to the improvement of management of education systems is the strengthening of examination systems and the building of national capacity to conduct research on education. Improvements in testing will make it better able to serve its four purposes—curriculum development, measurement of performance, certification, and selection—and in the long term such improvements may be expected to pay for themselves in increased educational efficiency. In the short and medium term, however, significant sums will be required for additional personnel, training, equipment, and technical support. Early investments are needed to improve examination systems so that they may play properly supportive roles in the implementation of new policies.

Applied research on education, and the training to do it, also costs money, which under conditions of extreme austerity in the public sector is not readily available. The payoff to such expenditures is not usually immediate or even precisely attributable to specific interventions. And yet the quality of national educational development programs depends vitally on first-rate operations-oriented research and greater knowledge of internal and external efficiency. This kind of analytical capacity is generated as much by actually doing such work as by formal training to do it. International aid is a crucial source of support for both.

• Second, ready access to the ongoing experience of other countries in formulating and implementing education policies should be provided by the international community to African countries that embark on national education reform. As countries grapple with common issues—such as equivalency programs in secondary education, consolidation of academic programs in higher education, and establishment of systems for providing textbooks in primary schools—intensive collaboration that enables countries to share their accumulating experience will pay high dividends. Serving as a catalyst for such sharing of experience is a function nicely suited to donors.

• Third, the international community could establish and finance a source of high-quality technical expertise that is nonpolitical and beholden to no international donor or government in particular. African governments could call upon this expertise for help in formulating policies at the outset and in monitoring, evaluating, and correcting them during implementation. Small teams that regularly make intensive visits over several months or even years would support but not supplant locally constituted task forces or commissions. Interaction of the national commission with the outside technical expertise would initially produce a package of policies together with a detailed plan for their implementation—that is, an educational development program—ready to be considered for financing by the government and appraised by the international donor community. The interaction between national commission and outside technical expertise might continue as the program attracts funding and enters implementation. This could take the form of collaborative efforts in the ongoing evaluation of policies and in the formulation of recommendations for refinements on the basis of accumulating experience. If this technical support is provided in sensible ways, African national capacity to engage in this sort of continuous policy planning and analysis should be significantly enhanced.

Program Implementation

The international community should also help to finance the implementation of the programs themselves. Sound educational development programs will typically require more resources, sustained over a longer period, than can be mobilized internally. Countries that have demonstrated their willingness to address policy issues should have access to increased, longer-term, and more flexibly proffered international aid. To the extent that a country's program involves thoroughgoing reform, there are likely to be substantial one-time transition costs to a new and more sustainable policy regime. In countries with severe foreign exchange constraints, revitalization measures are likely to claim a large share of foreign exchange to import essential nonsalary inputs to learning.

In many cases the necessary policy changes constitute a sharp break with the past; their implementation must be carefully phased and corrections made as implementation proceeds. The international community can be very helpful in this process, but only to the extent that its support of the development program is seen from the beginning as a long-term commitment. Aid must have continuity over time, something it has too often lacked in the past. Disbursements should be made in sequence with the achievement of agreed-upon policy objectives, as verified in periodic joint reviews of the development program.

A promising approach for marshaling and coordinating international assistance is the use of country-specific donor consortia. Already a number of African governments have successful experience in submitting their macroeconomic structural adjustment and development programs to meetings of prospective international supporters for their review and appraisal. The World Bank has supported Consultative Group meetings in which to appraise together with other donors the macroeconomic policy framework of a country's adjustment program, while the UNDP Round Tables have been used to coordinate donor support for a country's projects within an investment program. The education sector needs its own mechanism that builds upon the strengths of both these devices.

Once an African government has prepared its own strategy for educational development—has decided on the necessary policy reforms and identified the operational means and resource requirements for implementing them—the international community can be invited to a forum in which the strategy is presented in some detail and thoroughly reviewed, and broad agreement reached with respect to external support. In 1986 there were two useful precedents for this approach. Ghana's ambitious education sector adjustment program was the subject of a meeting of donors in Vienna that was an adjunct to the World Bank Consultative Group set up to consider Ghana's overall adjustment program. The UNDP organized a Round Table on Education for Burundi, chaired by the minister of education and held in Bujumbura.

Some governments may wish to invite the World Bank to arrange similar special Consultative Group meetings to review their education sector development program; other governments may wish to ask the UNDP to arrange a special Round Table for this purpose. In still other instances, governments may wish to rely on the good offices of the ad hoc technical support teams, suggested above, to organize a meeting. Whatever the mechanism, the important point is that each African country would have an opportunity to meet periodically with all prospective donors, to review the policy framework and operational programs of its long-term educational development strategy, to monitor progress in its implementation, and to agree collectively on resource requirements and sources. The result would be much better coordination of aid in support of the priority needs of the recipient country.

This discussion of how international assistance should be organized brings us next to the question of how the money should be spent.

Future Amounts and Targeted Areas of Aid to African Education

Whether or not new organizational forms take root, the challenges of educational development in Africa today and the recent patterns of international assistance for African education suggest that the focus of aid urgently needs modification. This will of course be easier to achieve to the extent that African governments have embraced the need for policy reform and the donor community has improved the organization of its activities.

Of the three dimensions of education reform, the first (adjustment policies to diversify financing and reduce unit costs, thereby economizing public resources) will usually not depend on a fresh injection of financial resources. Two possible exceptions are the establishment of student loan schemes and, in some countries, the reduction or redeployment of excess personnel by offering one-time compensation to those involved. But in general the implementation of adjustment policies does not entail the purchase of goods or services and thus presents few opportunities for increased international financial aid. Contingent upon African countries' vigorous implementation of adjustment policies in the education sector, however, the international donor community has a vital role in enabling African governments to implement the other two dimensions of change—revitalization and selected expansion of education systems. In both these areas, there is an immediate and continuing requirement for more resources. This study concludes, therefore, with a discussion of aid for these two purposes.

Aid for Revitalization

INSTRUCTIONAL MATERIALS. The revitalization of African educational systems depends first and foremost on correcting the imbalance between salary and nonsalary recurrent expenditures. Nothing short of a massive resurgence of the flow of nonsalary inputs to learning is required. Instructional materials are central in this effort. For primary schools, textbooks and writing materials are the essential elements. For general secondary schools, the need is for textbooks and consumable supplies for laboratory demonstrations. In addition, secondary technical schools require substantial amounts for the maintenance and repair of equipment, and for spare parts, to make the workshops functional again. In tertiary institutions, the priorities are libraries (including multiple copies of standard textbooks), maintenance and repair of equipment, and consumables for laboratories and workshops. At all three levels, but particularly for secondary and tertiary education, maintenance of the physical plant is the second priority for nonsalary recurrent expenditure.

To get a rough sense of the volume of resources required, assume that by 1988 there will be roughly 63 million African children in primary education, 16 million in secondary, and 0.5 million in tertiary, and that the cost per student of providing an initial stock of materials is, respectively, $9, $18, and $90. The start-up costs, incurred over three years, would approximate $900 million. Thereafter, roughly one-third of that amount would be required annually to replace texts and ensure continued flows of consumables; provision would also have to be made for expanding enrollments (for example at 4 percent, 8 percent, and 0.5 percent annually for primary, secondary, and tertiary education, respectively). A reasonable target phased in over ten years (1991 to 2000) would be to have 60 percent recovery of replacement costs of materials from primary students and their families, and 95 percent cost recovery for secondary and tertiary materials. On these assumptions, the difference between replacement requirements and amounts recovered would decline over the decade from $322 million to $134 million; the total nonrecovered operational cost for that decade would approximate $2.4 billion. By the beginning of the next century, then, the shortage of instructional materials in African classrooms can be resolved for a total of about $3.3 billion. This level of response would not seriously burden the international development assistance community. This total would equal 33 percent of direct education aid under the pessimistic (and, indeed, unacceptable) assumption that the 1981–83 average annual amount of aid will not increase in the thirteen years from 1988 to 2000.

REPAIR AND MAINTENANCE OF EQUIPMENT AND PHYSICAL PLANT. When public resources for education contracted as a result of the economic crisis in Africa, typically the first casualty was funds for the maintenance of capital assets—physical plant and major items of equipment. Maintenance was deferred so long that many countries now face an immense burden of costly repairs. Particularly serious is the condition of equipment for technical subjects in secondary and tertiary institutions, but such fundamental items as electrical and water supply systems, sewage, lighting and ventilation systems, and even roofs and windows are also in desperate need of repair. Precise calculations of the financial requirements are beyond the scope of this study. A rough estimate of $500 per tertiary student, $100 per secondary technical student, and $20 per general secondary student suggests an order of magnitude of $600 million. In the context of an overall educational development program and agreements to ensure and protect a budgetary allocation adequate to cover preventative maintenance in the future, international donors should be willing to finance this backlog of necessary rehabilitation. In some cases it will be more economical to replace obsolete equipment with state-of-the-art items than to repair and then maintain the old.

Aid for Selective Expansion

PROGRESS TOWARD UNIVERSAL PRIMARY EDUCATION. Two aspects of resuming the advance toward universal primary education are especially appropriate subjects of international aid: getting the classrooms built and ensuring that students who will fill them are intellectually and physically ready to learn.

In the context of rapid growth of the school-age population and continuing public austerity, local communities should continue to assume the principal responsibility for financing the construction of primary schools. Nevertheless, African governments can, with the help of international aid, give vitally important support. Leading candidates for (donor-financed) government assistance include: applied research on low-cost construction techniques; the establishment of reasonable standards for the use of space and materials; the training and even the salaries of some workers, such as school construction foremen; and the provision of certain standard materials that are either unavailable or priced much higher at the community level.

But much more important than this, if an African government is vigorously implementing a comprehensive package of reforms that includes the expansion of primary education, international donors should be prepared to disburse a reasonable portion of the funds allocated to the overall program once classroom construction is completed. More bluntly, the expansion of primary education is so central to long-term African development that, even though aid funds may not be the optimal source of finance for primary school construction, the disbursement of those funds (for the purchase of other inputs to the education system or even for general balance of payments support) should be in some measure contingent upon the successful performance of primary school construction.

In addition to classrooms, teachers, and instructional materials, primary pupils need to have benefited from and continue to enjoy minimum standards of health and nutrition in order to learn while in school. In view of the sobering record of childhood disease and malnutrition in Africa, it is time to delineate the parameters of the problem, assess the likely implications for education systems, and identify practical solutions. These activities deserve international financial assistance.

STAFF DEVELOPMENT FOR THE EDUCATION SYSTEM. The quality of staff is obviously essential to the quality of learning. For primary education, more teachers will be required very soon if enrollment rates are to be maintained and then grow. At the secondary level, significant expansion will probably depend on widespread utilization of new distance learning technologies, for which a new style of teacher will be needed. It takes professional and financial resources to develop cost-effective systems of continuous in-service pedagogical support for and training of teachers at both levels, and such systems are appropriate objects of aid.

For secondary and tertiary institutions in Africa, less concerned in the short-run with expansion, new staff must be trained to replace expatriates; and in most countries current staff with inadequate academic credentials and insufficient professional experience need opportunities to upgrade their knowledge and skills. Ultimately most of this activity should take place in African universities. As a practical matter, however, much of the required staff development for the tertiary system cannot be conducted in Africa for the rest of this century. Although it is extremely important to expand opportunities for African staff (present and prospective) to enroll in formal programs of postgraduate study in universities abroad, the requirements for staff development extend far beyond this solution. Whatever the form of staff development, international aid must help to finance it.

DISTANCE EDUCATION FOR SECONDARY AND TERTIARY EDUCATION. Distance education—via self-study schools and extramural programs—offers a highly efficient mechanism for expanding secondary and higher education. For successful implementation, both forms depend on examination systems to ensure quality and provide accreditation. Self-study schools bring students together in simple classrooms, supervised by a community member, to follow lessons on radio and to work from texts and exercise books; they are highly cost-effective for lower and upper secondary education. They enjoy the added attraction of providing learning opportunities in small communities, a powerful device both for extending access to females and for reducing costly enrollments in boarding institutions.

Extramural programs differ from self-study schools principally in that they do not bring students together in supervised classrooms; unit costs are thereby further reduced, and individuals who are employed full time can still continue their studies. Extramural programs typically rely heavily on print, but may also utilize radio and occasional tutorial and laboratory instruction at a campus during evenings, weekends, or vacation periods. Extramural programs are particularly suitable for in-service and postsecondary education.

The international community can assist with the development of distance education in three important ways. First, as individual countries invest in self-study schools and extramural programs, aid can appropriately finance the capital costs and development of sound course materials and the necessary examination systems. Second, a rich variety of correspondence material is now available from universities throughout the world. Most of this is for university-level courses, but basic secondary courses in mathematics and science also exist. As a partial substitute for sending undergraduates for study abroad, external funding agencies could provide the foreign exchange for individuals to enroll in extramural correspondence courses without leaving their country. A good example of such a program, tailored particularly for the needs of developing countries, is an M.Sc. course in agricultural economics offered by an eminent British university.

Third, and most important, a number of donors could collaborate to help finance an African distance teaching center. Such a center would serve three main purposes: (a) it would provide a repository of experience and expertise to assist individual countries in establishing or improving their own distance teaching capacity; (b) it would prepare basic courses that could be adapted at minimal expense by national authorities for their own use (for example, in specialized courses or in conventional secondary schools and universities); and (c) it would offer extramural programs directly to at least a limited number of students. The latter activity would strengthen its own course development and provide a service especially welcome to small countries that are not in a position to invest heavily in this area themselves. An African distance teaching center could be set up in various ways; one alternative would be a semiautonomous entity, rather like the International Institute of Educational Planning (IIEP), under the Unesco umbrella.

TRAINING. International aid to training is now mostly of two quite different sorts. First, in donor-financed projects in all sectors, assistance is often given to train those responsible for building, operating, or maintaining various elements of the project. Experience with such project-related training has been generally favorable, although its focus on discrete projects usually has precluded longer-term attention to developing local training institutions. Second, international aid for training has supported the construction of vocationally oriented secondary schools, usually to provide graduates with specific job skills for agriculture, commerce, or industry. Although evaluation of the economic impact of such schools is in its infancy, it is known that industrial technical schools (and to a lesser extent, agricultural ones) are enormously expensive relative to more general secondary education in mathematics and science and that when graduates of those technical schools enter the labor market, the outcome—in terms of jobs and earnings—is often less successful than what was envisioned.

In this situation, international aid should strengthen training in three areas. First, for projects outside the education sector, increases in the proportion of resources devoted to project-related training will have a high payoff. At the same time, however, local training capacity in key economic sectors needs to be developed; sector-related investments to build the capacity of training institutions merit donor support. Second, aid for job-specific training in secondary schools should concentrate on maximizing the utilization of existing schools and minimizing their unit costs; all such assistance should provide for rigorous evaluation to determine whether labor market returns are in fact being realized.

Third, and most important, international donors should expand their support for the development and utilization of training institutions that serve employers and that are partially controlled and financed by them. These institutions would provide training programs mostly for existing employees or those newly hired for a specific assignment; upon completion of the training they would receive a certificate rather than an academic degree; and the menu of course offerings would evolve with labor market needs. Assisting in the development and financing of such employment-related training institutions, in the context of an overall education sector development program, is a high priority for international aid.

EXPANDED CAPACITY FOR GRADUATE EDUCATION AND RESEARCH. Beyond rationalizing the provision of undergraduate tertiary education, Africa must intensify efforts to develop its own capacity to conduct research and to provide postgraduate education and research training of world-class standards in fields central to African development. Leading candidates for attention in this respect are agriculture and health (including the natural sciences that underlie them), management (including the underlying social sciences), and engineering.

Determining which institutions will participate in postgraduate programs of excellence, in which fields and at what levels, will not be easy—for African governments or for their international partners. Questions of international and regional comparative advantage must be squarely faced, since resources will never be sufficient for every country in Africa or even for the continent as a whole to develop capacity at the highest level in all fields and subfields. Ultimately decisions must be made discipline by discipline and in light of an assessment of regional requirements. Sometimes an institution serving as the site for a program of excellence in one field may also need to be the site for programs in closely related fields if professional interaction is essential and facilities and equipment may be shared. Scale and sustainability are crucial matters. Fragmentation in space and time will defeat the purpose. Some internationalization of management control and finance may provide prudent insurance against such risks.

Here there is a strong case for African governments and funding agencies to establish jointly some overall coordinating mechanism to ensure reasonable efficiency in developing the concept of programs of excellence. A useful first step would be to appoint a small but very high-level study group to consider the evidence and render a judgment on the feasibility, desirability, and organization of, and the most important fields and possible sources of finance for, a sustained effort to transform the quality of African postgraduate education and research.

A Call to Action

The new era in international assistance for African education and training should commence without delay. Donors and African governments need now to come together to determine what concrete steps should be taken to support the adjustment, revitalization, and selective expansion of African education. This study will have served its purpose if it stimulates African governments to rethink policies for educational development, encourages international agencies to improve and enlarge their aid, and helps all parties form a new partnership to provide Africa with the stock of human skills indispensable for development in the next decades and beyond.

Bibliography

Background papers commissioned for this study are indicated by an asterisk. The word "processed" describes works that are reproduced from typescript by mimeograph, xerography, or similar means. Such works may not be cataloged or commonly available through libraries or may be subject to restricted circulation.

African Development Bank. 1986. *Education Sector Strategy Paper*. Abidjan.

Aklilu Habte, George Psacharopoulos, and Stephen P. Heyneman. 1983. "Education and Development: Views from the World Bank." World Bank, Washington, D.C.

Armitage, Jane, and Richard Sabot. 1987. "Efficiency and Equity Implications of Subsidies to Secondary Education in Kenya." In David Newbery and Nicholas Stern, eds., *The Theory of Taxation for Developing Countries*. New York: Oxford University Press.

Auerhan, Jan, S. Ramakrishnan, R. Romain, G. Stoikov, L. Tiburcio, and P. Torres. 1985. "Institutional Development in Education and Training in Sub-Saharan African Countries." Education and Training Department Discussion Paper EDT22. World Bank, Washington, D.C. Processed.

Avalos, Beatrice, and Wadi D. Haddad. 1981. *Review of Teacher Effectiveness Research in Africa, Middle East, Malaysia, Philippines and Thailand: A Synthesis of Results*. Ottawa: International Development Research Centre.

Behrman, Jere, and Nancy Birdsall. 1983. "The Quality of Schooling: The Standard Focus on Quantity Alone Is Misleading." *American Economic Review* 73 (December): 926–46.

Benson, Charles. 1987. "Taxonomies of Skill Development: A Search for Criteria to Predict the Relative Efficiency of Alternative Programs of Occupational Training." Education and Training Department Discussion Paper. World Bank, Washington, D.C. Processed.

Bertrand, Trent, and Robert Griffin. 1984. "Financing Education in Kenya." Country Policy Department Discussion Paper. World Bank, Washington, D.C. Processed.

Birdsall, Nancy. 1983. "Demand for Primary Schooling in Rural Mali: Should User Fees Be Increased?" Country Policy Department Discussion Paper 1983-8. World Bank, Washington, D.C. Processed.

_____. 1985. "Cost Recovery in Health and Education: Bank Policy and Operations." Population, Health, and Nutrition Department, World Bank, Washington, D.C. Processed.

*Bowcock, Dianne C. 1985. "Languages of Sub-Saharan Africa: A Listing by Country." Education and Training Department, World Bank, Washington, D.C. Processed.

Bowman, Mary Jean, and Richard H. Sabot. 1982. "Human Resources in Africa: A Continent in Rapid Change." Paper presented at the 1982 Conference of African Governmental Experts on Technical Cooperation among African Countries on Human Resources Development and Utilization, April. Processed.

Bray, Mark. 1986. *New Resources for Education*. London: Commonwealth Secretariat.

Caldwell, J. C. 1979. "Education as a Factor in Mortality Decline: An Examination of Nigerian Data." *Population Studies* 33: 395–413.

Caldwell, J. C., and Pat Caldwell. 1985. "Education and Literacy as Factors in Health." In Scott B. Halstead, Julia A. Walsh, and Kenneth S. Warren, eds., *Good Health at Low Cost*. New York: Rockefeller Foundation.

Cochrane, Susan H. 1979. *Fertility and Education: What Do We Really Know?* Baltimore, Md.: Johns Hopkins University Press.

———. 1986. "The Effects of Education on Fertility and Mortality." Education and Training Department Discussion Paper EDT26. World Bank, Washington, D.C. Processed.

Cochrane, Susan H., Donald J. O'Hara, and Joanne Leslie. 1980. *The Effects of Education on Health*. World Bank Staff Working Paper 405. Washington, D.C.

———. 1982. "Parental Education and Child Health: Intracountry Evidence." *Health Policy and Education* 2 (March): 213–50.

Colclough, Christopher. 1980. *Primary Schooling and Economic Development: A Review of the Evidence*. World Bank Staff Working Paper 399. Washington, D.C.

Court, David, and Kabiru Kinyanjui. 1986. "African Education: Problems in a High-Growth Sector." In Robert J. Berg and Jennifer Seymour Whitaker, eds., *Strategies for African Development*. Berkeley: University of California Press.

Denison, Edward. 1979. *Accounting for Slower Economic Growth*. Washington, D.C.: Brookings Institution.

Dorsey, B. J. 1986. "Development and Reform in Education—Zimbabwe: A Case Study." Paper presented at the 1986 Comparative and International Education Society Conference, Toronto, Canada. Processed.

Dougherty, Christopher. 1987. "Cost-Effectiveness of Training Delivery Modes: A Review." Education and Training Department Discussion Paper EDT73. World Bank, Washington, D.C. Processed.

Dutcher, Nadine. 1982. *The Use of First and Second Languages in Primary Education: Selected Case Studies*. World Bank Staff Working Paper 504. Washington, D.C.

Eastern and Southern African Universities Research Programme. 1987. *University Capacity Utilization in Eastern and Southern Africa*. London: James Currey.

ECA (Economic Commission for Africa). 1984. *Human Resources in Africa*. Monograph 13. New York: United Nations.

———. 1985. *Report of the Second Conference of Vice-Chancellors, Presidents, and Rectors of Institutions of Higher Learning in Africa, Mbabane, Swaziland, February 1985*. E/ECA/CM.11/47. Addis Ababa.

———. 1986. *Africa's Development Priorities and the Role of Institutions of Higher Learning: The Next Five Years*. ECA/AAU Third Conference of Vice-Chancellors, Presidents, and Rectors of Institutions of Higher Learning in Africa, Harare, Zimbabwe, January 1987. E/ECA/AAU/ED/86/3. Addis Ababa.

Eicher, Jean Claude. 1984. *Educational Costing and Financing in Developing Countries: Focus on Sub-Saharan Africa*. World Bank Staff Working Paper 655. Washington, D.C.

Eisemon, T. O. 1986. "Benefitting from Basic Education in Developing Countries: A Review of Research on the Educational Antecedents of School Effects." Centre for Cognitive and Ethnographic Studies, McGill University, Toronto, Canada. Processed.

Foster, P. J. 1965. "The Vocational School Fallacy in Development Planning." In C. A. Anderson and M. J. Bowman, eds., *Education and Economic Development*. Chicago: Aldine.

———. 1982. "The Educational Policies of Postcolonial States." In Lascelles Anderson and Douglas M. Windham, eds., *Education and Development: Issues in the Analysis and Planning of Post-Colonial Societies*. Lexington, Mass.: Lexington Books.

*———. 1985. "Education in Sub-Saharan Africa: Some Preliminary Issues." Education and Training Department, World Bank, Washington, D.C. Processed.

*Fryer, Michelle L. 1986. "Females as Beneficiaries of Bank Operations in Africa." Education and Training Department, World Bank, Washington, D.C. Processed.

Fuller, Bruce. 1985. "Raising School Quality in Developing Countries: What Investments Boost Learning?" Education and Training Department Discussion Paper EDT7. World Bank, Washington, D.C. Processed.

Haddad, Wadi D. 1978. *Educational Effects of Class Size*. World Bank Staff Working Paper 280. Washington, D.C.

———. 1979. *Educational and Economic Effects of Promotion and Repetition Practices*. World Bank Staff Working Paper 319. Washington, D.C.

_____. 1985. "Teacher Training: A Review of World Bank Experience." Education and Training Department Discussion Paper EDT21. World Bank, Washington, D.C. Processed.

Hakuta, Kenji, and Catherine Snow. 1986. "The Role of Research in Policy Decisions about Bilingual Education." In *A Report of the Compendium of Papers on the Topic of Bilingual Education of the Committee on Education and Labor, House of Representatives, 99th Congress, 2d Session, 28–40*. Gainesville: Univeristy of Florida, Teacher Training Project for Bilingual and English to Speakers of Other Languages.

Haveman, Robert H., and Barbara L. Wolfe. 1984. "Schooling and Economic Well-Being: The Role of Non-Market Effects." *Journal of Human Resources* 19 (3): 377–407.

Hawes, Hugh, and T. Coombe, eds. 1986. *Education Priorities and Aid Responses in Sub-Saharan Africa*. London: Institute of Education, University of London.

Heyneman, Stephen P. 1980a. *The Evaluation of Human Capital in Malawi*. World Bank Staff Working Paper 420. Washington, D.C.

_____. 1980b. "Instruction in the Mother Tongue: The Question of Logistics." *Journal of Canadian and International Education* 9 (2): 88–94.

_____. 1983. "Education during a Period of Austerity: Uganda, 1971–1981." *Comparative Education Review* 27 (October): 403–13.

Heyneman, Stephen P., and Dean Jamison. 1980. "Textbook Availability and Other Determinants of Student Learning in Uganda." *Comparative Education Review* 24 (June): 206–20.

Heyneman, Stephen P., and William Loxley. 1983. "The Effect of Primary-School Quality on Achievement across Twenty-nine High- and Low-Income Countries." *American Journal of Sociology* 88, no. 6 (June): 1162–94.

Hicks, Norman, and Jahangir Boroumand. 1980. *Economic Growth and Human Resources*. World Bank Staff Working Paper 408. Washington, D.C.

*Hinchliffe, Keith. 1985. *Issues Related to Higher Education in Sub-Saharan Africa*. World Bank Staff Working Paper 780. Washington, D.C.

*_____. 1986. "The Monetary and Non-Monetary Returns to Education in Africa." Education and Training Department Discussion Paper EDT46. World Bank, Washington, D.C. Processed.

Horn, Robin, and Ana-Maria Arriagada. 1986. "The Educational Attainment of the World's Population: Three Decades of Progress." Education and Training Department Discussion Paper EDT37. World Bank, Washington, D.C. Processed.

Houle, Cyril. 1973. *The External Degree*. San Francisco, Calif.: Jossey-Bass.

Huffman, Wallace, and Joseph A. Klock. Forthcoming. "Assistance for Education." In Anne O. Krueger, C. Michalopoulos, and Vernon W. Ruttan, eds., *The Impact of Development Assistance to LDCs*. Baltimore, Md.: Johns Hopkins University Press.

ILO (International Labour Organisation). 1982. *Paper Qualification Syndrome and Unemployment of School Leavers*. Addis Ababa.

Imhoof, Maurice, and Philip R. Christensen, eds. 1986. *Teaching English by Radio: Interactive Radio in Kenya*. Washington, D.C.: Academy for Educational Development, Inc.

Inkeles, Alex, and D. H. Smith. 1974. *Becoming Modern: Individual Change in Six Developing Countries*. Cambridge, Mass.: Harvard University Press.

Jamison, Dean. 1982. "Reduced Class Size and Other Alternatives for Improving Schools: An Economist's View." In Gene V. Glass, Leonard S. Cahen, Mary Lee Smith, and Nikola N. Filby, eds., *School Class Size*. Beverly Hills, Calif.: Sage Publications.

Jamison, Dean, and Peter Moock. 1984. "Farmer Education and Farm Efficiency in Nepal: The Role of Schooling, Extension Services, and Cognitive Skills." *World Development* 12 (January): 67–86.

Jimenez, Emmanuel. 1986a. "The Public Subsidization of Education and Health in Developing Countries: A Review of Equity and Efficiency." *World Bank Research Observer* 1, no. 1 (January): 111–30.

_____. 1986b. "The Structure of Educational Costs: Multiproduct Cost Functions for Primary and Secondary Schools in Latin America." *Economics of Education Review* 5: 25–40.

Kaluba, L. H., and P. P. W. Achola. 1985. "Community Financing of Schools in Commonwealth SADCC Countries, A Non-Government View from Zambia." Paper presented at the Commonwealth Regional Workshop with Special Reference to Southern Africa, Gaborone, Botswana. Commonwealth Secretariat, London. Processed.

King, Kenneth. 1986. "Manpower, Technology, and Employment in Africa: Internal and External Policy Agendas." In Robert J. Berg and Jennifer Seymour Whitaker, eds., *Strategies for African Development*. Berkeley: University of California Press.

*Knight, J. B., and Richard H. Sabot. 1986. "Overview of Educational Expansion, Productivity and Inequality: A Comparative Analysis of the East African Natural Experiment." Education and

Training Department Discussion Paper EDT48. World Bank, Washington, D.C. Processed.

*Lau, Lawrence, and Dean Jamison. Forthcoming. "Education and Economic Growth in Sub-Saharan Africa." Population and Human Resources Department, World Bank, Washington, D.C. Processed.

Lee, Kiong Hock. Forthcoming. "Universal Primary Education: An African Dilemma." Education and Training Department Discussion Paper. World Bank, Washington, D.C. Processed.

Lindauer, D. L. 1984. "Public Sector Pay in Africa: An Analytical Framework." Country Policy Department, World Bank, Washington, D.C. Processed.

Lindauer, D. L., O. A. Meesook, and P. Suebsaeng. 1986. "Government Wage Policy in Africa: Summary of Findings and Policy Issues." Country Policy Department Discussion Paper 1986-24. World Bank, Washington, D.C. Processed.

Livingstone, Ian D. 1985. "Perceptions of the Intended and Implemented Mathematics Curriculum." Urbana: University of Illinois. Processed.

Lockheed, Marlaine, Dean Jamison, and Lawrence Lau. 1980. "Farmer Education and Farm Efficiency: A Survey." *Economic Development and Cultural Change* 29 (October): 37–76.

Lucas, R. E. B., and O. Stark. 1985. "Motivations to Remit: Evidence from Botswana." *Journal of Political Economy* 93 (October): 901–18.

MacMillan, Deborah L. 1981. "Language Policies for African Primary Education: Summary of the Anglophone Research Literature." Population and Human Resources Division Discussion Paper 81-28. World Bank, Washington, D.C. Processed.

Malawi, Government of. 1984. *The Impact of the Increase in School Fees on Primary School Enrollments in 1983.* Lilongwe: Ministry of Education and Culture.

Mass, Jacob van Lutsenburg, and Geert Criel. 1982. *Distribution of Primary School Enrollments in Eastern Africa.* World Bank Staff Working Paper 511. Washington, D.C.

Mbanefoh, G. F. 1980. "Sharing the Cost and Benefits of University Education in Nigeria." *International Journal of Educational Development* 1 (July): 231–43.

McMahon, Walter W. 1987. "The Relation of Education and R&D to Productivity Growth in the Developing Countries of Africa." *Economics of Education Review* 6 (2): 183–94.

Michael, Robert. 1982. "Measuring Non-Monetary Benefits of Education: A Survey." In Walter W. McMahon and Terry G. Geske, eds., *Financing Education: Overcoming Inefficiency and Inequity.* Urbana: University of Illinois Press.

Middleton, John, Habteselassie Woldemariam, and Carolyn Mayo-Brown. 1986. "Management in World Bank Education Projects: Analysis of Experience." Education and Training Department Discussion Paper EDT42. World Bank, Washington, D.C. Processed.

*Millot, Benoit, François Orivel, and Jean-Bernard Rasera. 1987. "L'aide extérieure à l'éducation en Afrique sub-saharienne." Education and Training Department Discussion Paper EDT65. World Bank, Washington, D.C. Processed.

Mingat, Alain. 1985. "La diversification des sources de financement de l'enseignement supérieur en Afrique francophone." Material for a seminar at the Economic Development Institute, World Bank, Washington, D.C. Processed.

Mingat, Alain, and George Psacharopoulos. 1985. "Financing Education in Sub-Saharan Africa: Issues of Equity and Efficiency of Investment—Some Policy Alternatives." *Finance & Development* 22 (March): 35–38.

Mingat, Alain, and Jee-Peng Tan. 1985a. "Improving the Quantity-Quality Mix in Education: A Simulation of Policy Tradeoffs." Education and Training Department Discussion Paper EDT15. World Bank, Washington, D.C. Processed.

_____. 1985b. "Subsidization of Higher Education versus Expansion of Primary Enrollments: What Can a Shift of Resources Achieve in Sub-Saharan Africa?" *International Journal of Educational Development* 5 (4): 259–68.

_____. 1986. "Expanding Education through User Charges: What Can Be Achieved in Malawi and Other LDCs?" *Economics of Education Review* 5 (3): 273–86.

_____. Forthcoming. "The Economic Returns to Investment in Project-Related Training: Some Evidence from World Bank Projects." *International Review of Education* 34 (2).

Moock, Peter. 1981. "Education and Technical Efficiency in Small-Farm Production." *Economic Development and Cultural Change* 29 (July): 723–39.

Mundangepfupfu, R. M. 1986. "Economies in the Provision of Facilities for Teaching Secondary School Science." Economic Development Institute, Education and Training Design Division, World Bank, Washington, D.C. Processed.

Neumann, Peter H. 1980. *Publishing for Schools: Textbooks and the Less Developed Countries.* World Bank Staff Working Paper 398. Washington, D.C.

Noor, Abdun. 1985. "Strengthening Educational

Management: A Review of World Bank Assistance, 1963–83." Education and Training Department, World Bank, Washington, D.C. Processed.

Oduntan, S. O. 1975. "The Health of Nigerian Children of School Age." Regional Office, World Health Organization, Brazzaville.

Organization of African Unity. 1981. *Lagos Plan of Action for the Economic Development of Africa 1980–2000.* Geneva: International Institute for Labour Studies.

———. 1985. *Africa's Priority Programme for Economic Recovery 1986–1990.* Twenty-first Session of the Assembly of Heads of State and Government of the Organization of African Unity. Addis Ababa.

Osundare, Niyi. 1983. "Agonies of a Tottering Tower." *West Africa* (September 12): 2121–22.

Paul, Samuel. 1982. *Managing Development Programs: The Lesson of Success.* Boulder, Colo.: Westview.

Perraton, Hilary, ed. 1982. *Alternative Routes to Formal Education: Distance Teaching for School Equivalency.* Baltimore, Md.: Johns Hopkins University Press.

*Perraton, Hilary, Clifford H. Block, Michelle L. Fryer, Peter L. Spain, and Michael Young. 1986. "Distance Education: An Economic and Educational Assessment of Its Potential for Africa." Education and Training Department Discussion Paper EDT43. World Bank, Washington, D.C. Processed.

Psacharopoulos, George. 1982. "The Economics of Higher Education in Developing Countries." *Comparative Education Review* 26 (June): 139–59.

———. 1984. "The Contribution of Education to Economic Growth: International Comparisons." In John Kendrick, ed., *International Productivity Comparisons and the Causes of Slowdown.* Cambridge, Mass.: Ballinger.

———. 1985. "Returns to Education: A Further International Update and Implications." *Journal of Human Resources* 20 (Fall): 583–604.

———. 1987. "To Vocationalize or Not to Vocationalize? That Is the Curriculum Question." *International Review of Education* 33 (2): 187–212.

Psacharopoulos, George, and Ana-Maria Arriagada. 1986. "The Educational Attainment of the Labor Force: An International Comparison." *ILO Review* 125, no. 5 (September–October): 561–74.

Psacharopoulos, George, and William Loxley. 1985. *Diversified Secondary Education and Development: Evidence from Colombia and Tanzania.* Baltimore, Md.: Johns Hopkins University Press.

Psacharopoulos, George, and Maureen Woodhall. 1985. *Education for Development: An Analysis of Investment Choices.* New York: Oxford University Press.

Rogers, D. C. 1972. "Student Loan Programs and the Returns to Investment in Higher Levels of Education in Kenya." *Economic Development and Cultural Change* 2 (January): 243–59.

Romain, Ralph. 1985. "Lending in Primary Education: Bank Performance Review, 1962–1983." Education and Training Department Discussion Paper EDT20. World Bank, Washington, D.C. Processed.

Schultz, T. P. 1975. "The Value of the Ability to Deal with Disequilibria." *Journal of Economic Literature* 13 (September): 827–46.

———. 1985. "School Expenditures and Enrollments, 1960–1980: The Effect of Income, Prices and Population Growth." Discussion Paper 487. Economic Growth Center, Yale University, New Haven, Conn.

Smock, A. C. 1981. *Women's Education in Developing Countries: Opportunities and Outcomes.* New York: Praeger.

*Somerset, H. C. A. 1985. "The Quality of Elementary Education in Africa: Some Key Issues." Education and Training Department, World Bank, Washington, D.C. Processed.

———. 1987. "Examination Reforms: The Kenya Experience." Education and Training Department Discussion Paper EDT64. World Bank, Washington, D.C. Processed.

Stoikov, V. L. 1975. *The Economics of Recurrent Education and Training.* Geneva: International Labour Office.

Stromquist, N. P. 1986. *Empowering Women through Knowledge: Policies and Practices in International Cooperation in Basic Education.* Palo Alto, California: School of Education, Stanford University.

Tan, Jee-Peng. 1985. "Private Direct Cost of Secondary Schooling in Tanzania." *International Journal of Development Economics* 5 (1): 1–10.

Tan, Jee-Peng, Kiong Hock Lee, and Alain Mingat. 1984. *User Charges for Education: The Ability and Willingness to Pay in Malawi.* World Bank Staff Working Paper 661. Washington, D.C.

Thevenin, Tania. 1981. "Pedagogical Implications of Language Policy in African Schools: A Review of the Francophone Literature." Population and Human Resources Division Discussion Paper 81-29. World Bank, Washington, D.C. Processed.

Thobani, Mateen. 1983. *Charging User Fees for Social Services: The Case of Education in Malawi.* World Bank Staff Working Paper 572. Washington, D.C.

Tipple, Graham, and Susan Tipple. 1983. "The Use of Student Protest." *West Africa* (July 18): 1654–55.

Unesco (United Nations Educational, Scientific and Cultural Organization). 1961. *Final Report*. Conference of African States on the Development of Education in Africa, Addis Ababa, May. Paris.

———. 1976. *Education in Africa: Evolution, Reforms, Prospects*. Conference of Ministers of Education of African Member States, Lagos, January 27–February 4, 1976. Paris.

———. 1982a. *Development of Education in Africa: A Statistical Review*. Conference of Ministers of Education and Those Responsible for Economic Planning in African Member States, Harare, June 28–July 3, 1982. Paris.

———. 1982b. *Education and Endogenous Development in Africa: Trends—Problems—Prospects*. Paris.

———. 1983. *African Languages as Instructional Media*. Dakar: Unesco Regional Office for Education in Africa.

———. 1985. *African Community Languages and Their Use in Literacy and Education*. Dakar: Unesco Regional Office for Education in Africa.

UNICEF (United Nations Children's Fund). 1985. *Within Human Reach: A Future for Africa's Children*. New York.

United Nations. Annual, 1966–85. *Yearbook of National Accounts Statistics*. New York.

———. 1986. *Programme of Action for African Economic Recovery and Development 1986–1990*. A/RES/S-13/2. New York.

Wheeler, David. 1980. *Human Resource Development and Economic Growth in Developing Countries: A Simultaneous Model*. World Bank Staff Working Paper 407. Washington, D.C.

*Windham, Douglas M. 1987. "Internal Efficiency and the African School." Education and Training Department Discussion Paper EDT47. World Bank, Washington, D.C. Processed.

Wolff, Laurence. 1985. *Controlling the Costs of Education in Eastern Africa: A Review of Data, Issues, and Policies*. World Bank Staff Working Paper 702. Washington, D.C.

Woodhall, Maureen. 1983. *Student Loans as a Means of Financing Higher Education: Lessons from International Experience*. World Bank Staff Working Paper 599. Washington, D.C.

World Bank. 1980a. *Education*. Sector Policy Paper. Washington, D.C.

———. 1980b. *World Development Report 1980*. New York: Oxford University Press.

———. 1981. *Accelerated Development in Sub-Saharan Africa: An Agenda for Action*. Washington, D.C.

———. 1984. *Toward Sustained Development in Sub-Saharan Africa: A Joint Program of Action*. Washington, D.C.

———. 1986a. *Financing Adjustment with Growth in Sub-Saharan Africa, 1986–90*. Washington, D.C.

———. 1986b. *Population Growth and Policies in Sub-Saharan Africa*. Washington, D.C.

———. 1986c. *Financing Education in Developing Countries: An Exploration of Policy Options*. Washington, D.C.

Young, Michael, H. Perraton, J. Jenkins, and T. Dodds. 1980. *Distance Teaching for the Third World: The Lion and the Clockwork Mouse*. London: Routledge.

Appendix

List of Tables *121*
Introduction *123*
    Key to Tables *124*
    Alphabetical List of Countries *124*
    Countries Classified by Linguistic and Economic Status *124*
Tables
    A. Education Indicators *125*
    B. Economic and Social Indicators *153*
    C. Supplementary and Summary Tables *166*
Technical Notes
    A. Education Indicators *173*
    B. Economic and Social Indicators *179*
    C. Supplementary and Summary Tables *183*
    Data Sources *184*
Maps *following page 185*
    1. Total Population, 1984
    2. Population Density, 1984
    3. Language Groups, 1984
    4. Income Groupings, 1984
    5. Enrollment in Primary Schools, 1960
    6. Enrollment in Primary Schools, 1983

List of Tables

A. Education Indicators

A-1. Primary Enrollment   *125*
A-2. Secondary Enrollment   *126*
A-3. Distribution of Secondary Enrollment by Type of Education   *127*
A-4. Tertiary Enrollment   *128*
A-5. Distribution of Tertiary Enrollment by Field of Study, circa 1983   *129*
A-6. Total Enrollment   *130*
A-7. Gross Primary Enrollment Ratios   *131*
A-8. Gross Secondary Enrollment Ratios   *132*
A-9. Gross Tertiary Enrollment Ratios   *133*
A-10. Teachers and Schools   *134*
A-11. Student-Teacher Ratios   *135*
A-12. Student Flow and Indicators of Efficiency   *136*
A-13. Percentage of Students Enrolled in Private Schools   *137*
A-14. Total Public Expenditure on Education   *138*
A-15. Distribution of Total Public Expenditure on Education by Recurrent or Capital Component   *139*
A-16. Public Recurrent Expenditure on Education by Level of Education   *140*
A-17. Public Recurrent Expenditure per Primary Pupil   *141*
A-18. Public Recurrent Expenditure per Secondary Student   *142*
A-19. Public Recurrent Expenditure per Tertiary Student   *143*
A-20. Distribution of Public Recurrent Expenditure on Primary Schools by Purpose, circa 1983   *144*
A-21. Distribution of Public Recurrent Expenditure on Secondary Schools by Purpose, circa 1983   *145*
A-22. Distribution of Public Recurrent Expenditure on Tertiary Education by Purpose, circa 1983   *146*
A-23. Average Salaries of Primary and Secondary Teachers, circa 1983   *147*
A-24. External Aid to African Education and Training by Source, 1981–83 Average   *148*
A-25. Concessional Education Sector Aid from OECD and OPEC Members by Recipient Country, 1981–83 Average   *149*
A-26. External Education Sector Aid from OECD and OPEC Members by Level and Type of Education   *150*
A-27. External Education Sector Aid from OECD and OPEC Members by Purpose   *151*
A-28. External Public Debt of the Education Sector   *152*

B. Economic and Social Indicators

B-1. Basic Indicators   153
B-2. Languages of Sub-Saharan Africa   154
B-3. Population Growth and Projections   157
B-4. School-Age Population Growth and Projections   158
B-5. Demography and Fertility   159
B-6. Urbanization   160
B-7. Labor Force   161
B-8. Growth of Production   162
B-9. Central Government Expenditure   163
B-10. Disbursements of Official Development Assistance (ODA)   164
B-11. External Public Debt Service Ratios   165

C. Supplementary and Summary Tables

C-1. Selected Comparative Statistics for Countries with Fewer than a Half Million People   166
C-2. Summary Table: Enrollment Levels, Ratios, and Growth Rates, Selected Years, 1960–83   166
C-3. Estimated Average Number of Years of Education Attained by Working-Age Population   167
C-4. Adult Literacy   168
C-5. Cross-National Comparisons of Achievement in Mathematics, Reading, and Science   169
C-6. Countries Grouped by Gross Primary Enrollment Ratios   170
C-7. Enrollment Characteristics and Education Expenditure by Secondary Enrollment Group   171
C-8. Indicators of Unit Cost by Secondary Enrollment Group   172
C-9. Percentage of Nationals among Teaching Staff in Postprimary Education   172

Introduction

The appendix tables provide information on the principal features of educational, social, and economic development for thirty-nine countries in Sub-Saharan Africa. Excluded are Namibia and South Africa, all North African countries, and (with the exception of table C-1) six countries with populations of less than one-half million people in 1984 (Cape Verde, Comoros, Djibouti, Equatorial Guinea, São Tomé and Principe, and the Seychelles).

The education indicators in part A were calculated from data supplied by Unesco and supplemented with information from World Bank data files and country documentation. The social and economic indicators in part B are collected annually by the World Bank on its developing member countries, and the tables were prepared in collaboration with the Economic Analysis and Projections Department and the Population, Health and Nutrition Department of the World Bank. The data presented in part C supplement or summarize those displayed in parts A and B. Socioeconomic statistics are given through 1984, but internationally comparable educational statistics were available only through 1983. This is an unfortunate end-year because, in many respects, 1983 was the worst year of the economic crisis, and it is possible that a number of educational indicators have subsequently begun to improve.

Although considerable effort has been made to standardize the data, statistical methods, coverage, practices, and definitions differ from country to country. Moreover, weaknesses in developing countries' statistical systems limit the availability and reliability of the data. The indicators should, therefore, be used to characterize the trends and major differences between countries and country groups rather than to show precise quantitative measures of those trends and differences.

The format of parts A and B follows that used in the Bank's *World Development Report*. Countries are classified into two major economic groups—low-income and middle-income economies. The twenty-five countries with per capita incomes of less than $400 are classified as low-income economies. The fourteen middle-income economies are those with per capita incomes of greater than $400. The economies are further classified to distinguish low-income semiarid from other low-income economies and middle-income oil exporters from middle-income oil importers.

Within each economic group, countries are listed in ascending order of income per capita with the exceptions of Angola, Chad, and Mozambique, for which per capita income could not be calculated. The alphabetical list below shows the table reference number of each country.

Summary measures of all indicators appear in the bands within each table. The letter "w" following a summary measure indicates a weighted mean; the letter "m," a median; and the letter "t," a total. Readers should exercise caution in comparing the summary measures for different indicators, groups, and years or periods. Data coverage is not uniform for all indicators, and variations around central tendencies can be large. The technical notes, which outline the methods, concepts, definitions, and data sources, should be referred to before using any of the data.

The tables also provide summary measures for countries grouped by language. Those that could not be classified as either Anglophone or Francophone are included in the "Other" category.

Key to Tables

In the tables, the following symbols are used:
- . Not available.
- (.) Less than half the unit shown.
- ./. Data included in another category.
- * Data are for a year other than that specified.
- † Estimated or provisional data.
- w Weighted mean.
- m Median.
- t Total.

Because of rounding, the totals and subtotals shown in the tables may not correspond to the sums of their components. For data comparability and coverage, see the technical notes following the appendix tables.

Alphabetical List of Countries

In the appendix tables countries are listed in their economic group in ascending order of GNP per capita. For Angola, Chad, and Mozambique, however, no GNP per capita could be calculated, and each country is listed at the end of its appropriate group. The reference numbers in the alphabetical list below reflect the order in the tables.

Country	#	Country	#
Angola	39	Malawi	9
Benin	17	Mali	1
Botswana	33	Mauritania	26
Burkina Faso	2	Mauritius	34
Burundi	12	Mozambique	25
Cameroon	36	Niger	3
Central African Rep.	15	Nigeria	35
Chad	6	Rwanda	18
Congo	37	Senegal	24
Cote d'Ivoire	30	Sierra Leone	20
Ethiopia	7	Somalia	5
Gabon	38	Sudan	23
Gambia	4	Swaziland	32
Ghana	22	Tanzania	11
Guinea	21	Togo	14
Guinea-Bissau	10	Uganda	13
Kenya	19	Zaire	8
Liberia	27	Zambia	28
Lesotho	29	Zimbabwe	31
Madagascar	16		

Countries Classified by Linguistic and Economic Status

Francophone (n = 18)	Anglophone (n = 16)	Other (n = 5)
Low-income semiarid (n = 6)		
2 Burkina Faso	4 Gambia	5 Somalia
6 Chad		
1 Mali		
3 Niger		
Low-income other (n = 19)		
17 Benin	22 Ghana	7 Ethiopia
12 Burundi	19 Kenya	10 Guinea-Bissau
15 Central African Republic	9 Malawi	25 Mozambique
21 Guinea	20 Sierra Leone	
16 Madagascar	23 Sudan	
18 Rwanda	11 Tanzania	
24 Senegal	13 Uganda	
14 Togo		
8 Zaire		
Middle-income oil importers (n = 9)		
30 Côte d'Ivoire	33 Botswana	
26 Mauritania	27 Liberia	
	29 Lesotho	
	34 Mauritius	
	32 Swaziland	
	28 Zambia	
	31 Zimbabwe	
Middle-income oil exporters (n = 5)		
36 Cameroon	35 Nigeria	39 Angola
37 Congo, The		
38 Gabon		

Table A-1. Primary Enrollment

		Total (thousands)					Average annual growth rate (percent)		Females as a percentage of total		
		1960	1970	1980	1983*		1960–80	1980–83	1960	1970	1983*
Low-income economies	t	6796	13185	25803	28064	w	6.9	2.8	31	38	43
						m	6.6	3.1	30	36	40
Low-income semiarid	t	250	648	1276	1389	w	8.5	2.9	24	32	35
						m	8.7	3.9	29	33	36
1 Mali		65	204	291	293		7.8	0.2	28	36	37
2 Burkina Faso		57	105	202	277		6.6	11.1	29	37	37
3 Niger		27	89	229	250		11.4	3.0	30	35	36
4 Gambia		7	17	43	61		9.6	11.8	31	31	38
5 Somalia		23	50	272	221		13.2	−6.7	25	24	36
6 Chad		72	183	239	289		6.2	4.8	11	25	27
Low-income other	t	6546	12537	24527	26674	w	6.8	2.8	32	39	44
						m	6.1	3.1	31	37	41
7 Ethiopia		224	655	2131	2497		11.9	5.4	24	31	38
8 Zaire		1550	3088	4207	4655		5.1	3.4	27	37	43
9 Malawi		285	363	810	847		5.4	1.5	36	37	42
10 Guinea-Bissau		18	28	75	75		7.4	0.2	30	30	33
11 Tanzania		455	856	3368	3553		10.5	1.8	34	40	49
12 Burundi		92	182	176	301		3.3	19.6	24	33	40
13 Uganda		593	1110	1521	1617*		4.8	3.1	32	40	43*
14 Togo		103	229	506	457		8.3	−3.3	28	31	39
15 Central African Rep.		68	176	246	291		6.7	5.8	19	33	35
16 Madagascar		450	938	1311	1487†		5.5	4.3	44	46	48†
17 Benin		89	155	380	428*		7.5	6.2	28	31	33*
18 Rwanda		264	419	705	762		5.0	2.6	31	44	48
19 Kenya		781	1428	3927	4324		8.4	3.3	32	41	48
20 Sierra Leone		86	166	300	348		6.4	5.1	34	40	41
21 Guinea		97	191	258	284		5.0	2.5	26	32	32
22 Ghana		503	967	1417	1453		5.3	0.8	35	43	44
23 Sudan		344	826	1464	1599		7.5	3.0	27	38	41
24 Senegal		129	263	420	533		6.1	8.3	32	39	40
25 Mozambique		416	497	1307	1163		5.9	−3.8	38	34	43
Middle-income oil importers	t	1400	2571	4252	5566	w	5.7	9.4	42	44	47
						m	6.6	5.0	45	45	48
26 Mauritania		11	32	91	107*		11.0	8.9	19	28	39*
27 Liberia		59	120	227	230		7.0	0.4	29	33	40
28 Zambia		288	695	1042	1194		6.6	4.6	40	45	47
29 Lesotho		136	183	245	278*		3.0	6.5	62	60	58*
30 Côte d'Ivoire		239	503	1000	1160		7.4	5.1	26	36	41
31 Zimbabwe		484	736	1235	2131		4.8	14.6	45	45	48
32 Swaziland		34	69	112	130		6.1	5.0	50	49	50
33 Botswana		36	83	172	198		8.1	4.9	59	53	53
34 Mauritius		112	150	129	139		0.7	2.5	47	49	49
Middle-income oil exporters	t	3657	5215	17013	17715	w	8.0	1.4	36	38	46
						m	6.3	3.3	34	43	48
35 Nigeria		2913	3516	13788	14384		8.1	1.1	37	37	.
36 Cameroon		468	923	1379	1564		5.6	4.3	33	43	46
37 Congo, People's Rep.		116	241	391	423*		6.3	4.0	34	44	49*
38 Gabon		57	101	155	166*		5.1	3.3	38	48	49*
39 Angola		104	434	1301	1178*		13.5	−4.8	33	36	46*
Sub-Saharan Africa	t	11853	20971	47068	51345	w	7.1	2.9	34	39	44
						m	6.6	3.4	32	37	42
Francophone countries	t	3953	8022	12185	13727	w	5.8	4.1	30	38	42
						m	6.2	4.3	28	36	40
Anglophone countries	t	7117	11285	29799	32484	w	7.4	2.9	37	40	46
						m	6.5	3.2	35	41	47
Other	t	784	1665	5085	5134	w	9.8	0.3	33	33	40
						m	11.9	−3.8	30	31	38

* Figures with an asterisk are for 1982; those with a dagger are estimates. See the technical notes. Figures for Chad, Guinea, Nigeria, and Zimbabwe are for 1984.

Table A-2. Secondary Enrollment

		Total (thousands) 1960	1970	1980	1983*		Average annual growth rate (percent) 1960–80	1980–83	Females as a percentage of total 1960	1970	1983*
Low-income economies	t	510	1800	4497	6014	w	11.5	10.2	25	30	33
						m	11.4	8.9	26	27	31
Low-income semiarid	t	15	75	211	284	w	14.3	10.3	18	21	28
						m	14.1	11.2	17	23	30
1 Mali		5	35	68	76		14.4	4.2	17	22	28
2 Burkina Faso		3	11	28	36		11.7	9.3	27	28	34
3 Niger		1	7	39	48		18.1	7.4	17	27	27
4 Gambia		2	5	10	14		9.1	14.1	26	24	31
5 Somalia		2	7	44	63		16.1	13.1	9	16	34
6 Chad		2	11	24	46		13.8	17.4	7	8	15
Low-income other	t	495	1725	4285	5730	w	11.4	10.2	25	31	33
						m	10.0	6.5	27	28	33
7 Ethiopia		26	135	439	580		15.3	9.7	14	25	36
8 Zaire		55	248	1293	2152		17.1	18.5	24	22	28
9 Malawi		3	12	20	24		9.6	6.3	22	27	29
10 Guinea-Bissau		1	4	5	10		6.4	26.1	40	36	19
11 Tanzania		22	45	79	82		6.5	1.3	32	29	35
12 Burundi		3	8	19	26		9.5	11.6	37	20	37
13 Uganda		28	77	128	145*		8.0	6.4	21	25	33*
14 Togo		5	22	133	102		17.4	−8.6	23	22	25
15 Central African Rep.		2	11	45	58		16.6	8.9	15	19	26
16 Madagascar		29	113	189	225†		9.8	5.7	33	40†	44†
17 Benin		5	18	90	125*		15.7	17.7	27	30	28*
18 Rwanda		6	10	11	15		2.6	11.4	35	33	34
19 Kenya		26	136	428	517		15.0	6.5	32	30	40
20 Sierra Leone		8	35	57	78		10.0	11.0	27	28	28
21 Guinea		10	63	98	98		12.4	−0.2	10	21	28
22 Ghana		191	552	668	754		6.5	4.1	27	38	37
23 Sudan		45	133	384	507		11.4	9.7	14	28	41
24 Senegal		13	59	96	114		10.4	5.9	27	29	33
25 Mozambique		15	43	103	121		10.0	5.6	36	38	30
Middle-income oil importers	t	79	262	642	1042	w	11.1	17.5	30	33	37
						m	15.1	6.0	32	39	40
26 Mauritania		1	4	22	28*		19.8	12.2	5	11	24*
27 Liberia		3	17	55	53		15.1	−0.7	16	23	29
28 Zambia		5	56	102	115		16.0	4.1	23	33	36*
29 Lesotho		3	7	25	29*		10.9	8.2	53	54	60*
30 Côte d'Ivoire		12	70	238	269		16.0	4.1	12	22	29
31 Zimbabwe		28	50	75	416		5.0	53.6	36	39	40
32 Swaziland		2	8	24	29		14.1	6.5	45	44	49
33 Botswana		1	5	21	25		18.5	6.0	48	46	54
34 Mauritius		24	45	82	79		6.4	−1.1	32	40	47
Middle-income oil exporters	t	205	535	3007	4063	w	14.4	10.6	22	32	38
						m	14.2	5.5	21	30	39
35 Nigeria		167	357	2364	3400		14.2	9.5	21	32	.
36 Cameroon		16	77	234	289		14.5	7.2	17	29	38
37 Congo, People's Rep.		6	34	188	210*		18.8	5.5	28	30	41*
38 Gabon		3	10	29	33*		12.3	5.5	16	29	40*
39 Angola		14	58	191	132*		14.2	−16.8	40	42	33*
Sub-Saharan Africa	t	793	2597	8146	11119	w	12.4	10.9	25	31	34
						m	13.8	6.5	26	29	33
Francophone countries	t	178	811	2845	3946	w	14.9	11.5	24	26	31
						m	14.4	7.3	20	25	29
Anglophone countries	t	558	1539	4520	6268	w	11.0	11.5	25	34	39
						m	10.5	6.4	27	31	37
Other	t	58	247	781	906	w	13.9	5.1	26	31	34
						m	14.2	9.7	36	36	33

* Figures with an asterisk are for 1982; those with a dagger are estimates. See the technical notes. Figures for Chad, Nigeria, and Zimbabwe are for 1984.

Table A-3. Distribution of Secondary Enrollment by Type of Education

| | | \multicolumn{6}{c|}{Percentage of all secondary students enrolled in:} | \multicolumn{6}{c|}{Percentage of all female secondary students enrolled in:} |
| | | General | | Teacher training | | Vocational/ technical | | General | | Teacher training | | Vocational/ technical | |
		1970	1983*	1970	1983*	1970	1983*	1970	1983*	1970	1983*	1970	1983*
Low-income economies	w	85	93	7	3	8	4	86	94	7	3	7	3
	m	90	92	3	3	9	5	88	92	3	2	5	6
Low-income semiarid	w	89	91	3	2	8	7	89	87	3	3	8	10
	m	88	92	4	2	7	6	90	87	3	1	4	8
1 Mali		86	92	5	4	10	5	88	86	4	3	9	10
2 Burkina Faso		82	88	3	1	15	12	73	83	1	(.)	25	16
3 Niger		91	96	7	2	3	2	88	.	12	.	(.)	.
4 Gambia		94	93	3	1	4	6	96	91	3	1	1	8
5 Somalia		96	85	1	3	3	12	97	87	1	5	2	8
6 Chad		86	94	4	0	10	5	92	94	3	(.)	5	6
Low-income other	w	85	93	7	3	8	4	85	94	8	3	7	3
	m	90	91	3	3	9	5	88	93	5	2	6	4
7 Ethiopia		94	.	2	.	5	.	91	.	1	.	8	.
8 Zaire		75	.	16	.	10	.	72	.	18	.	9	.
9 Malawi		91	92	7	6	2	3	89	92	11	8	(.)	(.)
10 Guinea-Bissau		78	91	9	7	13	3	82	97	9	3	9	(.)
11 Tanzania		92	87	8	12	(.)	1	88	87	12	12	(.)	1
12 Burundi		49	57	38	30	14	14	33	53	65	38	1	10
13 Uganda		84	91*	8	6*	7	3*	.	91*	.	8*	.	1*
14 Togo		90	94	1	0	10	6	83	94	(.)	(.)	16	5
15 Central African Rep.		86	94	2	1	12	5	75	87	5	1	20	12
16 Madagascar		90	.	2	.	9	.	93	.	2	.	6	.
17 Benin		96	.	1	.	3	.	98	.	(.)	.	1	.
18 Rwanda		72	37	16	37	12	26	66	21	18	49	16	31
19 Kenya		93	96	5	3	2	2	93	96	7	3	(.)	2
20 Sierra Leone		96	.	2	.	2	.	97	.	2	.	1	.
21 Guinea		95	92	2	1	3	7	95	89	2	2	3	9
22 Ghana		60	96	17	2	23	2	56	98	19	2	25	(.)
23 Sudan		97	94	2	2	1	5	98	95	2	2	(.)	3
24 Senegal		90	91	1	1	9	8	88	93	1	(.)	11	7
25 Mozambique		62	87	3	3	35	10	.	93	.	1	.	6
Middle-income oil importers	w	93	94	2	5	5	1	93	98	3	1	4	1
	m	92	95	3	1	4	3	94	95	4	1	5	2
26 Mauritania		91	92*	9	4*	(.)	5*	.	95*	.	4*	.	2*
27 Liberia		92	95	2	1	5	4	94	95	2	1	5	4
28 Zambia		93	95	3	3	3	2	94	94	4	4	2	2
29 Lesotho		82	97*	10	(.)*	8	3*	80	97*	11	(.)*	8	3*
30 Côte d'Ivoire		90	85	2	14	7	1	90	.	3	.	7	.
31 Zimbabwe		99	100	(.)	(.)	2	(.)	97	100	(.)	(.)	3	(.)
32 Swaziland		95	98	3	1	2	1	94	.	5	.	1	.
33 Botswana		75	89	5	4	19	7	77	89	6	6	16	5
34 Mauritius		.	99	.	(.)	.	1	.	100	.	(.)	.	(.)
Middle-income oil exporters	w	81	89	7	2	12	9	82	78	6	2	12	20
	m	82	89	3	2	16	10	85	73	3	1	12	13
35 Nigeria		82	90	9	2	9	8	85	.	8	.	7	.
36 Cameroon		73	76	4	1	23	23	68	73	3	1	29	26
37 Congo, People's Rep.		89	89*	2	1*	10	10*	88	86*	1	1*	11	13*
38 Gabon		83	68*	1	13*	16	19*	87	73*	1	14*	12	13*
39 Angola		76	95*	3	2*	21	3*	79	.	5	.	16	.
Sub-Saharan Africa	w	85	91	6	3	9	6	85	92	7	3	8	5
	m	90	92	3	2	8	5	88	93	3	2	7	5
Francophone countries	w	83	85	7	5	10	10	83	82	7	3	10	15
	m	87	91	3	1	10	8	88	87	3	1	9	10
Anglophone countries	w	86	92	7	2	7	5	87	96	7	2	6	1
	m	92	95	5	2	3	3	94	95	5	2	2	2
Other	w	85	90	2	3	13	7	87	91	3	3	10	7
	m	78	89	3	3	13	7	86	93	3	3	8	6

* Figures with an asterisk are for 1982. See the technical notes.

Table A-4. Tertiary Enrollment

		Total (thousands)					Average annual growth rate (percent)		Females as a percentage of total		
		1960	1970	1980	1983*		1960–80	1980–83	1960	1970	1983*
Low-income economies	t	12	72	197	234	w	15.0	5.9	10	15	19
						m	13.0	5.3	12	13	21
Low-income semiarid	t	(.)	2	13	20	w	.	14.9	.	12	16
						m	.	21.3	.	13	17
1 Mali		(.)	0.7	5.1	5.8*		.	6.6	.	11	12*
2 Burkina Faso		(.)	0.2	1.6	3.4		.	28.6	.	15	22
3 Niger		(.)	(.)	1.4	2.5		.	21.3	.	.	22
4 Gambia		(.)	(.)	(.)	(.)		.	.	.	.	.
5 Somalia		0.1	1.0	2.9	3.0		18.3	1.1	13	13	11
6 Chad		(.)	(.)	2.0†	5.0†		.	35.7	.	.	.
Low-income other	t	12	70	184	214	w	14.6	5.2	10	15	19
						m	12.4	4.7	12	14	21
7 Ethiopia		0.9	4.5	14.4	16.0		14.9	3.6	5	8	11
8 Zaire		0.9	12.4	28.5	32.9		18.9	4.9	.	6	9
9 Malawi		(.)	1.1	2.2	2.4*		.	4.4	.	23	28*
10 Guinea-Bissau		(.)	(.)	(.)	(.)		.	.	.	.	.
11 Tanzania		(.)	2.0	5.0	6.2		.	7.4	.	17	17
12 Burundi		(.)	0.5	1.9	2.1		.	3.4	.	6	29
13 Uganda		1.3	4.2	5.9	7.3*		7.9	11.2	12	18	27*
14 Togo		(.)	0.9	4.8	4.0		.	−5.9	.	12	15
15 Central African Rep.		(.)	0.2	1.7	2.4		.	12.2	.	13	10
16 Madagascar		0.7	5.7	22.6	32.6*		19.0	20.1	23	32	.
17 Benin		(.)	0.3	4.0	6.3*		.	25.5	.	7	16*
18 Rwanda		(.)	0.6	1.2	1.4		.	5.3	.	9	14
19 Kenya		1.0	7.8	13.0	22.2		13.7	19.5	16	15	19
20 Sierra Leone		0.3	1.2	1.8	2.0†		9.4	3.6	11	16	25†
21 Guinea		(.)	2.0	18.3	13.2*		.	−7.8	.	8	22*
22 Ghana		1.5	5.4	15.5	12.9		12.4	−5.9	11	14	22
23 Sudan		4.0	14.3	28.7	37.5*		10.4	14.3	5	13	27*
24 Senegal		1.4	5.0	13.6	11.8		12.0	−4.6	17	17	21
25 Mozambique		(.)	2.0	1.0	1.1		.	3.2	.	44	36
Middle-income oil importers	t	1	15	47	56	w	19.2	5.8	20	24	31
						m	12.7	0.0	22	22	30
26 Mauritania		(.)	(.)	0.6	0.6*		.	(.)	.	.	10*
27 Liberia		0.5	1.1	4.9	3.5		12.1	−10.6	21	22	26†
28 Zambia		(.)	1.4	7.5	8.1*		.	3.9	.	15	22*
29 Lesotho		0.2	0.4	2.2	2.7		12.7	7.1	22	34	59
30 Côte d'Ivoire		0.3	4.4	19.6	17.9*		23.2	−4.4	11	14	18*
31 Zimbabwe		0.3	5.0	8.3	19.0		18.1	23.0	25	42	42
32 Swaziland		(.)	0.2	1.9	1.7		.	−3.6	.	39	41
33 Botswana		(.)	(.)	0.9	1.4		.	15.9	.	.	44
34 Mauritius		0.1	2.0	1.0	0.7		12.2	−11.2	.	5	30
Middle-income oil exporters	t	8	29	93	148	w	13.4	16.7	.	15	15
						m	15.6	10.8	.	15	15
35 Nigeria		7.0	22.0	69.7	120.0		12.2	14.5	7	15	.
36 Cameroon		(.)	2.7	11.5	13.3		.	5.0	.	8	14
37 Congo, People's Rep.		0.4	1.8	7.3	8.5*		15.6	7.9	7	5	14*
38 Gabon		(.)	0.2	2.0	3.0*		.	22.5	.	15	26*
39 Angola		0.1	2.3	2.2	2.7*		16.7	10.8	.	40	16*
Sub-Saharan Africa	t	21	116	337	437	w	14.9	9.1	10	16	21
						m	13.2	5.3	12	15	22
Francophone countries	t	4	38	148	167	w	20.2	4.1	16	13	15
						m	18.9	6.0	14	11	15
Anglophone countries	t	16	68	169	248	w	12.4	13.7	9	17	27
						m	12.2	7.1	12	16	27
Other	t	1	10	21	23	w	15.7	3.6	6	23	13
						m	16.7	3.4	9	27	14

* Figures with an asterisk are for 1982; those with a dagger are estimates. See the technical notes. Figures for Chad and Zimbabwe are for 1984.

Table A-5. Distribution of Tertiary Enrollment by Field of Study, circa 1983

		\multicolumn{4}{c}{Arts}	\multicolumn{5}{c}{Sciences}	Other	\multicolumn{3}{c}{Percentage of all females enrolled in:}
		All arts	Education	Social sciences	Commerce & business	All sciences	Natural sciences	Medical sciences	Math & engineering	Agriculture		Arts	Sciences	Other
Low-income economies	w	55	10	34	11	42	9	10	11	12	4	69	29	3
	m	63	12	39	9	35	5	8	10	8	(.)	75	22	(.)
Low-income semiarid	w	.	.	.	.	.	.	.	.	.	.	.	.	.
	m	.	.	.	.	.	.	.	.	.	.	.	.	.
1 Mali		71	32	21	18	29	(.)	6	12	10	(.)	80	20	(.)
2 Burkina Faso		72	./.	67	5	28	5	6	5	12	(.)	86	14	(.)
3 Niger		.	.	.	.	.	.	.	.	.	.	.	.	.
4 Gambia		.	.	.	.	.	.	.	.	.	.	.	.	.
5 Somalia		.	.	.	.	.	.	.	.	.	.	.	.	.
6 Chad		.	.	.	.	.	.	.	.	.	.	.	.	.
Low-income other	w	54	9	34	11	43	10	10	11	12	4	68	30	3
	m	58	13	39	9	37	9	8	10	7	(.)	75	24	(.)
7 Ethiopia		46	14	26	7	53	19	8	9	18	(.)	59	40	1
8 Zaire		.	.	.	.	.	.	.	.	.	.	.	.	.
9 Malawi		43	15	12	17	34	(.)	(.)	9	25	22	30	22	48
10 Guinea-Bissau		.	.	.	.	.	.	.	.	.	.	.	.	.
11 Tanzania		65	40	16	9	35	1	12	14	7	(.)	75	24	(.)
12 Burundi		69	11	39	19	29	5	8	11	5	2	.	.	.
13 Uganda		65	22	25	17	35	10	7	12	6	(.)	83	17	(.)
14 Togo		68	33	35	./.	32	14	8	6	4	(.)	82	18	(.)
15 Central African Rep.		86	24	56	7	14	3	5	2	3	(.)	93	7	(.)
16 Madagascar		55	2	46	7	45	14	17	12	1	(.)	.	.	.
17 Benin		73	14	47	12	27	5	8	8	5	(.)	82	18	(.)
18 Rwanda		55	9	47	./.	45	9	15	11	10	(.)	70	30	(.)
19 Kenya		29	12	9	8	48	5	6	17	20	23	.	.	.
20 Sierra Leone		.	.	.	.	.	.	.	.	.	.	.	.	.
21 Guinea		19	7	./.	12	81	13	5	9	54	(.)	34	66	(.)
22 Ghana		54	3	44	7	46	16	10	13	7	(.)	67	33	(.)
23 Sudan		73	3	46	24	26	1	6	9	9	1	77	19	4
24 Senegal		60	4	54	2	39	14	20	3	3	1	58	40	2
25 Mozambique		53	14	39	(.)	47	3	10	21	13	(.)	59	41	(.)
Middle-income oil importers	w	73	33	33	7	27	6	6	12	3	1	90	10	0
	m	68	27	26	16	28	7	3	13	2	1	83	13	(.)
26 Mauritania		.	.	.	.	.	.	.	.	.	.	.	.	.
27 Liberia		.	.	.	.	.	.	.	.	.	.	.	.	.
28 Zambia		58	26	16	17	41	8	7	24	2	1	83	17	(.)
29 Lesotho		.	.	.	.	.	.	.	.	.	.	.	.	.
30 Côte d'Ivoire		70	18	49	4	28	6	7	13	2	1	.	.	.
31 Zimbabwe		89	70	20	(.)	11	2	4	2	2	(.)	94	6	(.)
32 Swaziland		60	13	32	15	40	20	(.)	./.	20	(.)	78	22	(.)
33 Botswana		89	28	38	23	11	11	(.)	(.)	(.)	(.)	96	4	(.)
34 Mauritius		66	39	5	22	27	(.)	2	14	10	7	83	13	5
Middle-income oil exporters	w	62	15	40	7	39	13	11	11	4	(.)	.	.	.
	m	71	9	41	14	29	10	9	13	1	(.)	.	.	.
35 Nigeria		59	16	38	5	41	14	12	11	4	(.)	.	.	.
36 Cameroon		76	8	41	27	23	13	3	8	(.)	(.)	88	12	(.)
37 Congo, People's Rep.		84	14	69	./.	16	10	5	./.	1	(.)	75	25	(.)
38 Gabon		71	9	51	11	29	5	9	14	1	(.)	.	.	.
39 Angola		36	1	18	16	64	7	20	31	6	(.)	.	.	.
Sub-Saharan Africa	w	59	14	36	9	40	11	10	11	8	2	74	24	2
	m	65	14	39	12	34	7	7	11	6	(.)	79	20	(.)
Francophone countries	w	61	10	43	8	38	10	11	9	8	(.)	64	35	(.)
	m	71	11	47	11	29	8	8	9	4	(.)	81	19	(.)
Anglophone countries	w	60	17	33	10	37	9	9	12	7	3	80	17	3
	m	63	19	23	16	35	7	6	12	7	(.)	81	18	(.)
Other	w	46	12	26	8	55	17	9	13	16	(.)	59	40	(.)
	m	46	14	26	7	47	7	10	21	13	(.)	.	.	.

Table A-6. Total Enrollment

		Total (thousands)					Average annual growth rate (percent)		Females as a percentage of total enrollment		
		1960	1970	1980	1983*		1960–80	1980–83	1960	1970	1983*
Low-income economies	t	7318	15057	30496	34312	w	7.4	4.0	31	37	40
						m	7.0	3.7	29	34	38
Low-income semiarid	t	265	725	1500	1693	w	9.1	4.1	23	30	33
						m	9.0	5.0	28	32	35
1 Mali		70	239	364	375		8.6	1.0	27	34	35
2 Burkina Faso		60	116	231	316		7.0	11.1	29	36	36
3 Niger		28	96	269	300		12.0	3.7	29	34	34
4 Gambia		9	22	53	75		9.5	12.1	30	29	37
5 Somalia		25	59	318	287		13.6	−3.4	23	23	35
6 Chad		74	194	265	339		6.6	6.4	11	24	25
Low-income other	t	7053	14332	28996	32619	w	7.3	4.0	31	38	41
						m	6.7	3.6	31	36	39
7 Ethiopia		250	795	2584	3093		12.4	6.2	23	30	37
8 Zaire		1606	3349	5529	6839		6.4	7.3	27	36	38
9 Malawi		288	375	832	874		5.4	1.6	36	37	42
10 Guinea-Bissau		19	32	79	85		7.3	2.2	31	31	31
11 Tanzania		478	903	3451	3641		10.4	1.8	34	39	48
12 Burundi		96	191	197	330		3.7	18.8	25	32	40
13 Uganda		622	1191	1655	1770		5.0	3.4	32	39	42
14 Togo		109	251	645	563		9.3	−4.4	28	30	36
15 Central African Rep.		70	188	293	352		7.5	6.3	19	32	33
16 Madagascar		480	1057	1523	1743		5.9	4.6	43	45	.
17 Benin		94	174	474	560		8.4	8.6	28	31	32
18 Rwanda		270	430	717	778		5.0	2.8	31	44	48
19 Kenya		809	1571	4368	4863		8.8	3.6	32	40	47
20 Sierra Leone		95	202	359	428		6.9	6.1	33	38	38
21 Guinea		106	257	374	395		6.5	1.4	25	29	31
22 Ghana		696	1525	2101	2219		5.7	1.8	33	41	41
23 Sudan		392	973	1877	2144		8.1	4.5	25	36	41
24 Senegal		143	327	529	659		6.7	7.6	32	37	38
25 Mozambique		431	542	1411	1285		6.1	−3.1	38	34	41
Middle-income oil importers	t	1480	2848	4942	6664	w	6.2	10.5	41	43	45
						m	7.1	5.1	44	45	47
26 Mauritania		12	36	113	136		11.9	9.5	18	26	36
27 Liberia		62	138	287	287		7.9	0.0	28	32	38
28 Zambia		293	752	1151	1317		7.1	4.6	39	44	46
29 Lesotho		139	191	272	309		3.4	6.7	62	60	57
30 Côte d'Ivoire		251	577	1258	1446		8.4	4.8	26	34	38
31 Zimbabwe		513	791	1318	2566		4.8	18.1	44	45	47
32 Swaziland		36	78	138	160		6.9	5.2	50	48	49
33 Botswana		37	88	194	225		8.6	5.1	58	53	53
34 Mauritius		136	198	211	218		2.2	1.1	45	46	49
Middle-income oil exporters	t	3870	5779	20113	21926	w	8.6	2.9	36	38	45
						m	8.2	3.9	34	41	45
35 Nigeria		3086	3894	16221	17904		8.7	2.5	36	36	.
36 Cameroon		484	1002	1625	1866		6.2	4.7	32	41	44
37 Congo, People's Rep.		122	277	586	641		8.2	4.6	34	42	46
38 Gabon		60	111	187	201		5.9	3.9	37	46	47
39 Angola		117	495	1494	1313		13.6	−6.2	33	36	45
Sub-Saharan Africa	t	12667	23684	55551	62901	w	7.7	4.2	34	38	42
						m	7.1	4.6	32	36	40
Francophone countries	t	4134	8870	15177	17840	w	6.7	5.5	30	37	39
						m	6.9	4.7	28	34	36
Anglophone countries	t	7691	12892	34488	38999	w	7.8	4.2	36	39	45
						m	7.0	4.1	35	40	46
Other	t	843	1922	5886	6062	w	10.2	1.0	32	33	39
						m	12.4	−3.1	31	31	37

* Data in this column are rounded sums of data in tables A-1, A-2, and A-4. For some countries the year differs.

Table A-7. Gross Primary Enrollment Ratios

		\multicolumn{12}{c}{Number enrolled as a percentage of age group}
		\multicolumn{4}{c}{Total}	\multicolumn{4}{c}{Male}	\multicolumn{4}{c}{Female}
		1960	1970	1980	1983*	1960	1970	1980	1983*	1960	1970	1980	1983*
Low-income economies	w	31	46	64	64	43	57	74	73	19	34	53	56
	m	24	36	58	58	35	51	67	65	14	27	41	44
Low-income semiarid	w	10	19	28	27	15	27	36	36	4	12	19	19
	m	9	18	29	27	13	24	36	34	4	13	20	19
1 Mali		9	22	25	23	13	30	32	30	5	15	18	18
2 Burkina Faso		9	13	21	27	13	17	26	34	5	10	15	20
3 Niger		6	14	27	26	8	19	33	34	3	10	20	19
4 Gambia		14	24	52	68	20	34	68	85	9	15	36	51
5 Somalia		7	11	30	21	10	17	38	28	3	5	22	15
6 Chad		17	35	36†	38	29	52	52†	55	4	17	20†	21
Low-income other	w	34	50	69	69	47	61	79	78	21	37	57	61
	m	30	41	64	62	50	57	81	87	18	30	49	49
7 Ethiopia		7	16	35	38	11	23	46	46	4	10	23	29
8 Zaire		54	88	90	90	80	110	104	103	29	65	75	77
9 Malawi		38	36	61	58	50	46	74	68	26	26	49	48
10 Guinea-Bissau		24	39	67	62	35	57	95	87	14	23	41	39
11 Tanzania		24	34	93	87	33	41	100	91	16	27	86	84
12 Burundi		21	30	29	45	33	42	35	55	10	20	22	36
13 Uganda		47	58	58	57*	64	70	67	65*	30	30	42	49*
14 Togo		44	71	123	102	64	98	152	124	25	44	94	80
15 Central African Rep.		30	64	72	77	50	88	93	102	11	41	51	54
16 Madagascar		56	90	101	104†	63	99	111	110†	49	82	92	99†
17 Benin		26	36	64	67*	38	51	89	92*	15	22	40	43*
18 Rwanda		49	68	64	62	69	76	67	64	30	60	61	60
19 Kenya		47	58	104	100	64	67	109	104	30	48	99	97
20 Sierra Leone		20	34	45	54	27	40	55	64	14	27	36	44
21 Guinea		20	33	35	36	30	45	47	49	11	21	23	23
22 Ghana		46	64	73	79	60	73	81	89	32	54	65	70
23 Sudan		20	38	50	49	29	47	59	59	11	29	41	39
24 Senegal		27	41	46	53	37	51	55	63	18	32	36	42
25 Mozambique		51	47	75	79	64	62	87	91	39	31	64	68
Middle-income oil importers	w	55	70	85	99	64	78	93	105	47	62	76	92
	m	51	74	91	100	59	75	94	94	41	67	92	102
26 Mauritania		6	14	34	37*	11	20	44	45*	2	8	24	29*
27 Liberia		36	56	76	70	52	75	95	85	21	36	57	55
28 Zambia		51	90	98	100	61	99	103	105	40	80	92	95
29 Lesotho		92	87	102	110*	73	71	85	94*	109	101	120	126*
30 Côte d'Ivoire		43	58	75	77	59	71	92	92	25	45	58	62
31 Zimbabwe		74	74	88	131	83	81	94	136	66	66	82	127
32 Swaziland		57	87	106	111	58	91	107	114	57	83	105	109
33 Botswana		39	65	91	96	36	63	82	89	41	67	100	102
34 Mauritius		94	94	108	112	97	94	109	112	90	93	108	113
Middle-income oil exporters	w	42	46	101	94	55	56	115	131	31	35	87	112
	m	54	85	115	118	67	98	117	133	37	75	114	119
35 Nigeria		42	37	98	89	54	46	113	.	31	27	83	.
36 Cameroon		57	89	104	108	77	103	114	117	37	75	95	98
37 Congo, People's Rep.		81	130	160	163*	108	147	166	168*	55	114	155	159*
38 Gabon		54	85	115	118*	67	89	117	120*	41	81	114	117*
39 Angola		17	75	124	134*	23	98	132	146*	11	53	115	121*
Sub-Saharan Africa	w	36	48	76	75	48	59	87	80	24	36	64	63
	m	38	56	73	77	50	63	87	89	25	32	58	57
Francophone countries	w	38	60	69	71	53	75	81	82	23	46	57	60
	m	29	50	64	65	44	62	78	78	16	36	46	48
Anglophone countries	w	40	47	86	84	52	55	97	87	29	36	75	75
	m	44	58	90	88	56	69	89	89	31	42	82	84
Other	w	16	27	52	51	21	36	63	59	10	18	38	42
	m	17	39	67	62	23	57	87	87	11	23	41	39

* Figures with an asterisk are 1982; those with a dagger are estimates. See the technical notes. Figures for Chad, Guinea, Nigeria, and Zimbabwe are for 1984.

Table A-8. Gross Secondary Enrollment Ratios

Number enrolled as a percentage of age group

		Total 1960	1970	1980	1983*	Male 1960	1970	1980	1983*	Female 1960	1970	1980	1983*
Low-income economies	w	3	8	14	17	4	11	19	23	1	5	9	12
	m	2	5	11	12	3	8	15	17	1	3	7	8
Low-income semiarid	w	1	2	6	7	1	4	8	10	0.2	1	3	4
	m	1	3	6	7	1	4	9	10	0.2	1	3	3
1 Mali		1	5	7	7	1	8	11	10	0.2	2	4	4
2 Burkina Faso		1	1	3	4	1	2	4	5	0.3	1	2	3
3 Niger		0.3	1	5	6	1	2	7	9	0.1	1	3	3
4 Gambia		4	7	13	19	6	12	19	27	2	4	8	12
5 Somalia		1	3	11	14	2	5	16	19	0.2	1	6	10
6 Chad		0.4	2	4†	6	1	4	6†	11	0.1	0.3	1†	2
Low-income other	w	3	9	15	19	5	12	21	25	2	5	10	13
	m	2	7	14	15	3	10	16	19	1	4	7	8
7 Ethiopia		1	4	9	11	2	6	11	14	0.3	2	7	8
8 Zaire		2	9	34	52	4	13	48	73	1	4	20	30
9 Malawi		1	2	4	4	2	3	6	6	0.4	1	2	2
10 Guinea-Bissau		3	8	6	11	3	11	10	19	2	6	2	4
11 Tanzania		2	3	3	3	2	4	4	4	1	2	2	2
12 Burundi		1	2	3	4	1	3	5	5	1	1	2	3
13 Uganda		3	6	7	8*	5	9	11	10*	1	3	4	5*
14 Togo		2	7	34	24	4	11	52	36	1	3	17	12
15 Central African Rep.		1	4	14	16	2	7	21	24	0.3	2	7	8
16 Madagascar		4	12	14†	15†	5	14	16†	17†	3	9	13†	14†
17 Benin		2	5	16	22*	2	6	25	32*	1	3	9	12*
18 Rwanda		2	2	2	2	3	3	2	3	1	1	1	1
19 Kenya		2	9	18	19	3	12	21	23	2	5	15	16
20 Sierra Leone		2	8	14	15	3	12	19	19	1	5	9	9
21 Guinea		2	13	16	15	4	21	23	21	1	5	9	8
22 Ghana		19	42	37	38	28	52	46	48	10	31	28	28
23 Sudan		3	7	16	19	5	10	20	22	1	4	12	16
24 Senegal		3	10	11	12	4	14	15	17	2	6	7	8
25 Mozambique		2	5	5	6	3	6	8	8	2	4	3	4
Middle-income oil importers	w	4	10	17	25	5	13	21	31	3	7	12	19
	m	2	9	19	21	3	13	22	27	2	6	13	23
26 Mauritania		1	2	10	12*	1	4	16	19*	(.)	0.4	4	6*
27 Liberia		2	10	23	21	4	15	33	30	1	4	13	12
28 Zambia		2	13	17	17	2	17	22	22	1	8	12	12
29 Lesotho		3	7	17	19*	3	7	14	16*	3	7	20	23*
30 Côte d'Ivoire		2	9	19	20	3	13	26	27	1	4	12	11
31 Zimbabwe		6	7	8	39	7	9	8	46	4	6	6	31
32 Swaziland		5	18	39	43	5	21	40	44	4	16	38	42
33 Botswana		1	7	19	21	2	9	18	19	1	6	21	23
34 Mauritius		22	30	48	51	30	35	49	53	14	25	47	49
Middle-income oil exporters	w	3	5	20	23	4	7	25	27	1	3	14	18
	m	3	8	19	23	4	11	25	27	1	5	14	17
35 Nigeria		3	4	19	23	4	6	23	.	1	3	14	.
36 Cameroon		2	7	19	21	4	11	24	27	1	4	13	16
37 Congo, People's Rep.		4	20	83	87*	6	28	95	104*	2	12	70	70*
38 Gabon		3	8	21	23*	4	12	25	28*	1	5	17	18*
39 Angola		2	8	19	12*	2	9	25	14*	2	6	7	7*
Sub-Saharan Africa	w	3	7	16	20	4	10	21	24	1	4	11	13
	m	2	7	14	16	3	9	19	19	1	4	9	10
Francophone countries	w	2	7	18	23	3	10	26	32	1	3	11	14
	m	2	6	14	15	3	9	18	20	1	3	8	8
Anglophone countries	w	4	8	17	21	6	11	21	22	2	5	13	14
	m	3	7	17	19	4	11	20	22	1	5	12	16
Other	w	1	5	9	10	2	7	13	13	1	3	6	7
	m	2	5	9	11	2	6	11	14	2	4	6	7

* Figures with an asterisk are for 1982; those with a dagger are estimates. See the technical notes. Figures for Chad, Nigeria, and Zimbabwe are for 1984.

Table A-9. Gross Tertiary Enrollment Ratios

Number enrolled as a percentage of age group

		Total 1960	1970	1980	1983*	Male 1960	1970	1980	1983*	Female 1960	1970	1980	1983*
Low-income economies	w	0.2	0.6	0.9	1.1	0.3	0.9	1.4	1.6	0.1	0.2	0.3	0.3
	m	0.2	0.5	0.6	0.9	0.3	0.7	1.0	1.5	0.1	0.1	0.2	0.3
Low-income semiarid	w	.	0.3	0.4	0.7	.	0.3	0.6	1.3	.	.	0.1	0.2
	m	.	0.3	0.3	0.6	.	0.3	0.5	1.0	.	0.1	0.1	0.2
1 Mali		.	0.2	0.3	0.9*	.	0.3	0.5	1.8*	.	(.)	0.1	0.2*
2 Burkina Faso		.	(.)	0.3	0.6	.	0.1	0.5	0.9	.	(.)	0.1	0.3
3 Niger		.	.	0.3	0.5	.	.	0.5	0.8	.	.	0.1	0.2
4 Gambia		.	.	.	.	.	.	.	.	.	.	.	.
5 Somalia		.	0.4	0.6	0.6	.	0.7	1.2	1.0	.	0.1	0.1	0.1
6 Chad		.	.	0.5†	1.2†	.	.	1.0†	2.4†	.	.	(.)†	(.)†
Low-income other	w	0.2	0.6	1.0	1.1	0.3	1.0	1.5	1.6	0.1	0.2	0.4	0.4
	m	0.2	0.5	0.9	1.1	0.3	0.8	1.6	1.8	0.1	0.2	0.3	0.3
7 Ethiopia		.	0.2	0.4	0.5	.	0.4	0.8	1.0	.	(.)	0.2	0.1
8 Zaire		0.1	0.7	1.2	1.2	0.1	1.3	2.0	2.1	(.)	0.1	0.2	0.2
9 Malawi		.	0.3	0.4	0.4*	.	0.5	0.7	0.7*	.	0.1	0.2	0.7*
10 Guinea-Bissau		.	.	.	.	.	.	.	.	.	.	.	.
11 Tanzania		.	0.2	0.3	0.4	.	0.3	0.5	0.6	.	0.1	0.1	0.1
12 Burundi		.	0.2	0.6	0.6	.	0.3	0.9	0.8	.	(.)	0.3	0.3
13 Uganda		0.2	0.5	0.5	0.6*	0.4	0.8	0.8	0.9*	0.1	0.2	0.2	0.3*
14 Togo		.	0.5	2.2	1.7	.	0.9	3.8	2.9	.	0.1	0.6	0.5
15 Central African Rep.		.	0.1	0.9	1.2	.	0.2	1.7	2.2	.	(.)	0.1	0.2
16 Madagascar		0.2	1.0	3.1	3.5*	0.2	1.3	3.0	4.2*	0.1	0.6	1.7	2.6*
17 Benin		.	0.1	1.3	2.0*	.	0.3	2.1	3.5*	.	(.)	0.5	0.7*
18 Rwanda		.	0.2	0.3	0.3	.	0.4	0.5	0.5	.	(.)	0.1	0.1
19 Kenya		0.1	0.8	0.9	0.9	0.2	1.5	1.5	1.5	(.)	0.2	0.4	0.3
20 Sierra Leone		0.1	0.5	0.6	0.6†	0.2	0.8	1.0	1.0†	(.)	0.1	0.2	0.2†
21 Guinea		.	0.6	4.4	3.0*	.	1.0	7.2	4.8*	.	0.1	1.7	1.3*
22 Ghana		0.2	0.8	1.5	1.8	0.4	1.3	2.4	2.8	0.1	0.2	0.6	0.8
23 Sudan		0.4	1.2	1.8	2.1*	0.7	2.0	2.5	3.1*	(.)	0.3	0.9	1.2*
24 Senegal		0.5	1.5	2.8	2.2	0.8	2.4	4.5	3.6	0.2	0.5	1.0	0.9
25 Mozambique		.	0.3	0.1	0.1	.	0.3	0.1	0.1	.	0.2	0.1	0.1
Middle-income oil importers	w	0.2	0.9	1.9	2.1	0.3	1.4	2.8	2.9	0.1	0.4	1.1	1.2
	m	0.1	0.9	1.6	2.1	0.3	1.4	1.6	2.5	0.1	0.3	1.1	0.9
26 Mauritania		.	.	0.4	0.4*	.	.	0.7	0.8*	.	.	0.1	0.1*
27 Liberia		0.5	0.9	2.9	2.1	0.8	1.5	4.3	3.2	0.2	0.4	1.6	1.1
28 Zambia		.	0.4	1.6	1.6*	.	0.7	2.3	2.5*	.	0.1	0.7	0.7*
29 Lesotho		0.2	0.4	1.8	2.2	0.3	0.6	1.6	1.9	0.1	0.3	2.0	2.5
30 Côte d'Ivoire		0.1	0.9	2.9	2.4*	0.2	1.4	4.6	3.7*	(.)	0.3	1.1	0.9*
31 Zimbabwe		0.1	1.2	1.3	2.6	0.2	1.4	1.6	3.1	0.1	1.0	1.1	2.2
32 Swaziland		.	0.6	3.9	3.0	.	0.8	4.8	3.6	.	0.4	3.1	2.5
33 Botswana		.	.	1.1	1.6	.	.	1.4	1.8	.	.	0.9	0.4
34 Mauritius		0.1	2.6	1.1	0.6	0.3	5.1	1.4	0.8	(.)	0.2	0.7	0.4
Middle-income oil exporters	w	.	0.5	1.9	2.0	.	0.8	2.3	2.6	.	0.1	0.4	0.4
	m	.	0.5	2.2	2.1	.	0.8	3.5	4.0	.	0.1	0.7	1.0
35 Nigeria		0.2	0.5	2.2	2.1	0.3	0.8	3.7	.	(.)	0.1	0.7	.
36 Cameroon		.	0.5	1.5	1.6	.	1.0	2.6	2.9	.	0.1	0.4	0.4
37 Congo, People's Rep.		0.4	1.7	5.6	6.0*	0.8	3.3	9.6	10.5*	0.1	0.2	1.6	1.6*
38 Gabon		.	0.2	2.2	3.3*	.	0.4	3.5	5.0*	.	0.1	1.0	1.7*
39 Angola		.	0.5	0.3	0.4*	.	0.6	0.5	0.6*	.	0.4	0.1	0.1*
Sub-Saharan Africa	w	0.2	0.6	1.2	1.4	0.3	0.9	1.6	1.8	0.1	0.2	0.4	0.4
	m	0.2	0.5	1.1	1.2	0.3	0.8	1.6	2.0	0.1	0.2	0.5	0.4
Francophone countries	w	0.2	0.6	1.4	1.6	0.2	1.1	2.1	2.4	0.1	0.2	0.4	0.4
	m	0.2	0.5	1.3	1.4	0.2	0.9	2.1	2.7	0.1	0.1	0.4	0.4
Anglophone countries	w	0.2	0.6	1.3	1.5	0.4	1.0	1.6	1.8	0.1	0.2	0.5	0.6
	m	0.2	0.6	1.3	1.6	0.3	0.8	1.6	1.9	0.1	0.2	0.7	0.6
Other	w	.	0.3	0.4	0.4	.	0.4	0.6	0.7	.	0.1	0.1	0.1
	m	.	0.4	0.4	0.5	.	0.5	0.7	0.8	.	0.2	0.1	0.1

* Figures with an asterisk are for 1982; those with a dagger are estimates. See the technical notes. Figures for Nigeria and Zimbabwe are for 1984.

Table A-10. Teachers and Schools

| | | Teachers (thousands) |||| Number of primary schools (thousands) || | Number of primary students per school ||
| | | Primary || Secondary |||||||
		1960	1983*	1960	1983*	1960	1983*		1960	1983*
Low-income economies	t	153	657	29	140	41	80	w	124	273
								m	141	246
Low-income semiarid	t	5	35	1	12	2	7	w	147	201
								m	128	228
1 Mali		1.4	7.9	0.3	4.5	0.4	1.3*		162	225*
2 Burkina Faso		1.5	4.1	0.2	1.5	0.4	1.2		142	231
3 Niger		0.6	6.9	0.1	1.7	0.3	1.7		89	147
4 Gambia		0.2	2.4	0.1	0.8	0.1	0.2		70	303
5 Somalia		0.8	9.5	0.1	3.0	0.2	1.3		114	170
6 Chad		0.8	4.5	0.1	.	0.3	1.2		241	240
Low-income other	t	148	622	28	128	39	73	w	123	280
								m	143	249
7 Ethiopia		6.8	46.7	2.1	13.2	1.1	7.6		204	329
8 Zaire		38.8	112.0	3.1	.	.	.		.	.
9 Malawi		7.0	14.5	0.2	1.2	3.2	2.4*		89	353
10 Guinea-Bissau		0.5	3.3	0.1	0.5*	.	.8*		.	97*
11 Tanzania		10.1	85.3	1.1	4.2	3.3	10.0*		138	355*
12 Burundi		.	6.1	.	1.5	1.3	0.9		71	335
13 Uganda		18.5	44.4*	2.0	7.0*	6.0	4.9*		99	330*
14 Togo		1.6	10.2	0.2	4.4	0.6	2.3		172	199
15 Central African Rep.		1.2	4.2	0.1	1.0*	0.4	0.9		169	324
16 Madagascar		6.4	.	1.5	.	2.6	.		173	.
17 Benin		2.2	11.3*	0.2	.	0.6	2.7*		149	159*
18 Rwanda		.	14.1	.	1.1	3.2	1.6		82	476
19 Kenya		18.6	117.7	1.6	20.4	5.2	12.0		150	360
20 Sierra Leone		2.4	10.2	0.5	3.7	0.6	1.4		144	249
21 Guinea		1.8	7.9	0.4	5.1*	0.6	2.6*		161	109*
22 Ghana		16.2	52.3	12.0	36.5	5.1	8.4		99	173
23 Sudan		8.4	47.8	2.2	20.2	2.4	6.8*		143	235*
24 Senegal		3.0	12.9	.	4.9	.	2.2		.	243
25 Mozambique		4.4	20.8	0.7	3.5	3.2	5.9		130	197
Middle-income oil importers	t	35	143	3	35	7	18	w	159	314
								m	138	260
26 Mauritania		0.6	2.4*	0.0	0.9*	0.2	0.6*		57	179*
27 Liberia		1.9	7.0	0.3	1.7	0.6	1.7		98	139
28 Zambia		5.8	25.9	0.4	4.8	.	3.1		.	385
29 Lesotho		2.5	5.3*	0.2	1.5*	1.0	1.1*		136	253*
30 Côte d'Ivoire		5.8	32.1	0.6	8.9	1.7	5.8		141	200
31 Zimbabwe		12.7	54.0	.	10.4	2.7	4.2		179	507
32 Swaziland		0.9	3.9	0.1	1.5*	0.3	0.5		115	260
33 Botswana		1.2	6.4	0.1	1.4*	0.2	0.5		182	397
34 Mauritius		3.1	6.0	1.1	3.6	0.3	0.3		375	496
Middle-income oil exporters	t	114	474	11	108	19	14	w	171	236
								m	151	236
35 Nigeria		97.1	399.5	8.8	91.9	15.5	.		188	.
36 Cameroon		10.0	31.0	0.7	9.8	.	5.5		.	284
37 Congo, People's Rep.		2.2	7.3*	0.3	4.9*	0.6	1.4*		193	302*
38 Gabon		1.3	3.8*	0.2	1.7*	0.5	0.9*		114	184*
39 Angola		2.9	32.0*	0.8	.	2.0	6.3*		52	187*
Sub-Saharan Africa	t	301	1273	43	283	67	112	w	141	275
								m	141	246
Francophone countries	t	79	279	8	52	14	33	w	132	231
								m	149	228
Anglophone countries	t	207	882	31	211	47	57	w	147	315
								m	138	330
Other	t	15	112	4	20	7	22	w	118	235
								m	122	187

* Figures with an asterisk are for years other than those specified. See the technical notes.

Table A-11. Student-Teacher Ratios

		\multicolumn{9}{c}{Student-teacher ratios}
		\multicolumn{4}{c}{Primary}	\multicolumn{4}{c}{Secondary}	\multicolumn{2}{c}{Tertiary}
		1970	1975	1980	1983*	1970	1975	1980	1983*	1970	1983*
Low-income economies	w	42	42	43	40	19	23	25	25	10	11
	m	43	41	42	39	21	21	22	23	9	8
Low-income semiarid	w	44	48	40	39	18	18	21	21	8	8
	m	40	44	42	37	21	20	21	21	7	9
1 Mali		40	41	42	37	15	17	.	17	5	12*
2 Burkina Faso		44	47	54	62	23	20	25	24	5	10
3 Niger		39	39	43	36	.	.	.	28	7*	8*
4 Gambia		27	26	24	25	20	19	16	18	.	.
5 Somalia		33	57	33	23	24	21	21	21	17	6*
6 Chad		68	68	.	64	21	.	.	.	12	.
Low-income other	w	42	42	43	41	19	24	25	25	10	11
	m	44	43	44	41	20	21	22	21	9	7
7 Ethiopia		49	44	64	54	28	35	44	44	9	11
8 Zaire		43	.	.	42	23	.	.	.	9	.
9 Malawi		43	61	65	58	16	18	21	19	8	8*
10 Guinea-Bissau		45	34	23	23	18	10	10	19*	.	.
11 Tanzania		41	54	42	42	18	20	.	20	5*	4*
12 Burundi		37	31	35	49	11	19	.	18	5	7*
13 Uganda		34	34	34	36*	23	21	.	21*	9	11*
14 Togo		58	60	55	45	25	39	.	23	18	11*
15 Central African Rep.		64	67	60	69	22	.	62	58	.	6
16 Madagascar		65	61	55	.	20	.	.	.	18	46*
17 Benin		41	53	48	38*	23	31	.	.	9	7*
18 Rwanda		60	50	59	54	13	16	12	14	6	4*
19 Kenya		34	33	38	37	21	25	25	25	.	7*
20 Sierra Leone		32	32	28	34	20	19	.	21	6*	7*
21 Guinea		44	40	36	36	23	.	.	19*	.	10*
22 Ghana		30	31	29	28	17	22	22	21	6	.
23 Sudan		47	37	34	34	17	21	20	25	12	4*
24 Senegal		45	41	46	41	.	.	22	23	17	14*
25 Mozambique		69	85	81	56	17	.	36	35	9	3*
Middle-income oil importers	w	42	42	41	39	21	21	22	30	8	6
	m	40	40	41	36	21	21	21	24	6	9
26 Mauritania		24	35	41	45*	22	27	28	31*	.	.
27 Liberia		36	41	41	33	17	17	.	31	.	.
28 Zambia		47	48	49	46	.	.	21	24	7	10*
29 Lesotho		46	53	48	52*	22	22	.	19*	7	.
30 Côte d'Ivoire		45	45	39	36	21	.	.	30	20	.
31 Zimbabwe		40	40	44	40	.	18	20	40	.	.
32 Swaziland		40	38	34	33	17	21	17	18*	5	7*
33 Botswana		36	33	32	31	15	17	18	16*	5	10
34 Mauritius		32	26	20	23	25	30	26	22	4	3
Middle-income oil exporters	w	38	36	46	37	21	34	35	36	9	14
	m	46	48	49	44	21	33	36	33	11	12
35 Nigeria		34	34	.	36	21	.	.	37	8	15*
36 Cameroon		48	51	52	50	29	33	35	30	12	.
37 Congo, People's Rep.		62	59	54	58*	33	42	37	39*	15	25*
38 Gabon		46	48	45	44*	19	22	19	19	.	5*
39 Angola		44	32	40	37*	15	.	38	.	9	8*
Sub-Saharan Africa	w	41	40	43	39	20	24	26	30	9	12
	m	43	41	42	39	21	21	22	23	9	8
Francophone countries	w	47	51	49	44	22	29	31	27	12	13
	m	45	48	47	45	22	25	27	24	11	10
Anglophone countries	w	36	37	38	37	19	22	22	30	8	13
	m	36	36	34	35	19	21	21	21	7	7
Other	w	51	47	54	46	21	34	38	38	9	9
	m	45	44	40	37	18	21	36	28	9	7

* Figures with an asterisk are for years other than those specified. See the technical notes.

Table A-12. Student Flow and Indicators of Efficiency

		Primary								Secondary					
		Repeaters as a percentage of total enrollment		Proportion of cohort reaching the final grade (cohort = 1000)				Cost per completer as a multiple of cost per completer if no dropout or repetition		Repeaters as a percentage of total enrollment		Percentage of students progressing from last grade of primary to first grade of secondary general education			
				Total		Female						Total		Female	
		1970	1983a	1970	1983b	1970	1983b	1970	1983b	1970	1983a	1970	1983b	1970	1983b
Low-income economies	w	17	13					2.0	2.0	7	10	44	43	45	41
	m	21	15	615	498	556	530	1.8	1.6	10	16	29	36	31	39
Low-income semiarid	w	23	21					1.8	2.1	20	22	29	33	30	40
	m	19	16	536	703	542	702	1.8	1.9	11	11	29	39	29	48
1 Mali		26	33*	462	400	.	.	1.8	2.3	28	39*	33	42	.	.
2 Burkina Faso		16	17	536	703	542	702	1.5	1.6	11	15	13	22	13	.
3 Niger		19	15*	602	793	.	.	1.9	1.4	8	7*	24	35	20	28
4 Gambia		13	13	956	915	865	898	1.2	1.3	.	3	42	44	37	48
5 Somalia		.	.	.	.	.	.	.	2.1	.	.	100	50	88	49
6 Chad		27	.	285	293	200	201	2.6	4.0	11	.	12	19	.	.
Low-income other	w	16	12					2.0	2.0	6	10	45	43	45	41
	m	22	15	660	489	569	509	1.8	1.6	10	16	29	36	31	39
7 Ethiopia		.	12*	.	498	.	509	.	1.9	.	.	57	93	49	91
8 Zaire		23	18	.	.	.	.	2.2	1.6	11	8	40	71	37	62
9 Malawi		.	15	322	321	207	.	2.0	2.8	.	.	15	7	.	.
10 Guinea-Bissau		.	30	.	147	.	164	2.4	4.3	.	16	39	68	.	61
11 Tanzania		2	1*	841	757	.	644	1.6	1.4	.	.	16	8	14	7
12 Burundi		22	14	354	943	356	865	1.8	1.3	5	8*	16	8	15	7
13 Uganda		.	10*	.	757	.	644	1.4	1.4	.	.	.	13	.	11
14 Togo		34	36	676	257	586	180	4.2	3.3	19	34	27	31	28	27
15 Central African Rep.		28	35*	401	468	362	265	2.5	2.3	10	23*	23	36	21	40
16 Madagascar		29	.	.	.	.	.	2.5	2.7	13	.	41	.	41	.
17 Benin		19	22*	627	557	569	551	1.5	1.7	12	21*	28	40	31	39
18 Rwanda		30	12	.	412	.	376	3.8	2.0	3	5	7	4	6	2
19 Kenya		5	13*	744	607	679	.	1.3	1.5	(.)	.	28	35	28	33
20 Sierra Leone		.	.	.	480	.	.	.	.	10	.	58	73	56	72
21 Guinea		.	29	.	408	.	298	1.8	1.3	.	38	82	69	79	64
22 Ghana		3	2*	716	744	652	688	1.2	1.1	3	2*	105	.	100	.
23 Sudan		2	(.)*	.	.	.	.	1.4	1.2	5	.	50	53	40	54
24 Senegal		20	15	660	835	.	782	1.4	1.3	11	16	29	29	27	31
25 Mozambique		28	29	.	212	.	152	.	3.8	.	24	.	40	.	39
Middle-income oil importers	w	12	8					1.8	1.4	14	14	29	44	29	50
	m	13	13	771	812	639	639	1.7	1.4	11	12	30	45	33	47
26 Mauritania		15	17*	.	795	.	506	1.5	1.4	11	11*	18	39	.	20
27 Liberia		.	.	.	.	.	.	.	1.3	28	.	47	63	40	55
28 Zambia		2	1*	771	828	640	720	1.8	1.2	.	.	23	21	25	.
29 Lesotho		20	23*	405	375	490	458	2.7	1.7	.	.	44	45	39	41
30 Côte d'Ivoire		25	25	841	889	638	864	1.4	1.4	11	16	27	30	22	29
31 Zimbabwe		.	1	.	.	.	.	.	1.4	.	.	30	74	31	72
32 Swaziland		11	13	627	630	659	639	1.8	1.5	10	6	47	68	45	67
33 Botswana		(.)	6	809	904	.	.	1.5	1.1	.	.	30	31	28	30
34 Mauritius		.	.	.	.	.	.	.	.	.	12*	36	54	34	53
Middle-income oil exporters	w	28	32					.	.	12	25	30	40	30	38
	m	33	31	598	614	577	645	.	.	11	20	27	39	28	45
35 Nigeria		.	.	.	.	.	.	.	.	.	.	34	.	35	.
36 Cameroon		26	30*	598	670	577	645	.	.	11	17	17	26	15	23
37 Congo, People's Rep.		33	31*	720	676	691	680	1.6	1.7	17	37*	37	73	36	73
38 Gabon		33	32*	504	557	439	558	1.7	1.9	10	20*	19	27	20	.
39 Angola		.	36*	.	.	.	.	.	.	.	.	.	50	.	45
Sub-Saharan Africa	w	17	14					1.9	1.8	8	12	39	43	38	42
	m	20	16	627	607	577	599	1.8	1.5	11	16	30	40	31	41
Francophone countries	w	25	22					2.1	1.9	12	14	31	44	30	40
	m	26	23	598	614	556	555	1.8	1.7	11	16	26	31	22	29
Anglophone countries	w	4	6					1.6	1.5	3	3	43	34	43	37
	m	3	8	744	744	652	644	1.5	1.4	7	4	36	45	36	51
Other	w	28	22					2.4	2.9	.	24	61	63	52	59
	m	28	29	.	225	.	164	2.4	3.0	.	20	57	50	69	49

a. Figures with an asterisk are for 1982.
b. Figures are for the most recent available year. See the technical notes.

Table A-13. Percentage of Students Enrolled in Private Schools

		Primary				Secondary			
		1970	1975	1980	1983*	1970	1975	1980	1983*
Low-income economies	w	9.5	7.8	3.9	3.4	23.4	18.0	14.5	8.3
	m	7.4	6.4	3.3	1.9	24.2	19.4	10.2	9.3
Low-income semiarid	w	8.5	5.7	4.1	4.5	17.2	17.5	20.1	24.3
	m	7.4	6.6	4.2	4.1	17.8	14.1	24.7	44.4
1 Mali		6.3	6.0	4.2	4.1	13.6	10.8	8.3	8.4
2 Burkina Faso		3.5	7.2	8.4	8.2	36.1	42.5	51.0	50.2
3 Niger		6.1	4.6	3.1	2.3	22.0	14.1	15.5	.
4 Gambia		31.4	16.4	15.1	14.4	.	45.6	33.8	44.4
5 Somalia		25.1	0.0	0.0	0.0	.	.	.	.
6 Chad		8.4	9.7	.	.	6.8	6.1	.	.
Low-income other	w	9.6	7.9	3.9	3.3	23.8	18.0	14.3	7.8
	m	7.8	6.4	2.8	0.4	36.3	20.8	6.7	8.4
7 Ethiopia		28.1	28.6	15.6	12.5	11.2	7.1	7.2	7.3
8 Zaire		0.0	0.0	0.0	0.0	0.0	0.0	0.0	0.0
9 Malawi		11.2	10.2	6.8	.	.	13.4	1.4	.
10 Guinea-Bissau		.	.	.	.	.	.	.	.
11 Tanzania		3.3	3.7	0.2	0.3	24.2	30.1	41.0	44.2
12 Burundi		93.9	92.6	4.3	11.0	36.3	21.6	6.2	7.4
13 Uganda		.	.	.	.	.	.	.	.
14 Togo		33.9	28.6	23.3	22.7	38.6	20.8	12.0	12.4
15 Central African Rep.		0.0	0.0	0.0	0.0	2.3	1.7	0.9	9.3
16 Madagascar		24.4	23.4	.	.	70.3	49.1	31.3	.
17 Benin		34.2	6.4	3.4	0.0	55.9	17.9	4.1	0.0
18 Rwanda		.	.	.	0.4	.	21.2	37.0	31.3
19 Kenya		3.4	0.0	.	.	42.4	49.0	59.9	33.2
20 Sierra Leone		78.5	77.5	.	.	.	.	.	.
21 Guinea		0.0	0.0	0.0	0.0	0.0	0.0	0.0	0.0
22 Ghana		2.1	.	2.8	.	.	.	.	.
23 Sudan		4.3	2.0	2.5	1.9	.	.	.	.
24 Senegal		12.4	12.3	11.1	9.5	.	30.0	30.1	31.2
25 Mozambique		0.0	0.0	0.0	0.0	37.5	.	0.0	0.0
Middle-income oil importers	w	49.2	46.4	38.6	57.2	32.9	34.8	34.7	55.6
	m	29.3	27.8	25.9	26.0	51.2	34.3	35.4	35.7
26 Mauritania		0.0	0.0	0.0	0.0	0.0	0.0	0.0	0.0
27 Liberia		34.3	34.6	35.5	29.6	51.2	38.2	44.2	35.7
28 Zambia		27.4	24.4	0.6	.	.	.	.	.
29 Lesotho		100.0	100.0	98.4	98.5	.	88.9	89.9	.
30 Côte d'Ivoire		21.8	18.6	15.0	11.2	25.0	28.0	30.1	31.5
31 Zimbabwe		86.8	86.6	83.5	88.2	.	.	.	64.5
32 Swaziland		76.2	80.4	79.8	79.8	59.6	45.4	40.6	38.1
33 Botswana		5.2	5.4	4.7	5.8	59.0	30.3	27.6	32.1
34 Mauritius		29.3	27.8	25.9	22.3	.	.	.	.
Middle-income oil exporters	w	35.9	22.6	17.4	18.1	30.4	26.2	19.1	22.4
	m	37.7	21.5	18.2	17.4	19.6	16.5	22.0	22.8
35 Nigeria		37.7	.	.	.	.	.	.	.
36 Cameroon		53.9	42.9	36.3	34.7	65.8	56.8	47.0	46.3
37 Congo, People's Rep.		0.0	0.0	0.0	0.0	0.0	0.0	0.0	0.0
38 Gabon		49.4	45.1	39.0	36.9	39.1	32.9	43.9	45.5
39 Angola		0.0	0.0	0.0	0.0	0.0	0.0	0.0	0.0
Sub-Saharan Africa	w	21.9	15.2	11.5	14.6	25.3	21.0	17.1	14.9
	m	17.1	10.0	4.3	5.8	30.6	21.4	21.6	21.8
Francophone countries	w	16.5	13.7	9.4	8.1	24.8	17.6	11.8	6.9
	m	8.4	7.2	4.2	3.2	23.5	19.4	12.0	8.9
Anglophone countries	w	27.4	18.6	15.9	29.1	40.3	44.6	53.6	45.8
	m	29.3	24.4	11.0	22.3	51.2	41.8	40.8	38.1
Other	w	12.0	10.0	6.6	6.2	13.2	5.5	4.3	5.1
	m	12.6	0.0	0.0	0.0	11.2	3.6	0.0	0.0

* Figures are for the latest available year. See the technical notes.

Table A-14. Total Public Expenditure on Education

		Public expenditure on education in constant 1983 dollars (millions)					Average annual growth rate			Public expenditure on education as a percentage of:							
										Total government expenditure				GNP			
		1970	1975	1980*	1983*		1970–80	1980–83	1970	1975	1980*	1983*	1970	1975	1980*	1983*
Low-income economies	t	.	.	.	.	w	2.1	−3.6	17.0	17.2	16.1	14.6	4.1	4.1	4.0	3.2
						m	6.7	−3.0	17.6	17.8	18.8	15.3	3.8	3.5	3.7	3.3
Low-income semiarid	t	.	.	.	.	w	9.4	−2.0	11.8	15.3	18.7	17.6	1.5	2.8	3.1	2.9
						m	9.0	−4.5	10.8	15.6	19.8	22.8	2.0	3.2	3.2	3.6
1 Mali		.	.	44.5	36.7		.	−6.2	.	.	30.8	37.2	.	.	4.6	3.7
2 Burkina Faso		.	.	28.3	33.6		.	5.9	.	.	19.8	23.9	.	.	2.6	3.2
3 Niger		20.5	34.6	57.2	46.9		10.8	−6.4	17.7	18.7	22.9	21.7	2.0	3.8	4.3	3.6
4 Gambia		2.8	5.7	6.6	11.8*		9.0	.	10.8	.	12.5	.	2.3	3.2	3.2	5.9*
5 Somalia		11.7	27.8	22.6	20.7		6.8	−2.9	7.6	12.5*	8.7	6.3	1.0	2.1	1.7	1.4
6 Chad		.	.	.	.		.	.	.	.	.	.	.	.	.	.
Low-income other	t	.	.	.	.	w	1.8	−3.8	17.2	17.3	15.8	14.3	4.2	4.2	4.1	3.2
						m	3.9	−2.8	17.7	17.8	18.1	15.3	3.9	3.5	3.8	3.1
7 Ethiopia		88.6	125.8	126.9	147.7		3.7	5.2	19.4	13.4	9.3	10.9	2.8	3.6	2.9	3.1
8 Zaire		289.6	.	265.5	.		−0.9	.	17.6	.	22.0	.	7.0	.	6.1	.
9 Malawi		30.1	23.8	38.4	32.8		2.5	−5.1	13.2	9.6	.	8.5	4.6	2.4	3.6	3.0
10 Guinea-Bissau		.	.	.	3.3		.	.	.	.	.	11.8	.	.	.	3.0
11 Tanzania		138.6	210.4	281.0*	255.2		8.2	−2.4	16.0	17.8	14.3*	15.3	4.5	5.4	5.9*	5.8
12 Burundi		.	.	.	37.8*		.	.	.	.	.	.	.	.	.	3.4*
13 Uganda		328.3	214.4	46.7	106.1		−17.7	31.4	17.8	17.0	11.3	.	3.9	2.5	0.7	1.3
14 Togo		12.1	23.5	46.3	41.9		14.4	−3.2	19.0	15.2	19.4	20.8	2.2	3.5	5.6	5.9
15 Central African Rep.		.	29.3	.	.		.	.	.	20.1	.	.	.	4.9	.	.
16 Madagascar		.	93.9	118.2	65.5		.	−17.8	.	18.5	.	.	.	3.2	3.7	2.3
17 Benin		.	.	.	.		.	.	.	.	.	.	.	.	.	.
18 Rwanda		19.2	25.0	36.4	48.3		6.6	9.9	26.6	25.3	21.6	24.0	2.3	3.5	2.7	3.1
19 Kenya		120.9	240.9	348.1	272.6		11.2	−7.8	17.6	19.4	18.1	15.3	5.0	6.3	6.9	4.8
20 Sierra Leone		26.5	32.4	38.9	36.6		3.9	−2.0	17.5	.	.	17.6	3.2	3.4	3.8	3.5
21 Guinea		.	.	.	70.5		.	.	.	.	.	12.7	.	.	.	4.0
22 Ghana		184.5	253.0	140.5	80.9		−2.7	−16.8	19.6	21.5	.	15.2	4.3	5.9	3.1	2.0
23 Sudan		159.1	221.7	305.7	.		6.8	.	12.6	14.8	.	.	3.9	4.6	4.6	.
24 Senegal		67.6	.	.	.		.	.	21.3	.	.	.	3.8	.	.	.
25 Mozambique		.	.	.	.		.	.	.	.	.	.	.	.	.	.
Middle-income oil importers	t	547.4	.	.	.	w	8.8	3.5	14.7	15.1	17.6	19.6	4.2	5.1	6.7	7.3
						m	10.8	0.4	14.8	14.4	16.0	17.6	3.4	3.7	6.3	5.5
26 Mauritania		19.5	.	.	.		.	.	21.9	.	.	.	3.3	.	.	.
27 Liberia		19.0	20.2	65.1	51.1		13.1	−7.7	9.5	11.6	24.3	13.2	2.5	2.4	6.3	5.3
28 Zambia		126.7	201.0	136.7	176.2*		0.8	13.5	10.9	11.9	9.7	15.2*	4.5	6.5	4.5	5.5*
29 Lesotho		7.3	.	.	24.9		.	.	22.0	.	.	17.9	3.0	.	.	3.9
30 Côte d'Ivoire		205.1	327.0	538.4*	544.7		11.3	0.3	19.3	19.0	29.8*	28.2	5.4	6.3	8.4*	9.1
31 Zimbabwe		128.2	170.2	329.1	428.8		9.9	9.2	.	.	13.7	17.6	3.4	3.6	6.6	7.6
32 Swaziland		14.7	19.9	27.6	32.2*		6.5	.	17.3	16.9	18.8	.	4.3	3.7	4.5	4.7*
33 Botswana		8.5	28.5	56.8	58.2		20.9	0.6	12.3	18.8	16.0	18.5	5.2	8.5	7.1	7.2
34 Mauritius		18.3	29.0	51.1	46.0		10.8	−3.4	11.5	9.6	11.6	10.3	3.1	3.6	5.3	4.3
Middle-income oil exporters	t	.	.	5468.2	.	w	5.9	−14.2	19.4	16.7	15.9	9.8	3.8	5.3	6.0	4.3
						m	5.8	−7.0	19.6	18.2	20.3	13.7	3.5	4.7	4.8	4.5
35 Nigeria		.	3071.5	4680.8*	2693.5		.	−16.8	.	16.5	15.7*	9.3*	.	5.5	6.4*	4.3*
36 Cameroon		109.7	147.1	182.4	234.4		5.2	8.7	19.6	21.3	20.3	17.2	3.5	3.9	3.3	3.6
37 Congo, People's Rep.		44.8	89.1	92.6	102.0*		7.5	.	23.7	18.2	23.6	19.2*	5.9	8.1	6.9	6.0*
38 Gabon		46.5	69.3	81.9	.		5.8	.	16.2	.	.	.	3.1	2.1	2.8	.
39 Angola		.	.	430.4*	372.2		.	−7.0	.	.	.	10.1	.	.	5.0*	4.7
Sub-Saharan Africa	t	.	.	.	.	w	4.4	−9.2	16.7	16.6	16.2	11.9	4.1	4.9	5.5	4.3
						m	6.8	−2.9	17.6	17.4	18.5	15.3	3.5	3.7	4.5	3.9
Francophone countries	t	.	.	.	.	w	5.7	0.3	19.5	18.7	24.2	25.7	4.6	4.3	5.1	5.0
						m	7.1	−1.5	19.5	18.9	22.0	21.7	3.4	3.8	4.3	3.6
Anglophone countries	t	.	.	.	.	w	3.7	−11.8	14.6	16.7	14.3	15.3	4.0	5.1	5.7	4.3
						m	7.5	−2.9	14.6	16.7	14.3	15.3	3.9	3.7	4.6	4.6
Other	t	.	.	.	.	w	4.1	−2.3	13.5	13.0	9.0	10.5	2.3	3.2	2.6	3.8
						m	5.2	−2.9	13.5	13.0	9.0	10.5	1.9	2.8	2.3	3.0

* Figures with an asterisk are for years other than those specified. See the technical notes.

Table A-15. Distribution of Total Public Expenditure on Education by Recurrent or Capital Component

		Recurrent expenditure						Capital expenditure					
		As a percentage of total public expenditure on education				Average annual growth rate		As a percentage of total public expenditure on education				Average annual growth rate	
		1970	1975	1980*	1983*	1970–80	1980–83	1970	1975	1980*	1983*	1970–80	1980–83
Low-income economies	w	85.6	87.7	88.2	90.1	2.6	−1.2	14.4	12.3	11.8	9.9	0.1	−11.3
	m	89.0	89.6	91.1	95.7	5.0	−0.8	11.0	10.4	8.9	4.3	5.3	−20.3
Low-income semiarid	w	95.9	84.9	77.6	94.1	4.7	4.5	4.1	15.1	22.4	5.9	.	−37.1
	m	94.4	83.7	91.1	96.7	5.0	1.7	5.6	16.3	8.9	3.3	.	−28.1
1 Mali		.	.	98.8	98.9	5.0	−6.2	.	.	1.2	1.1	.	−8.2
2 Burkina Faso		.	.	93.0	99.2	4.4	8.2	.	.	7.0	0.8	.	−48.0
3 Niger		93.8	87.0	47.0	96.7	3.4	19.1	6.2	13.0	53.0	3.3	37.3	−62.9
4 Gambia		94.4	78.1	88.1	68.6*	8.2	.	5.6	21.9	11.9	31.4*	17.5	.
5 Somalia		100.0	83.7	91.1	85.9	5.8	−4.8	(.)	16.3	8.9	14.1	.	13.5
6 Chad		.	.	.	.	.	.	.	.	.	.	.	.
Low-income other	w	85.3	87.9	89.1	89.6	2.4	−1.8	14.7	12.1	10.9	10.4	−1.3	−7.3
	m	88.4	91.0	90.7	95.3	4.8	−0.8	11.6	9.0	9.3	4.7	2.2	−20.3
7 Ethiopia		49.5	83.5	89.3	77.3*	10.0	12.3	50.5	16.5	10.7	22.7*	−11.3	76.4
8 Zaire		88.1	.	96.0	.	(.)	.	11.9	.	4.0	.	−11.1	.
9 Malawi		73.7	91.9	75.6	90.1	2.7	0.7	26.3	8.1	24.4	9.9	1.7	−29.7
10 Guinea-Bissau		.	.	.	99.0	21.8	−5.2	.	.	.	1.0	.	.
11 Tanzania		82.8	80.4	82.3*	87.2	8.1	−1.0	17.2	19.6	17.7*	12.8	8.5	−10.0
12 Burundi		.	.	.	89.1*	6.0	.	.	.	.	10.9*	.	.
13 Uganda		82.4	93.0	88.3	76.0	−17.1	25.0	17.6	7.0	11.7	24.0	−21.0	67.1
14 Togo		88.8	96.3	96.4	97.4	15.3	−2.9	11.2	3.7	3.6	2.6	2.2	−13.8
15 Central African Rep.		.	86.9	.	.	1.5	−0.4	.	13.1	.	.	.	.
16 Madagascar		.	95.2	93.5	98.0	0.9	−16.5	.	4.8	6.5	2.0	.	−44.6
17 Benin		.	.	.	.	5.9	.	.	.	.	.	.	.
18 Rwanda		98.8	99.9	84.7	99.3	5.0	15.9	1.2	0.1	15.3	0.7	37.5	−60.2
19 Kenya		93.9	95.4	92.1	96.0	10.9	−6.5	6.1	4.6	7.9	4.0	14.1	−26.7
20 Sierra Leone		89.0	90.2	95.3	95.3	4.6	−2.0	11.0	9.8	4.7	4.7	−4.6	−1.9
21 Guinea		.	.	.	97.4	4.6	−0.6	.	.	.	2.6	.	.
22 Ghana		87.8	77.9	73.2	89.2	−4.5	−11.1	12.2	22.1	26.8	10.8	5.3	−38.6
23 Sudan		93.4	89.6	92.2	.	6.6	.	6.6	10.4	7.8	.	8.5	.
24 Senegal		97.8	.	.	.	3.5	(.)	2.2	.	.	.	.	.
25 Mozambique		.	.	.	.	.	.	.	.	.	.	.	.
Middle-income oil importers	w	87.3	83.1	86.0	93.3	8.4	6.6	12.7	16.9	14.0	6.7	9.2	−17.5
	m	88.5	81.4	85.9	95.6	10.0	4.3	11.5	18.6	14.1	4.4	11.8	−27.4
26 Mauritania		95.0	.	.	.	6.4	16.7	5.0	.	.	.	.	.
27 Liberia		.	.	85.9	95.7	.	−4.6	.	.	14.1	4.3	.	−37.8
28 Zambia		79.2	76.9	95.1	99.9*	2.6	16.4	20.8	23.1	4.9	0.1*	−12.7	−85.4
29 Lesotho		91.3	.	.	93.7	.	.	8.7	.	.	6.3	.	.
30 Côte d'Ivoire		85.6	84.7	77.8*	89.5	10.1	3.9	14.4	15.3	22.2*	10.5	16.8	−16.9
31 Zimbabwe		96.1	91.8	97.4	95.6	10.0	8.5	3.9	8.2	2.6	4.4	5.4	30.3
32 Swaziland		85.7	78.1	80.0*	80.0*	5.8	.	14.3	21.9	20.0*	20.0*	10.2	.
33 Botswana		84.6	54.5	75.8	83.9	19.5	4.3	15.4	45.5	24.2	16.1	26.4	−11.9
34 Mauritius		92.0	87.4	89.9	98.8	10.5	−0.3	8.0	12.6	10.1	1.2	13.5	−52.7
Middle-income oil exporters	w	93.9	54.0	82.9	88.9	15.5	.	6.1	46.0	17.1	11.1	17.8	.
	m	95.6	83.1	82.1	91.2	5.6	.	4.4	16.9	17.9	8.8	14.8	.
35 Nigeria		.	51.0	82.9*	88.3*	15.5	−15.0	.	49.0	17.1*	11.7*	.	−26.8
36 Cameroon		92.2	83.5	81.3	79.1	3.9	7.7	7.8	16.5	18.7	20.9	14.8	12.8
37 Congo, People's Rep.		96.6	82.6	93.8	94.0*	7.2	.	3.4	17.4	6.2	6.0*	14.1	.
38 Gabon		95.6	85.0	72.3	.	2.9	.	4.4	15.0	27.7	.	27.1	.
39 Angola		.	.	.	97.9*	.	.	.	.	.	2.1*	.	.
Sub-Saharan Africa	w	86.7	67.1	84.6	90.1	9.2	−7.0	13.3	32.9	15.4	9.9	4.1	−20.7
	m	91.7	85.0	88.8	95.3	5.8	−0.3	8.3	15.0	11.2	4.7	9.3	−21.8
Francophone countries	w	90.2	86.4	83.9	90.3	4.4	3.3	9.8	13.6	16.1	9.7	11.3	−17.3
	m	94.4	86.9	93.0	97.4	4.6	2.0	5.6	13.1	7.0	2.6	15.8	−30.7
Anglophone countries	w	86.9	63.2	84.7	89.9	11.1	−10.0	13.1	36.8	15.3	10.1	1.5	−23.6
	m	88.4	83.9	88.1	91.9	7.4	−0.6	11.6	16.1	11.9	8.1	8.5	−26.7
Other	w	55.4	83.6	89.6	91.9	9.4	6.0	44.6	16.4	10.4	8.1	−11.3	42.6
	m	74.8	83.6	90.2	91.9	10.0	−4.8	25.3	16.4	9.8	8.1	−11.3	45.0

* Figures with an asterisk are for years other than those specified. See the technical notes.

Table A-16. Public Recurrent Expenditure on Education by Level of Education

Percentage of public recurrent expenditure allocated to:

		Primary 1970	Primary 1975	Primary 1980*	Primary 1983*	Secondary 1970	Secondary 1975	Secondary 1980*	Secondary 1983*	Tertiary 1970	Tertiary 1975	Tertiary 1980*	Tertiary 1983*	Unspecified 1970	Unspecified 1975	Unspecified 1980*	Unspecified 1983*
Low-income economies	w	46	44	45	47	27	30	25	27	16	17	20	19	12	9	10	7
	m	49	44	44	43	25	26	27	29	13	19	19	19	12	10	11	10
Low-income semiarid	w	62	47	43	38	23	26	24	28	.	.	23	21	15	27	10	13
	m	62	44	44	36	26	26	26	26	.	.	17	21	12	12	13	19
1 Mali		65	40	39	33	20	26	25	37	5	23	25	21	10	12	11	9
2 Burkina Faso		.	43	32	31	.	26	20	17	.	25	34	26	.	6	14	26
3 Niger		61	.	.	36	25	.	.	31	3	.	.	21	12	.	.	13
4 Gambia		43	44	49	49*	26	21	32	26*	.	.	2	.	31	35	17	26*
5 Somalia		63	62	62	60*	27	26	27	25*	.	.	10	15*	11	12	1	0*
6 Chad		.	.	.	.	.	.	.	.	.	.	.	16	.	.	.	84
Low-income other	w	45	44	45	48	27	30	25	27	17	17	20	19	12	9	10	6
	m	49	45	44	46	24	29	28	29	14	17	19	18	11	8	10	9
7 Ethiopia		55	39	42	46*	36	41	30	29*	.	15	19	18*	9	6	9	8*
8 Zaire		.	44	47	.	.	35	28	.	.	21	25	.	.	0	0	.
9 Malawi		42	45	39*	39*	25	23	16*	15*	25	23	30*	27*	8	9	15*	19*
10 Guinea-Bissau		.	.	76	67*	.	.	16	15*	.	.	1	2*	.	.	8	17*
11 Tanzania		42	37	45	47*	23	22	14	30*	12	13	27	23*	24	28	15	0*
12 Burundi		.	45	.	39*	.	33	.	35*	.	20	.	24*	.	2	.	2*
13 Uganda		.	41	30	16	.	35	28	40	.	22	18	20	.	2	24	24
14 Togo		68	.	30	25*	23	.	31	26*	2	30	28	28*	7	70	11	21*
15 Central African Rep.		.	57	54	55	.	15	16	15	.	10	16	18	.	19	14	12
16 Madagascar		49	43	59	58	19	31	31	36	25	14	1	.	7	13	10	6
17 Benin		50	45	44	.	25	26	23	.	13	19	19	.	12	11	15	.
18 Rwanda		66	69	67	74	19	17	20	14	.	11	14	13	15	4	0	0
19 Kenya		49	65	48	65	32	19	15	15	14	11	14	13	6	5	23	8
20 Sierra Leone		.	.	.	40	.	.	.	31	.	.	.	17	.	.	.	12
21 Guinea		.	.	25	31	.	.	29	37	.	.	32	23	.	.	15	9
22 Ghana		39	25	29	32	34	37	43	41	.	17	18	17	27	22	10	10
23 Sudan		40	.	48	.	22	.	31	.	18	.	21	.	20	.	0	.
24 Senegal		.	47	44	49	.	29	27	28	.	21	27	19	.	3	2	4
25 Mozambique		.	.	.	.	.	.	.	.	.	.	.	.	.	.	.	.
Middle-income oil importers	w	40	43	48	49	33	34	34	32	11	15	13	15	15	8	6	4
	m	53	45	42	45	30	34	33	34	13	15	13	15	12	8	10	8
26 Mauritania		.	45	35	28*	.	40	50	32*	18	15	14	12*	82	1	1	28*
27 Liberia		.	.	18	30	.	.	27	16	.	.	19	32	.	.	37	23
28 Zambia		44	45	45	48*	30	25	26	34*	13	17	18	18*	12	13	11	0*
29 Lesotho		59	.	.	37*	21	.	.	35*	15	.	.	20*	5	.	.	9*
30 Côte d'Ivoire		29	37	39*	45	36	39	46*	40	14	19	15*	15	22	6	0*	0
31 Zimbabwe		48	49	67	61	34	34	21	24	7	8	8	11	12	8	5	5
32 Swaziland		.	32	41	47*	.	41	37	35*	.	19	13	10*	.	8	10	8*
33 Botswana		58	47	52	43	30	34	29	29	9	14	13	24	4	6	6	4
34 Mauritius		69	51	44	46	21	31	37	36	6	10	8	7	4	9	12	11
Middle-income oil exporters	w	.	.	.	34	.	.	.	54	.	.	.	.	.	.	.	12
	m	.	.	.	37	.	.	.	46	.	.	.	.	.	.	.	0
35 Nigeria		40	23	17*	33*	24	16	40*	56*	20	42	25*	11*	16	20	18*	0*
36 Cameroon		.	.	.	41	.	.	.	35	.	.	.	24	.	.	.	0
37 Congo, People's Rep.		49	34	36	48*	36	32	29	25*	10	29	24	.	5	5	11	27
38 Gabon		.	.	.	.	.	.	.	.	.	.	.	.	.	.	.	.
39 Angola		.	.	.	.	.	.	.	.	.	.	.	.	.	.	.	.
Sub-Saharan Africa	w	43	35	30	41	27	25	35	42	16	27	22	14	14	13	14	3
	m	49	44	44	43	25	30	28	31	13	18	18	18	12	9	11	9
Francophone countries	w	43	42	42	43	29	33	34	34	15	19	20	18	13	5	4	4
	m	55	45	41	39	24	30	28	32	11	19	22	21	12	6	11	9
Anglophone countries	w	42	32	26	40	26	21	35	45	17	30	22	13	15	16	16	3
	m	44	44	45	43	25	28	29	31	13	17	18	18	12	9	15	9
Other	w	57	43	46	48	34	38	29	29	.	15	17	17	9	4	8	7
	m	59	50	62	60	31	33	27	25	.	15	10	15	10	9	8	8

*Figures with an asterisk are for years other than those specified. See the technical notes.

Table A-17. Public Recurrent Expenditure per Primary Pupil

		Expenditure (constant 1983 dollars)				Expenditure as a percentage of GNP per capita				Expenditure on materials (current dollars)
		1970	1975	1980*	1983*	1970	1975	1980*	1983*	1983†
Low-income economies	w	53	45	36	32	.	.	.	.	2.3
	m	61	52	41	40	24	23	18	18	0.7
Low-income semiarid	w	105	58	51	49	.	.	.	.	2.4
	m	109	62	53	48	49	31	23	25	0.9
1 Mali		86	50	59	41	72	40	41	25	1.3
2 Burkina Faso		.	58	42	38	.	39	24	21	0.4
3 Niger		131	.	.	65	53	.	.	27	7.8
4 Gambia		67	78	67	80*	26	24	21	27*	.
5 Somalia		147	66	47	48	45	20	17	19	(.)
6 Chad		.	.	.	.	.	.	.	.	.
Low-income other	w	50	44	36	31	.	.	.	.	2.3
	m	46	43	36	30	18	22	16	12	0.7
7 Ethiopia		37	37	22	26*	33	35	19	23*	0.6
8 Zaire		.	35	29	.	.	18	18	.	.
9 Malawi		26	15	14	13	18	8	8	6	(.)
10 Guinea-Bissau		.	.	39	29	.	.	33	20	(.)
11 Tanzania		56	40	36*	30	24	16	12*	12	8.7
12 Burundi		.	61	.	63*	.	29	.	24*	0.8
13 Uganda		.	66	8	8	.	23	4	4	(.)
14 Togo		32	.	26	23	12	.	8	8	(.)
15 Central African Rep.		.	66	52	44	.	22	19	16	.
16 Madagascar		52	34	50	25	13	9	14	8	(.)
17 Benin		85	61	54	.	36	25	20	.	.
18 Rwanda		30	43	29	47	13	26	11	17	2.0
19 Kenya		39	52	39	39	18	19	13	12	1.0
20 Sierra Leone		.	.	.	40	.	.	.	12	.
21 Guinea		.	.	68	75	.	.	20	25	.
22 Ghana		66	41	21	16	13	10	6	5	1.6
23 Sudan		72	.	92	.	24	.	26	.	.
24 Senegal		.	120	98	101	.	30	27	23	3.6
25 Mozambique		.	.	.	.	.	.	.	.	.
Middle-income oil importers	w	74	101	129	121	.	.	.	.	1.3
	m	71	85	132	106	11	13	15	13	0.6
26 Mauritania		.	196	134	143	.	45	30	33	2.9
27 Liberia		.	.	43	63	.	.	8	13	0.7
28 Zambia		64	80	57	78*	9	13	10	15*	2.7
29 Lesotho		22	.	.	31	10	.	.	7	(.)
30 Côte d'Ivoire		100	152	171*	189	13	20	21*	27	2.8
31 Zimbabwe		80	89	173	122	11	12	24	17	(.)
32 Swaziland		.	56	81	100*	.	6	8*	11	0.6
33 Botswana		50	62	130	106	18	13	14	12	(.)
34 Mauritius		77	85	157	151	11	9	16	13	0.1
Middle-income oil exporters	w	.	.	.	.	.	.	.	.	.
	m	.	.	.	.	.	.	.	.	.
35 Nigeria		92	60	48*	55*	14	8	5*	7*	.
36 Cameroon		.	.	.	49*	.	.	.	6*	.
37 Congo, People's Rep.		87	79	79	.	14	10	9	.	0.1
38 Gabon		.	.	.	.	.	.	.	.	.
39 Angola		.	.	.	.	.	.	.	.	.
Sub-Saharan Africa	w	67	56	50	52	.	.	.	.	2.0
	m	67	61	51	48	16	19	16	15	0.6
Francophone countries	w	66	56	55	69	.	.	.	.	1.6
	m	85	61	54	49	14	26	20	23	1.3
Anglophone countries	w	70	57	50	50	.	.	.	.	2.4
	m	65	61	52	55	16	12	11	12	0.3
Other	w	45	42	26	28	.	.	.	.	0.5
	m	92	51	39	29	39	28	19	20	(.)

* Figures with an asterisk are for years other than those specified. See the technical notes.
† Figures are for the most recent available year. See the technical notes.

Table A-18. Public Recurrent Expenditure per Secondary Student

		Expenditure (constant 1983 dollars)				Expenditure as a percentage of GNP per capita				Expenditure (constant 1983 dollars)			Expenditure on materials (current dollars)
		1970	1975	1980*	1983*	1970	1975	1980*	1983*	General secondary 1983*	Teacher training 1983*	Vocational/ technical 1983*	1983†
Low-income economies	w	177	220	110	123	.	.	.	.	78	662	505	3.8
	m	258	213	145	165	127	119	62	64	152	900	446	0.8
Low-income semiarid	w	262	235	158	168	.	.	.	.	119	1122	514	2.9
	m	304	228	175	176	135	163	83	85	155	1734	292	2.8
1 Mali		156	148	163	176	130	119	113	110	74	1045	1583	1.9
2 Burkina Faso		.	307	186	154	.	207	107	85	184	2223	86	0.4
3 Niger		694	.	.	289	282	.	.	217	236	1734	1446	5.1
4 Gambia		137	135	186	188*	52	41	60	63*	155	2944	292	.
5 Somalia		451	857	127	71	139	267	44	28	33	644	198	3.6
6 Chad		.	.	.	.	.	.	.	.	.	.	.	.
Low-income other	w	173	219	109	119	.	.	.	.	73	605	502	3.8
	m	258	213	122	139	114	102	57	57	125	678	450	0.6
7 Ethiopia		116	179	77	74*	104	168	67	65*	.	.	.	0.9
8 Zaire		.	193	54	.	.	102	34	.	.	.	.	.
9 Malawi		452	318	228	183	311	168	131	124	181	(.)	598	0.5
10 Guinea-Bissau		.	.	125	49	.	.	104	50	28	184	446	(.)
11 Tanzania		573	599	39	823	249	246	15	343	231	850	4847	0.7
12 Burundi		.	422	.	594*	.	197	167	225*	.	.	.	1.0
13 Uganda		.	743	90	224	.	261	46	69	152	900	978	(.)
14 Togo		113	.	104	104	41	.	32	37	97	1201	131	1.3
15 Central African Rep.		.	161	84	59	.	54	30	21	.	.	.	.
16 Madagascar		173	202	181	104	42	52	50	33	.	.	.	0.2
17 Benin		364	213	120	.	154	89	45	.	.	.	.	.
18 Rwanda		360	346	558	451	156	209	212	167	.	.	.	0.4
19 Kenya		266	179	112	74	124	64	37	22	58	506	281	.
20 Sierra Leone		.	.	.	139	.	.	.	47	.	.	.	.
21 Guinea		.	.	222	259	.	.	67	86	.	.	.	.
22 Ghana		100	131	66	39	20	31	17	13	31	191	335	11.4
23 Sudan		250	.	228	.	84	.	64	.	.	.	.	.
24 Senegal		.	308	265	252	.	78	73	100	204	5578	455	7.3
25 Mozambique		.	.	.	.	.	.	.	.	.	.	.	.
Middle-income oil importers	w	612	597	609	456	.	.	.	.	365	3697	1503	1.0
	m	487	496	468	361	102	79	62	62	348	1539	945	0.5
26 Mauritania		.	1091	788	625	.	253	175	125	441	1804	3395	7.3
27 Liberia		.	.	270	148	.	.	49	33	116	1530	427	1.2
28 Zambia		543	496	325	536*	80	78	60	101*	399	1388	5286	2.1
29 Lesotho		198	.	.	282	88	.	.	73	230	11261	779	(.)
30 Côte d'Ivoire		896	842	89	726	117	110	11	109	532	9079	1326	(.)
31 Zimbabwe		847	752	915	310	118	97	128	42	310	(.)	(.)	0.5
32 Swaziland		.	371	337	361*	.	37	35	38*	348	1548	387	9.5
33 Botswana		431	373	599	568	150	79	64	62	493	1284	1111	(.)
34 Mauritius		79	121	204	208	11	13	20	18	206	(.)	510	0.1
Middle-income oil exporters	w	.	.	.	.	.	.	.	.	.	.	.	.
	m	.	.	.	.	.	.	.	.	.	.	.	.
35 Nigeria		535	286	65	392*	82	38	7	51*	327	3042	359	.
36 Cameroon		.	.	.	225*	.	.	.	27*	.	.	.	.
37 Congo, People's Rep.		462	230	134	.	73	29	16	.	112	1050	226	1.3
38 Gabon		.	.	.	.	.	.	.	.	.	.	.	.
39 Angola		.	.	.	.	.	.	.	.	.	.	.	.
Sub-Saharan Africa	w	306	278	325	287	.	.	.	.	249	2159	509	2.9
	m	362	308	195	223	111	93	62	62	194	1283	455	0.8
Francophone countries	w	391	289	176	306	.	.	.	.	262	3439	851	1.6
	m	362	269	181	252	124	106	67	86	194	1769	890	1.3
Anglophone countries	w	305	282	434	306	.	.	.	.	249	2084	425	4.1
	m	348	344	249	223	86	71	60	51	218	1283	510	0.5
Other	w	132	198	82	74	.	.	.	.	32	526	206	1.2
	m	284	518	125	71	122	218	67	34	31	414	322	0.9

* Figures with an asterisk are for years other than those specified. See the technical notes.
† Figures are for the latest available year. See the technical notes.

Table A-19. Public Recurrent Expenditure per Tertiary Student

		Expenditure (constant 1983 dollars)				Expenditure as a multiple of GNP per capita			
		1970	1975	1980*	1983*	1970	1975	1980*	1983*
Low-income economies	w	2791	3023	2313	1929	.	.	.	.
	m	3207	3090	2167	2197	13	15	9	10
Low-income semiarid	w	.	.	2280	1541	.	.	.	.
	m	.	.	2148	1337	.	.	15	11
1 Mali		1891	2517	2148	1337	16	20	15	8
2 Burkina Faso		.	23271	5540	2540	.	156	32	14
3 Niger		.	.	.	3818	.	.	.	14
4 Gambia		.	.	.	.	.	.	.	.
5 Somalia		.	.	711	891	.	.	3	4
6 Chad		.	.	.	351*	.	.	.	.
Low-income other	w	2811	2992	2315	2006	.	.	.	.
	m	4436	3090	2210	2538	11	13	8	10
7 Ethiopia		.	2060	1496	1565*	.	19	13	14*
8 Zaire		.	2316	2271	.	.	12	14	.
9 Malawi		5072	3120	3982	3365	35	17	23	16
10 Guinea-Bissau		.	.	.	.	.	.	.	.
11 Tanzania		6881	6987	12357*	8365	30	29	47*	35
12 Burundi		.	3459	.	3815*	.	16	.	14*
13 Uganda		.	7941	1258	2197	.	28	7	10
14 Togo		239	.	2798	2879	1	.	8	10
15 Central African Rep.		.	3603	2254	1754	.	12	8	6
16 Madagascar		4436	1480	.	.	11	4	.	.
17 Benin		11654	3090	2167	.	49	13	8	.
18 Rwanda		.	2458	3600	4354	.	15	14	16
19 Kenya		1979	2810	3402	1521	9	10	11	4
20 Sierra Leone		.	.	.	2962	.	.	.	9
21 Guinea		.	.	1218	1197	.	.	4	4
22 Ghana		.	3638	1195	619	.	9	3	2
23 Sudan		1850	.	2033	.	6	.	6	.
24 Senegal		.	2006	1849	.	.	5	5	.
25 Mozambique		.	.	.	.	.	.	.	.
Middle-income oil importers	w	3585	3678	3116	3456	.	.	.	.
	m	2462	2991	3205	4087	7	4	4	6
26 Mauritania		.	.	7756	10969	.	.	17	25
27 Liberia		.	.	2168	4405	.	.	4	9
28 Zambia		9317	3075	3118	3912*	14	5	6	7*
29 Lesotho		2462	.	.	1685	11	.	.	4
30 Côte d'Ivoire		5509	7191	3293*	4087	7	9	4*	6
31 Zimbabwe		1601	1544	2897	2287	2	2	4	3
32 Swaziland		.	2908	1489	1548*	.	3	2	2*
33 Botswana		.	4235	6316	8256	.	9	7	9
34 Mauritius		523	2231	3536	4480	1	2	3	4
Middle-income oil exporters	w	.	.	.	.	.	.	.	.
	m	.	.	.	.	.	.	.	.
35 Nigeria		7262	14621	13918*	2181*	11	20	15*	3*
36 Cameroon		.	.	.	3345	.	.	.	4
37 Congo, People's Rep.		2307	6579	2891	.	4	8	3	.
38 Gabon		.	.	.	.	.	.	.	.
39 Angola		.	.	.	.	.	.	.	.
Sub-Saharan Africa	w	4338	6461	5260	2365	.	.	.	.
	m	2462	3090	2798	2710	11	12	7	8
Francophone countries	w	4254	3114	2375	2759	.	.	.	.
	m	3371	3090	2535	3112	9	12	8	10
Anglophone countries	w	4358	8977	7533	2314	.	.	.	.
	m	2462	3120	3118	2625	11	9	6	6
Other	w	.	2060	1364	1458	.	.	.	.
	m	.	2060	1104	1228	.	19	8	9

* Figures with an asterisk are for years other than those specified. See the technical notes.

Table A-20. Distribution of Public Recurrent Expenditure on Primary Schools by Purpose, circa 1983

		Administration	Teachers' emoluments	Teaching materials	Scholarships	Welfare services	Not distributed
Low-income economies	w	1.7	87.2	5.8	0.9	3.6	0.8
	m	0.5	92.0	1.5	(.)	(.)	0.6
Low-income semiarid	w	6.4	81.9	4.0	(.)	5.8	2.0
	m	3.2	86.0	1.7	(.)	(.)	0.3
1 Mali		0.5	97.2	2.4	(.)	(.)	(.)
2 Burkina Faso		(.)	88.3	1.1	(.)	(.)	10.6
3 Niger		6.0	83.8	10.2	(.)	(.)	(.)
4 Gambia		.	.	.	.	.	.
5 Somalia		17.1	59.6	(.)	(.)	22.6	0.7
6 Chad		.	.	.	.	.	.
Low-income other	w	1.2	87.7	6.0	1.0	3.4	0.7
	m	0.3	93.9	1.5	(.)	(.)	0.8
7 Ethiopia		1.4	95.2	2.5	(.)	0.7	0.2
8 Zaire		.	.	.	.	.	.
9 Malawi		7.9	89.3	(.)	(.)	(.)	2.8
10 Guinea-Bissau		(.)	92.5	(.)	(.)	(.)	7.5
11 Tanzania		2.6	58.2	28.9	6.5	1.3	2.5
12 Burundi		(.)	98.4	1.4	(.)	(.)	0.3
13 Uganda		0.8	95.6	(.)	(.)	(.)	3.6
14 Togo		0.6	97.3	(.)	(.)	(.)	2.1
15 Central African Rep.		.	.	.	.	.	.
16 Madagascar		(.)	99.4	(.)	(.)	(.)	0.6
17 Benin		.	.	.	.	.	.
18 Rwanda		(.)	91.0	4.0	(.)	4.0	1.0
19 Kenya		2.1	85.3	2.6	(.)	10.0	(.)
20 Sierra Leone		.	.	.	.	.	.
21 Guinea		.	.	.	.	.	.
22 Ghana		(.)	98.4	1.6	(.)	(.)	(.)
23 Sudan		.	.	.	.	.	.
24 Senegal		./.	91.4	3.6	0.6	4.5	(.)
25 Mozambique		.	.	.	.	.	.
Middle-income oil importers	w	1.9	89.6	1.0	1.8	1.3	4.3
	m	0.2	89.6	0.6	(.)	0.1	(.)
26 Mauritania		0.2	97.9	1.9	(.)	(.)	(.)
27 Liberia		8.8	83.3	1.1	6.8	(.)	(.)
28 Zambia		7.2	89.6	3.1	(.)	0.2	(.)
29 Lesotho		(.)	99.9	(.)	(.)	(.)	0.1
30 Côte d'Ivoire		0.7	90.0	1.5	5.0	0.7	2.1
31 Zimbabwe		(.)	89.2	(.)	(.)	2.3	8.4
32 Swaziland		(.)	99.4	0.6	(.)	(.)	(.)
33 Botswana		(.)	85.8	(.)	(.)	(.)	14.2
34 Mauritius		13.0	80.8	(.)	./.	5.7	0.5
Middle-income oil exporters	w	.	.	.	.	.	.
	m	.	.	.	.	.	.
35 Nigeria		.	.	.	.	.	.
36 Cameroon		.	.	.	.	.	.
37 Congo, People's Rep.		(.)	99.4	0.1	0.5	0.0	0.0
38 Gabon		.	.	.	.	.	.
39 Angola		.	.	.	.	.	.
Sub-Saharan Africa	w	1.7	88.6	3.5	1.3	2.4	2.4
	m	0.3	91.2	1.1	(.)	(.)	0.4
Francophone countries	w	0.6	92.4	2.0	2.5	1.1	1.4
	m	(.)	97.2	1.5	(.)	(.)	0.3
Anglophone countries	w	2.1	86.7	4.4	0.8	2.9	3.1
	m	1.5	89.3	0.3	(.)	0.1	0.3
Other	w	4.6	87.7	1.9	(.)	5.2	0.8
	m	1.4	92.5	(.)	(.)	0.7	0.7

./. Expenditures are included with teachers' emoluments.

Table A-21. Distribution of Public Recurrent Expenditure on Secondary Schools by Purpose, circa 1983

		\multicolumn{6}{c}{Percentage of recurrent expenditure}
		Administration	Teachers' emoluments	Teaching materials	Scholarships	Welfare services	Not distributed
Low-income economies	w	1.1	75.8	6.2	0.9	5.1	8.5
	m	(.)	68.7	4.7	(.)	0.2	3.0
Low-income semiarid	w	6.1	52.4	8.4	(.)	6.1	3.4
	m	5.5	56.9	8.5	(.)	8.0	(.)
1 Mali		1.4	54.1	6.8	(.)	(.)	(.)
2 Burkina Faso		(.)	67.8	1.9	(.)	15.9	(.)
3 Niger		9.6	40.4	10.3	(.)	(.)	9.1
4 Gambia		.	.	.	.	.	.
5 Somalia		10.7	59.8	12.1	(.)	17.3	0.1
6 Chad		.	.	.	.	.	.
Low-income other	w	0.7	77.5	6.1	0.9	5.0	8.8
	m	(.)	74.7	4.0	(.)	0.2	6.7
7 Ethiopia		3.1	87.1	6.0	(.)	3.2	0.6
8 Zaire		.	.	.	.	.	.
9 Malawi		4.0	73.3	9.1	(.)	(.)	13.6
10 Guinea-Bissau		(.)	79.5	(.)	(.)	(.)	20.5
11 Tanzania		2.2	44.5	3.6	6.5	27.3	16.9
12 Burundi		(.)	67.8	2.3	(.)	28.5	1.5
13 Uganda		(.)	54.0	(.)	(.)	(.)	46.0
14 Togo		5.3	80.0	4.4	(.)	0.3	3.4
15 Central African Rep.		.	.	.	.	.	.
16 Madagascar		0.1	91.5	1.2	(.)	3.6	2.7
17 Benin		.	.	.	.	.	.
18 Rwanda		(.)	66.0	5.0	(.)	18.0	10.0
19 Kenya		(.)	69.5	(.)	(.)	(.)	30.5
20 Sierra Leone		.	.	.	.	.	.
21 Guinea		.	.	.	.	.	.
22 Ghana		(.)	90.7	9.0	(.)	(.)	0.3
23 Sudan		.	.	.	.	.	.
24 Senegal		(.)	76.1	11.0	0.6	(.)	(.)
25 Mozambique		.	.	.	.	.	.
Middle-income oil importers	w	3.3	67.4	1.3	2.4	5.4	21.0
	m	(.)	69.5	1.0	(.)	(.)	4.7
26 Mauritania		6.9	58.4	4.5	(.)	(.)	(.)
27 Liberia		18.3	62.8	3.5	6.8	(.)	(.)
28 Zambia		16.5	39.2	3.3	(.)	17.8	23.1
29 Lesotho		(.)	99.9	(.)	(.)	(.)	0.1
30 Côte d'Ivoire		(.)	69.5	(.)	5.0	(.)	30.5
31 Zimbabwe		(.)	78.5	1.0	(.)	11.5	9.0
32 Swaziland		(.)	87.4	12.6	(.)	(.)	(.)
33 Botswana		(.)	49.2	(.)	(.)	(.)	49.6
34 Mauritius		3.2	95.5	0.1	(.)	0.7	0.5
Middle-income oil exporters	w	.	.	.	.	.	.
	m	.	.	.	.	.	.
35 Nigeria		.	.	.	.	.	.
36 Cameroon		.	.	.	.	.	.
37 Congo, People's Rep.		(.)	83.9	1.8	0.5	4.0	0.4
38 Gabon		.	.	.	.	.	.
39 Angola		.	.	.	.	.	.
Sub-Saharan Africa	w	2.1	72.2	3.8	1.5	5.2	13.9
	m	(.)	69.5	3.4	(.)	0.2	3.0
Francophone countries	w	0.9	71.1	2.3	2.9	1.9	17.8
	m	(.)	67.8	4.4	(.)	0.3	1.5
Anglophone countries	w	2.6	72.2	4.6	0.8	7.2	12.5
	m	(.)	71.4	2.2	(.)	(.)	11.3
Other	w	4.2	82.8	6.8	(.)	5.3	1.0
	m	3.1	79.5	6.0	(.)	3.2	0.6

./. Expenditures are included with teachers' emoluments.

Table A-22. Distribution of Public Recurrent Expenditure on Tertiary Education by Purpose, circa 1983

		Percentage of recurrent expenditure					
		Administration	Teachers' emoluments	Teaching materials	Scholarships	Welfare services	Not distributed
Low-income economies	w	2.0	40.0	1.8	46.9	1.1	8.2
	m	(.)	52.0	0.2	44.9	(.)	2.4
1 Mali		(.)	20.9	1.4	77.8	(.)	(.)
2 Burkina Faso		7.8	9.4	7.6	65.3	7.2	2.7
3 Niger		(.)	(.)	(.)	59.6	(.)	40.4
9 Malawi		0.6	91.1	4.1	(.)	(.)	4.3
10 Guinea-Bissau		(.)	67.8	(.)	(.)	(.)	32.2
12 Burundi		(.)	59.8	(.)	40.2	(.)	0.1
14 Togo		3.4	44.1	0.4	49.6	0.3	2.1
18 Rwanda		./.	72.1	(.)	27.7	(.)	0.2
Middle-income economies	w	4.5	54.0	1.8	34.0	1.1	5.4
	m	(.)	73.2	(.)	25.6	(.)	0.3
26 Mauritania		13.0	17.5	7.5	62.1	(.)	(.)
28 Zambia		(.)	81.5	(.)	18.5	./.	(.)
29 Lesotho		(.)	100.0	(.)	./.	./.	(.)
30 Côte d'Ivoire		12.2	22.7	(.)	51.1	(.)	13.9
31 Zimbabwe		(.)	92.4	0.2	./.	6.0	1.5
32 Swaziland		(.)	90.0	10.0	(.)	(.)	(.)
33 Botswana		(.)	74.4	(.)	25.6	./.	(.)
34 Mauritius		(.)	100.0	(.)	./.	./.	(.)
37 Congo, People's Rep.		(.)	17.3	10.7	65.4	(.)	6.6
Sub-Saharan Africa	w	4.3	49.7	1.9	37.2	1.2	6.5
	m	(.)	67.8	0.1	33.9	(.)	0.9
Francophone countries	w	7.1	24.7	2.7	55.1	0.4	10.0
	m	(.)	20.9	0.4	59.6	(.)	2.1
Anglophone countries	w	(.)	87.3	0.6	9.2	2.5	0.9
	m	(.)	91.1	0.1	(.)	(.)	(.)
Other	w	(.)	67.8	(.)	(.)	(.)	32.2
	m	(.)	67.8	(.)	(.)	(.)	32.2

./. Expenditures are included with teachers' emoluments.

Table A-23. Average Salaries of Primary and Secondary Teachers, circa 1983

		Primary teachers — In current dollars	Primary teachers — As a multiple of income per capita	Secondary teachers — In current dollars	Secondary teachers — As a multiple of income per capita
Low-income economies	w	1361	.	3389	.
	m	1329	7.3	2577	12.2
Low-income semiarid	w	1773	.	1603	.
	m	2127	11.1	1902	9.2
1 Mali		1998	12.5	1003	6.3
2 Burkina Faso		2255	12.5	2501	13.9
3 Niger		2312	9.6	2919	12.2
4 Gambia		.	.	.	.
5 Somalia		985	3.9	1304	5.2
6 Chad		.	.	.	.
Low-income other	w	1332	.	3591	.
	m	1233	6.9	2599	12.4
7 Ethiopia		1139	10.0	2353	20.7
8 Zaire		.	.	.	.
9 Malawi		744	3.5	2599	12.4
10 Guinea-Bissau		1228	8.5	1501	10.3
11 Tanzania		662	2.8	6857	28.6
12 Burundi		1833	6.9	4010	15.2
13 Uganda		278	1.3	2487	11.3
14 Togo		1329	4.7	2577	9.2
15 Central African Rep.		.	.	.	.
16 Madagascar		.	.	.	.
17 Benin		.	.	.	.
18 Rwanda		2423	9.0	4061	15.0
19 Kenya		1233	3.6	1338	3.9
20 Sierra Leone		.	.	.	.
21 Guinea		.	.	.	.
22 Ghana		3070	9.9	5142	16.6
23 Sudan		.	.	.	.
24 Senegal		3211	7.3	4666	10.6
25 Mozambique		.	.	.	.
Middle-income oil importers	w	4120	.	8431	.
	m	3077	4.0	5314	10.0
26 Mauritania		6671	15.4	11331	26.2
27 Liberia		1801	3.8	3037	6.3
28 Zambia		3320	6.3	5541	10.5
29 Lesotho		1794	4.0	5314	11.9
30 Côte d'Ivoire		6093	8.6	15164	21.4
31 Zimbabwe		4118	5.6	7398	10.0
32 Swaziland		3077	3.3	5282	5.6
33 Botswana		2811	3.1	4987	5.4
34 Mauritius		2849	2.5	4300	3.7
Middle-income oil exporters	w	.	.	.	.
	m	.	.	.	.
35 Nigeria		.	.	.	.
36 Cameroon		.	.	.	.
37 Congo, People's Rep.		4966	4.8	5071	4.9
38 Gabon		.	.	.	.
39 Angola		.	.	.	.
Sub-Saharan Africa	w	2079	.	4651	.
	m	2255	5.6	4061	10.6
Francophone countries	w	3741	.	6655	.
	m	2367	8.8	4035	13.0
Anglophone countries	w	1804	.	4366	.
	m	2306	3.6	5065	10.2
Other	w	1120	.	2139	.
	m	1139	8.5	1501	10.3

Table A-24. External Aid to African Education and Training by Source, 1981–83 Average

		Millions of dollars							Total as a percentage of all aid to African education
		Education sector[a]			Project-related training[b]	Cost of hosting African students abroad[c]	Total		
		Overseas fellowships	Other	Sub-total					
OECD and OPEC members	t	168.2	617.3	785.5	394.4	189.8	1369.7	w	88.1
Concessional aid	t	168.2	589.2	757.4	366.9	189.8	1314.1	w	84.5
Bilateral	t	149.4	357.8	507.2	246.6†	189.8	943.6	w	60.7
France		23.4	182.8	206.2	.	73.2	279.4		18.0
Belgium		14.6	43.9	58.5	.	7.4	65.9		4.2
United Kingdom		15.7	24.2	39.9	.	23.8	63.7		4.1
United States		7.0	29.3	36.3	.	64.3	100.6		6.5
Germany, Federal Rep.		4.5	14.7	19.2	.	7.5	26.7		1.7
Italy		2.4	15.4	17.8	.	3.7	21.5		1.4
Sweden		0.3	23.0	23.3	.	0.0	23.3		1.5
Others and not distributed		81.5	24.5	106.0	246.6†	9.9	362.5		23.3
Multilateral	t	18.8	231.4	250.2	120.3	0.0	370.5	w	23.8
International Development Association		.	128.6	128.6	54.3	0.0	182.9		11.8
African Development Fund		0.0	33.7	33.7	14.6†	0.0	48.3		3.1
European Development Fund		13.2	26.6	39.8	.	0.0	39.8		2.6
United Nations Development Program		2.2	15.8	18.0	.	0.0	18.0		1.2
UNICEF		0.6	7.8	8.4	.	0.0	8.4		0.5
Others and not distributed		2.8	18.9	21.7	51.4†	0.0	73.1		4.7
Nonconcessional aid	t	0.0	28.1	28.1	27.5	0.0	55.6	w	3.6
IBRD		0.0	11.9	11.9	7.9	0.0	19.8		1.3
African Development Bank		0.0	16.2	16.2	19.6†	0.0	35.8		2.3
East European nonmarket economies and Cuba	t	32.8†	7.2†	40.0†	.	50.8†	90.8†	w	5.8†
Other (Egypt, India)	t	0.0	0.0	0.0	.	4.7	4.7	w	0.3
Nongovernmental organizations	t	9.8†	80.2†	90.0†	.	0.0†	90.0†	w	5.8†
Total	t	210.8	704.7	915.5	394.4	245.3	1555.2	w	100.0

† Figures with a dagger are estimates. See the technical notes.
a. Disbursements to central departments of education.
b. Aid for training in sectors other than education.
c. Host country subsidization of African students studying abroad, over and above any fellowships.

Table A-25. Concessional Education Sector Aid from OECD and OPEC Members by Recipient Country, 1981–83 Average

			Noncapital			Capital			Total		
			Dollars (millions)	As percentage of total recurrent education budget	Percentage going to females		Dollars (millions)	As percentage of total capital education budget		Dollars (millions)	Education aid as a percentage of total external aid	Education aid per capita
Low-income economies	t		468.9	w 18.8 m 19.7	35.2 32.6	t	107.2	w 31.2 m 47.7	t	576.1	w 10.4 m 11.0	2.41 2.94
Low-income semiarid	t		73.5	w 29.6 m 29.5	31.0 32.5	t	25.5	w 44.7 m 54.9	t	99.0	w 7.9 m 9.9	3.38 3.42
1 Mali			12.3	21.9	24.7		3.0	86.4		15.3	7.3	2.15
2 Burkina Faso			15.3	32.4	32.5		4.3	70.9		19.6	9.2	3.02
3 Niger			15.1	22.1	32.7		12.5	36.7		27.6	10.6	4.68
4 Gambia			3.0	26.6	43.6		2.4	38.8		5.4	11.3	7.71
5 Somalia			14.4	35.2	28.0		2.3	36.2		16.7	3.6	3.71
6 Chad*			13.4	55.5	.		1.0	100.0		14.4	22.3	3.13
Low-income other	t		395.4	w 17.6 m 17.0	36.0 32.6	t	81.7	w 28.1 m 47.7	t	477.1	w 11.1 m 13.1	2.28 2.56
7 Ethiopia			21.6	16.4	31.1		6.5	18.4		28.1	14.1	0.85
8 Zaire			40.2	10.6	24.8		5.0	26.2		45.2	13.0	1.47
9 Malawi			10.0	25.2	33.7		7.8	53.6		17.8	14.7	2.74
10 Guinea-Bissau*			.	.	.		.	.		.	.	.
11 Tanzania			30.7	11.9	.		8.1	18.4		38.8	5.7	1.96
12 Burundi			18.4	38.6	31.3		5.1	58.8		23.5	18.5	5.47
13 Uganda			2.1	2.3	37.8		2.2	11.1		4.3	3.2	0.32
14 Togo			10.7	18.7	27.9		3.6	74.3		14.3	18.5	5.11
15 Central African Rep.			13.7	33.9	22.1		2.2	84.6		15.9	17.7	6.63
16 Madagascar			20.0	19.7	40.7		1.9	14.6		21.9	8.7	2.38
17 Benin			8.7	12.9	27.2		4.1	47.7		12.8	15.9	3.46
18 Rwanda			9.9	17.0	29.6		5.9	52.1		15.8	10.5	2.87
19 Kenya*			124.5	26.9	47.2		.	.		124.5	25.7	6.88
20 Sierra Leone			7.6	17.1	33.9		3.2	63.8		10.8	13.1	3.38
21 Guinea			1.9	1.9	32.8		6.9	79.0		8.8	9.8	1.54
22 Ghana			9.4	11.1	31.1		1.8	9.3		11.2	7.9	0.92
23 Sudan			7.0	8.8	41.9		6.0	17.0		13.0	1.8	0.64
24 Senegal			50.6	33.1	32.6		9.1	.		59.7	21.0	9.95
25 Mozambique			8.4	.	42.1		2.3	.		10.7	5.1	0.83
Middle-income oil importers	t		95.9	w 6.5 m 11.1	43.6 44.8	t	21.9	w 12.0 m 28.0	t	117.8	w 11.4 m 10.7	4.16 4.16
26 Mauritania*			.	.	.		.	.		.	.	.
27 Liberia			6.5	11.3	37.8		2.0	26.8		8.5	7.8	4.25
28 Zambia			21.8	10.9	.		2.6	51.8		24.4	7.9	4.07
29 Lesotho			9.5	27.9	54.7		2.6	21.5		12.1	13.5	8.64
30 Côte d'Ivoire*			24.3	4.3	33.3		0.7	0.6		25.0	18.3	2.81
31 Zimbabwe			10.4	2.2	49.5		6.5	31.8		16.9	7.8	2.25
32 Swaziland			8.7	25.3	44.8		1.6	19.9		10.3	36.7	14.71
33 Botswana			12.4	20.7	47.7		5.3	35.5		17.7	17.4	19.67
34 Mauritius			2.3	4.5	38.7		0.6	29.1		2.9	6.1	3.22
Middle-income oil exporters	t		53.3	w 1.2 m 3.9	34.4 33.7	t	10.2	w 1.3 m 2.9	t	63.5	w 13.7 m 14.0	0.58 2.83
35 Nigeria			10.3	0.3	.		0.8	0.1		11.1	30.2	0.12
36 Cameroon			19.0	10.1	33.7		7.3	11.1		26.3	12.4	2.83
37 Congo, People's Rep.			12.8	10.8	.		0.2	2.9		13.0	14.0	7.65
38 Gabon			3.1	3.9	31.3		0.4	1.4		3.5	5.6	5.00
39 Angola			8.1	1.9	37.5		1.5	14.2		9.6	16.0	1.20
Sub-Saharan Africa	t		618.1	w 7.3 m 16.7	36.3 33.5	t	139.3	w 10.1 m 30.5	t	757.4	w 10.7 m 13.1	2.01 3.38
Francophone countries	t		289.4	w 13.5 m 18.7	30.7 31.3	t	73.2	w 19.0 m 49.9	t	362.6	w 13.2 m 13.0	3.15 3.13
Anglophone countries	t		276.2	w 4.9 m 11.9	44.5 40.3	t	53.5	w 6.1 m 24.2	t	329.7	w 9.8 m 11.3	1.61 3.38
Other	t		52.5	w 7.2 m 16.4	33.1 34.3	t	12.6	w 19.7 m 18.4	t	65.1	w 7.0 m 9.6	1.12 1.03

* Only partial information on education aid is available. Figures understate actual education aid.

149

Table A-26. External Education Sector Aid from OECD and OPEC Members by Level and Type of Education

		Dollars (millions) 1981–83 average		Primary	General	Teacher training	Vocational/ technical	Tertiary	Other and not distributed
				Source					
Concessional aid	t	757.4	w	7.4	16.0	6.2	16.9	34.2	19.3
Bilateral	t	507.2	w	3.4	20.9	3.0	14.9	42.4	15.4
France		206.2		0.9	34.1	0.9	20.2	39.4	4.5
Belgium		58.5		0.3	30.4	0.3	17.1	40.7	11.2
United Kingdom		39.9		0.3	19.8	5.0	5.0	56.6	13.3
United States		36.3		6.9	10.5	17.1	6.9	29.7	28.9
Germany, Federal Rep.		19.2		.	4.2	1.6	14.6	59.9	19.7
Italy		17.8		15.7	5.6	.	7.9	51.7	19.1
Sweden		23.3		29.6	2.1	3.0	18.5	15.5	31.3
Others		106.0		2.6	3.7	3.7	10.2	49.4	30.4
Multilateral	t	250.2	w	15.7	6.1	12.7	20.9	17.5	27.1
International Development Association		128.6		27.7	8.1	10.6	26.1	11.4	16.1
African Development Fund		33.7		(.)	8.9	44.5	31.8	2.6	12.2
European Development Fund		39.8		(.)	4.0	(.)	14.3	60.1	21.6
United Nations Development Program		18.0		2.8	1.7	10.6	12.8	25.0	47.1
UNICEF		8.4		39.3	(.)	13.1	2.4	(.)	45.2
Others		21.7		(.)	(.)	(.)	(.)	(.)	100.0
Nonconcessional aid	t	28.1	w	22.4	3.6	18.9	28.1	20.6	6.4
IBRD		11.9		27.7	8.4	10.9	26.1	11.8	15.1
African Development Bank		16.2		18.5	(.)	24.7	29.6	27.2	(.)
Total	t	785.5	w	8.0	15.6	6.7	17.3	33.7	18.7
				Recipient groups*					
Low-income semiarid	t	99.0	w	4.1	15.3	1.6	13.6	39.8	25.6
Low-income other	t	477.1	w	4.2	12.4	4.3	27.3	31.3	20.5
Middle-income oil importers	t	117.8	w	10.4	13.8	8.6	11.2	30.1	25.9
Middle-income oil exporters	t	63.5	w	3.4	15.2	13.2	28.0	22.1	18.1
Francophone countries	t	362.6	w	8.3	5.4	8.0	28.4	26.5	23.4
Anglophone countries	t	329.7	w	2.1	21.5	4.5	17.0	36.6	18.3
Other	t	65.1	w	7.2	6.9	2.6	27.7	23.4	32.2

* Concessional aid only.

Table A-27. External Education Sector Aid from OECD and OPEC Members by Purpose

		Dollars (millions) 1981–83 average		Capital	Technical assistance	Fellowships	Operating costs and supplies	Non-specified
					Source			
Concessional aid	t	757.4	w	26.4	44.3	16.9	10.9	1.5
Bilateral	t	507.2	w	7.4	57.5	20.5	12.7	1.9
France		206.2		2.4	82.6	11.4	3.8	(.)
Belgium		58.5		0.3	68.3	25.0	6.4	(.)
United Kingdom		39.9		2.0	55.4	39.3	3.3	(.)
United States		36.3		7.2	56.7	19.3	16.8	(.)
Germany, Federal Rep.		19.2		8.3	41.7	23.4	26.6	(.)
Italy		17.8		1.7	66.3	13.5	18.5	(.)
Sweden		23.3		24.1	25.4	0.7	49.9	(.)
Other		106.0		20.3	12.4	34.4	24.2	8.7
Multilateral	t	250.2	w	64.9	17.4	9.6	7.2	0.9
International Development Association		128.6		83.2	16.8	(.)	(.)	(.)
African Development Fund		33.7		86.8	8.3	1.9	3.0	(.)
European Development Fund		39.8		52.8	7.5	33.2	6.5	(.)
United Nations Development Program		18.0		(.)	64.2	12.2	23.6	(.)
UNICEF		8.4		9.5	23.8	7.1	59.5	0.1
Other		21.7		20.3	12.4	34.4	24.2	8.7
Nonconcessional aid	t	28.1	w	85.3	11.9	1.1	1.7	(.)
IBRD		11.9		83.2	16.8	(.)	(.)	(.)
African Development Bank		16.2		86.8	8.3	1.9	3.0	(.)
Total	t	785.5	w	28.5	43.1	16.4	10.6	1.4
					Recipient groups*			
Low-income semiarid	t	99.0	w	25.8	53.1	12.2	5.6	3.3
Low-income other	t	477.1	w	17.1	34.1	14.8	8.2	25.8
Middle-income oil importers	t	117.8	w	34.3	42.3	10.7	11.5	1.2
Middle-income oil exporters	t	63.5	w	44.4	34.5	11.7	8.7	0.7
Francophone countries	t	362.6	w	19.4	20.7	15.1	9.9	34.9
Anglophone countries	t	329.7	w	26.1	54.2	12.5	5.3	1.9
Other	t	65.1	w	31.8	32.7	11.6	20.4	3.5

* Concessional aid only.

Table A-28. External Public Debt of the Education Sector

		Debt outstanding and disbursed (millions of dollars)			Debt service profile (millions of dollars)								
					Actual						Projected*		
		1970	1980	1984	1970	1980	1981	1982	1983	1984	1985	1986	1987
Low-income economies	t	42.6	364.1	577.4	1.0	11.4	10.5	6.9	20.0	16.3	25.6	21.5	21.5
Low-income semiarid	t	0.2	42.4	101.1	0.0	0.3	0.5	2.2	4.2	1.6	3.7	5.8	5.9
1 Mali		0.1	20.4	24.8	(.)	0.1	0.3	0.2	0.3	0.3	0.3	0.4	0.5
2 Burkina Faso		0.0	3.5	9.8	0.0	(.)	(.)	(.)	0.1	0.1	0.1	0.1	0.1
3 Niger		0.0	0.2	22.6	0.0	(.)	(.)	1.6	3.6	0.9	1.4	3.1	2.9
4 Gambia		0.0	1.8	5.5	0.0	(.)	(.)	(.)	(.)	(.)	(.)	(.)	(.)
5 Somalia		0.0	11.6	33.6	0.0	0.1	0.1	0.2	0.2	0.2	1.7	2.1	2.2
6 Chad		0.1	4.9	4.8	0.0	0.0	0.0	(.)	(.)	0.2	0.1	0.1	0.1
Low-income other	t	42.4	321.7	476.3	1.0	11.1	10.1	4.8	15.8	14.7	21.9	15.7	15.7
7 Ethiopia		6.5	49.9	77.0	(.)	0.5	0.7	0.8	0.9	1.1	1.2	1.5	1.7
8 Zaire		0.9	6.7	8.4	0.3	(.)	0.1	0.1	0.1	0.2	0.1	0.3	0.3
9 Malawi		3.9	21.8	57.3	(.)	0.2	0.2	0.3	0.4	0.6	0.5	0.7	0.8
10 Guinea-Bissau		0.0	1.3	2.8	0.0	(.)	0.2	0.7	(.)	(.)	(.)	(.)	0.1
11 Tanzania		9.5	31.6	40.8	0.1	0.5	0.6	0.5	0.6	0.7	0.9	1.0	1.0
12 Burundi		0.0	9.9	29.8	0.0	0.1	0.1	0.1	0.1	0.1	0.3	0.3	0.4
13 Uganda		9.6	21.0	22.9	0.1	0.3	0.5	0.3	0.5	0.6	0.6	0.6	0.8
14 Togo		(.)	0.1	12.5	(.)	0.0	(.)	(.)	0.1	0.1	0.1	0.1	0.1
15 Central African Rep.		0.0	3.9	11.3	0.0	(.)	(.)	0.1	0.1	0.1	0.2	0.2	0.2
16 Madagascar		1.6	79.6	50.5	0.1	4.0	4.9	0.5	11.5	8.5	7.8	1.7	0.5
17 Benin		(.)	0.0	3.0	(.)	0.0	0.0	0.0	0.0	(.)	0.1	0.1	0.1
18 Rwanda		0.0	2.7	6.7	0.0	(.)	(.)	(.)	(.)	0.1	0.2	0.3	0.3
19 Kenya		8.4	22.3	43.8	(.)	0.5	0.5	0.6	0.8	1.0	1.4	1.9	2.1
20 Sierra Leone		(.)	8.9	14.4	0.0	0.1	0.1	0.1	0.1	0.2	0.3	0.3	0.3
21 Guinea		0.0	4.7	22.3	0.1	(.)	(.)	0.1	0.1	0.1	2.4	2.4	3.1
22 Ghana		2.0	2.3	2.1	0.3	0.0	0.0	0.1	(.)	0.1	0.1	0.1	0.1
23 Sudan		0.0	22.2	21.7	0.0	0.2	0.2	0.2	0.2	0.2	1.6	0.6	0.6
24 Senegal		0.0	32.7	49.1	0.0	4.7	1.9	0.4	0.3	0.8	4.1	3.6	3.2
25 Mozambique		.	.	.	.	.	.	.	.	.	.	.	.
Middle-income oil importers	t	5.3	235.6	214.7	0.3	43.7	33.0	39.3	39.0	22.9	38.7	32.0	32.6
26 Mauritania		0.0	3.2	8.9	0.0	1.2	0.9	0.1	(.)	(.)	0.2	0.2	0.2
27 Liberia		2.3	15.0	17.5	(.)	0.3	0.2	0.9	1.2	1.2	1.4	1.4	1.4
28 Zambia		0.4	39.8	52.5	0.2	4.9	4.3	4.9	6.3	5.9	5.8	5.8	5.8
29 Lesotho		0.0	0.0	4.9	0.0	0.0	0.0	0.0	(.)	(.)	(.)	0.1	0.1
30 Côte d'Ivoire		1.6	150.7	81.2	0.1	35.9	26.0	30.8	27.3	11.1	24.6	15.5	15.9
31 Zimbabwe		0.9	0.0	0.0	0.0	0.0	0.0	0.0	0.0	0.0	0.0	0.0	0.0
32 Swaziland		0.0	6.9	14.3	0.0	0.4	0.2	0.6	0.7	1.1	1.9	1.8	1.8
33 Botswana		0.0	8.1	22.1	0.0	0.5	0.6	0.8	1.2	1.7	3.1	5.4	5.5
34 Mauritius		0.1	11.9	13.4	(.)	0.6	0.7	1.3	2.1	1.9	1.6	1.8	1.9
Middle-income oil exporters	t	4.7	135.3	166.0	0.1	19.1	17.4	13.4	10.7	15.4	25.9	40.0	49.3
35 Nigeria		2.8	56.9	96.3	(.)	2.8	3.1	3.8	5.7	10.6	20.6	33.6	43.0
36 Cameroon		1.7	47.5	50.8	(.)	1.4	3.6	1.1	2.4	2.1	2.4	3.6	3.9
37 Congo, People's Rep.		0.0	5.5	10.7	0.0	0.1	0.5	1.0	1.0	1.1	1.3	1.1	0.9
38 Gabon		0.2	25.5	8.1	0.1	14.8	10.1	7.5	1.5	1.5	1.6	1.8	1.5
39 Angola		.	.	.	.	.	.	.	.	.	.	.	.
Sub-Saharan Africa	t	52.6	735.0	958.1	1.4	74.2	60.9	59.7	69.7	54.6	90.1	93.5	103.4
Francophone countries		4.7	333.9	378.0	0.6	59.0	44.3	44.5	39.3	20.8	41.0	34.9	35.6
Anglophone countries		41.4	338.2	466.7	0.8	14.6	15.6	13.5	29.3	32.6	46.1	55.0	63.8
Other		6.5	62.9	113.4	(.)	0.6	1.0	1.6	1.2	1.2	3.0	3.6	4.0

* Projected debt service is based on contractual obligations on debt outstanding at the end of 1984. It excludes the effect of subsequent debt relief agreements.

Table B-1. Basic Indicators

		Population (millions) mid-1984	Area (thousands of square kilometers)		Dollars 1984	GNP per capita Average annual growth rate (percent) 1965–84	Average annual rate of inflation 1965–73	Average annual rate of inflation 1973–84*	Life expectancy at birth (years) 1984
Low-income economies	t	259.2	15693	w m	210 260	−0.2 0.6	4.3 3.7	19.6 11.2	48 46
Low-income semiarid	t	30.9	4714	w m	160 190	0.2 1.1	4.1 3.9	12.2 10.0	45 45
1 Mali		7.3	1240		140	1.1	7.6	10.4	46
2 Burkina Faso		6.6	274		160	1.2	2.6	10.6	45
3 Niger		6.2	1267		190	−1.3	4.0	11.5	43
4 Gambia		0.7	11		260	1.1	3.0	10.4	42
5 Somalia		5.2	638		260	.	3.8	20.2	46
6 Chad		4.9	1284		.	.	4.5	.	44
Low-income other	t	228.3	10979	w m	220 260	−0.3 0.6	4.3 3.4	20.1 11.5	49 48
7 Ethiopia		42.2	1222		110	0.4	1.8	4.4*	44
8 Zaire		29.7	2345		140	−1.6	18.7	48.2*	51
9 Malawi		6.8	119		180	1.7	4.5	9.4	45
10 Guinea-Bissau		0.9	36		190	.	.	9.1	38
11 Tanzania		21.5	945		210	0.6	3.2	11.5*	52
12 Burundi		4.6	28		220	1.9	2.9	12.2	48
13 Uganda		15.0	236		230	−2.9	5.6	64.5	51
14 Togo		2.9	57		250	0.5	3.1	8.2	52
15 Central African Rep.		2.5	623		260	−0.1	3.0	13.8	49
16 Madagascar		9.9	587		260	−1.6	4.1	14.4	52
17 Benin		3.9	113		270	1.0	3.6	10.8	49
18 Rwanda		5.8	26		280	2.3	7.7	10.5	47
19 Kenya		19.5	583		310	2.1	2.3	10.8	54
20 Sierra Leone		3.7	72		310	0.6	1.9	15.4	38
21 Guinea		5.9	246		330	1.1	3.0	4.5	38
22 Ghana		12.3	239		350	−1.9	8.1	52.2	53
23 Sudan		21.3	2506		360	1.1	7.2	19.3	48
24 Senegal		6.4	196		380	−0.5	3.0	9.0	46
25 Mozambique		13.4	802		.	−2.0	4.5	11.8	46
Middle-income oil importers	t	32.4	3258	w m	630 610	1.1 1.5	3.2 4.3	10.6 11.1	54 54
26 Mauritania		1.7	1031		450	0.3	3.9	7.7	46
27 Liberia		2.1	111		470	0.5	1.5	6.7	50
28 Zambia		6.4	753		470	−1.4	5.8	10.5	52
29 Lesotho		1.5	30		530	5.9	4.4	11.9*	54
30 Côte d'Ivoire		9.9	323		610	0.8	3.0	11.1	52
31 Zimbabwe		8.1	391		760	1.5	1.1	11.4	57
32 Swaziland		0.7	17		790	4.0	4.3	14.0*	54
33 Botswana		1.0	600		960	8.4	4.4	9.8	58
34 Mauritius		1.0	2		1090	2.7	5.6	12.7	66
Middle-income oil exporters	t	117.5	3256	w m	710 970	1.9 2.9	8.5 5.8	13.7 13.4	50 51
35 Nigeria		96.5	924		730	2.7	10.3	13.4	50
36 Cameroon		9.9	475		800	2.9	5.8	12.7	54
37 Congo, People's Rep.		1.8	342		1140	3.7	4.6	12.3	57
38 Gabon		0.8	268		4100	5.9	5.8	15.5	51
39 Angola		8.5	1247		.	−5.7	6.9	18.4*	43
Sub-Saharan Africa	t	409.2	22207	w m	390 310	1.0 1.1	4.5 4.2	15.2 11.5	49 49
Francophone countries	t	120.7	10725	w m	330 355	1.0 1.1	4.2 4.5	14.0 12.1	49 51
Anglophone countries	t	218.3	7538	w m	520 245	1.7 0.2	5.9 3.0	16.2 10.5	50 46
Other	t	70.2	3944	w m	. 395	. 2.1	2.6 4.8	. 14.8	45 46

* Figures with an asterisk are for 1973–83, not 1973–84.

153

Table B-2. Languages of Sub-Saharan Africa

	Number of languages Total	Number of languages Principal	Principal languages*	Percentage of population speaking language as: Mother tongue	Percentage of population speaking language as: Second language	Language used as: Official language	Language used as: Lingua franca	Medium of instruction in: Lower primary	Medium of instruction in: Upper primary	Medium of instruction in: Post-primary
Low-income economies										
1 Mali	10	4	Bambara	31	20		x			
			Fulfulde	20						
			Arabic				x			
			French	low		x		x	x	x
2 Burkina Faso	10†	5	Mossi	50			x			
			French	low		x		x	x	x
3 Niger	7†	7	Hausa	46	24		x			
			Songhai		19					
			French	low		x		x	x	x
4 Gambia	8	5	Manding	41	19		x			
			Wolof	13			x			
			Fulfulde	14						
			English	low		x		x	x	x
5 Somalia	4†	4	Somali	95	2	x		x	x	x
			Arabic			x				
			English			x				
			Italian			x				
6 Chad	15†	3	Arabic	13	40		x	x	x	
			Sara	19	10		x	x		
			French	low	13	x		x	x	x
7 Ethiopia	70	4	Amharic	31	40	x	x	x	x	
			Tigrinya	14			x			
			Galla	35						
			English	low						x
8 Zaire	300	5	Swahili	36	13		x	x		
			Lingala	28	41		x	x		
			Luba	17			x	x		
			Kongo	12	18		x	x		
			French	low		x			x	x
9 Malawi	15†	4	Nyanja	50	10		x	x		
			Lomwe	15						
			Yao	14						
			English		5	x			x	x
10 Guinea-Bissau	NA	5	Crioulo				x			
			Portuguese	low		x		x	x	x
11 Tanzania	120	3	Sukuma	13						
			Swahili	.6	90	x	x	x	x	x
			English	low	15					x
12 Burundi	3	3	Rundi	99		x				
			Swahili		10					
			French	low		x		x	x	x
13 Uganda	30†	7	Runyankore	20		x				
			Luganda	18	20			x		
			Lwo	12		x				
			Swahili		35		x			
			Lugbara			x				
			Ateso/ Akarimo-jong			x				
			English	low		x			x	x
14 Togo	15†	4	Ewe	44	6		x	x		
			Kabiye		20			x		
			Hausa				x			
			French	low		x			x	x
15 Central African Rep.	10†	4	Banda	31						
			Gaya	29						
			Sango	25			x			
			French	low		x		x	x	x

Table B-2 *(continued)*

	Number of languages Total	Number of languages Principal	Principal languages*	Percentage of population speaking language as: Mother tongue	Percentage of population speaking language as: Second language	Language used as: Official language	Language used as: Lingua franca	Medium of instruction in: Lower primary	Medium of instruction in: Upper primary	Medium of instruction in: Post-primary
16 Madagascar	NA	2	Malagasy				x	x		
			French	low		x			x	x
17 Benin	10†	4	Fon-Ewe	60			x			
			Yoruba	13						
			Bariba	12						
			French	low		x		x	x	x
18 Rwanda	3†	3	Kinyarwanda	90	8	x		x		
			Swahili	10			x			
			French	low		x		x	x	x
19 Kenya	50	7	Swahili	5	60	x	x	x		
			Kikuyu	25		x				
			Luhya			x				
			Luo			x				
			Kamba			x				
			English	low		x		x	x	x
20 Sierra Leone	18	4	Mende	31	5		x			
			Temne	25	45					
			Krio				x			
			English	low		x		x	x	x
21 Guinea	15†	4	Malinke	30	18		x			
			Fulfulde	28	5					
			SouSou	16						
			French			x		x	x	x
22 Ghana	54	9	Dagbani	16		x				
			Ewe	12		x				
			Akan	40			x	x		
			Hausa		60		x			
			Adangme			x				
			Nzema			x				
			Ga			x				
			Dagaari			x				
			English	low		x			x	x
23 Sudan	100	13	Arabic	50	10	x	x	x	x	x
			Shilluk			x				
			Bari			x				
			Latuka			x				
			Zande			x				
			Kreish			x				
			Ndogo			x				
			Moru			x				
			English	low			x			
24 Senegal	10†	8	Wolof	42	40		x	x		
			Fula	19	5		x	x		
			Serer	15		x				
			Diola	7		x				
			Malinke	6			x	x		
			Soninke	3		x				
			Arabic		high					
			French	low		x			x	x
25 Mozambique	20	8	Portuguese	low		x		x	x	x
Middle-income oil importers										
26 Mauritania	5	6	Arabic	80	7	x				
			Fulfulde		13	x				
			Wolof			x				
			French	low		x		x	x	x

(Table continues on the following page.)

Table B-2 (continued)

	Number of languages — Total	Number of languages — Principal	Principal languages*	Percentage of population speaking language as: Mother tongue	Percentage of population speaking language as: Second language	Language used as: Official language	Language used as: Lingua franca	Medium of instruction in: Lower primary	Medium of instruction in: Upper primary	Medium of instruction in: Post-primary
27 Liberia	28	4	Bassa	14	23					
			Kpelle	20	40					
			Krio	40	50		x			
			English	low		x	x	x	x	x
28 Zambia	73	8	Bemba	31	25		x	x		
			Nyanja	11	42		x	x		
			Tonga	11		x				
			Kaonde			x				
			Lunda			x				
			Luvale			x				
			English	low		x			x	x
29 Lesotho	2	2	Sotho	95	4		x	x		
			English	low		x			x	x
30 Côte d'Ivoire	60	5	Akan	25						
			Dyula	16	50		x			
			Anyi-Baoule	20						
			Senoufo	12						
			French	low	35	x		x	x	x
31 Zimbabwe	20†	3	Shona	75			x	x	x	
			Ndebele	16		x		x		
			English	low		x				x
32 Swaziland	NA	3	Swati	90			x	x		
			English	low		x			x	x
33 Botswana	3	2	Tswana	90	9	x	x	x		
			English	low		x			x	x
34 Mauritius	NA	8	French	low		x				
			English	low		x				
35 Nigeria	350†	11	Hausa	30	20		x	x		
			Yoruba	20			x	x		
			Ibo	10		x				
			Fulfulde				x	x		
			Pidgin-English				x			
			Kanuri				x			
			Edo			x				
			Ijo			x				
			Efik			x				
			Idoma			x				
			English	low		x			x	x
36 Cameroon	200	9	Bamileke	27						
			Fang	18						
			Ewondo				x			
			Fulfulde				x			
			French			x		x	x	x
			English	low		x		x	x	x
37 Congo, People's Rep.	15†	4	Kongo	52			x			
			Teke	25						
			Lingala				x			
			French	low		x		x	x	x
38 Gabon	15†	4	Fang	30	20		x			
			Eshira	20						
			Pidgin-English				x			
			French	low		x		x	x	x
39 Angola	20	4	Kongo	15						
			Kimbundu	23						
			Umbundu	30	20					
			Portuguese	low	35	x		x	x	x

* Only those languages for which data were available are shown. See the technical notes for other principal languages.
† Estimates may understate the actual number.

Table B-3. Population Growth and Projections

		Average annual growth of population (percent)			Population (millions)			Hypothetical size of stationary population (millions)	Assumed year of reaching net reproduction rate of 1	Population momentum 1985
		1965–73	1973–84	1980–2000	1984	1990	2000			
Low-income economies	w	2.6	2.8	3.1						
	m	2.4	2.8	3.0	t 259	310	419			
Low-income semiarid	w	2.5	2.5	2.7						
	m	2.2	2.7	2.6	t 31	36	47			
1 Mali		2.6	2.6	2.6	7	9	11	36	2035	1.8
2 Burkina Faso		2.0	1.8	2.0	7	7	9	31	2040	1.6
3 Niger		2.3	3.0	3.2	6	7	10	36	2040	1.9
4 Gambia		2.1	3.5	2.6	1	1	1	3	2040	.
5 Somalia		3.5	2.8	3.0	5	6	8	30	2040	1.9
6 Chad		1.9	2.1	2.5	5	6	7	22	2040	1.8
Low-income other	w	2.6	2.9	3.1						
	m	2.4	2.8	3.1	t 228	274				371
7 Ethiopia		2.6	2.8	2.7	42	49	65	204	2040	1.9
8 Zaire		2.4	3.0	3.2	30	36	47	130	2030	1.9
9 Malawi		2.8	3.1	3.2	7	8	11	38	2040	1.9
10 Guinea-Bissau		1.2	3.9	2.1	1	1	1	4	2045	.
11 Tanzania		3.2	3.4	3.5	21	27	37	123	2035	2.0
12 Burundi		1.4	2.2	3.0	5	5	7	24	2035	1.9
13 Uganda		3.6	3.2	3.3	15	18	26	84	2035	2.0
14 Togo		3.8	2.8	3.3	3	4	5	16	2035	2.0
15 Central African Rep.		1.6	2.3	2.8	3	3	4	12	2035	1.8
16 Madagascar		2.4	2.8	3.1	10	12	16	48	2035	1.9
17 Benin		2.6	2.8	3.2	4	5	6	20	2035	2.0
18 Rwanda		3.1	3.3	3.6	6	7	10	40	2040	2.0
19 Kenya		3.8	4.0	3.9	20	25	35	111	2030	2.1
20 Sierra Leone		1.7	2.1	2.4	4	4	5	17	2045	1.8
21 Guinea		1.8	2.0	2.1	6	7	8	24	2045	1.8
22 Ghana		2.2	2.6	3.5	12	15	20	54	2030	1.9
23 Sudan		3.0	2.9	2.9	21	25	34	101	2035	1.9
24 Senegal		2.4	2.8	2.9	6	8	10	30	2035	1.9
25 Mozambique		2.3	2.6	3.0	13	16	21	67	2035	1.9
Middle-income oil importers	w	3.3	3.5	3.4						
	m	3.0	3.2	3.3	t 32	40	54			
26 Mauritania		2.3	2.1	2.7	2	2	3	8	2035	1.8
27 Liberia		2.8	3.3	3.2	2	3	4	11	2035	1.9
28 Zambia		3.0	3.2	3.4	6	8	11	35	2035	1.9
29 Lesotho		2.1	2.4	2.6	1	2	2	6	2030	1.8
30 Côte d'Ivoire		4.6	4.5	3.7	10	13	17	46	2035	2.1
31 Zimbabwe		3.4	3.2	3.4	8	10	13	33	2025	2.0
32 Swaziland		3.2	3.4	3.3	1	1	1	3	2030	.
33 Botswana		3.3	4.4	3.4	1	1	2	5	2025	2.0
34 Mauritius		2.0	1.4	1.5	1	1	1	2	2010	1.7
Middle-income oil exporters	w	2.5	2.8	3.3						
	m	2.4	3.1	3.3	t 118	144				198
35 Nigeria		2.5	2.8	3.4	96	118	163	528	2035	2.0
36 Cameroon		2.4	3.1	3.3	10	12	17	51	2030	1.9
37 Congo, People's Rep.		2.6	3.1	3.7	2	2	3	9	2025	1.9
38 Gabon		0.2	1.5	2.6	1	1	1	4	2035	.
39 Angola		2.1	3.1	2.7	9	10	13	43	2040	.
Sub-Saharan Africa	w	2.7	2.9							3.2
	m	2.4	2.8	3.1	t 409	494				670
Francophone countries	w	2.4	2.6							3.0
	m	2.6	3.0	3.2	t 121	144				194
Anglophone countries	w	2.7	3.0							3.3
	m	2.7	3.1	3.2	t 218	267				367
Other	w	2.6	2.7							2.8
	m	2.0	2.1	2.6	t 70	82				110

Table B-4. School-Age Population Growth and Projections

| | | Average annual growth rates, population of primary- and secondary-school-age children (percent) ||| | School-age population |||||| | As a percentage of total population ||
| | | 1960–70 | 1970–80 | 1980–2000 | | Primary (millions) ||| Secondary (millions) ||| | 1984 | 2000 |
						1984	1990	2000	1984	1990	2000			
Low-income economies	w	2.8	2.9	3.2								w	31.2	31.5
	m	2.7	2.8	3.1	t	45.6	54.4	75.7	34.8	42.4	58.1	m	31.5	31.9
Low-income semiarid	w	2.9	2.4	2.8								w	29.9	30.9
	m	2.6	2.6	2.8	t	5.0	5.9	8.1	4.3	5.0	6.7	m	30.1	31.2
1 Mali		2.7	3.0	2.7		1.3	1.5	2.0	1.1	1.2	1.6		31.6	31.5
2 Burkina Faso		2.2	2.4	2.1		1.1	1.2	1.5	1.0	1.1	1.4		31.5	31.9
3 Niger		3.0	2.7	3.5		1.0	1.3	1.8	0.9	1.1	1.7		30.5	32.7
4 Gambia		2.5	2.9	3.0		0.1	0.1	0.2	0.1	0.1	0.1		27.1	28.4
5 Somalia		4.7	1.4	3.4		0.9	1.1	1.5	0.5	0.6	0.8		25.4	27.2
6 Chad		2.3	1.9	2.6		0.7	0.8	1.2	0.7	0.8	1.1		29.8	30.8
Low-income other	w	2.8	3.0	3.3								w	31.3	31.6
	m	2.7	2.9	3.1	t	40.6	48.5	67.6	30.5	37.4	51.4	m	31.8	32.2
7 Ethiopia		2.8	2.9	2.8		6.8	7.6	11.1	5.5	6.6	8.1		29.3	29.4
8 Zaire		2.0	2.1	3.1		5.1	6.0	8.0	4.0	4.9	6.7		30.4	29.5
9 Malawi		2.8	2.9	3.3		1.5	1.8	2.5	0.6	0.7	1.0		31.0	31.1
10 Guinea-Bissau		2.8	2.8	1.9		0.1	0.2	0.2	0.1	0.1	0.1		26.7	26.0
11 Tanzania		3.4	3.5	3.8		4.2	5.0	7.5	2.7	3.5	5.0		31.8	33.9
12 Burundi		1.7	2.5	3.0		0.7	0.9	1.3	0.7	0.8	1.2		31.1	33.1
13 Uganda		4.3	3.5	3.6		3.0	3.8	5.3	2.0	2.5	3.6		33.4	36.2
14 Togo		3.2	2.7	3.5		0.5	0.6	0.9	0.5	0.6	0.8		33.1	34.6
15 Central African Rep.		1.7	3.2	2.6		0.4	0.5	0.7	0.4	0.4	0.6		32.0	32.1
16 Madagascar		2.8	2.7	3.1		1.7	2.0	2.6	1.5	1.8	2.6		32.8	32.2
17 Benin		2.9	2.9	3.4		0.7	0.9	1.2	0.6	0.8	1.1		34.4	35.4
18 Rwanda		3.5	3.9	3.5		1.4	1.5	2.3	0.7	0.8	1.3		37.2	34.9
19 Kenya		4.1	3.8	4.3		4.5	6.0	8.1	2.7	3.6	5.7		36.4	37.7
20 Sierra Leone		1.8	1.3	2.6		0.7	0.8	1.0	0.5	0.7	0.8		33.0	34.1
21 Guinea		1.4	1.7	2.3		0.9	1.0	1.3	0.7	0.8	1.1		27.2	27.8
22 Ghana		2.6	2.5	3.1		2.1	2.6	3.3	1.9	2.4	3.3		33.1	28.7
23 Sudan		2.2	3.2	3.0		3.5	4.1	5.5	2.7	3.3	4.4		28.8	29.7
24 Senegal		2.6	2.5	3.1		1.1	1.2	1.7	1.0	1.2	1.6		31.6	32.6
25 Mozambique		2.5	4.6	3.0		1.9	2.2	3.1	1.6	1.9	2.6		28.4	26.2
Middle-income oil importers	w	3.3	3.8	3.5								w	31.9	33.0
	m	3.0	3.5	3.6	t	5.9	7.3	10.3	4.5	5.5	8.0	m	31.2	32.0
26 Mauritania		2.7	2.2	2.8		0.3	0.4	0.5	0.2	0.3	0.3		31.2	33.1
27 Liberia		2.9	2.3	3.8		0.3	0.4	0.6	0.3	0.3	0.5		27.6	32.4
28 Zambia		3.0	3.6	3.5		1.3	1.6	2.2	0.7	0.9	1.3		30.6	31.4
29 Lesotho		2.6	2.4	3.0		0.3	0.3	0.4	0.2	0.2	0.3		27.3	29.9
30 Côte d'Ivoire		3.3	5.6	3.8		1.7	2.1	2.8	1.5	1.9	2.7		31.6	31.9
31 Zimbabwe		4.0	3.8	3.7		1.6	2.0	3.0	1.3	1.6	2.4		35.8	37.1
32 Swaziland		3.8	3.5	3.6		0.1	0.2	0.2	0.1	0.1	0.2		31.4	32.0
33 Botswana		3.2	4.2	3.6		0.2	0.3	0.4	0.1	0.2	0.2		33.0	33.5
34 Mauritius		2.6	0.0	0.3		0.1	0.1	0.2	0.2	0.2	0.2		29.0	24.8
Middle-income oil exporters	w	2.5	2.8	3.5								w	32.8	34.2
	m	2.5	2.7	3.5	t	20.2	24.7	35.0	18.3	22.8	32.5	m	30.3	34.5
35 Nigeria		2.6	2.7	3.5		17.0	20.7	29.2	15.2	18.9	27.0		33.3	34.5
36 Cameroon		2.5	3.0	4.1		1.6	2.1	3.0	1.4	1.8	2.8		30.3	34.8
37 Congo, People's Rep.		2.6	4.0	4.0		0.3	0.4	0.6	0.3	0.4	0.6		33.9	35.3
38 Gabon		1.0	2.2	3.1		0.1	0.1	0.2	0.1	0.1	0.2		27.5	31.5
39 Angola		2.3	2.7	2.9		1.2	1.4	1.9	1.3	1.6	2.1		30.1	30.0
Sub-Saharan Africa	w	2.8	2.9	3.3								w	31.7	32.4
	m	2.7	2.8	3.1	t	71.7	86.4	120.9	57.6	70.7	98.6	m	31.2	32.0
Francophone countries	w	2.4	2.7	3.2								w	31.3	31.8
	m	2.6	2.7	3.1	t	20.4	24.3	33.6	17.4	20.9	29.1	m	31.5	32.4
Anglophone countries	w	2.9	3.0	3.5								w	32.8	33.9
	m	2.9	3.1	3.5	t	40.4	49.7	69.6	31.2	38.5	55.9	m	31.6	32.2
Other	w	2.8	3.0	2.9								w	28.9	28.6
	m	2.8	2.8	2.9	t	10.9	12.4	17.7	9.0	10.9	13.7	m	28.4	27.2

Table B-5. Demography and Fertility

		Crude birth rate per thousand population 1965	Crude birth rate per thousand population 1984	Crude death rate per thousand population 1965	Crude death rate per thousand population 1984	Percentage change in: Crude birth rate 1965-84	Percentage change in: Crude death rate 1965-84	Total fertility rate 1984	Total fertility rate 2000
Low-income economies	w	48	47	22	18	-1.5	-18.3	6.6	5.5
	m	48	47	24	19	0.6	-24.0	6.5	5.6
Low-income semiarid	w	47	48	26	20	1.7	-21.2	6.5	6.0
	m	48	49	27	21	2.5	-21.8	6.5	6.0
1 Mali		50	48	27	20	-5.3	-26.7	6.5	5.9
2 Burkina Faso		46	47	24	21	2.2	-14.6	6.5	6.0
3 Niger		48	51	29	22	6.1	-26.0	7.0	6.4
4 Gambia		47	49	28	22	2.8	-19.9	6.5	5.5
5 Somalia		50	49	26	20	-1.4	-23.7	6.8	6.2
6 Chad		40	43	26	21	6.7	-19.6	5.6	5.5
Low-income other	w	48	47	22	18	-2.1	-17.4	6.6	5.5
	m	48	47	23	17	-0.4	-28.0	6.5	5.6
7 Ethiopia		44	41	19	24	-5.7	26.3	6.1	5.5
8 Zaire		48	45	21	15	-5.8	-28.3	6.1	4.9
9 Malawi		56	54	27	22	-4.3	-17.0	7.6	6.4
10 Guinea-Bissau		46	46	30	26	0.9	-11.1	6.0	5.6
11 Tanzania		49	50	22	16	2.6	-30.0	7.0	5.7
12 Burundi		47	47	24	19	-0.4	-24.0	6.5	5.9
13 Uganda		49	50	19	16	2.1	-18.6	6.9	5.7
14 Togo		50	49	23	16	-2.0	-30.5	6.5	5.4
15 Central African Rep.		34	42	24	17	-23.8	-32.0	5.6	5.4
16 Madagascar		44	47	21	15	6.6	-29.2	6.5	5.0
17 Benin		49	49	25	17	0.6	-29.3	6.5	5.4
18 Rwanda		52	52	17	19	0.8	8.4	8.0	6.7
19 Kenya		51	53	21	13	9.8	-37.4	7.9	5.6
20 Sierra Leone		48	49	33	26	1.0	-20.3	6.5	6.0
21 Guinea		46	47	30	26	1.3	-12.0	6.0	5.6
22 Ghana		50	46	20	14	-8.6	-29.5	6.4	4.7
23 Sudan		47	45	24	17	-3.6	-28.0	6.6	5.5
24 Senegal		47	46	23	19	-2.0	-17.9	6.6	5.5
25 Mozambique		49	45	27	18	-7.8	-32.2	6.3	5.7
Middle-income oil importers	w	48	45	19	14	-5.4	-26.3	6.6	4.8
	m	46	46	20	14	-2.1	-26.3	6.5	4.8
26 Mauritania		44	45	25	19	1.5	-25.1	6.2	5.9
27 Liberia		46	49	22	17	6.1	-25.2	6.9	5.7
28 Zambia		49	48	20	15	-2.1	-26.3	6.8	5.6
29 Lesotho		42	41	18	14	-4.5	-19.7	5.8	4.7
30 Côte d'Ivoire		44	45	22	14	2.4	-37.3	6.5	4.8
31 Zimbabwe		55	47	17	12	-14.2	-31.0	6.3	4.0
32 Swaziland		50	49	21	14	-1.4	-34.6	6.9	5.0
33 Botswana		53	46	19	12	-13.3	-36.3	6.7	4.7
34 Mauritius		37	21	8	7	-43.5	-21.9	2.7	2.3
Middle-income oil exporters	w	50	49	23	17	-1.6	-27.9	6.8	5.7
	m	41	47	22	16	9.3	-28.1	6.4	5.6
35 Nigeria		51	50	23	16	-3.4	-28.1	6.9	5.7
36 Cameroon		40	47	20	14	18.5	-28.5	6.7	5.6
37 Congo, People's Rep.		41	45	18	12	9.3	-31.4	6.2	5.6
38 Gabon		32	38	22	16	19.4	-26.6	4.9	5.4
39 Angola		49	47	29	22	-3.9	-26.0	6.4	5.9
Sub-Saharan Africa	w	48	47	23	17	-1.5	-23.3	6.6	5.5
	m	48	47	23	17	-0.4	-26.3	6.5	5.6
Francophone countries	w	47	47	23	17	1.5	-25.9	6.4	5.4
	m	49	48	24	19	1.0	-25.2	6.5	5.6
Anglophone countries	w	50	49	21	16	-1.8	-23.4	6.9	5.5
	m	47	47	22	16	-2.8	-28.6	6.4	5.5
Other	w	46	43	23	22	-5.5	-1.3	6.2	5.6
	m	50	50	27	22	6.1	-17.9	6.9	5.9

Table B-6. Urbanization

| | | Urban population |||| Percentage of urban population |||| Number of cities of over 500,000 persons ||
| | | As a percentage of total population || Average annual growth rate (percent) || In largest city || In cities of over 500,000 persons || ||
		1965	1984	1965–73	1973–84	1960	1980	1960	1980	1960	1980
Low-income economies	w	12	21	6.2	6.1	31	41	3	36		
	m	11	21	6.0	6.1	37	38	0	31	t 1	14
Low-income semiarid	w	11	20	6.2	5.5	.	33	0	0		
	m	11	20	5.6	8.7	.	34	0	0	t 0	0
1 Mali		13	19	5.4	4.5	32	24	0	0	0	0
2 Burkina Faso		6	11	6.5	4.8	.	41	0	0	0	0
3 Niger		7	14	7.0	7.1	.	31	0	0	0	0
4 Gambia		14	31	4.2	10.2	.	.	.	.	.	.
5 Somalia		20	33	6.4	5.4	.	34	0	0	0	0
6 Chad		9	21	6.9	6.5	.	39	0	0	0	0
Low-income other	w	12	21	6.3	6.2	31	42	3	42		
	m	11	21	5.9	6.1	37	47	0	38	t 1	14
7 Ethiopia		8	15	7.4	6.1	30	37	0	37	0	1
8 Zaire		19	39	5.9	7.1	14	28	14	38	1	2
9 Malawi		5	12	8.2	7.3	.	19	0	0	0	0
10 Guinea-Bissau		16	26	4.1	6.8	.	.	.	.	.	.
11 Tanzania		6	14	8.1	8.6	34	50	0	50	0	1
12 Burundi		2	3	1.4	3.3	.	.	0	0	0	0
13 Uganda		6	7	8.3	-0.1	38	52	0	52	0	1
14 Togo		11	23	6.4	6.5	.	60	0	0	0	0
15 Central African Rep.		27	45	4.4	4.6	40	36	0	0	0	0
16 Madagascar		12	21	5.3	5.5	44	36	0	36	0	1
17 Benin		11	15	4.5	5.0	.	63	0	63	0	1
18 Rwanda		3	5	6.0	6.6	.	.	0	0	0	0
19 Kenya		9	18	7.3	7.9	40	57	0	57	0	1
20 Sierra Leone		15	24	5.0	3.5	37	47	0	0	0	0
21 Guinea		12	27	5.0	6.2	37	80	0	80	0	1
22 Ghana		26	39	4.5	5.3	25	35	0	48	0	2
23 Sudan		13	21	6.3	5.5	30	31	0	31	0	1
24 Senegal		27	35	4.2	3.8	53	65	0	65	0	1
25 Mozambique		5	16	8.2	10.2	75	83	0	83	0	1
Middle-income oil importers	w	19	38	7.5	6.9	.	38	0	31		
	m	14	27	7.6	6.4	.	37	0	17	t 0	3
26 Mauritania		7	26	16.0	5.1	.	39	0	0	0	0
27 Liberia		23	39	5.3	6.0	.	.	0	0	0	0
28 Zambia		24	48	7.6	6.4	.	35	0	35	0	1
29 Lesotho		2	13	7.8	20.1	.	.	0	0	0	0
30 Côte d'Ivoire		23	46	8.2	8.3	27	34	0	34	0	1
31 Zimbabwe		14	27	6.8	6.1	40	50	0	50	0	1
32 Swaziland		6	19	5.8	12.9	.	.	.	.	.	.
33 Botswana		4	24	19.0	11.3	.	.	.	.	.	.
34 Mauritius		37	56	4.6	3.4	.	.	.	.	.	.
Middle-income oil exporters	w	15	31	4.9	5.2	17	19	19	52		
	m	16	40	4.7	5.4	26	21	0	21	t 2	10
35 Nigeria		15	30	4.7	5.2	13	17	22	58	2	9
36 Cameroon		16	41	7.3	8.2	26	21	0	21	0	1
37 Congo, People's Rep.		35	56	4.4	5.4	77	56	0	0	0	0
38 Gabon		21	40	4.0	4.6	.	.	.	.	.	.
39 Angola		13	24	5.8	6.6	.	.	.	.	.	.
Sub-Saharan Africa	w	13	25	6.0	5.9	28	36	0	47		
	m	13	24	6.0	6.1	37	37	0	26	t 3	27
Francophone countries	w	15	28	6.0	7.2	30	36	4	31		
	m	12	25	5.7	5.5	37	38	0	0	t 1	8
Anglophone countries	w	13	25	5.8	7.5	22	28	11	49		
	m	14	24	6.6	6.3	36	41	0	42	t 2	17
Other	w	9	18	7.0	6.4	37	46	0	33		
	m	13	24	6.4	6.6	.	37	0	37	t 0	2

Table B-7. Labor Force

		Percentage of population of working age		Percentage of labor force in:						Average annual growth of labor force		
				Agriculture		Industry		Services				
		1965	1984	1965	1980*	1965	1980*	1965	1980*	1965–73	1973–84	1980–2000
Low-income economies	w	53	51	84	79	7	8	9	13	2.2	2.2	2.8
	m	53	52	89	82	5	7	10	16	2.5	2.3	2.9
Low-income semi-arid	w	53	51	91	85	4	4	5	11	2.2	2.0	2.4
	m	53	52	90	85	3	5	7	11	2.0	2.5	2.4
1 Mali		53	50	90	86	1	2	8	13	2.2	1.9	2.4
2 Burkina Faso		53	52	89	87	3	4	7	9	1.6	1.4	1.7
3 Niger		51	51	95	91	1	2	4	7	2.1	2.8	3.0
4 Gambia		53	55	88	84	5	7	7	9	1.8	3.4	2.1
5 Somalia		49	52	81	76	6	8	13	16	3.8	2.6	2.6
6 Chad		55	56	92	83	3	5	5	12	1.6	2.3	2.3
Low-income other	w	52	51	83	78	7	8	10	14	2.2	2.2	3.0
	m	53	51	87	81	5	7	8	12	2.0	2.1	2.8
7 Ethiopia		52	51	86	80	5	8	8	12	2.2	2.2	2.5
8 Zaire		52	51	82	72	9	13	9	16	1.9	2.3	2.8
9 Malawi		51	48	92	83	3	7	5	9	2.3	2.5	2.7
10 Guinea-Bissau		.	52	89	82	5	4	6	14	.	.	.
11 Tanzania		53	50	92	86	3	5	6	10	2.6	2.6	3.2
12 Burundi		53	52	94	93	2	2	4	5	1.2	1.7	2.5
13 Uganda		53	49	91	86	3	4	6	10	3.1	2.2	3.2
14 Togo		52	50	78	73	8	10	13	17	3.2	2.0	2.9
15 Central African Rep.		57	55	89	72	3	6	8	21	1.1	1.6	2.4
16 Madagascar		54	50	.	80	.	3	.	9	1.9	2.0	2.9
17 Benin		52	50	83	70	5	7	12	23	2.1	2.0	2.6
18 Rwanda		51	51	94	93	2	3	3	4	2.7	2.8	3.1
19 Kenya		48	45	86	81	5	7	9	12	3.3	2.8	3.5
20 Sierra Leone		54	54	79	70	11	14	11	16	1.0	1.8	1.9
21 Guinea		55	53	87	81	6	9	6	10	1.2	1.2	1.8
22 Ghana		52	48	61	56	15	18	24	26	1.4	1.5	3.5
23 Sudan		53	52	82	71	5	7	13	22	2.8	2.4	2.8
24 Senegal		53	52	83	81	5	6	11	13	1.7	2.2	2.4
25 Mozambique		55	51	87	85	5	7	7	8	1.8	1.6	2.4
Middle-income oil importers	w	53	46	77	52	8	7	15	21	3.0	2.5	2.9
	m	52	52	81	70	5	9	11	17	2.3	2.3	2.7
26 Mauritania		52	53	90	69	3	9	7	22	1.9	2.3	2.1
27 Liberia		51	52	79	74	10	9	11	16	2.1	3.6	2.5
28 Zambia		51	49	79	73	8	10	13	17	2.3	2.1	3.1
29 Lesotho		56	53	92	86	3	4	6	10	1.7	1.8	2.3
30 Côte d'Ivoire		54	53	81	65	5	8	14	27	4.2	3.9	3.3
31 Zimbabwe		51	45	79	53*	8	13*	13	34*	2.7	1.5	3.4
32 Swaziland		53	49	85	74	5	9	10	17	2.6	2.2	2.7
33 Botswana		50	48	89	70	4	13	7	17	2.2	4.2	2.9
34 Mauritius		52	62	37	28	25	24	38	48	2.8	2.3	2.1
Middle-income oil exporters	w	53	50	68	69	12	11	20	20	1.7	2.0	3.2
	m	55	51	79	70	8	11	13	20	1.7	1.9	3.0
35 Nigeria		51	49	72	68	10	12	18	20	1.7	2.0	3.1
36 Cameroon		55	50	87	70	4	8	9	22	1.9	1.8	3.0
37 Congo, People's Rep.		55	51	66	62	11	12	23	26	1.9	1.9	3.7
38 Gabon		61	58	83	75	8	11	9	14	−0.2	0.3	2.0
39 Angola		55	52	79	74	8	10	13	17	1.5	2.6	2.7
Sub-Saharan Africa	w	53	51	81	75	7	9	12	16	2.1	2.2	2.8
	m	53	51	86	75	5	8	9	16	2.0	2.2	2.7
Francophone countries	w	54	53	85	78	6	8	9	15	2.0	2.1	2.8
	m	53	52	87	78	4	7	8	14	1.9	2.0	2.6
Anglophone countries	w	52	49	74	70	9	10	16	18	2.1	2.4	3.1
	m	52	49	84	74	5	9	11	17	2.3	2.3	2.9
Other	w	51	51	82	80	7	8	11	12	2.3	2.2	2.5
	m	54	52	86	80	5	8	8	14	2.0	2.4	2.6

* Figures with an asterisk are for years other than those specified.

Table B-8. Growth of Production

		\multicolumn{2}{c}{GDP}	\multicolumn{2}{c}{Agriculture}	\multicolumn{2}{c}{Industry}	\multicolumn{2}{c}{Manufacturing}	\multicolumn{2}{c}{Services[a]}
		1965–73	1973–84*	1965–73	1973–84*	1965–73	1973–84*	1965–73	1973–84*	1965–73	1973–84*
Low-income economies	w	4.0	1.6	2.8	.	6.6	.	.	.	4.1	.
	m	3.6	2.6	2.6	1.4	6.1	2.6	7.6	−0.1	4.5	3.4
Low-income semiarid	w	0.8	3.5	.	.	.	.	.	.	.	.
	m	2.8	2.9	0.9	1.6	5.1	5.2	.	.	4.5	4.5
1 Mali		3.1	4.1*	0.9	5.0*	5.1	0.6*	.	.	4.7	4.5*
2 Burkina Faso		2.4	2.9	.	1.3	.	5.2	.	.	.	3.2
3 Niger		−0.8	5.2*	−2.9	1.6*	13.2	10.9*	.	.	−1.5	5.9*
4 Gambia		4.5	2.0	4.5	.	4.4	.	.	.	4.5	.
5 Somalia		3.5	2.5	.	.	.	.	.	.	.	.
6 Chad		0.5	.	.	.	.	.	.	.	.	.
Low-income other	w	4.3	1.5	3.2	.	6.3	.	.	.	4.3	.
	m	3.8	2.3	2.9	1.2	6.2	2.6	7.6	−0.1	5.0	3.0
7 Ethiopia		4.1	2.3*	2.1	1.2*	6.1	2.6*	8.8	3.5*	6.7	3.6*
8 Zaire		3.9	−1.0*	.	1.4*	.	−2.0*	.	−5.0*	.	−1.1*
9 Malawi		5.7	3.3	.	2.5	.	3.3	.	.	.	4.0
10 Guinea-Bissau		.	2.1*	.	−3.1*	.	1.3*	.	.	.	12.1*
11 Tanzania		5.0	2.6*	3.1	.	6.9	.	8.7	.	6.2	.
12 Burundi		4.8	3.6*	4.7	2.3*	10.4	8.3*	.	.	3.0	5.3*
13 Uganda		3.6	−1.3*	3.6	−0.7*	3.0	−8.8*	.	.*	3.8	−0.4*
14 Togo		5.3	2.3*	2.6	1.1*	6.2	2.6*	.	.	7.3	3.0*
15 Central African Rep.		2.7	0.7	2.1	1.1	7.1	1.2	.	.	1.6	.
16 Madagascar		3.5	0.0	.	0.3	.	−3.0	.	.	.	0.9
17 Benin		2.2	4.6	.	2.7	.	7.9	.	.	.	5.1
18 Rwanda		6.3	5.4	.	.	.	.	.	.	.	.
19 Kenya		7.9	4.4	6.2	3.5	12.4	4.8	12.4	6.0	7.6	4.9
20 Sierra Leone		3.7	1.8	1.5	2.0	1.9	−2.5	3.3	1.8	7.1	3.7
21 Guinea		3.0	3.1	.	2.4	.	5.7	.	−2.0	.	2.3
22 Ghana		3.4	−0.9	4.5	0.2	4.3	−6.9	6.5	−6.9	1.1	0.4
23 Sudan		0.2	5.5	0.3	2.7	1.0	6.4	.	10.1	0.5	7.5
24 Senegal		1.5	2.6	0.2	−0.2	3.5	6.0	.	.	1.5	2.3
25 Mozambique		7.4	−2.2*	4.5	−2.4*	11.3	−6.5*	1.8	−6.0*	9.2	−0.4*
Middle-income oil importers	w	5.7	2.8	.	.	.	.	.	.	3.3	.
	m	5.5	3.6	6.4	1.1	4.3	0.9	.	3.3	7.6	3.1
26 Mauritania		2.6	2.3	−2.1	2.3	4.3	0.9	.	.	7.6	3.1
27 Liberia		5.5	0.2*	6.5	2.0*	6.2	−1.5*	13.2	0.5*	3.8	0.8*
28 Zambia		2.4	0.4	2.0	0.9	2.7	−0.1	9.8	0.8	2.3	0.6
29 Lesotho		3.9	5.0	.	.	.	.	.	.	.	.
30 Côte d'Ivoire		8.6	4.2	.	.	.	.	.	.	.	.
31 Zimbabwe		9.4	1.7	.	1.1	.	0.4	.	2.3	.	3.0
32 Swaziland		7.6	3.7*	8.0	4.9*	3.1	3.6*	.	5.7*	12.2	3.2*
33 Botswana		14.8	10.7	6.4	−4.0	30.2	15.6	.	8.2	10.6	10.8
34 Mauritius		2.3	3.6	.	−3.1	.	4.4	.	4.3	.	6.5
Middle-income oil exporters	w	8.3	0.8	2.4	.	19.0	.	13.2	.	7.3	.
	m	6.8	1.5	3.5	−0.3	14.5	6.5	11.5	9.9	5.2	5.5
35 Nigeria		9.7	1.3*	2.8	−0.9*	19.7	0.3*	15.0	10.7	8.8	4.0*
36 Cameroon		4.2	7.2*	4.7	1.8*	4.7	15.2*	7.5	9.9	3.6	7.3*
37 Congo, People's Rep.		6.8	8.1	4.1	0.4	9.3	12.7	.	.	6.7	6.9
38 Gabon		7.4	1.5	.	.	.	.	.	.	.	.
39 Angola		3.6	−5.7*	0.2	−5.5*	20.2	−5.0*	11.5	−8.5	2.7	−6.4*
Sub-Saharan Africa	w	6.4	1.3	2.6	.	15.0	.	.	.	5.9	.
	m	3.9	2.6	3.0	1.2	6.2	2.6	8.8	2.3	4.6	3.2
Francophone countries	w	6.4	1.3	2.6	.	15.0	.	.	.	5.9	.
	m	3.3	3.1	2.1	1.5	6.2	5.5	.	−2.0	3.6	3.2
Anglophone countries	w	7.8	1.1	3.0	.	16.0	.	.	.	6.7	.
	m	4.8	2.3	4.1	1.1	4.4	0.4	9.8	4.3	5.4	3.7
Other	w	4.6	−2.4	1.5	.	14.7	.	6.0	.	5.2	.
	m	3.9	2.1	2.1	−2.8	11.3	−1.9	8.8	−6.0	6.7	1.6

* Figures with an asterisk are for 1973–83, not 1973–84.
a. Services include the unallocated share of GDP.

162

Table B-9. Central Government Expenditure

		Defense 1972	Defense 1983*	Education 1972	Education 1983*	Health 1972	Health 1983*	Housing 1972	Housing 1983*	Economic services 1972	Economic services 1983*	Other 1972	Other 1983*	Total expenditure (percentage of GNP) 1972	Total expenditure (percentage of GNP) 1983*	Overall surplus/deficit (percentage of GNP) 1972	Overall surplus/deficit (percentage of GNP) 1983*
Low-income economies	w	13.2	10.3	15.5	15.9	5.2	4.5	5.7	5.0	20.9	21.5	39.5	42.8	21.0	20.1	−3.9	−4.4
	m	11.7	7.9	15.6	16.3	5.7	5.7	3.3	2.6	21.9	19.2	36.7	41.6	19.5	26.6	−2.9	−4.6
Low-income semiarid	w	18.7	18.3	12.6	21.2	6.3	5.9	5.3	11.2	18.5	15.7	38.6	27.8	14.0	40.5	−0.5	−8.5
	m	23.3	.	14.8	.	7.2	.	1.9	.	21.6	.	37.6	.	13.5	.	0.3	.
1 Mali		.	7.9	.	10.1	.	2.5	.	4.6	.	7.1	.	67.8	.	68.9	.	−18.4
2 Burkina Faso		11.5*	20.7	20.6*	19.6	8.2*	6.8	6.6*	8.0	15.5*	16.3	37.6*	28.6	10.9*	13.6	0.3*	0.9
3 Niger		.	.	.	.	.	.	.	.	.	.	.	.	.	.	.	.
4 Gambia		.	.	.	.	.	.	.	.	.	.	.	.	.	.	.	.
5 Somalia		23.3	.	5.5	.	7.2	.	1.9	.	21.6	.	40.5	.	13.5	.	0.6	.
6 Chad		24.6	.	14.8	.	4.4	.	1.7	.	21.8	.	32.7	.	18.1	.	−3.2	.
Low-income other	w	13.0	9.8	15.6	15.6	5.1	4.5	5.8	4.6	21.0	21.9	39.5	43.8	21.5	18.8	−4.2	−4.2
	m	11.1	7.9	15.8	16.3	5.7	5.7	3.9	2.3	22.9	19.2	36.6	41.6	19.8	26.6	−3.9	−4.6
7 Ethiopia		14.3	.	14.4	.	5.7	.	4.4	.	22.9	.	38.3	.	13.7	.	−1.4	.
8 Zaire		11.1	7.9*	15.2	16.3*	2.3	3.2*	2.0	0.4*	13.3	16.8*	56.1	55.4*	38.6	27.5	−7.5	−3.0
9 Malawi		3.1	6.2	15.8	13.4	5.5	6.8	5.8	1.3	33.1	35.2	36.7	37.1	22.1	32.0	−6.2	−7.7
10 Guinea-Bissau		.	.	.	.	.	.	.	.	.	.	.	.	.	.	.	.
11 Tanzania		11.9	.	17.3	.	7.2	.	2.1	.	39.0	.	22.6	.	19.7	.	−5.0	.
12 Burundi		10.3*	.	23.4*	.	6.0*	.	2.7*	.	33.9*	.	23.8*	.	19.9*	.	..	.
13 Uganda		23.1	17.0	15.3	12.9	5.3	4.6	7.3	2.6	12.4	9.5	36.6	53.4	21.8	4.5	−8.1	−1.2
14 Togo		.	6.8	.	19.6	.	5.7	.	8.2	.	18.2	.	41.6	.	34.1	.	−2.1
15 Central African Rep.		.	.	.	.	.	.	.	.	.	.	.	.	.	.	.	.
16 Madagascar		3.6	.	9.1	.	4.2	.	9.9	.	40.5	.	32.7	.	20.8	.	−2.5	.
17 Benin		.	.	.	.	.	.	.	.	.	.	.	.	.	.	.	.
18 Rwanda		25.6*	.	22.2*	.	5.7*	.	2.6*	.	22.0*	.	21.9*	.	11.7*	.	−2.5*	.
19 Kenya		6.0	13.8	21.9	20.6	7.9	7.0	3.9	0.7	30.1	24.6	30.2	33.3	21.0	26.6	−3.9	−5.1
20 Sierra Leone		.	4.2	.	14.8	.	6.2	.	1.5	.	32.1	.	41.2	.	21.2	.	−13.8
21 Guinea		.	.	.	.	.	.	.	.	.	.	.	.	.	.	.	.
22 Ghana		7.9	6.2*	20.1	18.7*	6.3	5.8*	4.1	6.8*	15.1	19.2*	46.6	43.3*	19.5	7.8	−5.8	−2.6
23 Sudan		24.1	9.5*	9.3	6.1*	5.4	1.3*	1.4	2.3*	15.8	23.5*	44.1	57.3*	19.2	16.9*	−0.8	−4.6*
24 Senegal		.	9.7	.	17.6	.	4.7	.	8.6	.	19.2	.	40.3	17.4	26.8	−0.8	−6.0
25 Mozambique		.	.	.	.	.	.	.	.	.	.	.	.	.	.	.	.
Middle-income oil importers	w	.	14.5	18.1	18.6	7.6	7.1	5.9	7.9	25.4	23.8	43.0	28.1	29.6	36.2	−11.1	−9.2
	m	.	7.5	16.3	16.6	7.7	7.3	12.3	5.3	25.6	25.7	42.5	41.2	25.2	35.6	−7.5	−8.1
26 Mauritania		.	.	.	.	.	.	.	.	.	.	.	.	.	.	.	.
27 Liberia		.	7.9	.	15.8	.	7.3	.	2.7	.	28.6	.	37.7	.	34.9	.	−10.6
28 Zambia		.	.	19.0	15.2*	7.4	8.4*	1.3	1.8*	26.7	23.9*	45.7	50.7*	34.0	41.5*	−13.8	−19.8*
29 Lesotho		.	.	19.5	17.4	8.0	7.2	6.5	1.3	24.5	29.4	41.5	44.7	16.6	27.6	−0.9	−2.8
30 Côte d'Ivoire		.	.	.	.	.	.	.	.	.	.	.	.	.	.	.	.
31 Zimbabwe		.	18.3	.	21.5	.	6.1	.	7.8	.	20.9	.	25.4	.	36.3	.	−6.9
32 Swaziland		.	.	.	.	.	.	.	.	.	.	.	.	.	.	.	.
33 Botswana		.	7.0	10.0	19.4	6.0	5.6	21.7	9.1	28.0	27.4	34.5	31.5	33.7	44.7	−23.8	11.5
34 Mauritius		0.8*	0.9	13.5*	15.6	10.3*	7.8	18.0*	21.1	13.9*	9.2	43.4*	45.3	16.3*	28.7	−1.2*	−9.3
Middle-income oil exporters	w	.	.	.	.	.	.	.	.	.	.	.	.	.	.	.	.
	m	.	.	.	.	.	.	.	.	.	.	.	.	.	.	.	.
35 Nigeria		40.2	.	4.5	.	3.6	.	0.8	.	19.6	.	31.4	.	10.2	.	−0.9	.
36 Cameroon		.	9.6	.	13.2	.	3.7	.	8.5	.	26.0	.	39.0	.	21.8	.	1.3
37 Congo, People's Rep.		.	.	.	.	.	.	.	.	.	.	.	.	.	43.9	.	−3.0
38 Gabon		.	.	.	.	.	.	.	.	.	.	.	.	.	.	.	.
39 Angola		.	.	.	.	.	.	.	.	.	.	.	.	.	.	.	.
Sub-Saharan Africa	w	20.2	11.4	13.2	16.6	5.1	5.4	5.2	6.6	21.2	22.8	35.1	37.2	17.8	25.0	−3.4	−4.8
	m	11.7	7.9	15.3	16.1	6.0	6.0	3.9	3.7	22.0	22.2	36.7	41.4	19.4	27.6	−2.5	−4.6
Francophone countries	w	10.7	10.5	14.7	16.4	3.2	4.0	4.5	7.3	19.4	21.3	47.5	40.5	26.9	28.6	−4.9	−2.3
	m	11.3	8.8	17.9	17.0	5.1	4.2	2.7	8.1	21.9	17.5	32.7	41.0	18.1	27.5	−2.5	−3.0
Anglophone countries	w	24.1	12.0	12.8	16.7	5.6	6.1	5.4	6.2	21.6	23.6	30.5	35.4	16.0	23.2	−3.3	−6.0
	m	9.9	7.5	15.8	15.7	6.3	6.5	4.1	2.5	24.5	24.3	36.7	42.3	19.7	28.1	−5.0	−6.0
Other	w	.	.	.	.	.	.	.	.	.	.	.	.	.	.	.	.
	m	.	.	.	.	.	.	.	.	.	.	.	.	.	.	.	.

* Figures with an asterisk are for 1973 or 1982.

Table B-10. Disbursements of Official Development Assistance (ODA)

		\multicolumn{7}{c	}{Net disbursements of ODA from all sources (millions of dollars)}		Per capita (dollars) 1984	As a percentage of GNP 1984
		1978	1979	1980	1981	1982	1983	1984			
Low-income economies	t	3517	4715	5397	5568	5616	5543	5619	w m	21.7 26.0	9.0 10.2
Low-income semiarid	t	851	867	1173	1142	1257	1038	1205	w m	38.9 36.2	22.6 17.3
1 Mali		163	193	267	230	210	215	320		43.6	32.0
2 Burkina Faso		159	198	212	217	213	184	188		28.7	19.7
3 Niger		157	174	170	193	259	175	162		26.1	14.8
4 Gambia		36	37	54	68	48	42	56		77.9	35.1
5 Somalia		212	179	433	374	462	327	363		69.4	.
6 Chad		125	86	35	60	65	95	115		23.6	.
Low-income other	t	2666	3848	4225	4425	4360	4505	4414	w m	19.3 22.1	8.2 8.3
7 Ethiopia		140	191	216	250	200	344	363		8.6	7.7
8 Zaire		317	416	428	394	348	317	314		10.6	10.1
9 Malawi		99	142	143	138	121	117	159		23.2	13.8
10 Guinea-Bissau		50	53	60	65	68	64	55		63.3	.
11 Tanzania		424	588	678	702	683	621	559		26.0	14.7
12 Burundi		75	95	117	122	127	142	141		30.7	15.0
13 Uganda		23	46	114	136	133	137	164		10.9	3.3
14 Togo		103	110	91	63	77	112	110		37.3	16.7
15 Central African Rep.		51	84	111	102	90	93	114		45.1	18.8
16 Madagascar		91	138	230	234	251	185	156		15.8	7.0
17 Benin		62	85	91	82	80	87	77		19.7	8.0
18 Rwanda		125	148	155	154	151	151	165		28.2	10.2
19 Kenya		248	351	397	449	485	402	431		22.1	7.5
20 Sierra Leone		40	54	93	61	82	66	61		16.5	6.2
21 Guinea		60	56	90	107	90	68	123		20.8	6.3
22 Ghana		114	169	193	148	142	110	216		17.5	4.4
23 Sudan		318	671	588	681	740	957	616		28.9	8.5
24 Senegal		223	307	262	397	285	322	333		52.2	14.8
25 Mozambique		105	146	169	144	208	211	259		19.3	4.9
Middle-income oil importers	t	819	946	1246	1200	1231	1153	1219	w m	37.6 37.1	6.8 9.4
26 Mauritania		238	167	176	231	193	172	168		101.5	24.6
27 Liberia		48	81	98	109	109	118	133		62.6	13.6
28 Zambia		185	277	318	231	309	216	238		37.1	9.4
29 Lesotho		50	64	91	101	90	104	97		65.8	17.6
30 Côte d'Ivoire		131	162	210	124	137	157	128		13.0	2.3
31 Zimbabwe		9	13	164	212	216	208	298		36.7	5.8
32 Swaziland		45	50	50	37	28	34	18		24.5	3.7
33 Botswana		69	100	106	97	102	104	103		99.2	11.6
34 Mauritius		44	32	33	58	48	41	36		35.1	3.5
Middle-income oil exporters	t	393	472	501	425	465	426	487	w m	4.1 19.0	0.5 2.5
35 Nigeria		43	27	36	41	37	48	33		0.3	0.0
36 Cameroon		178	270	265	199	212	130	188		19.0	2.5
37 Congo, People's Rep.		81	91	92	81	93	109	98		53.9	5.3
38 Gabon		44	37	56	44	62	64	76		93.1	2.5
39 Angola		47	47	53	61	60	76	93		10.9	1.3
Sub-Saharan Africa	t	4729	6133	7145	7192	7311	7122	7325	w m	17.9 28.2	4.1 8.3
Francophone countries	t	2383	2817	3059	3032	2944	2776	2976	w m	24.7 28.5	7.9 10.2
Anglophone countries	t	1793	2701	3155	3267	3370	3323	3216	w m	14.7 27.5	2.9 8.0
Other	t	553	615	931	893	998	1023	1134	w m	16.1 19.3	4.2 4.9

Table B-11. External Public Debt Service Ratios

		External public debt outstanding and disbursed Dollars (millions) 1970	1984		As a percentage of GNP 1970	1984		Interest payments on external public debt (millions of dollars) 1970	1984		Debt service as a percentage of: GNP 1970	1984	Exports of goods and services 1970	1984*
Low-income economies	t	3187	29014	w m	17.4 14.8	54.4 59.7	t	80	793	w m	1.3 1.0	3.5 2.2	5.2 4.2	. 11.3
Low-income semiarid	t	399	3387	w m	25.8 11.9	. 61.9	t	2	45	w m	0.6 0.3	. 2.3	3.3 3.8	. 8.0
1 Mali		238	960		88.1	95.9		(.)	7		0.3	1.7	1.4	8.0
2 Burkina Faso		21	407		6.4	42.6		(.)	7		0.6	2.3	6.2	.
3 Niger		32	678		8.7	61.9		1	27		0.6	6.1	3.8	.
4 Gambia		.	.		.	.		(.)	.		.	.	.	.
5 Somalia		77	1233		24.4	.		(.)	3		0.3	.	2.1	28.9
6 Chad		32	109		11.9	.		(.)	1		1.0	.	3.9	1.7
Low-income other	t	2788	25627	w m	16.7 15.2	53.6 59.5	t	77	748	w m	1.3 1.2	3.5 2.0	5.4 4.8	. 13.2
7 Ethiopia		169	1384		9.5	29.5		6	31		1.2	1.8	11.4	13.5
8 Zaire		311	4084		17.6	132.0		9	210		2.1	11.4	4.4	7.7*
9 Malawi		122	731		43.2	63.5		3	32		2.1	7.2	7.2	.
10 Guinea-Bissau		.	.		.	.		.	.		.	.	.	.
11 Tanzania		250	2594		19.5	68.0		6	30		1.2	1.9	4.9	.
12 Burundi		7	334		3.1	35.8		(.)	8		0.3	1.9	.	.
13 Uganda		138	675		7.3	13.5		4	32		0.4	1.7	2.7	.
14 Togo		40	659		16.0	100.1		1	37		0.9	10.1	2.9	26.3
15 Central African Rep.		24	224		13.5	37.1		1	6		1.6	2.0	4.8	8.0
16 Madagascar		93	1636		10.8	73.0		2	31		0.8	5.2	3.5	.
17 Benin		41	582		16.0	59.8		(.)	17		0.7	3.9	2.3	.
18 Rwanda		2	244		0.9	15.1		(.)	3		0.1	0.4	1.2	3.3
19 Kenya		319	2633		20.6	45.8		12	144		1.8	6.1	5.4	21.5
20 Sierra Leone		59	342		14.3	34.7		2	4		2.9	1.6	9.9	9.3
21 Guinea		312	1168		47.1	59.5		4	21		2.2	5.3	.	.
22 Ghana		495	1122		21.9	22.9		12	26		1.1	1.7	5.0	13.2
23 Sudan		307	5659		15.2	78.4		13	65		1.7	1.5	10.6	13.6
24 Senegal		100	1555		11.9	68.9		2	53		0.8	4.1	2.8	.
25 Mozambique		.	.		.	.		.	.		.	.	.	.
Middle-income oil importers	t	1352	11751	w m	24.5 16.8	67.5 56.4	t	51	674	w m	2.4 1.5	7.1 5.0	. 4.5	15.4 12.1
26 Mauritania		27	1171		13.9	171.2		(.)	23		1.7	6.2	3.1	12.8
27 Liberia		159	757		49.9	77.4		6	20		5.5	4.3	.	8.6
28 Zambia		623	2779		35.7	109.4		26	63		3.4	4.5	5.9	11.3
29 Lesotho		8	134		7.7	24.3		(.)	4		0.5	3.8	.	5.1
30 Côte d'Ivoire		256	4835		18.7	85.1		11	404		2.8	11.3	6.8	20.9
31 Zimbabwe		233	1446		15.7	28.4		5	119		0.6	5.4	.	20.0
32 Swaziland		.	.		.	.		.	.		.	.	.	.
33 Botswana		15	276		17.9	31.3		(.)	15		0.7	3.8	.	3.8
34 Mauritius		32	354		14.3	35.3		2	25		1.3	7.5	3.0	14.8
Middle-income oil exporters	t	755	14949	w m	. 12.1	. 23.2	t	27	1357	w m	. 0.8	. 4.4	. .	. 18.5
35 Nigeria		480	11815		4.8	16.3		20	1172		0.6	4.4	4.2	25.4
36 Cameroon		131	1738		12.1	23.2		4	107		0.8	3.0	3.1	8.6
37 Congo, People's Rep.		144	1396		53.9	76.2		3	78		3.3	13.7	.	18.5
38 Gabon		.	.		.	.		.	.		.	.	.	.
39 Angola		.	.		.	.		.	.		.	.	.	.
Sub-Saharan Africa	t	5294	55714	w m	15.1 15.2	36.3 59.5	t	158	2824	w m	1.2 1.0	4.4 4.1	5.1 4.1	18.7 12.8
Francophone countries	t	1810	21780	w m	19.2 13.5	65.5 65.4	t	40	1039	w m	1.5 0.8	6.3 4.7	4.3 3.3	14.0 8.3
Anglophone countries	t	3238	31317	w m	13.7 16.8	27.9 35.0	t	111	1751	w m	1.2 1.3	4.0 4.1	5.4 5.2	21.1 13.2
Other	t	246	2617	w m	. .	. .	t	7	34	w m	. .	. .	. .	. .

* Figures with an asterisk are for 1983, not 1984.

Table C-1. Selected Comparative Statistics for Countries with Fewer than a Half Million People

	Population (millions)[a]	GDP per capita (dollars)	Percentage of GNP devoted to education	Gross primary enrollment rate (percent)	Progression rate from primary to secondary	Percentage females in total enrollment
Cape Verde	0.30	349	10.6	.	14.7	48.0
Comoros	0.40	349	5.4[b]	103.0	32.1	40.0
Djibouti	0.40	480[a]	11.5	42.0[c]	24.9	39.4
Equatorial Guinea	0.40	190	.	78.1	14.4	42.0
São Tomé and Principe	0.10	706	5.9[b]	.	23.2	47.0
Seychelles	0.10	1,938	5.9	95.0[d]	21.9	50.7

Note: Figures are for latest available year.
a. World Bank (1983).
b. Unesco, *Statistical Yearbook*, 1986; figures are for 1982.
c. Includes 20,065 and 1,782 students in public and private schools, respectively. Excludes 2,500 students enrolled in independent private schools.
d. World Bank (1986); figure is for 1977.
Source: African Development Bank (1986).

Table C-2. Summary Table: Enrollment Levels, Ratios, and Growth Rates, Selected Years, 1960–83

	1960	1970	1975	1980	1983
Primary education					
Number of students	11,853	20,971	30,117	47,068	51,345
Index (1960 = 100)	100	177	254	397	433
Average annual growth rate					
from 1960 to:	.	5.9	6.4	7.1	6.6
from 1970 to:	.	.	7.5	8.4	7.1
from 1975 to:	.	.	.	9.3	6.9
from 1980 to:	.	.	.	.	2.9
Gross enrollment ratio	36	48	58	76	75
Secondary education					
Number of students	793	2,597	4,284	8,146	11,119
Index (1960 = 100)	100	327	540	1,027	1,402
Average annual growth rate					
from 1960 to:	.	12.6	11.9	12.4	12.2
from 1970 to:	.	.	10.5	12.1	11.8
from 1975 to:	.	.	.	13.7	12.7
from 1980 to:	.	.	.	.	10.9
Gross enrollment ratio	3	7	10	16	20
Tertiary education					
Number of students	21	116	216	337	437
Index (1960 = 100)	100	552	1,029	1,605	2,081
Average annual growth rate					
from 1960 to:	.	18.6	16.8	14.9	14.1
from 1970 to:	.	.	13.3	11.3	10.8
from 1975 to:	.	.	.	9.3	9.2
from 1980 to:	.	.	.	.	9.1
Gross enrollment ratio	0.2	0.6	0.8	1.2	1.4
All levels					
Number of students	12,667	23,684	34,617	55,551	62,901
Index (1960 = 100)	100	187	273	439	497
Average annual growth rate					
from 1960 to:	.	6.5	6.9	7.7	7.2
from 1970 to:	.	.	7.9	8.9	7.8
from 1975 to:	.	.	.	9.9	7.8
from 1980 to:	.	.	.	.	4.2

Note: Numbers of students in thousands. Based on tables A-1 to A-9.

Table C-3. Estimated Average Number of Years of Education Attained by Working-Age Population

		Average years of education				
		1965	1970	1975	1980	1983
Low-income economies	w	0.86	1.25	1.64	2.31	2.91
	m	0.44	0.79	1.20	1.71	2.20
Low-income semiarid	w	0.11	0.33	0.51	0.80	0.96
	m	0.11	0.30	0.42	0.75	0.90
1 Mali		0.11	0.30	0.59	0.94	1.12
2 Burkina Faso		0.09	0.22	0.38	0.56	0.67
3 Niger		.	.	0.28	0.48	0.64
4 Gambia		.	.	.	.	.
5 Somalia		0.17	0.30	0.42	.	.
6 Chad		.	0.56	0.91	1.26	1.47
Low-income other	w	0.94	1.36	1.87	2.56	3.31
	m	0.49	0.88	1.38	1.90	2.94
7 Ethiopia		0.06	0.17	.	.	.
8 Zaire		1.15	1.96	2.89	3.99	4.71
9 Malawi		1.77	2.26	2.69	3.10	3.41
10 Guinea-Bissau		.	.	.	.	.
11 Tanzania		0.31	0.70	1.13	1.56	.
12 Burundi		0.47	0.75	1.11	1.43	1.53
13 Uganda		0.42	0.93	1.43	1.90	2.18
14 Togo		0.50	1.08	1.88	3.06	3.85
15 Central African Rep.		.	0.75	1.38	2.14	2.62
16 Madagascar		0.41	1.18	2.13	3.20	3.97
17 Benin		0.40	0.78	1.22	1.77	2.22
18 Rwanda		1.49	2.11	2.67	3.07	3.27
19 Kenya		1.19	1.92	2.67	3.57	4.26
20 Sierra Leone		0.31	0.69	1.17	1.71	.
21 Guinea		0.49	0.80	1.20	1.58	.
22 Ghana		5.33	5.96	.	.	.
23 Sudan		0.55	0.84	1.19	1.70	2.03
24 Senegal		0.27	0.71	1.20	1.64	1.93
25 Mozambique		2.02	2.32	.	.	.
Middle-income oil importers	w	1.24	1.84	2.61	3.18	4.50
	m	1.31	1.81	2.73	3.65	4.27
26 Mauritania		.	.	.	.	.
27 Liberia		0.51	1.00	1.60	2.30	.
28 Zambia		.	1.54	2.51	3.65	4.27
29 Lesotho		2.62	3.68	4.72	5.63	6.17
30 Côte d'Ivoire		0.47	0.94	1.47	2.10	.
31 Zimbabwe		1.31	2.20	3.08	3.76	.
32 Swaziland		.	1.81	2.95	4.24	.
33 Botswana		.	.	2.03	2.84	3.37
34 Mauritius		5.00	6.11	7.50	.	.
Middle-income oil exporters	w	1.99	2.36	2.64	3.03	3.51
	m	0.67	1.43	2.36	3.08	3.56
35 Nigeria		2.40	2.72	2.85	3.08	3.46
36 Cameroon		0.65	1.43	2.36	3.36	3.97
37 Congo		0.69	1.87	3.50	5.63	.
38 Gabon		.	1.21	1.98	2.93	3.56
39 Angola		0.10	0.40	0.88	1.57	.
Sub-Saharan Africa	w	1.21	1.60	2.06	2.63	3.19
	m	0.50	1.04	1.60	2.30	3.32
Francophone countries	w	0.65	1.18	1.78	2.52	2.86
	m	0.47	0.87	1.38	2.10	2.42
Anglophone countries	w	1.83	2.23	2.34	2.75	3.29
	m	1.25	1.85	2.59	3.08	3.43
Other	w	0.42	0.58	0.72	1.57	.
	m	0.14	0.35	0.65	1.57	.

Table C-4. Adult Literacy

	Literates as percentage of adult population	
	1960	1985 or latest year
Low-income economies	7	33.8
Low-income semiarid	2	15.4
1 Mali	2	16.8
2 Burkina Faso	2	13.2
3 Niger	1	13.9
4 Gambia	6	25.1
5 Somalia	2	11.6
6 Chad	6	25.3
Low-income other	10	40.7
7 Ethiopia	1	55.2
8 Zaire	31	61.2
9 Malawi	.	41.2
10 Guinea-Bissau	5	31.4
11 Tanzania	10	.
12 Burundi	14	33.8
13 Uganda	25	57.3
14 Togo	10	40.7
15 Central African Rep.	7	40.2
16 Madagascar	.	67.5
17 Benin	5	25.9
18 Rwanda	16	46.6
19 Kenya	20	59.2
20 Sierra Leone	7	29.3
21 Guinea	7	28.3
22 Ghana	27	53.2
23 Sudan	13	.
24 Senegal	6	28.1
25 Mozambique	8	38.0
Middle-income oil importers	19	72.2
26 Mauritania	5	.
27 Liberia	9	35.0
28 Zambia	29	75.7
29 Lesotho	.	73.6
30 Côte d'Ivoire	5	42.7
31 Zimbabwe	39	74.0
32 Swaziland	.	67.9
33 Botswana	.	70.8
34 Mauritius	61	82.8
Middle-income oil exporters	16	56.2
35 Nigeria	15	42.4
36 Cameroon	19	56.2
37 Congo	16	62.9
38 Gabon	.	61.6
39 Angola	.	41.0
Sub-Saharan Africa	9	41.8
Francophone countries	7	40.2
Anglophone countries	18	58.3
Other	4	38.0

Note: Values for country groups are medians.

Table C-5. Cross-National Comparisons of Achievement in Mathematics, Reading, and Science

Country group	Mathematics		Reading comprehension		General science	
Industrial						
Francophone Belgium	0.81		1.00		0.79	
England and Wales	..		0.96		0.92	
Finland	0.76		1.00		0.93	
France	0.84		..		..	
Japan	1.00		..		1.00	
United States	0.72		0.91		1.00	
Average (country sample size)	0.79	(14)	0.94	(9)	0.90	(11)
Upper middle-income						
Chile	..		0.82		0.59	
Hong Kong	0.78		..		..	
Hungary	0.89		0.95		0.87	
Iran	..		0.53		0.52	
Average (sample size)	0.80	(3)	0.77	(3)	0.66	(3)
Lower middle-income						
Nigeria	0.53		..		..	
Swaziland	0.50		..		..	
Thailand	0.67		..		0.77	
Average (sample size)	0.57	(3)	..	(0)	0.77	(1)
Low-income						
India	..		0.72		0.59	
Malawi	..		0.46		0.69	
Average (sample size)	..	(0)	0.59	(2)	0.64	(2)

* The average number of items answered correctly by the sample of students in a particular country is expressed as the proportion of items answered correctly by the students in the highest scoring country. For further explanation and sources, see the technical notes.

Table C-6. Countries Grouped by Gross Primary Enrollment Ratios

Country group		Gross primary enrollment ratio	Enrollment growth rate minus growth rate of school-age population	Repeaters as percentage of primary enrollment	Females as percentage of primary enrollment	Pupil-teacher ratio	Public recurrent expenditure per pupil	Public education expenditures as percentage total public expenditures	Public recurrent expenditures on primary education as percentage of total public recurrent expenditures on education
Low primary enrollment	w	37		11	38	42	40	17.6	38
	m	37	1.1	16	37	41	49	17.2	34
Somalia		21	−10.2	.	36	23	48	6.3	60
Mali		23	−2.4	33	37	37	41	37.2	33
Niger		26	−0.7	15	36	36	65	21.7	36
Burkina Faso		27	8.8	17	37	62	38	23.9	31
Guinea		36	0.1	29	32	36	75	12.7	31
Mauritania		37	6.0	17	39	45	143	.	28
Ethiopia		38	2.4	12	38	54	26	10.9	46
Chad		38	2.0	.	27	64	.	.	.
Burundi		45	16.2	14	40	49	63	.	39
Sudan		49	−0.1	(.)	41	34	.	.	.
Medium primary enrollment	w	66		16	42	39	54	15.2	43
	m	67	−0.4	15	41	36	55	15.2	45
Senegal		53	5.4	15	40	41	101	.	49
Sierra Leone		54	2.4	.	41	34	40	17.6	40
Uganda		57	−0.4	10	43	36	8	.	16
Malawi		58	−1.8	15	42	58	13	8.5	39
Guinea-Bissau		62	−1.7	30	33	23	29	11.8	67
Rwanda		62	−1.3	12	48	54	47	24.0	74
Benin		67	2.9	22	33	38	.	.	.
Gambia		68	8.6	13	38	25	80	.	49
Liberia		70	−3.4	.	40	33	63	13.2	30
Côte d'Ivoire		77	1.7	25	41	36	189	28.2	45
Central African Rep.		77	2.7	35	35	69	44	.	55
Mozambique		79	−6.9	29	43	56	16	.	.
Ghana		79	−2.7	2	44	28	.	15.2	32
High primary enrollment	w	96		14	47	39	53	16.3	41
	m	106	0.0	18	48	42	29	16.3	46
Tanzania		87	−1.8	1	49	42	30	15.3	47
Nigeria		89	−2.4	.	.	36	55	9.3	33
Zaire		90	−0.3	18	43	42	.	.	.
Botswana		96	1.5	6	53	31	106	18.5	43
Zambia		100	1.2	1	47	46	39	15.2	48
Kenya		100	−0.9	13	48	37	78	15.3	65
Togo		102	−6.7	36	39	45	23	20.8	25
Madagascar		104	1.3	.	48	.	25	.	58
Cameroon		108	.0	30	46	50	49	17.2	41
Lesotho		110	3.5	23	58	52	31	17.9	37
Swaziland		111	1.6	13	50	33	100	.	47
Mauritius		112	1.8	.	49	23	151	10.3	46
Gabon		118	−0.6	32	49	44	.	.	.
Zimbabwe		131	11.2	1	48	40	122	17.6	61
Angola		134	−7.8	36	46	37	.	10.1	.
Congo, People's Rep.		163	−0.1	31	49	58	.	19.2	48
Sub-Saharan Africa	w	75		14	44	39	52	11.9	41
	m	77	0.0	16	42	39	48	15.3	43

Note: Gross primary enrollment ratios below 50 percent in 1983 are considered low, between 50 and 80 percent are medium, and above 80 percent are high.

Sources: Appendix tables A-1, A-7, A-11, A-12, A-14, A-16, and A-17.

Table C-7. Enrollment Characteristics and Education Expenditure by Secondary Enrollment Group

Country group		Gross secondary enrollment ratio	Ratio of secondary to primary enrollments	Progression rate from primary to secondary	Females as percentage of secondary enrollments	Public expenditure on education as percentage of GNP	Secondary as percentage of public recurrent expenditure on education
Low secondary enrollment	w	5	.07	18	30	3.0	29
	m	5	.10	16	32	3.3	30
Rwanda		2	.02	4	34	3.1	14
Tanzania		3	.02	8	35	5.8	30
Burkina Faso		4	.13	22	34	3.2	17
Burundi		4	.09	8	37	3.4	35
Malawi		4	.03	7	29	3.0	15
Chad		6	.16	19	15	.	.
Mozambique		6	.10	40	30	.	.
Niger		6	.19	35	27	3.6	31
Mali		7	.26	42	28	3.7	37
Uganda		8	.09	13	33	1.3	40
Medium secondary enrollment	w	15	.18	46	37	4.9	31
	m	15	.21	45	33	4.0	30
Ethiopia		11	.23	93	36	3.1	29
Guinea-Bissau		11	.13	68	19	3.0	15
Angola		12	.11	50	33	4.7	.
Mauritania		12	.26	39	24	.	32
Senegal		12	.21	29	33	.	28
Somalia		14	.29	50	34	1.4	25
Guinea		15	.34	69	28	4.0	37
Madagascar		15	.15	.	44	2.3	36
Sierra Leone		15	.22	73	28	3.5	31
Central African Rep.		16	.20	36	26	.	15
Zambia		17	.10	21	36	5.5	34
Gambia		19	.24	44	31	5.9	26
Kenya		19	.12	35	40	4.8	15
Lesotho		19	.10	45	60	3.9	35
Sudan		19	.32	53	41	.	.
Côte d'Ivoire		20	.23	30	29	9.1	40
High secondary enrollment	w	30	.29	57	33	4.4	49
	m	24	.23	54	39	5.3	35
Liberia		21	.23	63	29	5.3	16
Cameroon		21	.18	26	38	3.6	35
Botswana		21	.13	31	54	7.2	29
Benin		22	.29	40	28	.	.
Gabon		23	.20	27	40	.	.
Nigeria		23	.24	.	.	4.3	56
Togo		24	.22	31	25	5.9	26
Ghana		38	.52	.	37	2.0	41
Zimbabwe		39	.20	74	40	7.6	24
Swaziland		43	.22	68	49	4.7	35
Mauritius		51	.57	54	47	4.3	36
Zaire		52	.46	71	28	.	.
Congo, People's Rep.		87	.50	73	41	6.0	25
Sub-Saharan Africa	w	20	.22	43	34	4.3	42
	m	16	.20	40	33	3.9	31

Note: Gross secondary enrollment ratios below 10 percent in 1983 are considered low, between 10 and 20 percent are medium, and above 20 percent are high.

Sources: Appendix tables A-1, A-2, A-8, A-12, A-14, and A-16.

Table C-8. Indicators of Unit Cost by Secondary Enrollment Group
(median)

	1970	1975	1980	1983
Public expenditure per secondary student (constant 1983 dollars)				
Low secondary enrollment	452	346	207	256
Medium secondary enrollment	250	255	186	163
High secondary enrollment	397	230	204	225
Sub-Saharan Africa	362	308	195	223
Public expenditure per secondary student (as percentage of GNP per capita)				
Low secondary enrollment	249	207	122	115
Medium secondary enrollment	88	78	64	60
High secondary enrollment	78	38	35	37
Sub-Saharan Africa	111	93	62	62
Public expenditure per secondary student (as multiple of expenditure per primary pupil)				
Low secondary enrollment	10.3	8.1	11.1	9.6
Medium secondary enrollment	3.5	5.2	3.2	3.1
High secondary enrollment	4.8	4.8	4.0	3.6
Sub-Saharan Africa	5.6	5.6	3.8	4.1
Secondary student-teacher ratio				
Low secondary enrollment	17	19	23	19
Medium secondary enrollment	21	21	22	24
High secondary enrollment	22	22	21	23
Sub-Saharan Africa	21	21	22	23
Secondary repetition rate (percent)				
Low secondary enrollment	9	12	10	12
Medium secondary enrollment	11	13	10	16
High secondary enrollment	11	11	19	17
Sub-Saharan Africa	10	12	10	16

Note: Gross secondary enrollment ratios below 10 percent in 1983 are considered low, between 10 and 20 percent are medium, and above 20 percent are high.
Sources: Appendix tables A-11, A-12, A-17, and A-18.

Table C-9. Percentage of Nationals among Teaching Staff in Postprimary Education

Country	Year	Secondary	Higher
Benin	1979	97.3	66.7
Botswana	1976	25.5	21.4
Burundi	1976	37.2	.
Central African Republic	1978	.	34.2
Côte d'Ivoire	1978	47.0	51.2
Equitorial Guinea	1978	69.0	.
Gabon	1977	16.4	16.5
Gambia	1979	75.9	85.7
Guinea Bissau	1978	83.4	.
Kenya	1978	80.0	.
Liberia	1978	77.0	.
Malawi	1977	71.4	.
Mali	1978	97.1	40.5
Mauritania	1977	39.7	.
Niger	1977	40.0	.
Rwanda	1979	73.9	52.3
Senegal	1978	73.7	49.0
Swaziland	1980	74.7	.
Togo	1979	92.0	77.0
Mean	—	65.1	49.5
Median	—	74.3	50.1

Source: Unesco (1982).

Technical Notes

Where possible, definitions for the technical notes have been taken from the *World Development Report*, published annually by the World Bank, the Unesco *Statistical Yearbook*, and other official publications.

All monetary growth rates are in constant prices. In the tables on Education Indicators, growth rates have been computed with the use of the compound growth rate equation

$$X_t = X_0(1 + r)^t$$

where X is the variable, t is time, and r is the growth rate. In the tables on Social and Economic Indicators, growth rates have been computed with the use of the least-squares method. The least-squares growth rate is estimated by regressing the annual values of the variable in the relevant period, using the logarithmic form

$$\log X_t = a + bt + e_t$$

where X_t is the value of the variable X in year t, a is the intercept, b is the slope coefficient, and e_t is the error term. The growth rate is equal to (antilog b) − 1, which is equivalent to the logarithmic transformation of the compound growth rate equation.

A. Education Indicators

Tables A-1, A-2, A-4, and A-6. Enrollment

Unless otherwise noted, enrollment includes students of all ages in both public and private schools. Enrollment growth rates are calculated with the use of the compound growth equation described above. The percentage of females enrolled at each level is the number of females enrolled divided by total enrollment; the means are weighted by total enrollment.

Mean enrollment growth rates are computed from group enrollment totals of those countries for which data for the first and last years of the growth period are available. Means for the percentage of females are computed from group totals of female and total enrollment.

To obtain a close approximation of enrollment in 1983, only data for 1982–84 are reported. Where data for these years were unavailable, the least-squares regression line was fitted to enrollment data from 1970 to obtain enrollment estimates. These estimates should not be interpreted as precise quantitative indications of enrollment. They are included only to obtain more valid aggregate measures for 1983 than would be possible without them.

Table A-1. Liberia: Data include preprimary enrollment.

Table A-2. Botswana (1970): Data refer to schools maintained and aided by the government.

Table A-4. Côte d'Ivoire (1970): Data refer to

institutions under the Ministry of Education only. Nigeria (1970): Data at the tertiary level include teacher education. Swaziland: Data on students enrolled include students studying abroad.

Table A-3. Distribution of Secondary Enrollment by Type of Education

General education refers to education in secondary schools—high schools, middle schools, lyceums, gymnasiums, and the like—which require at least four years of primary preparation, are not intended to prepare students directly for a specific trade or occupation, and offer courses of study the completion of which is a minimum condition for admission to a university. Schools that provide both academic and vocational training are also under this heading. Teacher training refers to education in secondary schools that train students for the teaching profession. Vocational and technical education covers education provided in secondary schools that prepare students for a trade or occupation other than teaching. Such schools vary greatly as to the type and duration of training.

Mean percentages are weighted by total secondary enrollment. The data shown are for 1981–83 except for Nigeria and Chad (1984) and Mauritania and Swaziland (1980).

Ghana (1970): Middle schools are classified as primary schools.

Ghana (1980): Commercial schools are included under general education rather than vocational and technical education. Because of reorganization, data on teacher training are not comparable with data for previous years.

Tanzania (1970): Vocational education is included under general education.

Tanzania (1983): Data for general education include only part of vocational education.

Uganda: Data refer only to schools maintained and aided by the government.

Table A-5. Distribution of Tertiary Enrollment by Field of Study

Definitions of levels and of the composition of fields of study follow the International Standard Classification of Education (ISCED) system. The ISCED defines twenty fields of study in higher education, here reduced to two broad areas, Arts and Sciences, which are divided into three and four subareas, respectively. The Arts area consists of education, the social sciences, and commerce and business administration.

In turn, education includes education science and teacher training, and the social sciences include the fine and applied arts, the humanities, religion and theology, the social and behavioral sciences, law, home economics, mass communication and documentation, and the service trades. The Sciences area is made up of the natural sciences, the medical sciences, agriculture, and mathematics and engineering. The medical sciences include health and hygiene; agriculture includes forestry and fisheries; and mathematics and engineering include computer sciences, architecture and town planning, transport and communications, and trade, craft, and industrial programs. The category "other" covers other or unspecified fields of study.

The means for the distribution of enrollment by field of study are weighted by total tertiary enrollment; those for the percentage of all females enrolled are weighted by tertiary female enrollment.

Owing to the unavailability of data for the years before 1980, only the most recent year for which data were available is represented. The figures for Cameroon, Malawi, and Nigeria are for 1980; the data for all other countries are for either 1982 or 1983.

Burkina Faso: Education is included under social sciences.

Burundi: The social and behavioral sciences are under commerce and business administration.

Cameroon: Data refer to universities and degree-granting institutions only.

Central African Republic: Education includes humanities, religion, and theology.

Congo: Commerce and business administration and mass communication and documentation are under social sciences; mathematics and computer sciences are under natural sciences.

Guinea: Law is under commerce and business administration; humanities, religion, theology, social and behavioral sciences, mathematics, and computer sciences are under education.

Kenya: Humanities, religion, theology, and other and unspecified subjects are under education.

Malawi: Data refer to universities and degree-granting institutions only.

Rwanda: Commerce and business administration are under social sciences.

Swaziland: Data refer to universities and equivalent degree-granting institutions only. Mathematics and computer sciences are under natural sciences.

Togo: Mass communication and documentation are under social sciences; humanities, religion, theology, and fine and applied arts are under education.

Zambia: Humanities, religion, and theology are

under social sciences; architecture, town planning, and trade, craft, and industrial programs are under engineering.

Zimbabwe: Data refer to universities and equivalent degree-granting institutions only. Commerce and business administration are under social sciences, and mathematics and computer sciences are under natural sciences.

Tables A-7, A-8, and A-9. Enrollment Ratios

Estimates of total, male, and female enrollment of students of all ages are expressed as percentages of the total, male, and female populations of school age to obtain gross enrollment ratios. The gross primary enrollment ratio describes the capacity of a school system in relation to the size of the official school-age population. For example, a ratio of 100 percent indicates that the number of children actually enrolled, including those outside the official age range, is equivalent to the size of the official primary-school-age population. It does not mean that all children of official primary school age are actually enrolled; if the ratio were so misinterpreted, it would overstate the actual enrollment picture in those countries in which a sizable proportion of students are younger or older than the official age owing to early or delayed entry or to repetition.

Many countries consider primary school age to be 6–11 years and secondary school age to be 12–18 years, but others do not. The differences in national systems of education and durations of schooling are reflected in the primary and secondary ratios. For tertiary education, the total enrollment of all ages is divided by the population ages 20–24.

The means are weighted by the school-age populations.

The enrollment data used to compute the gross enrollment ratios appear in tables A-1, A-2, and A-4. The estimates of school-age population are from the data files of the United Nations Population Division and of the World Bank.

Table A-10. Teachers and Schools

In general, data in this table cover both public and private schools. Data on teachers refer to both full-time and part-time teachers. The great differences among countries in the proportions of part-time teachers may affect the comparability of data, particularly the pupil-teacher ratios in table A-11. The means for the average number of students per school are weighted by the number of schools.

Figures marked with an asterisk are for 1981 or 1982 except for Chad, Nigeria, and Zimbabwe (1984). For Burkina Faso, Ethiopia, Mali, Mauritania, Mauritius, Swaziland, Togo, and Zambia secondary data refer to secondary general education only.

Botswana (1970): Data on secondary education refer to schools maintained and aided by the government.

Burkina Faso (1983): Data on primary teachers refer to public education.

Kenya (1983): Secondary teachers include trainers of secondary teachers.

Malawi: Secondary teachers include trainers of secondary teachers.

Senegal (1982): Data on secondary teachers refer to public education.

Tanzania: Primary school data refer to schools maintained and aided by the government.

Table A-11. Student-Teacher Ratios

Student-teacher ratios are obtained by dividing the number of students enrolled by the number of full-time and part-time teachers. The means are computed from group totals of enrollment and teachers. The years of data coverage are the same as those for tables A-1, A-2, A-4, and A-10.

Chad: Data on primary education exclude Islamic private education.

Uganda: Data for primary and secondary education refer to schools maintained and aided by the government.

Table A-12. Student Flow and Indicators of Efficiency

The figures for repeaters as a percentage of enrollment are computed by dividing the total number of students who repeat a grade by the number of students enrolled in both public and private institutions. Where data on repeaters in private institutions were not available, Unesco estimates of these figures were used. In some cases the estimates reflect the proportion of repeaters in private schools for previous years. Where no information was available, data on repeaters were adjusted to reflect the incidence of private enrollment. In no case did the missing data constitute more than 5 percent of total enrollment.

Reconstructed cohort analysis was used to derive the proportion of entering students who can be expected to complete the final year of primary school given the prevailing dropout rates. This method uses promotion, repetition, and dropout rates to simulate the progression of an entering cohort ($n = 1,000$)

through the primary school cycle, deriving for each grade and year the number of pupils who are promoted, repeat the same grade the following year, or drop out.

Cost per completer of primary school is an efficiency index that is defined as the ratio of the total number of student years invested in each primary school completer (given prevailing promotion, repetition, and dropout rates) to the number of years in the school cycle. The index value shows the average cost per completer in relation to the prescribed cost and was derived by means of cohort analysis (described above). For example, an index of 1.5 indicates that the cost to the system per graduate was 50 percent greater than if there had been no repeaters or dropouts.

Progression from the last grade of primary school to the first grade of secondary school indicates the proportion of pupils enrolled in the final grade of primary school who enroll in the first grade of secondary school in general education the following year. The rate is derived by subtracting the number of repeaters in the first grade of secondary general education in year t from the total enrollment in year $t + 1$ and dividing this figure by the enrollment in the final grade of primary school in year t.

The completion, cost, and progression figures shown are for the most recent year for which promotion, repetition, and dropout rates were available. In general, the data cover the years 1980–83.

The means for the percentage of repeaters, cost per completer, and progression to secondary school are weighted by total enrollment, the number of years in the school cycle, and total enrollment in the last grade of primary school, respectively.

Table A-13. Percentage of Students Enrolled in Private Schools

The number of students enrolled in private schools is expressed as a percentage of all students enrolled in both public and private institutions for primary and secondary education. Care should be taken when interpreting these figures since some countries classify aided (subsidized) schools as private and others do not.

The means are weighted by primary or secondary enrollment. All data shown are for the most recent year, generally between 1980 and 1983.

Table A-14. Total Public Expenditure on Education

Total public expenditure on education includes both capital and recurrent expenditure at every level of administration according to the constitution of the country—that is, central or federal government, state governments, provincial or regional authorities, and local authorities, unless otherwise indicated in the notes on specific countries, below. Total public expenditure is expressed in constant 1983 U.S. dollars. Local currencies were converted by applying the GDP deflator and the 1983 official exchange rate. The figures for education expenditure expressed as a percentage of GNP and as a percentage of total government expenditure were computed with constant dollar GNP and total government expenditure. GNP data are from the World Bank; total government expenditure data are from Unesco, supplemented with information from World Bank data files.

The weighted total expenditure growth rates reflect the real growth of total education expenditure for those countries for which data are available for both the first and the last years of the growth period. The growth rates were computed by aggregating the figures for all countries that had data for both years and applying the compound growth formula. The means for education expenditure as a percentage of GNP and of total government expenditure are weighted by constant dollar GNP and total government expenditure, respectively.

All 1983 figures marked with an asterisk are for 1982 except for Nigeria (1984) and, notably, Burundi, Congo, The Gambia, and Swaziland (1981). Total education expenditure for the four last-named countries are shown but are not included in the calculation of growth rates for 1980–83. All 1980 figures marked with asterisks are for 1979 except for Nigeria and Angola (1981).

Angola: Data refer to expenditures of the Ministry of Education only.

Ethiopia (1982): Data include foreign aid.

Kenya (1983): Data refer to expenditures of the Ministry of Basic and Higher Education only.

Madagascar (1970): Data include foreign aid for tertiary education; for 1980–83 expenditure on tertiary education is not included.

Somalia (1980, 1983): Data refer to expenditures of the Ministry of Education only.

Tanzania (1983): Data refer to expenditures of the Ministry of Education only.

Table A-15. Distribution of Total Public Expenditure on Education by Recurrent or Capital Component

Recurrent expenditure refers to expenditure on administration, emoluments of teachers and of supporting teaching staff, schoolbooks and other teaching materials, scholarships, welfare services, and maintenance of school buildings. Capital expenditure covers expenditure on land, buildings, construction, equipment, and the like, as well as loan transactions. For the methodology for computing growth rates and for the years and sources of data, see the notes to table A-14.

Table A-16. Public Recurrent Expenditure on Education by Level of Education

Public recurrent expenditures on primary, secondary, and tertiary education are expressed as percentages of total public recurrent expenditure on education. The unspecified category is treated as a residual and includes expenditure on other types of education (for example, adult education) and all expenditure that could not be attributed to any of the three levels of formal education. The latter may include expenditure on administration for which there is no breakdown by level of education.

The means for primary, secondary, and tertiary education are weighted by recurrent expenditure in constant 1983 dollars; the means for the unspecified expenditure is a residual—that is, 100 minus the sum of the percentages for primary, secondary, and tertiary education.

The Gambia: Except for 1980, only teachers' emoluments are distributed by level of education.

Mali: Scholarships and allocations for study abroad for all levels of education are included under higher education.

Swaziland: Data refer to expenditure of the Ministry of Education only.

Uganda: Data refer to expenditure of the Ministry of Education only.

Tables A-17, A-18, and A-19. Public Recurrent Expenditure per Student

Public recurrent expenditure per primary pupil and secondary student is expressed in 1983 constant dollars and as a percentage of constant dollar income per capita; tertiary per student expenditure is expressed as a multiple of constant dollar GNP per capita. Per student expenditure on teaching materials is expressed in current dollars. All means are weighted by total enrollment at the respective level of education.

The 1983 per student expenditure figures marked with an asterisk are for 1982 except for Nigeria (1984) and Burundi, Congo, The Gambia, and Swaziland (1981). The 1980 figures marked with an asterisk are for 1979 except for Angola and Nigeria (1981). Per student expenditure on materials was computed using the most recent data available. See also notes to tables A-20 and A-21.

Tables A-20, A-21, and A-22. Distribution of Public Recurrent Expenditure by Purpose

Public recurrent expenditures on administration, teachers' emoluments, teaching materials, scholarships, and welfare services are expressed as percentages of total recurrent expenditure on primary, secondary, and tertiary education. Administration includes emoluments of administrative staff and other expenditures of central and local administrations. Teachers' emoluments are salaries and additional benefits paid to teachers and to other auxiliary teaching staff. The category teaching materials covers expenditures directly related to instructional activities, such as the purchase of textbooks and other scholastic supplies. Scholarships include all forms of financial aid granted to students for studies in the country or abroad. The category welfare services refers to expenditure on boarding school meals, transport, medical services, and the like. Expenditures that cannot be classified in one of these categories and expenditures connected with the operation and maintenance of buildings and equipment are included in "amount not distributed."

The means are weighted by total public recurrent expenditure for the respective level of education in constant 1983 dollars.

Figures for Guinea-Bissau, Mali, Somalia, and Zambia are for 1982. Figures for Burundi, Congo, Ethiopia, Ghana, Senegal, Swaziland, and Togo are for 1981. The figure for Tanzania is for 1979.

Burundi: Data refer to expenditure of the Ministry of Education only.

Senegal: Data refer to expenditure of the ministries of Primary and Secondary Education only.

Swaziland: Data refer to expenditure of the Ministry of Education only.

Table A-23. Average Salaries of Primary and Secondary Teachers

Teachers' salaries are expressed in current U.S. dollars converted at official exchange rates. Caution should be exercised when interpreting average teachers' salaries. The figures were computed by applying the percentage of public recurrent education expenditure allocated to teachers' emoluments, as shown in tables A-20 and A-21, to the recurrent public education expenditure on primary and secondary education for the same year and dividing by the number of teachers shown in table A-10. The data on number of teachers and for expenditures may not be for the same year in every case. The means for average teachers' salaries are weighted by the total number of teachers.

Tables A-24, A-25, A-26, and A-27. External Aid to African Education and Training

External aid to education and training consists of loans and grants made on concessional and nonconcessional financial terms by all bilateral, multilateral, and private sources. Bilateral sources of funding that are not listed but are included under "others" are Canada, Denmark, the Netherlands, Switzerland, and all other OECD and OPEC members whose aid represents less than 3 percent of total aid to education and training. The "others" category under multilateral funding agencies includes Unesco, the World Health Organization (WHO), and other agencies whose aid represents less than 1 percent of total aid to education. Aid to education from the U.S.S.R. is included in the total for the East European nonmarket economies, and aid from private sources is captured in the total for nongovernmental organizations.

The value of aid to education is the average annual aid disbursed or committed between 1981 and 1983, converted from local currencies by applying single-year official exchange rates. Aid from IDA, IBRD, the African Development Bank, and the African Development Fund are average commitments. For all other external funding sources, average net disbursements are shown.

The breakdown of direct aid to education between capital and recurrent expenditures is inconsistent in tables A-25 and A-27 owing to differences in the sources for the two tables and in the way these sources treat technical assistance. Technical assistance that is used to build capacity is classified by some sources as an investment item rather than as a recurrent expenditure.

Aid to the education sector refers to the value of capital and noncapital aid disbursed to central departments of education. Capital aid is the value of external assistance for construction and equipment. Noncapital aid includes the value of overseas fellowships, technical assistance, and financial support for the operating costs of education, for the purchase of supplies, and for miscellaneous expenses. Fellowships include external assistance for tuition, fees, and living expenses for African students studying abroad. Aid for technical assistance refers to the cost of foreign nationals who work for the recipient country.

Aid for project-related training (PRT) reflects the estimated value of external financial assistance for training in sectors other than education. Because data on assistance for project-related training are available only for the World Bank (IDA and IBRD), all other figures are estimates. The estimates are calculated by applying to the total aid of the other external sources of funding the ratio of PRT to total aid observed for the World Bank.

The cost of hosting African students at colleges and universities abroad is an estimate of the indirect costs, over and above any fellowships, incurred by the host countries. In countries where no fees are charged, the subsidization equals the full teaching costs. In the United States tuition and fees account for approximately two-thirds of an estimated $7,000 annual per student cost. The level of subsidization estimated for the United States is also applied to African students studying in the United Kingdom.

The data on external aid to the education sector from OECD and OPEC countries are drawn from annual reports prepared in each country by the local United Nations Development Programme (UNDP) office on external aid and from the financial reports of the U.S. Agency for International Development (USAID), the World Bank, the African Development Bank, and the African Development Fund. A more complete description of the data and sources is available in Millot, Orivel, and Rasera (1987).

Table A-28. External Public Debt of the Education Sector

The data on debt in the appendix tables are from the World Bank Debtor Reporting System. The dollar figures shown are in current U.S. dollars converted at official exchange rates.

Outstanding and disbursed external public debt is the amount of public and publicly guaranteed loans that has been disbursed to the education sector, net of repayments of principal and writeoffs at year's end. Public loans are external obligations of public debtors, including the national government and its agencies and autonomous public bodies. Publicly guaranteed loans are external obligations of private debtors that are guaranteed for repayment by a public entity. Because of unavailability of data at the country level, the data do not cover nonguaranteed private debt. Debt service is the sum of interest payments and repayments of principal on external public and publicly guaranteed debt.

The data in this table should be used with caution. Sufficient information is not always available to enable accurate sectoral allocations to be made.

Frequently debt can only be assigned to an unallocated sector. All values should thus be considered as lower bounds.

B. Economic and Social Indicators

Table B-1. Basic Indicators

The estimates of population for mid-1984 are based on data from the United Nations Population Division or on World Bank data sources. Refugees not permanently settled in the country of asylum are generally considered to be part of the population of their country of origin. Data on area are from the FAO *Production Yearbook, 1984.*

GNP measures the total domestic and foreign output claimed by residents and is calculated without making deductions for depreciation. The 1984 GNP and GNP per capita figures are calculated according to the *World Bank Atlas* method. To smooth the impact of fluctuations in prices and exchange rates, a conversion factor, computed as the average of the actual and deflated exchange rates for the base period 1982–84, is applied to 1984 GNP converted at current purchaser values. The resulting GNP in U.S. dollars is divided by the midyear population to derive the 1984 per capita GNP.

The average annual rate of inflation is the growth rate of the GDP implicit deflator and shows annual price movements for all goods and services produced in an economy. The GDP deflator is first calculated by dividing, for each year of the period, the value of GDP at current purchaser values by the value of GDP at constant purchaser values, both in national currency. The least-squares method is then used to calculate the growth rate of the GDP deflator for the period.

Life expectancy at birth indicates the number of years a newborn child would live if the mortality patterns prevailing at the time of its birth were to remain constant throughout its life. Data are from the United Nations Population Division, supplemented by World Bank estimates.

The means for GNP per capita and life expectancy are weighted by population. Those for average annual rates of inflation are weighted by the share of country GDP valued in current U.S. dollars for the entire period.

Table B-2. Languages of Sub-Saharan Africa

The number of languages refers to the estimated number of indigenous languages spoken in each country. The figures shown are not exact and are intended only to differentiate, in a general way, between linguistically heterogeneous and homogeneous countries.

Principal languages include indigenous languages spoken by at least 10 percent of a country's population and any other language that serves as an official language, lingua franca, or medium of instruction in the country's education system. Several names are sometimes used for the same language; equivalent language names are listed at the end of the notes for this table. The percentage of the population speaking a language is the sum of the percentages that speak it as a mother tongue and as a second language.

The official language (or languages) is the language recognized and promoted for use in official domains such as law courts, national speeches, and public documents and is often the language of instruction. The percentage of speakers of the official language is estimated only roughly, if at all, and is usually directly related to the percentage of the population that completes several years of formal education. A lingua franca is a common language used as a means of communication among groups of people whose mother tongues differ.

A language is defined as a medium of instruction when it is used to teach a variety of subjects in the curriculum; it is not considered a medium of instruction when it is taught only as a subject. Instruction is here divided into three levels: lower primary, upper primary, and postprimary. Lower primary refers to the first three or four years of primary education, upper primary to the last half of primary instruction, and postprimary to secondary schools and to universities, colleges, and other postsecondary schools.

The data in this table are based on Bruhn (1984); Center for Applied Linguistics (1984); Morrison and others (1972); Skinner (1985); and Tadadjeu (1980). The table was compiled by a consultant to the World Bank, Dianne C. Bowcock.

Other principal languages

Burkina Faso: Mande, Senufo, Fulfulde
Cameroon: Bassa, Duala, Hausa
The Gambia: Arabic
Guinea-Bissau: Balante, Fulfulde, Malinke
Kenya: Nandi
Mauritania: Berber, Soninke
Mauritius: Creole (French), Bhodjpuri, Chinese, Hindi, Telegu, Urdu
Mozambique: Sena, Shona, Ndau, Mallua, Chope, Tsonga, Makonde
Niger: Fulfulde, Tuareg, Kanuri, Tamahiq
Sudan: Nuba, Fuv, Dinka, Nuer

Language names

Name used in table B-2	Equivalent
Akan	Twi-Fanti
Bambara	See Manding
Bemba	CiBemba
Dagbani	Mole-Dagbani
Dyula	See Manding
Fulfulde	Fulani, Peul, Fulbe, Fula, Ful, Pulaar, Adamawa
Galla	Oromo
Ganda	Luganda
Gaya	Gbaya
Ibo	Igbo
Kabiay	Kabre
Kanuri	Manga, Lare, Kagama, Bornu, Sirata
Kongo	KiKongo, Kituba, Kingala
Lingala	Bangala, Ngala, Mangala
Luba	CiLuba, Tshiluba
Luhya	Lukuya
Malinke	See Manding
Manding	Bambara, Dyula, Mandinka, Malinke, Mande, Jula, Dioula, Mandekan, Kangbe, Mandingo
Mossi	More
Nganguela	Ganguela
Ngbandi	Banda
Nyanja	Chinyanja, Chewa, Chichewa
Rundi	Kirundi
Sango	A pidgin "based on Ngbandi," (Morrison, p. 200)
Song'ai	Songhay, Songhai, Sonay
Sotho	Sesotho
Swahili	Kiswahili, Mbalazi, Tanga
Swati	Swazi, Siswati
Tamahiq	Tamacheq, Tamasheq
Teke	Lali, Lari
Rswana	Setswana
Wolof	Oulof, Olof, Jolof

Tables B-3 and B-4. Population Growth and Projections

The population growth rates are period averages calculated from midyear population estimates. All means are weighted by each country's share in the aggregate population.

The estimates of population for mid-1984 are based on data from the United Nations Population Division and from World Bank data files. In many cases they take into account the results of recent population censuses. Refugees not permanently settled in the country of asylum are generally considered to be part of the population of their country of origin.

To make population projections, data on total population by age and sex, fertility and mortality rates, and international migration in the base year 1980 are projected at five-year intervals on the basis of generalized assumptions until the population becomes stationary.

To project fertility rates, the year in which fertility will reach replacement level (see the definition below) is estimated. These estimates are speculative and are based on trends in crude birth rates, total fertility rates (see notes to table B-5 for definitions), female life expectancy at birth, and the performance of family planning programs. For most countries in Sub-Saharan Africa total fertility rates are assumed to remain constant for some time and then to decline until replacement level is reached. For a few countries they are assumed to increase until 1990–95 and then to decline.

Mortality rates are projected as a function of the female primary enrollment ratio and life expectancy in 1980–85. For a given life expectancy at birth the annual increments during the projection period are larger in countries with a primary school enrollment ratio greater than 70 percent and a life expectancy of up to 62.5 years. At higher life expectancies the increments are the same.

Migration rates are based on past and present trends in migration flows. For most countries future net migration rates are assumed to be zero by 2000, but for a few they are assumed to be zero by 2025.

The 1980 base-year estimates are from updated files of the United Nations "World Population Prospects as Assessed in 1982," from the most recent issues of the United Nations *Population and Vital Statistics Report,* from World Bank country data, and from national population censuses.

The net reproduction rate (NRR) indicates the number of daughters a newborn girl would bear during her lifetime, assuming fixed age-specific fertility and mortality rates. An NRR of 1 indicates that fertility is at replacement level. At this rate, childbearing women, on average, bear only enough daughters to replace themselves in the population.

A stationary population is one in which age-specific and sex-specific mortality rates have not changed over a long period, whereas age-specific fertility rates have remained at replacement level (NRR = 1). In such a population the birth rate is constant and is equal to the death rate, the age structure is constant, and the growth rate is zero.

Population momentum is the tendency for population growth to continue beyond the time that replacement-level fertility (NRR = 1) has been reached. The momentum of a population in year t is measured as a ratio of the ultimate stationary population to the population in year t, assuming that fertility remains at replacement level from year t on.

The estimates of the hypothetical size of the stationary population and the assumed year of reaching replacement-level fertility are speculative and should not be regarded as predictions. They are included to show the long-run implications of recent fertility and mortality trends on the basis of highly stylized assumptions. A more complete description of the methods and assumptions used in calculating the estimates is available in Vu (1986).

Table B-5 Demography and Fertility

The crude birth and death rates indicate the number of live births and deaths per thousand population in a year. The total fertility rate represents the number of children that would be born to a woman if she were to live until the end of her childbearing years and bear children in accordance with prevailing age-specific fertility rates.

The means for all indicators are weighted by each country's share in the aggregate population. The data sources are the same as those cited in the notes to table B-4.

Table B-6. Urbanization

The data on urban population as a percentage of total population are from United Nations, *Estimates and Projections of Urban, Rural and City Populations 1950–2025: The 1982 Assessment*, 1985, supplemented by data from various issues of the United Nations *Demographic Yearbook* and from the World Bank.

The growth rates of urban population are calculated from World Bank population estimates; the estimates of urban population shares are calculated from the sources cited in tables B-1, B-3, and B-4. Data on urban agglomeration are from United Nations, *Patterns of Urban and Rural Population Growth*, 1980.

Because estimates in this table are based on different national definitions of what is "urban," cross-country comparisons should be made with caution.

The means for urban population as a percentage of total population are calculated from country percentages weighted by each country's share in the aggregate population; the other means are weighted in the same fashion, using urban population.

Table B-7. Labor Force

The population of working age refers to the population ages 15–64. The estimates are based on World Bank population estimates for 1984 and previous years. The means are weighted by population.

The labor force refers to economically active persons ages 10 years and over, including the armed forces and the unemployed but excluding housewives, students, and other economically inactive groups. The agricultural sector consists of agriculture, forestry, hunting, and fishing. Industry consists of mining, manufacturing, construction, and electricity, water, and gas. All other branches of economic activity are categorized as services. Estimates of the sectoral distribution of the labor force are from ILO, *Labor Force Estimates and Projections, 1950–2000*, 1986, and from the World Bank. Means are weighted by the size of the labor force.

The labor force growth rates are derived from World Bank population projections and from ILO data on age-specific activity rates in the source cited above. The application of the ILO activity rates to the Bank's latest population estimates may be inappropriate for some countries in which there have been important changes in unemployment and underemployment, in international and internal migration, or in both. The projected growth rates for the labor force should therefore be used with caution. The summary measures for 1965–73 and 1973–84 are country growth rates weighted by each country's share in the aggregate labor force in 1973; those for 1980–2000 are weighted by each country's share in the aggregate labor force in 1980.

Table B-8. Growth of Production

GDP measures the final output of goods and services produced by an economy—that is, by residents and nonresidents—regardless of the allocation to domestic and foreign claims and without deductions for depreciation. Sectoral definitions are described in the notes to table B-7.

The figures for GDP are dollar values converted from local currency by using the single-year official exchange rates. For a few countries where the official exchange rate does not reflect the rate effectively applied to actual foreign exchange transactions, an alternative conversion factor is used.

Growth rates were calculated from constant price series using the least-squares method.

Table B-9. Central Government Expenditure

Central government expenditure comprises current and capital expenditure by all government offices, departments, establishments, and other bodies that are agencies or instruments of the central authority of a country. The shares of government expenditure by category are calculated from national currencies.

Defense comprises all expenditure on the maintenance of military forces, including the purchase of military supplies and equipment, construction, recruiting, and training. Expenditure on strengthening public services to meet wartime emergencies, the training of civil defense personnel, research and development, and the administration of military aid programs is also included.

Education comprises expenditure on the provision, management, inspection, and support by central governments of preprimary, primary, and secondary schools, of universities and colleges, and of vocational, technical, and other training institutions. Also included is expenditure on the general administration and regulation of the education system, on research, and on such subsidiary services as transport, school meals, and medical and dental services in schools. The differences between the percentages shown in this table and those in table A-14 are attributable to differences in the years of the data.

Health covers public expenditure on hospitals, medical and dental centers, and clinics that have a major medical component; on national health and medical insurance schemes; and on family planning and preventive care. Also included is expenditure on the administration and regulation of relevant government departments, hospitals and clinics, health and sanitation, and national health and medical insurance schemes and on research and development.

Housing and community amenities covers public expenditure on housing, including the support of housing and slum clearance activities, community development activities, and sanitary services. Social security and welfare covers compensation to the sick and temporarily disabled for loss of income; payments to the elderly, the permanently disabled, and the unemployed; and family, maternity, and child allowances. The welfare category also includes the cost of welfare services such as care of the aged, the disabled, and children, as well as the cost of general administration, regulation, and research associated with social security and welfare services.

Economic services includes public expenditure associated with the regulation, support, and more efficient operation of business, economic development, the redress of regional imbalances, and the creation of employment opportunities. Among the activities included are research, trade promotion, geological surveys, and inspection and regulation of particular industries. The five major categories of economic services are fuel and energy, agriculture, industry, transport and communication, and other economic affairs and services.

The category "other" covers expenditure on the general administration of government not included elsewhere. For a few countries it also includes amounts that could not be allocated to other components.

Overall surplus or deficit is defined as current and capital revenue and grants received, less total expenditure less lending minus repayments.

The means for the percentage distribution of central government expenditure are computed from group totals for the expenditure components and central government expenditure in current dollars. Those for total government expenditure as a percentage of GNP are computed from group totals for the above total expenditures and GNP in current dollars; those for overall surplus or deficit as a percentage of GNP are computed from overall surplus or deficit in current dollars and GNP in current dollars.

The data on central government expenditure are from IMF, *Government Finance Statistics Yearbook*, 1986, from IMF data files, and from World Bank country documentation. The accounts of each country are reported using the system of definitions and classifications in the IMF *Manual on Government Finance Statistics*. Because of differences in data coverage, however, the components of central government expenditure may not be comparable among countries.

Table B-10. Disbursements of Official Development Assistance (ODA)

Net disbursements of ODA from all sources consist of loans and grants made on concessional financial terms by all bilateral agencies and multilateral sources with the object of promoting economic development and welfare. Net disbursements equal gross disbursements less payments to funding sources for amortization. Net disbursements are shown per capita and as a percentage of GNP.

The means of per capita ODA are computed from group aggregates for population and for ODA; those for ODA as a percentage of GNP are computed from group totals for ODA and for GNP in current U.S. dollars.

Table B-11. External Public Debt Service Ratios

External public debt outstanding and disbursed represents public and publicly guaranteed loans drawn at year's end, net of repayments of principal and writeoffs. To estimate external public debt as a percentage of GNP, public debt is converted into U.S. dollars from currencies of repayment at end-of-year official exchange rates. GNP is converted from national currencies into current dollars by the method described in the notes to table B-8. The mean ratios of external debt to GNP are weighted by current dollar GNP.

Interest payments are actual payments made on the disbursed and outstanding public and publicly guaranteed debt in foreign currencies, goods, or services. They include commitment charges on undisbursed debt when such information is available.

Debt service is the sum of actual repayments of principal (amortization) and actual payments of interest made in foreign currencies, goods, or services on external public and publicly guaranteed debt. The mean ratios of public debt and debt service to GNP are weighted by GNP in current dollars. The mean ratios of debt service to exports of goods and services are weighted by exports of goods and services in current dollars.

C. Supplementary and Summary Tables

Table C-1. Selected Comparative Statistics for Countries with Fewer Than a Half Million People

Unless otherwise noted, these data come from African Development Bank (1986). All such entries are based on the most recent information available, generally from the years 1979, 1980, or 1981. Other data sources are listed in the notes to the table.

Table C-3. Estimated Average Number of Years of Education Attained by Working-Age Population

The average number of years of education is the ratio of educational stock to working-age population. The educational stock series was constructed as a weighted sum of the enrollment of students by level (primary, secondary, and postsecondary) during the previous fifty-eight years. The working-age population is the population ages 15–64. For details see Lau and Jamison (forthcoming).

Table C-4. Literacy

The adult literacy rate is the percentage of persons ages 15 and over who can read and write. The 1960 data are from *World Development Report 1983* and other World Bank data sources. These data are based primarily on information from Unesco, supplemented by World Bank data. Because these data are normally gathered in large-scale demographic surveys and censuses, they often are not available for the more recent year. For some countries the estimates are for years other than, but generally not more than two years distant from, those specified. Thus the series are not comparable for all countries. Data for 1985 or for the latest year are from Unesco, *The Current Literacy Structure in the World*, 1985.

Table C-5. Cross-National Comparisons of Achievement in Mathematics, Reading, and Science

The figures for mathematics are based on data from the International Association for the Evaluation of Educational Achievement (IEA) Second Study of Mathematics, as reported in Livingstone (1985). Tests in five subfields of mathematics were administered in participating countries to students age 13.

The figures for reading comprehension and general science for Malawi are based on Heyneman (1980). Scores for countries other than Malawi are from tests administered by the IEA to students age 10 and are not strictly comparable with the scores for Malawi. The tests in Malawi were administered by a World Bank study team in only two districts, Mulanje and Nsanje, to students whose average age was 16. The questions were in English rather than in the vernacular languages of the districts. (After the first few years of primary school, instruction in Malawi is given in English as well as in the vernacular.)

Table C-6. Gross Primary Enrollment Ratios

All figures are for 1983. All are percentages except for the figures for public recurrent expenditure per pupil, which are in 1983 dollars. The averages shown are weighted means (w) and medians (m).

Table C-7. Enrollment Characteristics and Education Expenditures by Secondary Enrollment Groups

All figures are for 1982. The averages shown are weighted means (w) and medians (m).

Data Sources

Education Indicators

National sources.
Unesco (United Nations Educational, Scientific and Cultural Organization) data tape.
_____. Various years. *Statistical Yearbook*. Paris.
_____. 1982. *Education and Endogenous Development in Africa: Trends—Problems—Prospects*. Paris.
_____. 1985. *Female Participation in Higher Education*. Paris.
World Bank country documentation and data files.

External Aid to Education

Millot, Benoit, François Orivel, and Jean-Bernard Rasera. 1987. "L'aide extérieure à l'éducation en Afrique sub-saharienne." Education and Training Department Discussion Paper EDT65. World Bank, Washington, D.C. Processed.
United Nations Development Programme data files.
USAID (U.S. Agency for International Development) country documentation.
World Bank documentation.

Economic and Social Indicators

African Development Bank. 1986. *Education Sector Policy Paper*. Abidjan.
FAO (Food and Agriculture Organization). 1985. *Food Aid Bulletin* (October). Rome.
_____. *Food Aid in Figures*. Rome.
_____. Various years. *Production Yearbook*. Rome.
_____. Various years. Standard computer tape for *Production Yearbook*.
IMF. 1986. *Government Finance Statistics Yearbook*. Vol. 9. Washington, D.C.
National sources.
Sawyer, Malcolm. 1976. *Income Distribution in OECD Countries*. OECD Occasional Studies. Paris.
United Nations Department of International Economic and Social Affairs. Various years. *Demographic Yearbook*. New York.
_____. Various years. *Statistical Yearbook*. New York.
_____. 1981. *A Survey of National Sources of Income Distribution Statistics*. Statistical Papers, Series M., no. 72. New York.
_____. 1985. *National Accounts Statistics Compendium of Income Distribution Statistics*. Statistical Papers, series M, no. 79. New York.
UNIDO (United Nations Industrial Development Organization). Data files.
World Bank. 1983. *World Development Report 1983*. New York: Oxford University Press.
_____. 1986. *Social Indicators of Development*. Washington, D.C.: World Bank.
_____. Country documentation and data files.

Balance of Payments and Debt

OECD (Organisation for Economic Co-operation and Development). Various years. *Development Co-operation*. Paris.
_____. 1986. *Geographical Distribution of Financial Flows to Developing Countries*. Paris.
IMF balance of payments data files.
World Bank Debtor Reporting System.

Languages

Bruhn, Thea C. 1984. "African Lingua Francas." Center for Applied Linguistics. Washington, D.C. Processed.
Center for Applied Linguistics. 1984. Country status reports. Washington, D.C.
Morrison, Donald G., R. C. Mitchell, J. N. Paden, and H. M. Stevenson, eds. 1972. *Black Africa*. New York: Free Press.
Skinner, Neil. 1985. Table, "Sub-Saharan Africa Less the Republic of South Africa and Islands: Degree of Multilingualism." Madison: University of Wisconsin. Processed.
Tadadjeu, Maurice. 1980. "A Model for Functional Trilingual Educational Planning in Africa." Paris: Unesco.

Population

United Nations Department of International Economic and Social Affairs. Various years. *Demographic Yearbook*. New York.
_____. Various years. *Population and Vital Statistics Report*. New York.
_____. 1980. *Patterns of Urban and Rural Population Growth*. New York.
_____. 1982. "Infant Mortality: World Estimates and Projections, 1950–2025." *Population Bulletin of the United Nations*, no. 14. New York.
_____. 1982. "World Population Prospects as Assessed in 1982." Updated printouts. New York.
_____. 1983. *World Population Trends and Policies: 1983 Monitoring Report*. New York.
_____. 1985. *Estimates and Projections of Urban, Rural and City Populations, 1950–2025; The 1982 Assessment*. New York.

Vu, My T. 1985. *World Population Projections 1985. Short- and Long-Term Estimates by Age and Sex with Related Demographic Statistics.* Baltimore, Md.: Johns Hopkins University Press.
World Bank data files.

Labor Force

ILO (International Labour Organisation). 1982. *Paper Qualification Syndrome and Unemployment of School Leavers.* Addis Ababa.

———. 1986. *Labour Force Estimates and Projections, 1950–2000.* 3rd ed. Geneva.

ILO tapes.
World Bank data files.

Student Achievement

Heyneman, Stephen P. 1980. *The Evaluation of Human Capital in Malawi.* World Bank Working Paper 420. Washington, D.C.

Lau, Lawrence, and Dean Jamison. Forthcoming. "Education and Economic Growth in Sub-Saharan Africa." Population and Human Resources Department, World Bank, Washington, D.C. Processed.

Livingstone, Ian D. 1985. "Perceptions of the Intended and Implemented Mathematics Curriculum." Urbana: University of Illinois. Processed.

Unesco. 1985. *The Current Literacy Structure in the World.* Paris.

MAP 1
SUB-SAHARAN AFRICA
TOTAL POPULATION
1984

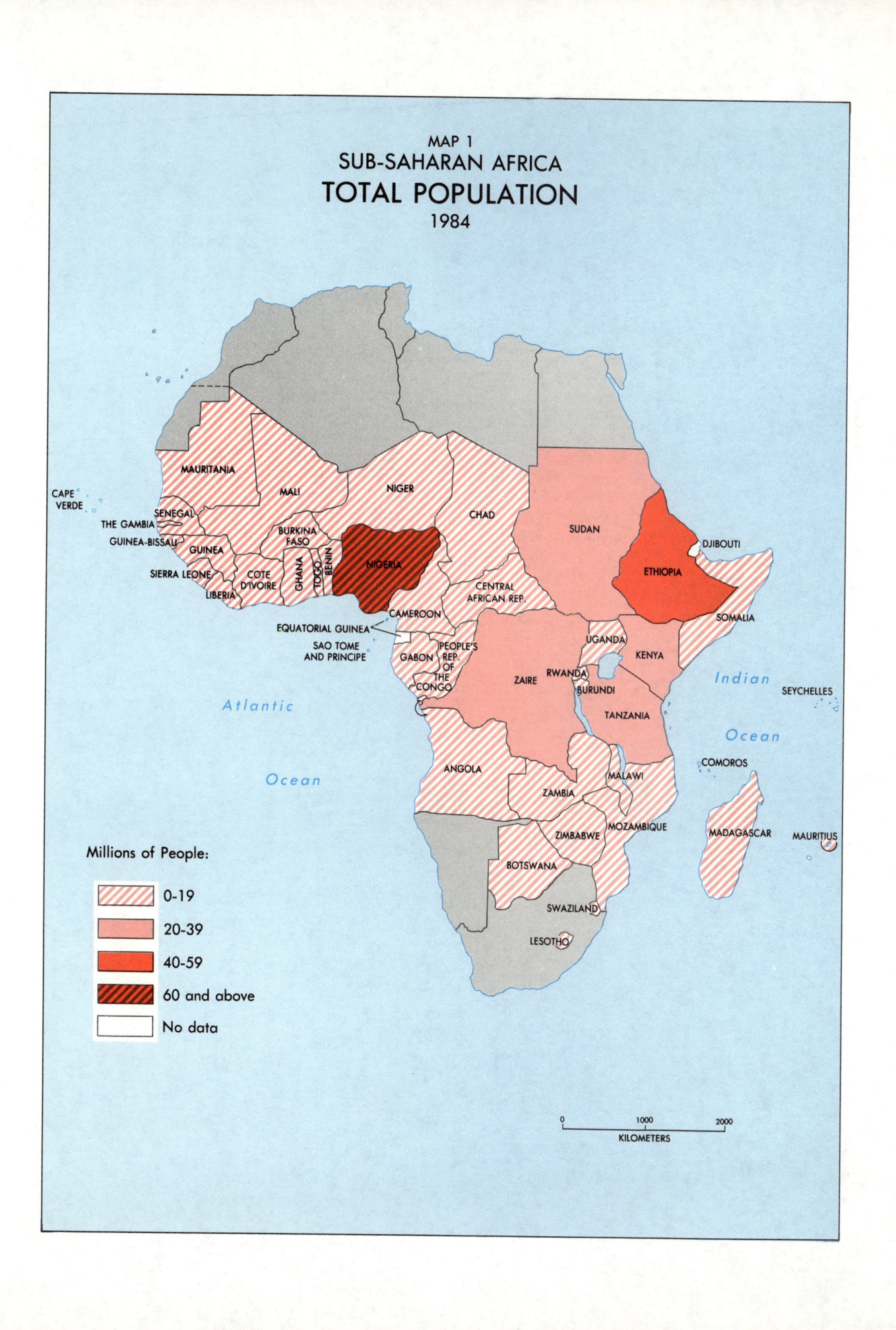

Millions of People:
- 0-19
- 20-39
- 40-59
- 60 and above
- No data

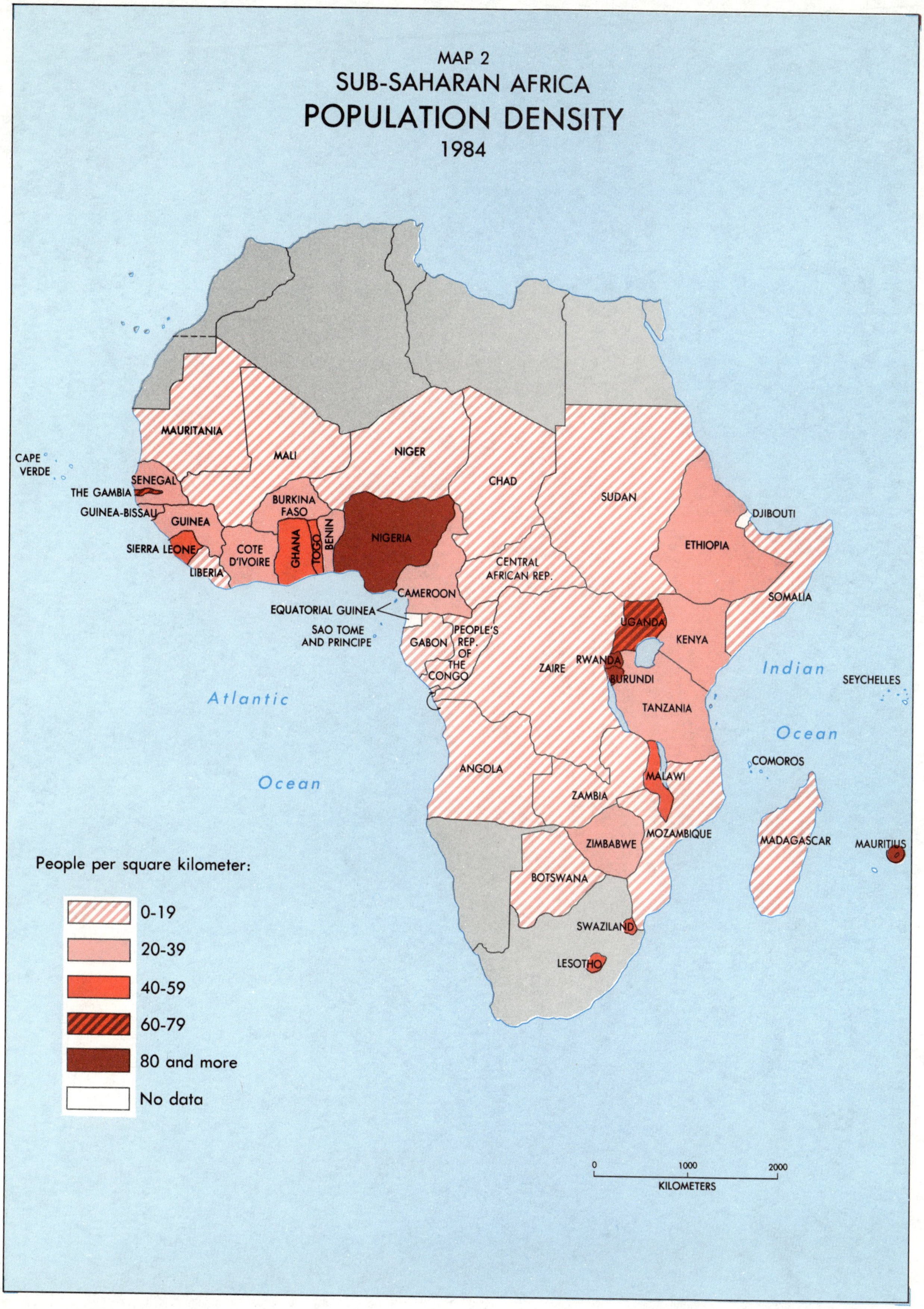
MAP 2
SUB-SAHARAN AFRICA
POPULATION DENSITY
1984
MAURITANIA
MALI
NIGER
CHAD
SUDAN
CAPE VERDE
SENEGAL
THE GAMBIA
GUINEA-BISSAU
GUINEA
SIERRA LEONE
LIBERIA
COTE D'IVOIRE
BURKINA FASO
GHANA
TOGO
BENIN
NIGERIA
CAMEROON
CENTRAL AFRICAN REP.
ETHIOPIA
DJIBOUTI
SOMALIA
EQUATORIAL GUINEA
SAO TOME AND PRINCIPE
GABON
PEOPLE'S REP. OF THE CONGO
ZAIRE
UGANDA
KENYA
RWANDA
BURUNDI
TANZANIA
Atlantic
Ocean
Indian
Ocean
SEYCHELLES
COMOROS
ANGOLA
ZAMBIA
MALAWI
MOZAMBIQUE
MADAGASCAR
MAURITIUS
ZIMBABWE
BOTSWANA
SWAZILAND
LESOTHO
People per square kilometer:
0-19
20-39
40-59
60-79
80 and more
No data
0
1000
2000
KILOMETERS

MAP 3
SUB-SAHARAN AFRICA
LANGUAGE GROUPS
1984

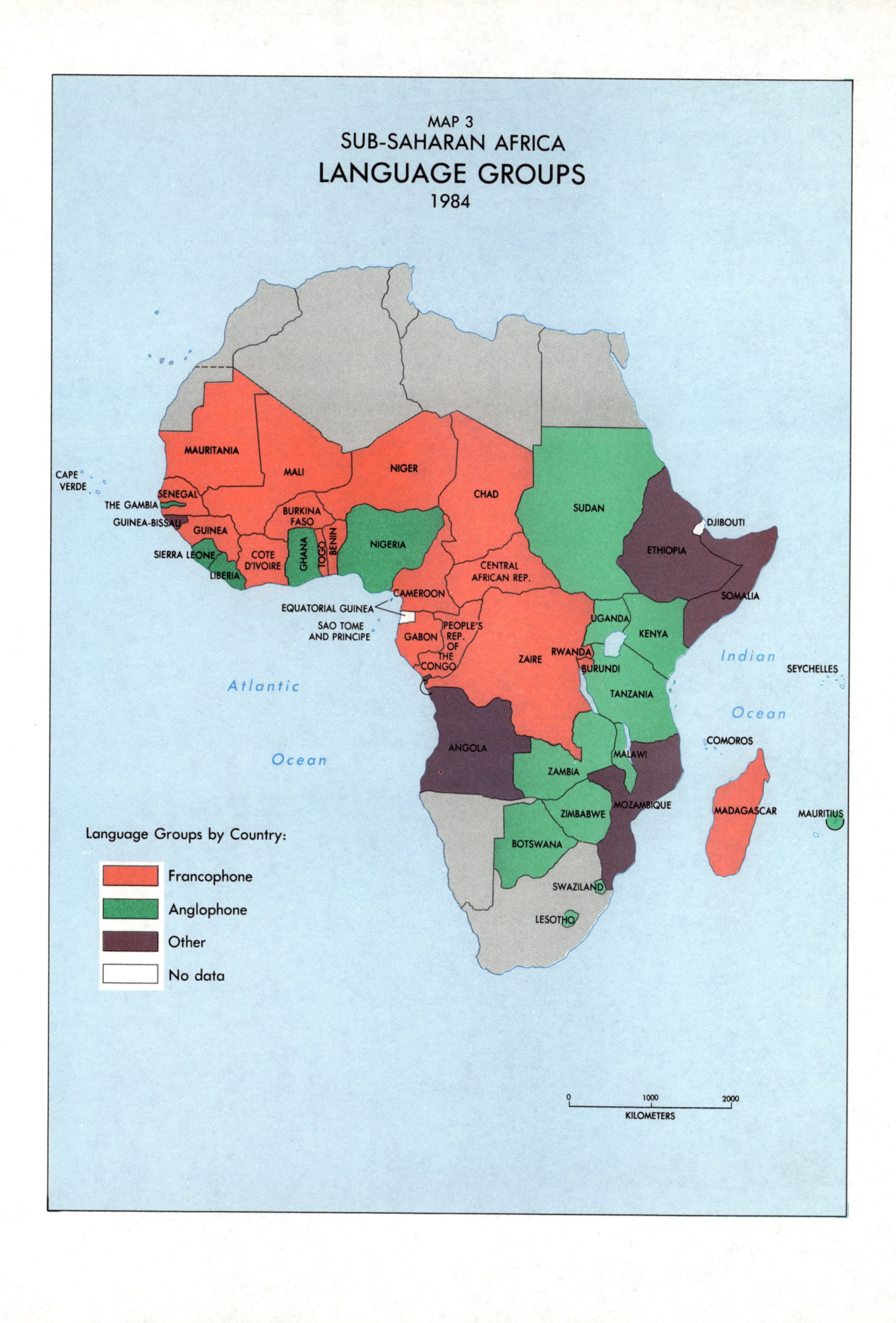

Language Groups by Country:

- Francophone
- Anglophone
- Other
- No data

0 1000 2000
KILOMETERS

MAP 4
SUB-SAHARAN AFRICA
INCOME GROUPINGS
1984

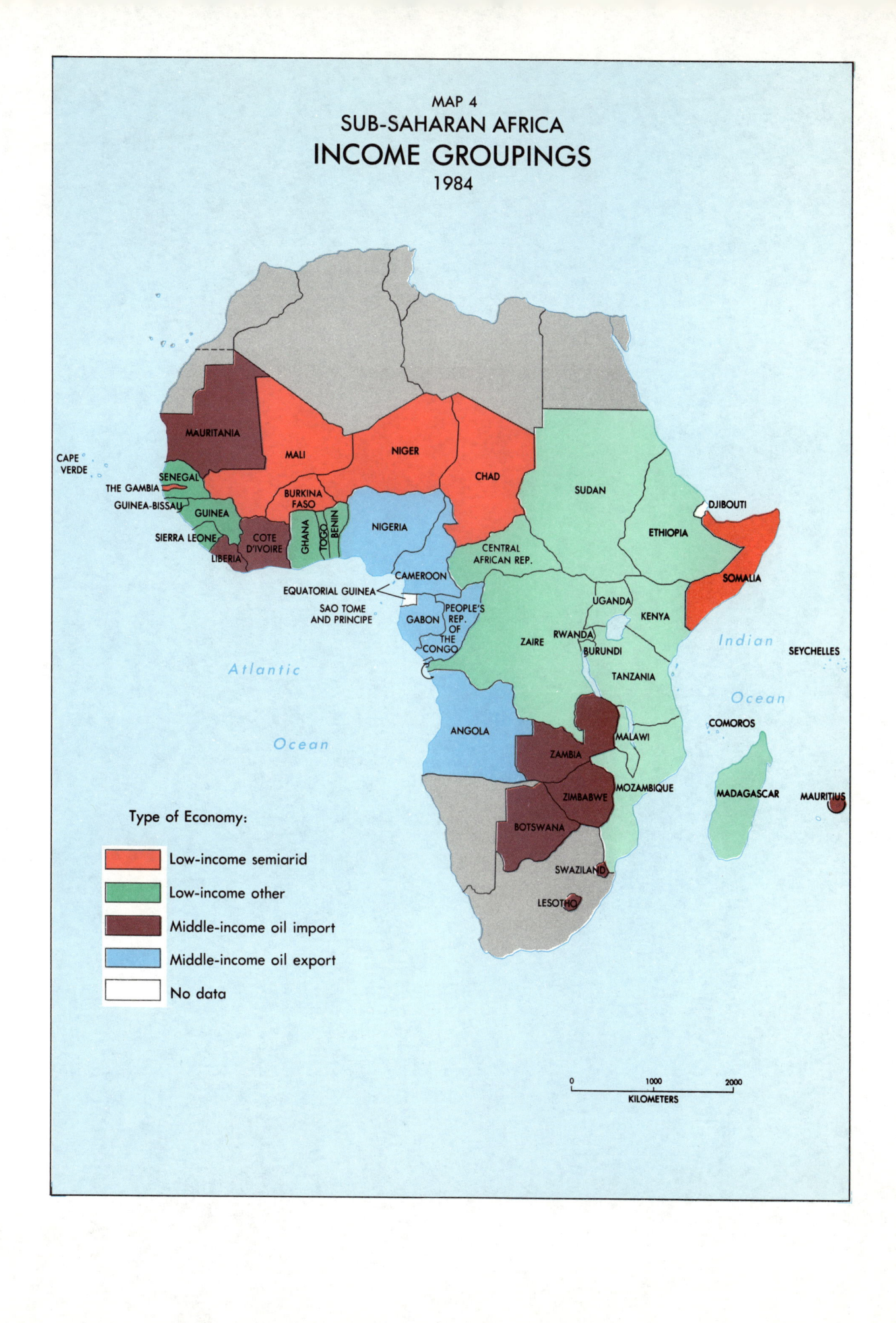

Type of Economy:

- Low-income semiarid
- Low-income other
- Middle-income oil import
- Middle-income oil export
- No data

0 — 1000 — 2000 KILOMETERS

MAP 4
SUB-SAHARAN AFRICA
INCOME GROUPINGS
1984

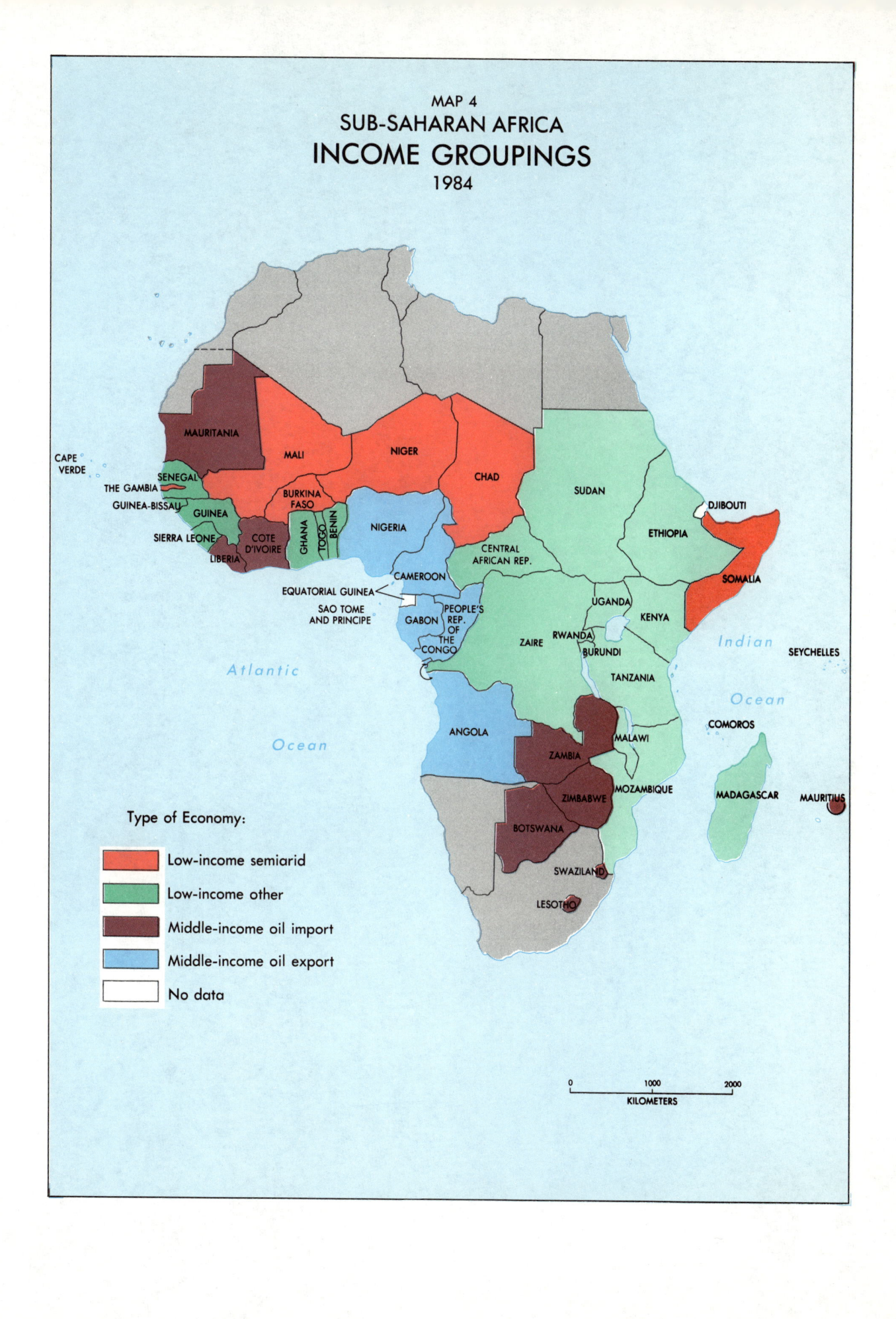

Type of Economy:

- Low-income semiarid
- Low-income other
- Middle-income oil import
- Middle-income oil export
- No data

0 — 1000 — 2000 KILOMETERS

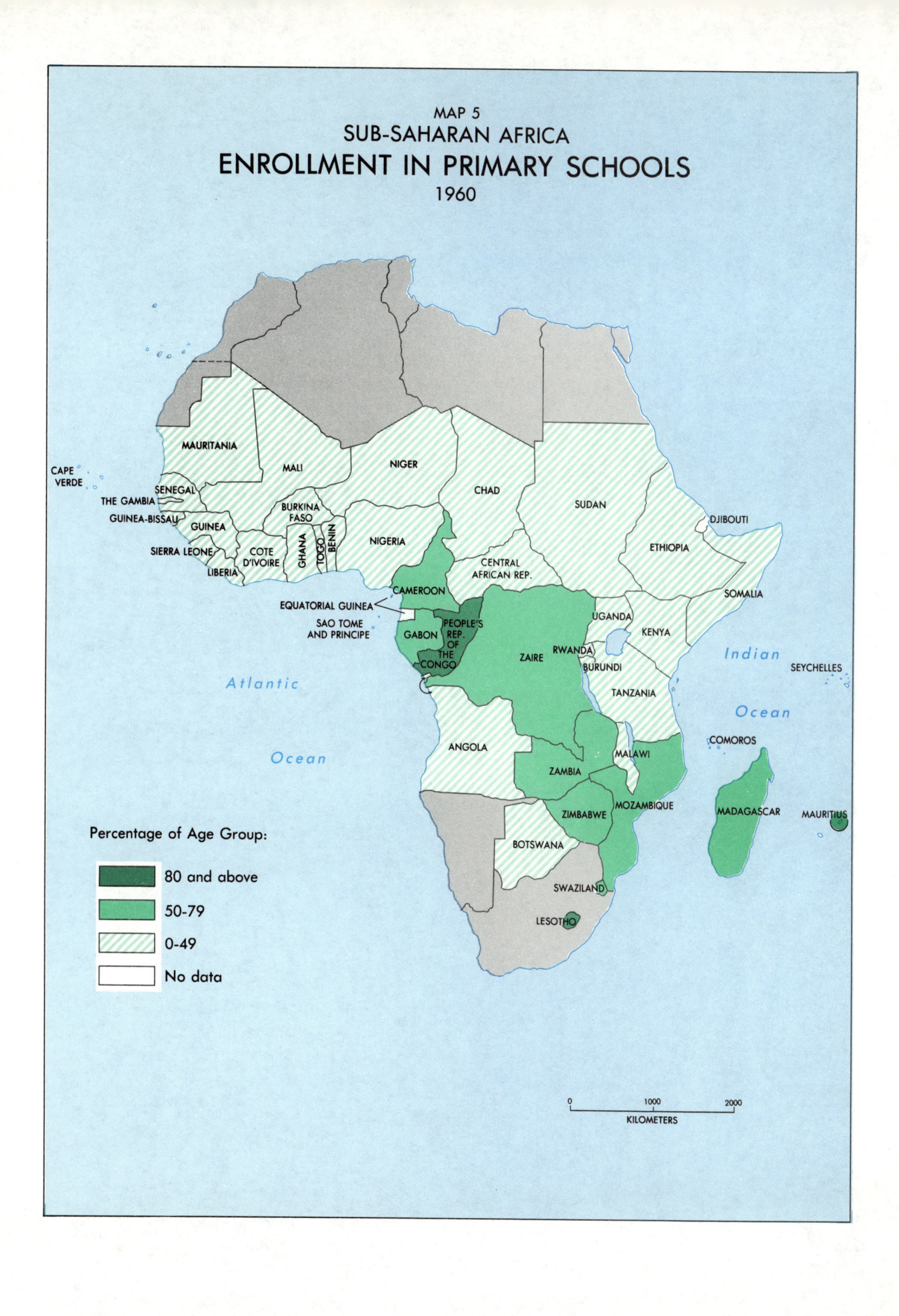

MAP 5
SUB-SAHARAN AFRICA
ENROLLMENT IN PRIMARY SCHOOLS
1960

Percentage of Age Group:
- 80 and above
- 50-79
- 0-49
- No data

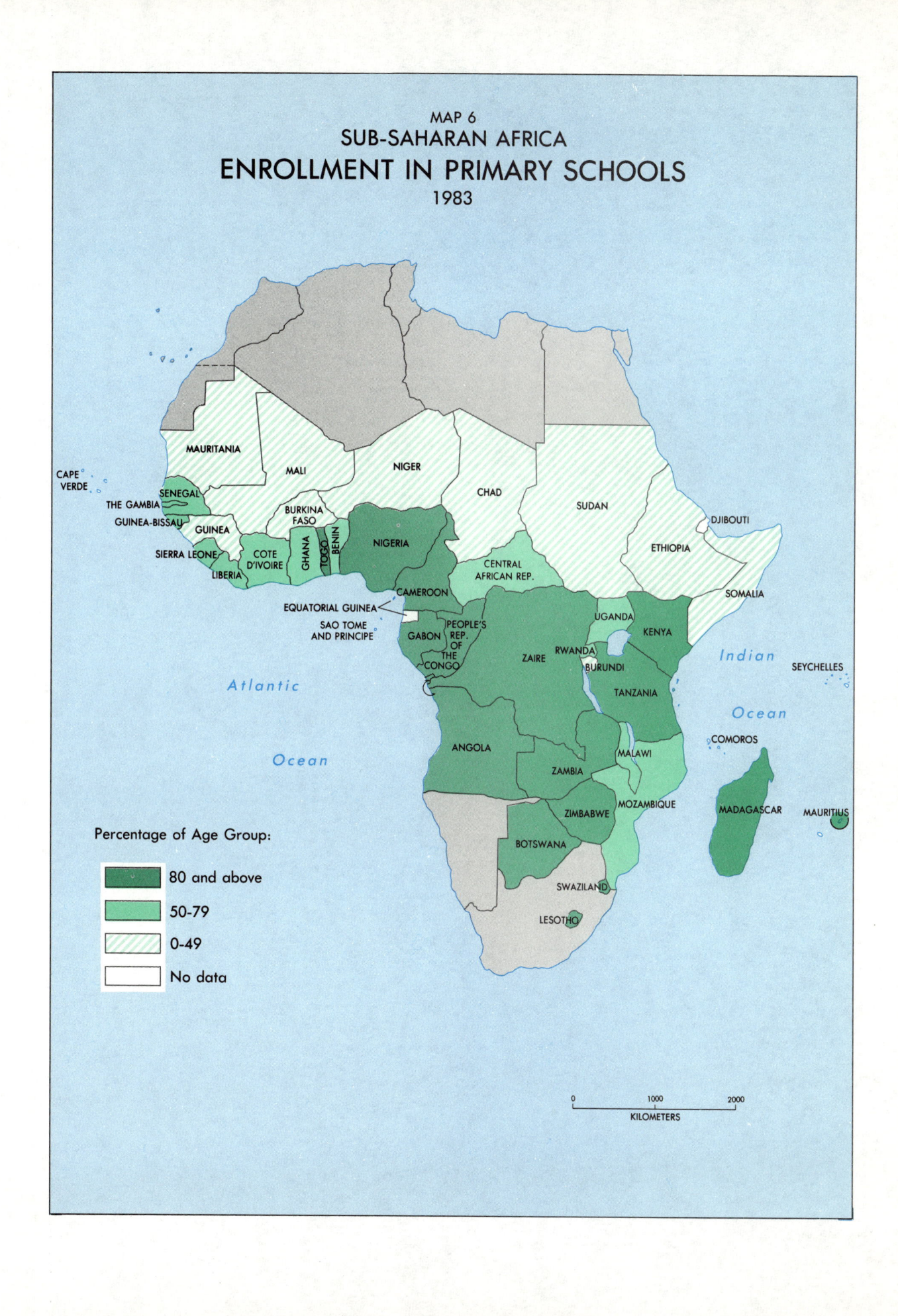

MAP 6
SUB-SAHARAN AFRICA
ENROLLMENT IN PRIMARY SCHOOLS
1983

Percentage of Age Group:
- 80 and above
- 50-79
- 0-49
- No data